Literary Construction of Identity
in the Ancient World

Literary Construction of Identity in the Ancient World

Proceedings of the Conference
Literary Fiction and the Construction of Identity in Ancient Literatures:
Options and Limits of Modern Literary Approaches
in the Exegesis of Ancient Texts

Heidelberg, July 10–13, 2006

Edited by

HANNA LISS and MANFRED OEMING

Winona Lake, Indiana
EISENBRAUNS
2010

Library of Congress Cataloging-in-Publication Data

Literary construction of identity in the ancient world : proceedings of a
 conference, literary fiction and the construction of identity in ancient
 literatures : options and limits of modern literary approaches in the
 exegesis of ancient texts, Heidelberg, July 10–13, 2006 / edited by Hanna
 Liss and Manfred Oeming.
    p.   cm.
 Includes bibliographical references and indexes.
 ISBN 978-1-57506-190-0 (hardback : alk. paper)
 1. Identity (Psychology) in literature—Congresses.   2. Literature,
Ancient—History and criticism—Congresses.   3. Bible as literature—
Congresses.   I. Liss, Hanna.   II. Oeming, Manfred.
    PN56.I42L58   2010
    880.09—dc22
                                                              2010005674

Contents

Part 1
Thinking of Ancient Texts as Literature

Part 2
The Identity of Authors and Readers

Part 3
Fiction and Fact

Part 4
Rereading Biblical Poetry

Part 5
Modeling the Future
by Reconstructing the Past

Preface

Encountering an ancient text not only as a historical source but also as a literary artifact entails an important paradigm shift. In recent years, this shift has taken place in classical and Oriental philology. Biblical scholars, Egyptologists, and classical philologists have been pioneers in supplementing traditional historical-critical exegesis with more-literary approaches. This has led to a wealth of new insights. While the methodological consequences of this shift have been discussed within each discipline, there has not yet been an attempt to discuss its validity and methodology on an interdisciplinary level. In 2007, the Faculty of Bible and Biblical Interpretation at the Hochschule für Jüdische Studien, Heidelberg, and the Faculty of Theology at the University of Heidelberg invited scholars from the U.S., Canada, the Netherlands, Israel, and Germany to examine these issues. Under the title "Literary Fiction and the Construction of Identity in Ancient Literatures: Options and Limits of Modern Literary Approaches in the Exegesis of Ancient Texts," experts in Egyptology, classical philology, ancient Near Eastern studies, biblical studies, Jewish studies, literary studies, and comparative religion came together to present current research and debate open questions.

Different texts or text genres do not all have the same connection to reality. Not every author wants to report historical events. Many if not most intend to shape the world view and identity of those who read them by taking recourse to fictional creativity. When readers interact with texts, it would be absurd to assume otherwise. This is a commonplace truth for contemporary literary communication; however, religious fundamentalism in all religions shows clearly that the same assumptions are not always held when reading ancient literatures. It is thus the responsibility of philologists, who are concerned with teaching and explaining these texts in church, synagogue, school, and university, to address what ancient authors 2,500 or even 3,000 years ago may have intended with the texts they wrote. Is it possible to show the beginnings of fictional imagination in these contexts? What might be its cause, and how could later readers recognize fictional imagination in ancient texts?

Each representative of a total of 23 different disciplines has dealt with literary theory in regard to his or her area of research. So far, their insights have not been received beyond the boundaries of their own discipline. In the 19th century, the situation was quite different when, for example, Protestant biblical scholarship related closely to classical philology and contemporary ancient Near Eastern studies. Today, the various disciplines must first agree whether anything is to be gained from interdisciplinary interaction and how different areas of research may learn from each other. The Heidelberg conference created the framework for an important milestone in this kind of methodological reflection. The present volume has organized the various contributions along thematic lines that show how similar issues are dealt with in different disciplines.

Much gratitude goes to the various individuals and institutions who made the conference and the publication of this volume possible: The Deutsche Forschungsgemeinschaft, the Lautenschläger Stiftung, and the Stiftung Universität Heidelberg for their generous financial support; Dr. Joachim Vette for translating; and Kai-Jo Petzold and Dr. Verena Hug for gathering and copy editing the various manuscripts.

Prof. Dr. HANNA LISS
Prof. Dr. MANFRED OEMING
Heidelberg, December 2009

Abbreviations

General

A.	Louvre Museum siglum
Akk.	Akkadian
ANE	ancient Near East
AO	tablets in the collections of the Musée du Louvre
Aram.	Aramaic
ASV	American Standard Version
BM	tablets in the collections of the British Museum
chap(s).	chapter(s)
col(s).	column(s)
cstr.	construct
Dar.	Darius
DNa	Inscription A from the tomb of Darius at Naqs-i Rustam
DtrH	Deuteronomistic Historian
E	Elohistic writer/source
EASJ	European Association of Jewish Studies
fem.	feminine
frag(s)./fr(s).	fragment(s)
Gr.	Greek
Heb.	Hebrew
K	tablets in the Kouyunjik collection of the British Museum
KJV	King James Version
LXX	Septuagint
Mnmt	monument
mp	masculine plural
ms	masculine singular
MS(S)	manuscript(s)
MT	Masoretic Text
N	tablets from Nippur in the collections of the University Museum of the University of Pennsylvania, Philadelphia
NA	Neo-Assyrian
NAB	New American Bible
NB	Neo-Babylonian
Nbk.	Nebuchadnezzar
Nbn.	Nabonidus
ND	field numbers of tablets excavated at Nimrud (Kalhu)
NinA	"Niniveh A" in R. Borger. *Die Inschriften Asarhaddons: Königs von Assyrien. AfO Beiheft 9*. Graz, Austria: Published by the editor, 1956
NJPSV	New Jewish Publication Society Version
NKJV	New King James Version
NRSV	New Revised Standard Version
n.s.	new series
obv.	obverse
OT	Old Testament
pl.	plural

PN	personal name
ptc.	participle
R	redactor
R.	Rabbi
rev.	reverse
RJE	redactor of the JE sources
RSV	Revised Standard Version
Sam.	Samaritan
Sm.	tablets in the collections of the British Museum
suff.	suffix
SV	Subject-Verb word order
Syr.	Syriac
TDA	Tell Deir ʿAlla Balaam Inscription
Vulg.	Vulgate
v(v).	verse(s)
WDSP	Wadi ed-Daliyeh Samaria Papyri

Reference Works

AASOR	Annual of the American Schools of Oriental Research
AB	Anchor Bible
ABD	Freedman, D. N. (editor). *The Anchor Bible Dictionary.* 6 vols. Garden City, NY: Doubleday, 1992
ABL	R. F. Harper (editor). *Assyrian and Babylonian Letters Belonging to the Kouyunjik Collections of the British Museum.* 14 vols. Chicago: University of Chicago Press, 1892–1914
ABRL	Anchor Bible Reference Library
ADAJ	*Annual of the Department of Antiquities of Jordan*
AEM	*Archives épistolaires de Mari*
AfO	*Archiv für Orientforschung*
AfOB	Archiv für Orientforschung Beiheft
AHw	Von Soden, W. *Akkadisches Handwörterbuch.* 3 vols. Wiesbaden: Harrassowitz, 1965–81
AJBA	*Australian Journal of Biblical Archaeology*
AJP	*American Journal of Philology*
AJSL	*American Journal of Semitic Languages and Literatures*
AnBib	Analecta Biblica
ANET	Pritchard, J. B. (editor). *Ancient Near Eastern Texts Relating to the Old Testament.* 3rd ed. Princeton: Princeton University Press, 1969
AnSt	*Anatolian Studies*
AOAT	Alter Orient und Altes Testament
AOS	American Oriental Series
AP	Cowley, A. E. (editor). *Aramaic Papyri of the Fifth Century* B.C. Oxford: Clarendon, 1923
AS	Assyriological Studies
ATD	Das Alte Testament Deutsch
AuOr	*Aula orientalis*
AUWE	Ausgrabungen in Uruk-Warka: Endberichte
BA	*Biblical Archaeologist*
BAR	*Biblical Archaeology Review*

BAR Int. Series British Archaeological Reports, International Series
BASOR *Bulletin of the American Schools of Oriental Research*
BBB Bonner Biblische Beiträge
BDB Brown, F., S. R. Driver, and C. A. Briggs. *Hebrew and English Lexicon of the Old Testament.* Oxford: Clarendon, 1907
BEATAJ Beiträge zur Erforschung des Alten Testaments und des antiken Judentum
BETL Bibliotheca ephemeridum theologicarum lovaniensium
BHS Elliger, K., and W. Rudolph (editors). *Biblia Hebraica Stuttgartensia.* Stuttgart: Deutsche Bibelgesellschaft, 1984
Bib *Biblica*
BibInt *Biblical Interpretation*
BIN Babylonian Inscriptions in the Collection of James B. Nies
BiOr *Bibliotheca Orientalis*
BJRL *Bulletin of the John Rylands University Library of Manchester*
BJS Brown Judaic Studies
BKAT Biblischer Kommentar: Altes Testament
BN *Biblische Notizen*
BR *Biblical Research*
BTAVO Beihefte zum Tübinger Atlas des Vorderen Orients
BWANT Beiträge zur Wissenschaft vom Alten und Neuen Testament
BZ *Biblische Zeitschrift*
BZAW Beihefte zur Zeitschrift für die Alttestamentliche Wissenschaft
BZNW Beihefte zur Zeitschrift für die Neutestamentliche Wissenschaft
CAD Oppenheim, A. L., et al. (editors). *The Assyrian Dictionary of the Oriental Institute of the University of Chicago.* Chicago: The Oriental Institute of the University of Chicago, 1956–
CAH *Cambridge Ancient History*
CahRB Cahiers de la Revue biblique
CAT Dietrich, M., O. Loretz, and J. Sanmartín. *The Cuneiform Alphabetic Texts from Ugarit, Ras Ibn Hani, and Other Places.* 2nd ed. Münster: Ugarit-Verlag, 1995
CBQ *Catholic Biblical Quarterly*
CHI *Cambridge History of Iran.* Cambridge: Cambridge University Press, 1968–91
CHJ Davies, W. D., and Louis Finkelstein (editors). *Cambridge History of Judaism.* 2 vols. Cambridge: Cambridge University Press, 1984–90
COS Hallo, W. W. (editor). *The Context of Scripture.* 3 vols. Leiden: Brill, 1997–2003
CP *Classical Philology*
CT Cuneiform Texts from the British Museum
CW *Classical World*
DDD Toorn, K. van der, B. Becking, and P. W. van der Horst (editors). *Dictionary of Deities and Demons in the Bible.* Leiden: Brill, 1995
DJD Discoveries in the Judaean Desert
DMOA Documenta et Monumenta Orientis Antiqui
ErIsr *Eretz-Israel*
EvT *Evangelische Theologie*
FAT Forschungen zum Alten Testament
FB Forschung zur Bibel

FGH	Jacoby, F. (editor). *Die Fragmente der griechischen Historiker*. Leiden: Brill, 1954–64
FOTL	Forms of the Old Testament Literature
FRLANT	Forschungen zur Religion und Literatur des Alten und Neuen Testaments
FuB	*Forschungen und Berichte*
GB	[Gesenius, Wilhelm, and] Gotthelf Bergsträsser. *Hebräische Grammatik*. 29th ed. 2 vols. Leipzig: Hinrichs, 1918–29. Reprinted, Hildesheim: Olms, 1962
GCCI	Dougherty, R. P. *Goucher College Cuneiform Inscriptions*. 2 vols. New Haven, CT: Yale University Press, 1923–33
GKC	Kautzsch, E. (editor). *Gesenius' Hebrew Grammar*. Translated by A. E. Cowley. 2nd ed. Oxford: Oxford University Press, 1910
GTA	Göttinger theologischer Arbeiten
HALAT	Koehler, L., and W. Baumgartner, et al. (editors). *Hebräisches und aramäisches Lexikon zum Alten Testament*. 4 vols. Leiden: Brill, 1967–90
HAR	*Hebrew Annual Review*
HAT	Handbuch zum Alten Testament
HdA	Weippert, H. *Vorderasien, 2/1: Palästina in vorhellenistischer Zeit*. Handbuch der Archäologie. Munich: Beck, 1988
HNT	Handbuch zum Neuen Testament
HO	Handbuch der Orientalistik
HS	*Hebrew Studies*
HSM	Harvard Semitic Monographs
HSS	Harvard Semitic Studies
HTKAT	Herders theologischer Kommentar zum Alten Testament
HTR	*Harvard Theological Review*
HUCA	*Hebrew Union College Annual*
ICC	International Critical Commentary
IEJ	*Israel Exploration Journal*
IOS	*Israel Oriental Studies*
JANES(CU)	*Journal of the Ancient Near Eastern Society (of Columbia University)*
JAOS	*Journal of the American Oriental Society*
JBL	*Journal of Biblical Literature*
JBTh	*Jahrbuch für biblische Theologie*
JCS	*Journal of Cuneiform Studies*
JEA	*Journal of Egyptian Archaeology*
JESHO	*Journal of Economic and Social History of the Orient*
JHS	*Journal of Hebrew Scriptures*. http://www.jhsonline.org
JJS	*Journal of Jewish Studies*
JNES	*Journal of Near Eastern Studies*
JNSL	*Journal of Northwest Semitic Languages*
JQR	*Jewish Quarterly Review*
JRS	*Journal of Roman Studies*
JSJ	*Journal for the Study of Judaism*
JSJSup	Journal for the Study of Judaism, Supplement
JSOT	*Journal for the Study of the Old Testament*
JSOTSup	Journal for the Study of the Old Testament, Supplements
JSS	*Journal of Semitic Studies*
JTS	*Journal of Theological Studies*

JTVI	*Journal of the Transactions of the Victoria Institute*
KAI	Donner, H., and W. Röllig. *Kanaanäische und aramäische Inschriften.* Wiesbaden: Harrassowitz, 1962–64
KAT	Kommentar zum Alten Testament
KEK	Kritisch-exegetischer Kommentar über das Neue Testament
KS	*Kirjath-Sepher*
LÄ	Helck, W., E. Otto, and W. Westendorf (editors). *Lexikon der Ägyptologie.* 7 vols. Wiesbaden: Harrassowitz, 1972–92
LHB/OTS	Library of Hebrew Bible/Old Testament Studies
LSJ	Liddell, H. G., and R. Scott. *Greek-English Lexicon.* Revised by H. S. Jones. Oxford: Clarendon, 1968
LTQ	*Lexington Theological Quarterly*
MD	*Materiali e discussioni per l'analisi dei testi classici*
MDAIK	*Mitteilungen des deutschen archäologischen Instituts, Abteilung Kairo*
MdB	*Le Monde de la Bible*
NABU	*Nouvelles assyriologiques brèves et utilitaires*
Nbk.	Strassmaier, J. N. *Inschriften von Nabuchodonosor, König von Babylon (604–561 v. Chr.).* Leipzig: Pfeiffer, 1889
Nbn.	Strassmaier, J. N. *Inschriften von Nabonidus, König von Babylon (555–538 v. Chr.).* Leipzig: Pfeiffer, 1889
NCB	New Century Bible
NEAEHL	Stern, E. (editor). *New Encyclopaedia of Archaeological Excavations in the Holy Land.* 4 vols. Jerusalem: Israel Exploration Society and Carta / New York: Simon & Schuster, 1993
NEchtB	Neue Echter Bibel
NTOA	Novum Testamentum et Orbis Antiquus
NTT	*Norsk Teologisk Tidsskrift*
OBO	Orbis biblicus et orientalis
OEANE	Meyers, E. M. (editor). *The Oxford Encyclopaedia of Archaeology in the Near East.* 5 vols. New York: Oxford University Press, 1997
OLA	Orientalia Lovaniensia Analecta
Or	*Orientalia*
OrAnt	*Oriens antiquus*
OTL	Old Testament Library
OTS	Oudtestamentische Studiën
PCPS	*Publications of the Cambridge Philological Society*
PEQ	*Palestine Exploration Quarterly*
PIHANS	Publications de l'Institut historique: Archéologique néerlandais de Stanboul
PJB	*Palästina-Jahrbuch*
PMLA	*Publications of the Modern Language Association*
QUCC	*Quaderni urbinati di cultura classica*
RA	*Revue d'assyriologie et d'archéologie orientale*
RB	*Revue biblique*
RGG	Galling, K. (editor). *Die Religion in Geschichte und Gegenwart.* 4th ed. Tübingen: Mohr Siebeck, 2000
RGTC	Répertoire géographique des textes cunéiformes
SBAW	Sitzungsberichte der Bayerischen Akademie der Wissenschaften
SBLABS	Society of Biblical Literature Archaeology and Biblical Studies
SBLDS	Society of Biblical Literature Dissertation Series

SBLMS	Society of Biblical Literature Monograph Series
SBLSP	Society of Biblical Literature Seminar Papers
SBLSymS	Society of Biblical Literature Symposium Series
SBLWAW	Society of Biblical Literature Writings from the Ancient World
Sem	*Semitica*
SHANE	Studies in the History of the Ancient Near East
SNTSMS	Society for New Testament Studies Monograph Series
STDJ	Studies on the Texts of the Desert of Judah
TA	*Tel Aviv*
TAD	Porten, B., and A. Yardeni. *Textbook of Aramaic Documents from Ancient Egypt.* 4 vols. Hebrew University Department of History of the Jewish People, Text and Studies for Students. Jesrusalem: Academon, 1986–99
TAPA	*Transactions of the American Philological Association*
TCL	Textes cunéiformes: Musée du Louvre
TDOT	Botterweck, G. J., and H. Ringgren (editors). *Theological Dictionary of the Old Testament.* Grand Rapids, MI: Eerdmans, 1974–
ThR	*Theologische Rundschau*
TLZ	Theologische Literaturzeitung
Transeu	*Transeuphratène*
ThWAT	Botterweck, G. J., and H. Ringgren (editors). *Theologisches Wörterbuch zum Alten Testament.* Stuttgart: Kohlhammer, 1970–
TRE	Krause, G., and G. Müller (editors). *Theologische Realenzyklopädie.* Berlin: de Gruyter, 1977–
TUAT	Kaiser, Otto (editor). *Texte aus der Umwelt des Alten Testaments.* Gütersloh: Mohn, 1984–
TuM	Texte und Materialien der Frau Professor Hilprecht Collection Babylonian Antiquities im Eigentum der Universität Jena
TynBul	*Tyndale Bulletin*
UF	*Ugarit-Forschungen*
VAB	Vorderasiatische Bibliothek
VS	Vorderasiatische Schriftdenkmäler der Königlichen (Staatlichen) Museen zu Berlin
VT	*Vetus Testamentum*
VTSup	Vetus Testamentum Supplements
WBC	Word Biblical Commentary
WHJP	World History of the Jewish People
WMANT	Wissenschaftliche Monographien zum Alten und Neuen Testament
WUNT	Wissenschaftliche Untersuchungen zum Neuen Testament
WZKM	*Wiener Zeitschrift für die Kunde des Morgenlandes*
YCS	Yale Classical Studies
ZA	*Zeitschrift für Assyriologie*
ZABR	*Zeitschrift für altorientalische und biblische Rechtsgeschichte*
ZAH	*Zeitschrift für Althebraistik*
ZÄS	*Zeitschrift für ägyptische Sprache und Altertumskunde*
ZAW	*Zeitschrift für die Alttestamentliche Wissenschaft*
ZBKAT	Zürcher Bibelkommentare: Altes Testament
ZDPV	*Zeitschrift des deutschen Palästina-Vereins*
ZTK	*Zeitschrift für Theologie und Kirche*

PART 1

Thinking of Ancient Texts as Literature

Memory, Narration, Identity:
Exodus as a Political Myth

JAN ASSMANN
University of Konstanz

> How do we know it's us without our past?
> —John Steinbeck, *Grapes of Wrath*

What Are Political Myths?

Christopher Flood proposes distinguishing between sacred and political myths.[1] Sacred myths are primarily concerned with the general structure and meaning of cosmos and reality; political myths concentrate on the narrative construction of collective identity. There is a distinction, no doubt, but I wonder whether it should be described as sacred versus political. Sacredness seems to be present on both sides of the distinction and to be inherent in the very notion of myth. Both cosmos and collective identity are sources of sacredness and are, therefore, productive of sacred narratives. Instead of sacred and political myths, we should perhaps speak of myths sacralizing cosmos and reality, and myths sacralizing society and history. The first type is concerned with what may be called *historia divina*, the latter with *historia humana*. Both, however, are sacred in the sense of founding or foundational power and authority. The political myth with which this essay is particularly concerned, the myth of Moses and Exodus, is the most prominent example of a political myth of highest sacredness.

Political myths are based on or made of mythicized history; they are the form, to quote Claude Lévi-Strauss, in which societies "interiorize their history in order to make it the motor of their development."[2] With regard to this motivating and mobilizing effect of political mythmaking, Anthony Smith, one of the leading theorists on nations and nationalism, used the French term *mythomoteur*, which

---

1. Christopher Flood, *Political Myth: A Theoretical Introduction* (New York, 1996) 3–12.
2. C. Lévi-Strauss, *La pensée sauvage* (Paris, 1962) 309 (translation mine).

3

might be translated into English as 'mythomotorics'. I shall come back to this term on several occasions within this paper.

In serving the construction of collective identity, political myths are a form of memory. Memory is the faculty that enables us to form an identity, both on the personal and on the collective level. Identity, in its turn, is related to time; we could call it a "diachronic identity." "Time is the stuff," wrote the sociologist Thomas Luckmann, "of which a human self is built."[3] Luckmann distinguishes three forms of time: inner, social, and historical time, corresponding to three forms of identity: an inner, subjective self; a social self or person as a carrier of social roles and ascriptions; and a historical or, rather, cultural identity. Memory is the locus where and the mechanism by which this synthesis of time and identity is brought about. It is the faculty allowing us to orient ourselves in time and to form a diachronic identity. Memory research distinguishes between episodic and semantic memory.[4] Our episodic or autobiographical memory concerns what we ourselves lived through, whereas semantic memory is about what we have learned. With reference to this distinction, one could perhaps say that political myths or interiorized histories form the "episodic memory" of a society, whereas myths sacralizing cosmos and reality correspond to its semantic memory.

Do groups such as societies, peoples, and nations "have" a memory in a way that is comparable to individuals? Certainly not: "having" a memory requires a brain. For this reason, the use of the term *memory* with reference to groups, objects, archives, and so on is often criticized as purely and illicitly metaphorical. However, human memory not only is *embodied* and requires a brain as the material carrier of its embodiment, it also is *embedded* and requires social and cultural frames for its embedment. With regard to embedment, the term *memory* is not a metaphor but a metonym based on material contact between a remembering mind and a reminding object; or more generally speaking, "reminding frames of memory," to use the term of Maurice Halbwachs.[5]

---

3. T. Luckmann, "Remarks on Personal Identity: Inner, Social and Historical Time," in *Identity: Personal and Socio-Cultural* (ed. A. Jacobon-Widding; Stockholm, 1983) 67–91; quotation from p. 69.

4. Endel Tulving, "Episodic and Semantic Memory," in *Organization of Memory* (ed. Endel Tulving and Wayne Donaldson; New York: Academic Press, 1972) 382–402.

5. Maurice Halbwachs, *Les Cadres sociaux de la mémoire* (Paris, 1925); repr. 1975 with a foreword by F. Châtelet (Archontes 5; Paris: Mouton); critical reedition by G. Namer (Paris: Albin Michel, 1994).

Halbwachs only acknowledged social frames, but it seems obvious that human memory is also embedded into cultural frames, such as, for example, the landscape or townscape in which we grew up, the texts we learned, the feasts we celebrated, the churches or synagogues we frequented, the music we listened to and, above all, the stories we were told and by and in which we live.

Political myths belong to this sphere of cultural memory but in a very special way. Aleida Assmann distinguishes between "having" and "making" a memory.[6] Groups that cannot be said to "have" a memory tend to make themselves one. This collectively made or instituted memory is what Aleida Assmann calls "political memory." Political memory is an "imaginary institution" in the sense spoken of by Cornelius Castoriadis.[7] Among the many possible symbolizations and representations of political memory such as monuments, anniversaries, holidays, celebrations, parades, national museums and libraries, and other official *lieux de mémoire*, myths seem to hold the most prominent place. They are the stories in and by which a society or community imagines itself.

Coming back to our initial distinction between two sources of sacredness, cosmos and ethnos, we may state that the first source has "run dry" since ancient cosmotheism gave way first to monotheism and then to secularization. The other source, however, proved to be secularization-resistant. Political myths are still flourishing and constitute perhaps the only form in which a certain element of sacredness still survives in our secular world.[8] There does not seem to exist anything that might supersede or replace political myths in a way similar to the way that sacred myths were superseded by world religions or the Enlightenment. On the contrary, the Enlightenment proved to be a particularly prolific generator of political myths. Political myths are only replaced by new political myths. Unlike cosmos and reality, human history proves an inexhaustible source of sacralization. I will cite just the most conspicuous example, the history of the holocaust. In Israel, as well as in Germany, the United States, Europe in general, and in ever-increasing parts of the rest of the world, this event has

---

6. Aleida Assmann, "Memory, Individual and Collective," in *The Oxford Handbook of Contextual Political Analysis* (ed. Robert E. Goodin and Charles Tilly; Oxford: Oxford University Press, 2006) 210–24.

7. Cornelius Castoriadis, *L'institution imaginaire de la société* (Paris, 1975).

8. See, e.g., Anthony D. Smith, *Chosen Peoples: Sacred Sources of National Identity* (Oxford, 2003).

become a foundational story and a central part of political memory, represented in a numberless variety of big and small monuments, museums, anniversaries, novels, history books, films, school books, teaching units, and other forms in which a nation or a society makes itself a memory. Because political myths cannot be secularized, they must be carefully observed and analyzed. Facts may be correct or incorrect, but myths are beyond true and false. Their truth lies in their function, and their value in the use to which they are put.[9] They can be helpful: keeping the memory of the holocaust alive in the form of a foundational story is certainly helpful in bringing about more humane forms of society, approaching the ideal of a decent society as outlined by Avishai Margalit;[10] but they may also be dangerous, such as the Kosovo myth proved to be in the 1990s. Myths tend to be performed; there is a strong relationship between myth and ritual. In the form of political rituals, the sacredness of the group is acted out, and the community is transformed into a *ritual communitas* in Victor Turner's sense. This can always lead to collective zealotry and fanaticism. Critical attention is therefore necessary. A first step toward a critical analysis may be an attempt to distinguish the various types and motifs of political mythmaking.

A Short Typology of Political Mythmaking

There are, first of all, myths of origin. The Franks and Normans traced their origin back to ancient Troy; the Dutch to the Batavians; the Polish nobility to the Sarmatians; the Scots even to Scota, the daughter of the pharaoh of the exodus.[11] Another widespread type is represented by myths of liberation. They normally tell the deeds of a savior hero who managed to free his or her people from oppression or occupation,

---

9. "Der politische Mythos ist also weder eine positive Realität noch reine Fiktion, er ist eine wirksame Fiktion," Jeanne Hersch writes in "Mythos und Politik," in *Die Wirklichkeit des Mythos* (ed. Kurt Hoffmann; Munich, 1965) 86; see also A. Dörner and L. Vogt, "Der Wahlkampf als Ritual: Zur Inszenierung der Demokratie in der Multioptionsgesellschaft," *Aus Politik und Zeitgeschichte* (B 15–16/2002): "Politische Mythen sind nicht wahr oder falsch. Es handelt sich um 'wirksame Fiktionen,' die politischen Sinnentwürfen eine besondere Evidenz verleihen."

10. Avishai Margalit, *The Decent Society* (Cambridge, MA, 1996).

11. For the Franks, Normans, and Troy, see, e.g., Frantisek Graus, *Lebendige Vergangenheit: Überlieferung im Mittelalter und in den Vorstellungen vom Mittelalter* (Cologne, 1975) 81–89. Compare with similar myths concerning the Bohemians (pp. 89–109), Bavarians (pp. 109–11), and Saxons (pp. 112–44). On "Scota," see Smith, *Chosen Peoples*, 124–25.

such as Moses, Arminius the Cheruscan (Hermann der Cherusker), Joan of Arc,[12] William Tell.[13] A third type of political mythology is represented by myths of the Golden or Heroic Age. These myths boom in times that are experienced as periods of suffering and decline. Nineteenth-century Germany, which considers its political situation of an agglomeration of counties, princedoms, dukedoms, and kingdoms to be a *Zerrissenheit* 'dismemberment', invents an originally united Germania and draws from this myth the energy to form a united nation-state in 1871.[14] The same image of dismemberment characterizes the self-image of ancient Egypt during foreign domination. During this period, the ancient ritual of reassembling the dismembered corpse of Osiris assumes a political meaning. The various parts of the corpse are equated with the nomes of Egypt and the ritual reassembling of Osiris symbolizes the restoration of the political integrity of Egypt.[15]

Most typically, however, the experience of suffering, decline, or oppression gives origin to myths of martyrdom and resistance that may be subsumed in the category of *passion myths*. Myths of martyrdom, centered on the death of a hero, are for example, the myth of Kerbela with the murder of Husain in 680 C.E., which is annually enacted by millions of Shi'ites and Alevites in the Ashura Feast; and the myth of Kosovo with the death of King Lazar and a number of fighters in 1389 C.E., who were afterward placed on the calendar of saints by the Serbian Orthodox Church. Related to myths of suffering is a messianic element that fosters hope for the advent or return of an avenger or savior king or leader who will bring an end to the present sufferings and introduce a period of bliss or a return of the Golden Age. The earliest examples date back to ancient Egypt.[16] In the same category belong ancient Israelite and more recent Jewish messianism; the Shi'ite hope for the return of the 12th Imam; the German myth of Kyffhäuser, a mountain under which the emperor Barbarossa sleeps, awaiting his

---

12. Yves Bizeul, "Theorien der politischen Mythen und Rituale," *Politische Mythen und Rituale in Deutschland, Frankreich und Polen* (Berlin, 2000) 33–34; G. Krumeich, *Jeanne d'Arc in der Geschichte: Historiographie, Politik, Kultur* (Sigmaringen, 1992); Marina Warner, *Joan of Arc: The Image of Female Heroism* (Harmondsworth, 1983).

13. Jean-Pierre Bergier, *Wilhelm Tell: Realität und Mythos* (Munich, 1982).

14. Rudolf Speth, *Nation und Revolution: Politische Mythen im 19. Jahrhundert* (Opladen, 2000).

15. See my *Mind of Egypt* (New York, 2002).

16. Idem, "Königsdogma und Heilserwartung: Politische und kultische Chaosbeschreibungen in ägyptischen Texten," in *Apocalypticism in the Mediterranean World and in the Near East* (ed. D. Hellholm; Tübingen, 1983) 345–77.

hour of return; and the various myths and cults known as "cargo cults" that are widespread among peoples oppressed by colonization.[17]

Another and perhaps the most typical element of political myth-making is the idea of divine election or chosenness. The biblical representation became the model for many political myths all over the world and, in some form or another, the Jewish model of the chosen people is still operative even in modern ideas of nationhood and nation states.[18] The concept of *chosenness* is always connected with the idea of a mission. A people is chosen for a purpose, to achieve a given goal, to fulfill a certain mission. The people of Israel is chosen to live according to the Law that the Lord himself issued through Moses, to become thereby a holy people, and to give the other peoples of the earth an example of a political system in conformity with the will of God. The complex of chosenness and sense of mission exist in a national and an imperial form. In the same way that Israel became the model for many movements of nation-building, Rome became the model for imperialism. The "First Rome" was chosen to provide the political stage for Jesus to appear and to spread his message over the world; the Italian-German empire of the Middle Ages and early modernity considered itself the continuation of the Roman Empire—"das heilige römische Reich deutscher Nation." Byzantium called itself the "Second Rome," and Moscow the "Third Rome" with the mission of spreading Christianity, followed by the Soviet Union, which saw its mission as the spread of communism and the advancement of the world revolution. In our days, the U.S.A. is expanding its empire with missionary zeal to spread democracy, human rights, capitalism, and a market economy.

To sum up, chosenness is always linked to a sense of mission regarding a particular agenda. The national model ("Israel") sees its mission as marking the differences, forming an outpost, a bulwark, a stronghold, or an avant-garde of truth in the midst of enemies and pagans. The imperial model ("Rome"), on the other hand, sees its mission as annihilating the difference and the plurality, unifying the world, and universalizing its vision of truth, justice, and order.

---

17. V. Lanternari, *Movimenti religiosi di libertà e di salvezza dei popoli oppressi* (Rome, 1960); ET by L. Sergio, *The Religions of the Oppressed: A Study of Modern Messianic Cults* (New York: Knopf, 1963); P. Worsley, *The Trumpet Shall Sound: A Study of "Cargo" Cults in Melanesia* (New York: Schocken, 1968).

18. See Smith, *Chosen Peoples*.

The Biblical Story of the Exodus

After this perhaps all-too clear-cut taxonomy of political myth-making, let us focus on a particular narrative that combines almost all of the motifs of political mythology that we encountered in the previous survey. This is the biblical story of the exodus. It begins as a story of suffering; turns into a story of liberation; culminates in the story of election, legislation, and mission; and ends as a story of conquest. This example shows that we are dealing with narrative plot structures that may fuse, intersect, and superimpose on each other in various ways.

To treat the exodus as a political myth may provoke two objections. One concerns the "political" element. Is this not a religious myth? What is political in the story of God's rescuing his chosen people from Egyptian slavery? The answer was given by Michael Walzer 20 years ago.[19] Whatever its original meaning in the Hebrew Bible, the story of the exodus has played an immensely important role in politics from early modernity until the present day. Religion and politics cannot be kept apart; they are intimately intertwined in this story. Its reception points to its political core.

The second objection concerns the element of "myth." Is the exodus a "myth" in the same sense as Greek myths; is Moses a hero similar to Heracles, for example?[20] Not in the same sense, I would answer, but in the sense of a foundational story that takes place on the plane of human history and turns a historical experience into a formative memory; thus, in the sense of a political myth.

The text begins as a story of suffering and oppression that uncannily foreshadows Nazi-German concentration camps and turns into a story of liberation when God, at the apex of oppression, sent Moses as a liberator. The central message of this part of the story, underlined by the ten-times-repeated motif of the plagues, is that the Hebrews were not *expelled* from Egypt but *liberated by force* and against the will of Pharaoh. Up to this point, we are dealing with a **myth of origin and of liberation**.

With the events surrounding Mt. Sinai, we enter the second phase, where the story turns into a **myth of election**. God elected the Israelites as his people, and the Israelites turned, by accepting the contract, from a formless mass into a completely new form of human society: a

---

19. Michael Walzer, *Exodus and Revolution* (New York, 1985).

20. For the question of biblical myth, see Michael Fishbane, *Biblical Myth and Rabbinic Mythmaking* (Oxford: Oxford University Press, 2003).

people or nation of God, living according to divine law which, unlike all existing law codes and legal practices, regulates all aspects of their lives because it consists of three different kinds of law:

1. judicial laws (*mišpāṭîm* in Hebrew), which correspond to Egyptian, Babylonian, and other ancient laws;
2. moral laws (*miṣwôt*), which in other civilizations belong instead to the wisdom traditions; and
3. ritual and purity laws (*ḥukkîm*), which in other cultures would apply only to the sphere of priests and the cult.

The combination of these three different kinds of prescriptions—legal, educational, and ritual—must be considered a revolutionary innovation, something unheard of in the ancient world. It is much more than a law code and amounts to something like a script or blueprint that covers all of human life, collective and individual, and is to be performed or "fulfilled" by everyone, always, and everywhere. The text stresses the novelty of this form of community. 'And ye shall be to me', says God, 'a kingdom of priests and a holy nation' (*wĕ-tihyû-lî memlĕḱet kōhănîm wĕgôy qādôš*, Exod 19:6): the world has never seen anything like this before. This is the purpose for which God has chosen them as his people and the task that they must fulfill: to live as a kingdom of priests and a holy nation. This is the central scene of the narrative from which all its surrounding scenes, exodus, wilderness, and conquest, receive their meaning.

The third phase of the narrative, which I will call "wilderness," is a story of crises, in which the new construction is constantly put to the test and in which the people constantly fail and arouse the wrath of God. The two outstanding scenes are the "Golden Calf" (Exodus 32–34) and the "spies" (Numbers 14). The first scene occurs when Moses is still on Mt. Sinai receiving the tablets and when the people, despairing of seeing Moses again after 40 days of absence, relapse into paganism and idolatry. God is resolved to break the covenant, to annihilate the people, and to create a new nation with Moses alone, but Moses persuades him to change his mind. Nevertheless, the people are severely punished for this transgression; 3,000 fall under the sword of the Levite camp police.

Whereas this event may be interpreted as a religious or theological crisis, the crisis with the spies is purely political. The two scenes are clearly parallel and highlight the inseparable union of religion and politics that is characteristic of this myth. When the spies whom Moses had sent out to Canaan return, their report arouses fear and despair among the people; they want to return to Egypt and rebel against

Moses. Again, God decides in his wrath to destroy the people and to create a new nation with Moses, and Moses manages again to persuade God to change his verdict from death to lifelong imprisonment. "Your dead bodies," says God to the Israelites, "shall fall in this wilderness, and of all your number from twenty years old and upward . . . not one will enter the land that I promised you" (Num 14:29). Forty years of wandering in the desert is the time necessary to let a generation of culprits pass away and a new and innocent generation take over.

There are many more scenes like this, when the people rebel against Moses, even wanting to kill him; when they "murmur" against God or Moses and show their unwillingness to follow him any farther. This is undoubtedly the leading theme of the third part of the myth, and we should ask about its narrative function. As is well known, Sigmund Freud went so far as to postulate a real lynching of Moses, because he needed this crime for his psycho-historical interpretation.[21] For the Bible, however, the decisive semantic element is not a single *event* of real murder but a constant attitude of resistance to Moses, even to the point of wishing to kill him. Why does the biblical narrative insist on ascribing to the people of Israel this abiding resistance to the covenant, this "stiff-neckedness" as it is called, this attitude of aversion and rejection? What could be the semantic function of such an unflattering character trait in a foundational story such as this, where the birth of a nation is told and even extolled? Why all this Israel-bashing in a story that lays the cultural foundations of Israel?

The answer, in my view, is found in the theme of the two generations. The covenant is given to the old generation but actually is accepted and realized only by the young generation, which is emphatically distanced from and acquitted of "the sins of the fathers." This motif gives the story the significance of a conversion and a radical turning away from the past. Israel failed but is given a second opportunity, which will be used by the second generation.

The fourth part of the story (after liberation, election, and rebellion/conversion) is told in the book of Joshua, which is not part of the Torah or Pentateuch. It is, however, anticipated in the books of the Torah, especially in Deuteronomy, in the form of prescriptions and stipulations. This fourth phase is the immigration into Canaan which,

---

21. Sigmund Freud, *Moses and Monotheism* (trans. Catherine Jones; New York: Vintage, 1955); James Strachey, trans., *Moses and Monotheism: The Standard Edition of the Complete Psychological Works of Sigmund Freud*, vol. 23 (London: Hogarth, 1964; henceforth referred to as SE) 1–137.

since this is a country inhabited by many peoples, assumes the character of a military conquest.

The prescriptions for dealing with the Canaanites, that is, the aboriginal population of the country, are of a shocking brutality and violence. The law of warfare as codified in the book of Deuteronomy makes an important distinction between dealing with Canaanites and dealing with other cities. Other cities, which are far away, may be "normally" conquered. They should be besieged, offered voluntary submission and, if they reject this offer, be destroyed: the men killed and the women, children, and cattle looted and brought home. Canaanite cities, however, which are not far away but nearby, must not be offered peace and submission, nor may they be conquered and looted. With them, the ban must be executed, leaving nothing alive, destroying everything, and yielding no booty.[22]

The same treatment must be applied to Israelite cities that turn away from the Law and adopt Canaanite customs.[23] The apostates are treated in the same way as the Canaanites, and both are treated differently from complete outsiders. This leads to the supposition that there might be a stronger link between Hebrews and Canaanites, which could explain the strange distinction between distant and Canaanite cities. Could it be that Canaan is just a narrative symbol for the heathen, the unconverted, and the apostates among the Israelites' own ranks? Could it be that conquest, therefore, is but another narrative symbol of conversion? This would correspond to the archaeological record, which so far has not produced any evidence for large-scale conquest, invasion, and destruction in Late Bronze Age and early Iron Age Palestine.[24] The same, by the way, applies to the exodus, for which archaeological or epigraphical evidence is also missing. Could it be that *exodus*, like *conquest*, is just another metaphor for conversion?

---

22. Thus you shall do to all the towns far distant from you, which are not of the towns of these nations. Only, of the towns of these people that the LORD your God is about to give you in estate, you shall let no breathing creature live, but you shall surely put them under the ban: the Hittite and the Amorite, the Canaanite and the Perizzite, the Hivite and the Jebusite, as the LORD your God has charged you, so that they will not teach you to do according to all the abhorrent things that they did for their gods, and you would offend the LORD your God. (Deut 20:15–17 NRSV)

23. The model for these regulations is obvious: this is precisely the punishment with which the Assyrians threatened their vassals.

24. See, e.g., Israel Finkelstein and Neil Asher Silberman, *The Bible Unearthed: Archaeology's New Vision of Ancient Israel and the Origin of Its Sacred Texts* (New York, 2001).

The whole narrative in its four phases of exodus, election, wilderness, and conquest is about the establishment and adoption of a new identity. The exodus is about separation from the old life, wilderness concerns the enormous difficulties and conflicts connected with collective conversion to a new life and identity, and conquest is about dealing with the unconverted or relapsing majority. The Hebrews as the story depicts them were pagans, polytheists, and idolaters themselves before slowly and reluctantly converting to monotheism and iconoclasm; and they were always prone to being lured into assimilation.[25] "Exodus" is about separation from one's former life in oppression and dependence; "wilderness" is about the conflict with an older, backward-looking generation; and "conquest" is about conflict with the unconverted, mainstream culture, with fighting the danger of assimilation and relapse.

The whole myth thus turns out to be centered on identity in terms of difference, conflict, and separation. Separation, however, is not a goal in its own right but the precondition for adopting a new identity as it is laid down by the Law. Separation is the condition for being chosen, and the award is the Promised Land. Chosenness and promise belong together. Chosenness concerns the future.

The relationship between chosenness and the future lies in the idea of a goal to achieve or a task to fulfill. The election of a whole people for partnership with God is a revolutionary idea that can be read as an inversion of the Mesopotamian and Egyptian concepts of a *hieros gamos* between deity and king. I cannot go into details here, but the idea seems to be to replace the king with the people of Israel. According to the Egyptian royal myth, Pharaoh is chosen in order to fulfill two tasks: to provide the altars with offerings for the gods and to establish justice for humankind. In both respects, the people of Israel appears to be the successor of Pharaoh, being commissioned to live a life of justice and ritual purity or sanctity.

But the case of Israel is more specific, because there is the idea of the divine promise that goes far beyond the Promised Land. It is about filling the earth with the seed of Abraham, making the people of God more numerous than the stars in heaven, and making them the avant-garde of what, in the end of time, will become the universal truth, the

---

25. Compare the section in the Passover *Haggadah*:

One must begin with degradation and end with praise. How? One begins and tells that at first our ancestors, in the days of Terah and before him, were deniers and mistakenly followed nothingness and idol worship; and one finishes with the true faith that The Holy One, blessed be He, brought us close to and separated us from those in error and drew us close to His Oneness.

kingdom of God, the end of all separation, conflict, and persecution. With this universal, eschatological, and at times even apocalyptic perspective, the biblical myth of chosenness transcends the realm of the political and lays the foundations for what is called, since St. Augustine, "sacred history" or "salvation history." This, of course, is a religious and not a political idea, even though it had enormous political consequences.

In its secularized forms, moreover, such as communism and socialism, it is still a powerful political narrative. The ideas of chosenness and promise imply a thoroughgoing linearization of cultural time. They made the past narratable back to the first day of creation and the future predictable to the end of time. The five books of Moses are the first attempt at creating a historical narrative that covers the entire stretch of time from creation to the present. The king-lists of Mesopotamia and Egypt also attempt to cover the totality of past time, which they calculate to be much longer than is allowed for by biblical chronology; but they are not narrative. They are just tools of chronological calculation, unrelated to identity and memory.

This brings us back to the point from which we began: the concept of memory. Memory enables us to orient ourselves in time and to form out of the stuff of time a "diachronic identity." Political myths are about forming a collective or political identity, and they achieve this by giving time the form of a narrative structure and charging this structure with values, emotions, and ideals. This connection between memory, identity, and time is particularly evident in the biblical myth of the exodus. Identity is its most obvious aspect. The whole myth is about establishing a new identity, which is laid out in the form of a law code framed by a historical narrative. Without the narrative, the law code could not exert its *formative* function and force, and without the law code, the narrative would not exert its *normative* claim. Both the narrative and the Law constitute a script or blueprint of the new identity. The Law would not make much sense without the narrative, because it would not appear as a means of liberation; and the narrative would not make much sense without the Law, because it would not become clear into which kind of freedom the people had been liberated out of the house of serfdom. This ligature of Law and narrative is a unique feature of this particular political myth, and it is linked to the unique character of the political identity that it founds.

The aspect of memory comes to the forefront at a liminal stage of the narrative between "wilderness" and "conquest," when the people reach the shores of the Jordan River, which they are about to cross. On the eve of this crossing, Moses, who is doomed to stay on the east side, gives a farewell speech in which he devises for his people a very elaborate, collective mnemonic. Moses' main concern is to transform the living memory of the group into a cultural memory that can be transmitted to future generations. The whole book of Deuteronomy is grounded by a deep anxiety about forgetting.[26] Moses' mnemonic is designed as a compensation for his absence and a fortification against the vulnerability of memory confronted with radical changes. It includes no less than seven different devices:

1. Inscription on the heart, that is, learning by heart the text of the Torah
2. Education: teaching the children and the children's children the Law
3. Conversational remembering: constantly discussing the Torah, at home and abroad, by day and by night
4. Marking body and boundary by binding the text on the forehead and by affixing it to the doorpost of one's house
5. Celebrating the three commemorative feasts, Pesah, Shavuot, and Sukkot, all of which provide a frame for collective commemoration of the sojourn in Egypt, the exodus, and the Torah
6. Inscription and publication of the Law on steles covered with plaster
7. Oral poetry: Moses teaches the Israelites a song dealing with the event of the exodus that they are requested to learn by heart and to transmit orally to future generations (chap. 32)

The prerequisite for these mnemonics is canonization of the text of the Law: to add nothing, to subtract nothing, to change nothing (Deut 4:2).

Nietzsche, in his *Genealogy of Morals*, deals with the question how to make human beings a memory and shows how civil society depends on the "fabrication of memory." The book of Deuteronomy is the most elaborate and explicit answer to this question. Two facts are important: (1) the inauguration of this memory occurs at the liminal stage between

---

26. Only take heed and watch yourselves diligently, lest you forget the things that your eyes have seen or they slip from your mind all the days of your life: but teach them to your children and your children's children. (Deut 4:9, based on the NRSV)

When the LORD your God has brought you into the land that he swore to your ancestors . . . to give you—a land with fine, large cities that you did not build . . . when you have eaten your fiill, take care that you do not forget the LORD, who brought you out of the land of Egypt, out of the house of slavery. (Deut 6:10–12, NRSV)

Take care that you do not forget the LORD your God, by failing to keep his commandments. . . . When you have eaten your fill and have built fine houses . . . then do not exalt yourself, forgetting the LORD your God, who brought you out of the land of Egypt. (Deut 8:11–14, NRSV)

wilderness and conquest, and even more important, (2) the Torah, the Pentateuch, ends here. The book of Joshua, which provides the last act of the narrative and is in every other respect its logical continuation, is cut off from the Torah, which is the most canonical, the most sacred, and the most didactic part of the Hebrew Bible.

From a narratological point of view, the story of the exodus, as in every other ethnogenic narrative, draws an arc from no people to one people, defining peoplehood by number, autonomy, and territory and explaining how the children of Israel became numerous, acquired freedom and law (that is, autonomy), and took possession of their allotted territory. Why this drawing of the line after autonomy? The inauguration of memory and the recapitulation of the Law is one big closing line separating the first three acts of the story from its last act. The explanation lies in the newness of the identity thus founded.

With this remark, I pass the borderline between politics and religion. It seems obvious that we are dealing here with the foundation of an identity that is both political and religious. The decisive point, I think, is the aterritorial character of the experience that forms the content of the Mosaic mnemonic. Despite the inclusion of oral poetry, the Mosaic mnemonic is born out of the idea of script and writing. The leading idea is to surpass the principle of localization and to replace or at least complement territory with Scripture. Normally, a cultural memory is inseparably linked to places: religious centers, sacred trees or springs, rivers and valleys, groves or mountains, temples, towers, and castles— landmarks of all kinds.

Jewish memory, if we think of Jerusalem as a symbol of identity, makes no exception in this respect. But there is more to it, and this is perhaps the most important element. The "lost ten tribes" of the Israelites who were deported by the Assyrians from the Northern Kingdom in 722 B.C.E. lost together with their homeland their memory and identity because they lacked something like the Mosaic mnemonic. The deportees from the Southern Kingdom after 587 B.C.E., however, with the help of Deuteronomy, became the "people of the book" and were able to return as Jews to Jerusalem after 50 years of exile.

The new identity is aterritorial, thus laying the foundations not only for a new concept of nationhood but also for a "world religion." This may be the reason why the book of Joshua, which presents itself as the continuation of the ethnogenic narrative, telling the story of conquest, and stressing the connection between the chosen people and the Promised Land, was not accepted into the Torah. Some biblical scholars hold that it originally belonged in what was a Hexateuch and only later became disconnected from the Torah proper. After the experience of the exile, residing in the country no longer counted as the most decisive factor for the new identity of Jewishness. One could live in Babylonia or Egypt and still be a Jew. By means of Scripture, Jewishness became an identity independent of state and territory.

The Torah teaches the principle of double citizenship, of being in this world, without feeling totally at home in it, because it offers yet another realm of belonging. *Gēr ʾanōkî bā-ʾareṣ* 'I am a stranger on earth', we read in Ps 119:19, *ʾal-tastēr mimmenî miṣwōteikā* 'do not conceal your commandments from me'. Seen in this perspective, the exodus story symbolizes the transition from terrestrial alienation to a scriptural home—that is, a religious identity based on a canon of sacred Scripture and its continuous exegesis.

This is the mission that the Jewish people are called to fulfill, and it has set an example that, in the long run, has actually changed the world in the most profound way. All of the new religions emerging since antiquity, most of them monotheistic and most of them in opposition to older traditions and other religions that they reject as paganistic, developed canons of sacred Scripture and commentaries that translate the canonical texts into changing realities and conditions of understanding: Judaism and the Tanakh, Christianity and the Christian Bible, Islam and the Qurʾān, Buddhism and the Pāli Canon, Jainism and the Jaina Canon, the Sikh religion and the Adi Granth, Daoism, Confucianism, and so on down to the Mormons and the Book of Mormon.

This strong alliance between religions of this new type, the so-called world religions, and the formation of canons and commentaries once again illustrates the connection between memory and identity. The transition from ritual to textual continuity means a complete reorganization of the cultural memory in the same way as the transition from the ethnically and culturally determined religions of the ancient world to the new type of transcultural and transnational world religions meant a totally new construction of identity. The canon, in a way, functioned as a new transethnical homeland and as a new transcultural formation and education.

This rather theological interpretation amounts to a depoliticization of the exodus myth, which now appears as the foundation not of political but of religious identity. This shift of focus, I think, corresponds precisely to the course of history, from a politically motivated monolatry, a resistance movement against Assyrian and Babylonian oppression and against one's own collaborative establishment toward monotheism as a totally new form of religious, social, and political order. The exodus myth oscillates between a political narrative of liberation and a religious narrative of conversion and as such exemplifies the intricate connection between religion and politics.

Narrative Poetics and Hebrew Narrative: A Survey

JOACHIM VETTE
University of Heidelberg

Introduction

The following is a survey of narrative criticism or narrative poetics as an approach to understanding Old Testament narrative (hereafter: biblical narrative). This survey is presented from a specific point of view that needs to be made transparent from the outset. I am writing in English but from within a context of German biblical scholarship at the University of Heidelberg. Until recently, interest in narrative poetics was confined almost exclusively to an English and Hebrew context.[1] Narrative studies are a relatively new arrival to German biblical scholarship, a fact illustrated both by several recent publications and by a great deal of suspicion toward this exegetical approach. The diverging interests governing historical-critical approaches and narrative-critical approaches have given rise to no small amount of polemical bantering. As much as possible, I will refrain from entering into or evaluating this bantering.

The various influences that have enriched the analysis of biblical narrative, including structuralism and formalism, are too widespread to be adequately represented in a single essay. Instead, I will trace the development of narrative criticism and introduce its basic concerns by highlighting individual authors who have made special contributions to the study of narrative in general and biblical narrative in particular.[2] Among these, my focus will be on publications that deal

---

1. I will not be concerned with contributions published exclusively in Hebrew.

2. This overview is wider in scope and in depth than the very short article by C. Long Westfall in S. Porter, ed., *Dictionary of Biblical Criticism and Interpretation* (London: Routledge, 2007) 237–38. At the same time it is more limited than the broad overview of various synchronic approaches compiled in J. C. Exum and D. J. Clines, eds., *The New Literary Criticism and the Hebrew Bible* (JSOTSup 143; Sheffield: JSOT Press, 1993). I have omitted the works on narrative criticism that deal exclusively or primarily with New Testament texts,

primarily with general questions of biblical narrative. The large body of narrative-critical readings of single biblical narratives cannot enter into this discussion for reasons of space.[3]

Narrative criticism, narrative poetics, or narratology, as it is sometimes called, has often been accused of subjectivity, lacking methodology and clearly defined interpretive criteria. Some of this may be justified—"literary studies" does display a tendency toward exalting the interpretive genius of the individual interpreter—but this accusation also reflects the fact that many authors who engage in an analysis of Hebrew narrative poetics use tools and paradigms taken from the larger context of literary studies. However, authors who use narrative-critical approaches to biblical narrative rarely reflect on and explain these tools when presenting their interpretations. Although there are many textbooks on the methodology of historical-critical approaches, most narrative critics seem more interested in engaging in "close readings" than in communicating the tools used in this process. For this reason, it is necessary to bridge the disciplines of literary studies and biblical studies and begin with a brief description of the development of narrative analysis in general before moving on to the specifics of biblical narrative. Only in this way can we understand why narrative critics read the way they do.

The Development of Narrative Poetics

Lubbock and Forster: The Beginnings of Narrative Poetics

As much as individual books can be taken as the beginning point for a certain development, *The Craft of Fiction* by Percy Lubbock[4] and

---

such as R. Funk, *The Poetics of Biblical Narrative* (Sonoma, CA: Polebridge, 1988); M. Powell, *What Is Narrative Criticism?* (Minneapolis: Fortress, 1990); and D. Tolmie, *Narratology and Biblical Narratives: A Practical Guide* (San Francisco: International Scholars, 1999).

3. A few examples are: D. Gunn, "David and the Gift of the Kingdom," *Semeia* 3 (1975) 14–45; J. P. Fokkelman, *Narrative Art in Genesis* (Assen: Van Gorcum, 1975); P. D. Miscall, "The Jacob and Joseph Stories as Analogies," *JSOT* 6 (1978) 28–40; G. Wenham, "Coherence of the Flood Narrative," *VT* 28 (1978) 336–48; L. Eslinger, "Viewpoints and Points of View in 1 Samuel 8–12," *JSOT* 26 (1983) 61–76; J. C. Exum, "Isaac, Samson, and Saul: Reflections on the Comic and Tragic Visions," *Semeia* 32 (1984) 5–40; R. Polzin, "The Monarchy Begins: 1 Samuel 8–10," in *Society of Biblical Literature: Seminar Papers* (SBLSP 26; Atlanta: Scholars Press, 1987) 120–43; G. Chirichigno, "The Narrative Structure of Exodus 19–24," *Bib* 68 (1987) 457–79; E. van Wolde, "The Story of Cain and Abel: A Narrative Study," *JSOT* 52 (1991) 25–41; P. Satterthwaite, "Narrative Artistry in the Composition of Judges XX:29ff.," *VT* 42 (1992) 8–89; G. Nicol, "The Narrative Structure and Interpretation of Genesis XXVI," *VT* 46 (1996) 339–60; S. Brooks, "Saul and the Samson Narrative," *JSOT* 71 (1996) 19–25.

4. P. Lubbock, *The Craft of Fiction* (6th ed.; London, 1954), first published in 1921.

Aspects of the Novel by E. M. Forster[5] are a good place to begin when summarizing the development of narrative analysis in the 20th century. Both stand at the onset of a developing narrative poetics. Compared with dramatic or lyrical works, the systematic study of narrative as a literary form is a relatively late arrival to the scene of literary criticism. The achievement of these authors consists of laying down several basic paradigms for the study of narrative texts.

According to Forster, the basis of any narrative is a story.[6] This story, however, is not the same as the narrative; it is merely the basic material that an author shapes with various strategies in an attempt to create an artful composition.[7] This artful composition, or narrative discourse, is the sum of a series of decisions and selections made by the author. It is not the same as the story, nor is it an unmediated, direct representation of that story. The difference between story (in other words: the source for the discourse) and discourse becomes very apparent when looking at characters in a novel. Forster highlights the basic difference between "people in a novel" and "people like you and me, or Queen Victoria."[8] While narrative people and real people already differ fundamentally in the categories of birth, death, food, sleep, and love,[9] the main difference between *homo sapiens* and *homo fictus* is found on an epistemological level: members of the category *homo fictus* "are people whose secret lives are visible or might be visible," whereas "we are people whose secret lives are invisible."[10]

When interpreters or exegetes shift their attention from *what* is told to *how* something is told, they engage narrative texts on their discourse level in an attempt to describe and understand how and why a discourse is shaped in a particular fashion. Lubbock emphasizes that this sort of interaction with the discourse level requires the involvement of

---

5. E. M. Forster, *Aspects of the Novel* (London, 1927).

6. As Forster states with characteristic sarcasm:

The primitive audience was an audience of shock-heads, gaping round the campfire, fatigued with contending against the mammoth or the woolly rhinoceros, and only kept awake by suspense. What would happen next? The novelist droned on, and as soon as the audience guessed what happened next they either fell asleep or killed him. . . . Scheherazade survived because she managed to keep the king wondering what would happen next. (Ibid., 14)

7. Ibid., 43.

8. Ibid., 55.

9. Ibid., 60–62.

10. Ibid., 70. Lubbock argues that the "truth and force of the characters" are among the most powerful aspects in narrative (Lubbock, *Craft of Fiction*, 5).

the reader: reading narrative is not a passive consumption of information but a creative activity. In his words, "The reader of a novel—by
which I mean the critical reader—is himself a novelist."[11]

The distinction between story and plot, the clear separation between *homo fictus* and *homo sapiens*, and the emphasis on the creative
role of the reader paved the way for many aspects of narrative poetics.
These categories were an important step in separating the world of
narrative discourse from the world of story with all of its potential historical connections. Even though narrative discourse itself also remained an object of history, conditioned and affected by its immediate
historical context, this discourse was no longer directly connected to
the historical context of the subject matter contained in it.[12]

Wolfgang Kayser and Others: Moving from Source to Discourse

In the 1950s, the work of the German scholars Max Wehrli and
Wolfgang Kayser was influenced by trends in narrative analysis developed in an English-speaking context.[13] A movement away from the
historical context of the subject matter toward the structures of the
text itself characterizes their approach. Kayser saw this movement as
no less than a fundamental paradigm shift in literary studies:

---

11. Ibid., 17. See also p. 21.

12. A related highly important shift was the movement in the 1930s and 1940s from
the author and his "intention" to "the text itself." This movement comprised many different scholars who stood for what came to be known as "New Criticism." These "New
Critics" included W. K. Wimsatt, M. C. Beardsely, C. Brooks, R. Wellek, A. Warren, and
A. Tate. Although New Criticism no longer exists as it did in the first half of the last
century (see F. Lentricchia, *After the New Criticism* [London: Athlone, 1980]), many of its
tenets have become unquestioned axioms of literary analysis. For a discussion of New
Criticism as a literary and cultural phenomenon, see U. Halfmann, *Der Amerikanische
"New Criticism"* (Frankfurt a.M.: Athenäum, 1971); M. Jancovich, *The Cultural Politics of
the New Criticism* (Cambridge: Cambridge Univ. Press, 1993); W. Spurlin and M. Fischer,
eds., *The New Criticism and Contemporary Literary Theory: Connections and Continuities*
(New York: Garland, 1995); J. Barton, "The New Criticism," in *Reading the Old Testament:
Method in Biblical Study* (London: Darton, 1996).

13. M. Wehrli, *Allgemeine Literaturwissenschaft* (Bern: Francke, 1951) 21:

> Es ist nicht ganz unrichtig, wenn für das Debakel der deutschen Literaturwissen-
> schaft deren allzu "geistes"-wissenschaftliche Tendenz verantwortlich gemacht
> wurde und selbst Linien von Herder zur nazistischen Literatur gezogen werden
> konnten. Die eingetretene Ernüchterung kann nun umgekehrt eine größere
> Offenheit und methodische Unbefangenheit gegenüber den wissenschaftlichen
> Traditionen anderer Länder befördern. *Um so mehr, als diese ihrerseits, vor allem im
> angelsächsischen Bereich, eine lebendige und vielfältige Forschung gerade in den letzten
> 20 Jahren entwickelt haben.*

Italics mine; compare p. 83: "das klassisch gewordene Werk von E. M. Forster."

Emil Staiger hat wohl die Signatur der Zeit richtig gedeutet, als er in der Einleitung zu seinem Buch *Die Zeit als Einbildungskraft des Dichters* im Jahre 1939 sagte, dass die Literaturgeschichte "einer Erneuerung heute sehr bedürfe, dass sie in dem, was sie bisher getan, gesättigt sei, und, um zu dauern, gleichsam von vorn beginnen müsse."[14]

Like Forster, Kayser differentiates between story (*Stoff*) and discourse (*literarisches Werk*). The story, or source, is the content that also exists apart from its expression in a literary work and gives rise to it. Literary studies, according to Kayser, had suffered from a long-standing fixation on the source of a narrative—that is, the historical context of the story. By reducing literary analysis to the analysis of the source, scholars merely perpetuate a 'stench of historical preoccupation' (*Odium der Stoffhuberei*).[15] Instead, Kayser argues for an increased interest in the relationship between story and discourse (*Fabel und Werk*).[16] This sort of analysis should not proceed from fixed assumptions about how a piece of literature *should be* but from what *it is*.[17]

Recognizing that defining what narrative is remains problematic at best,[18] Kayser proposes a definition that begins with the fundamental activity of narration: narration occurs when content is related to an audience by a narrator who mediates between content and an audience.[19] This mediation stands at the core of that in which narrative analysis must be interested. By shaping chronological order, narrative perspective, and characters, the narrator determines how content is communicated to and received by his or her audience.[20] Kayser, as Lubbock before him, recognizes a lack of sufficiently defined analytical tools and terminology suited to describing this process. This was what prompted

---

14. "Emil Staiger correctly recognized the signs of the time when he stated in the introduction to his 1939 book *Die Zeit als Einbildungskraft des Dichters* that the studies in literary history 'were very much in need of renewal. They had grown complacent with what they had accomplished in the past and needed to start over in order to continue on.'" Cited from W. Kayser, *Das sprachliche Kunstwerk* (2nd ed.; Bern: Francke, 1951) 24 (translation mine). See also E. Staiger, *Die Kunst der Interpretation: Studien zur deutschen Literaturgeschichte* (Zurich: Atlantis, 1955).

15. Kayser, *Das sprachliche Kunstwerk*, 60.

16. Ibid., 82.

17. See Wehrli, *Allgemeine Literaturwissenschaft*, 40: "Die Lehre von der ars poetica hat schon längst den normativen Charakter einer sog. Regelpoetik abgestreift und ist zur beschreibenden und begründenden Wissenschaft geworden."

18. Compare Forster's expression: "The novel is most distinctly one of the moister areas of literature" (*Aspects of the Novel*, 25).

19. Kayser, *Das sprachliche Kunstwerk*, 198–202.

20. Ibid., 206, 210, and 355ff.

Wehrli to omit a discussion of narrative literature in his *Allgemeine Literaturwissenschaft*.[21] Kayser, however, makes a first attempt at addressing several of these aspects, such as perspective, setting, and time.

The analysis of time in narrative also stands at the center of the work of Günther Müller and his student Eberhard Lämmert.[22] Whereas Forster only discussed various possibilities of playing with chronological order in narrative, Müller and Lämmert focus on the matter of duration, of narrative time versus narrated time (*Erzählzeit und erzählte Zeit*). They recognize that the relationship between the length of the discourse and the time span narrated by this discourse is no matter of course but is the author's choice and is an important part of the strategies he or she uses to convey content to the reader.

Wayne Booth: The Craft of the Narrator

With the appearance of W. Booth's classic monograph *The Rhetoric of Fiction*,[23] the development of tools and terminology for the analysis of narrative took a large step forward. Booth's monograph, which is still a widely used text in fiction courses, created a theoretical framework that found wide acceptance. Booth works with the assumption that "narrative is an art, not a science, but this does not mean that we are necessarily doomed to fail when we attempt to formulate principles about it. There are systematic elements in every art, and criticism of fiction can never avoid the responsibility of trying to explain technical successes and failures by reference to general principles."[24]

Central to Booth's work is the distinction between the implied author and the real author. Following the tenet of the New Critics, who argued that analytical focus should be on the product of literary composition, not on the producer, Booth claims that readers have no access to the real author by means of the narrative composed by him or her. The agent of narration that becomes visible in the narrative is an entity separate from the persona of the real author. Booth refers to this agent of narration as the implied author: "We infer [the implied author] as an ideal, literary, created version of the real man; *he is the sum of his own choices*."[25] This narrator as implied author is, in a sense, the personified selection pro-

---

21. Wehrli, *Allgemeine Literaturwissenschaft*, 84–85.

22. G. Müller, *Morphologische Poetik: Gesammelte Aufsätze* (Darmstadt: Wissenschaftliche Buchgesellschaft, 1968); E. Lämmert, *Bauformen des Erzählens* (Stuttgart: Metzler, 1967).

23. W. Booth, *The Rhetoric of Fiction* (2nd ed.; Chicago: University of Chicago Press, 1983). The 1st edition appeared in 1961.

24. Ibid., 164.

25. Ibid., 75 (emphasis mine).

cess that shaped a story into narrative discourse. Booth distinguishes between dramatized and undramatized narrators as well as between reliable and unreliable narrators. Booth argues vehemently that the narrator's selection process is equally present on all levels of narrative, whether it is direct speech and dialogue ("showing") or description and commentary ("telling"). The implied author shapes the story no less or no more in direct speech than in description or commentary.

As the composition of a narrative involves selecting one narrative strategy over another, the result of this selection process provides the readers with an indication of the reasons behind the selection. Thus, a narrative text becomes a communicational matrix that embodies the intention of an implied author, an intention that he aims to convey to his or her readers by means of certain narrative strategies. Booth spends much time discussing how narrators are able to lead readers in a certain direction while impressing certain attitudes and value judgments on them (thus also the title "The *Rhetoric* of Fiction"). He posits that every reader comes to a text with certain interests, which he classifies as intellectual, qualitative, and practical interests.[26] These interests lead to reader expectations (which narrators then use to shape suspense and surprise) as well as leading readers to certain conclusions. For this communication to work, however, readers and implied authors must share a basic set of values. For "to pass judgment where the author intends neutrality is to misread. But to be neutral or objective where the author requires commitment is equally to misread."[27] Whether a good reader is required to follow what the author requires, or whether rebellion against the implied author's intention is acceptable is an issue that Booth does not address but that subsequently gains increasing importance.

Seymour Chatman: Characters in Narrative

The book *Story and Discourse* by Seymour Chatman[28] is another milestone in the description and analysis of what occurs when one writes or reads narrative. Chatman widens his focus beyond written texts to include narrative transmission in verbal, cinematic, balletic,

---

26. Ibid., 125ff.

27. Ibid., 144. Here we already find a description of what Sternberg later refers to as foolproof composition (see below).

28. S. Chatman, *Story and Discourse: Narrative Structure in Fiction and Film* (Ithaca, NY: Cornell Univ. Press, 1978). See also his earlier work: "New Ways of Analyzing Narrative Structure with an Example from Joyce's Dubliners," *Language and Style* 2 (1969) 3–36; idem, "The Structure of Narrative Transmission," in *Style and Structure in Literature: Essays in the New Stylistics* (ed. R. Fowler; Oxford, 1975) 213–58.

and pantomimic manifestations. Common to all these areas is the basic separation between what is told (the story, or content) and how it is told (the discourse or expression of the content). Each attempt at communicating the story through a particular discourse involves the participation of the audience or readership. Chatman refers to this process as "reading out."[29]

Chatman introduces a myriad of categories that continually refine the analysis of narrative texture. Stories consist of events and existents. Events (actions and happenings) are weighted according to their importance for the narrative logic (kernels and satellites) and constitute an array called plot.[30] Plots are shaped by chronological order and the relationship between narrated time and narrative time.[31] Plots can further be classified as plots of action, plots of character, and plots of thought. Whereas the events of a story are governed by time, the existents of a story are governed by space. For Chatman, the most important existents are the characters in a given story. Whereas Propp, following Aristotle, argued that characters are primarily products of action and thus of plot,[32] Chatman is insistent that characters are primarily defined by their specific character traits. He defines Forster's *homo fictus* not as a mere plot function but as a personality whose character determines the actions he or she performs. This personality is reconstructed by the reader "from evidence announced or implicit in an original construction and communicated by the discourse, through whatever medium."[33] Characters are paradigms of character traits that either remain constant throughout the narrative or change, thus creating suspense and surprise.

---

29. "From the surface or manifestation level of reading, one works through to the deeper narrative level. That is the process I call, technically, reading out" (Chatman, *Story and Discourse*, 41). By thus emphasizing the role of the reader in constituting the meaning of the text, Chatman also anticipates the later development of so-called reader-response criticism. For an introduction to this approach, see H. Jauss, "Literary History as a Challenge to Literary Theory," in *New Directions in Literary Theory* (ed. R. Cohen; London, 1974); W. Iser, *Der Akt des Lesens: Theorie ästhetischer Wirkung* (Munich: Fink, 1978); S. Fish, *Is There a Text in This Class? The Authority of Interpretive Communities* (Cambridge: Harvard Univ. Press, 1980).

30. Chatman, *Story and Discourse*, 54. "Each arrangement [of events] produces a different plot, and a great many plots can be made from the same story" (ibid., 43).

31. Compare Müller, *Morphologische Poetik*; and Lämmert, *Bauformen des Erzählens*.

32. V. Propp, *Morphology of the Folktale* (trans. L. Scott; ed. L. Wagner; 2nd ed.; Austin: Univ. of Texas Press, 1975) 20. The work was originally published in Russian in 1928.

33. Chatman, *Story and Discourse*, 119. See Lubbock, *Craft of Fiction*, 5.

Table 1. Classifications of Analepses and Prolepses

	External	*Internal*	*Mixed*	*Heterodiegetic*	*Homodiegetic*
Analepsis/ Prolepsis	Stays entirely outside the temporal frame of the main narrative.	Stays entirely within the temporal frame of the main narrative.	Starts before the time of the main narrative, includes this time frame up to the point where the anachronism occurred in the text.	Refers to subject matter other than the story of the main narrative.	Refers to the subject matter contained in the main narrative.

Gerard Genette: Narrative and Time

Müller and Lämmert had already focused on the issue of narrative and time in the late 1950s. Ten years later, the French scholar Gerard Genette once again dealt with this issue, creating an unparalleled system of classification for all temporal aspects of narrative.[34] Each narrative text is governed by temporal aspects internal to the discourse and temporal aspects brought to it externally by the process of reading, which itself occurs in time. Genette classifies these temporal processes as order, duration, and frequency. The order in narrative discourse is especially interesting when it deviates from "natural" chronological order. Based on whether these deviations move forward or backward in time, Genette speaks of prolepses and analepses, which he further classifies as summarized in table 1.[35] In his discussion of duration in narratives, Genette builds on the observations made by Müller and Lämmert and distinguishes descriptive pauses, scenes, summaries, and ellipses in narrative.[36] Frequency is an account of the repetitions within narrative discourse. Narratives can narrate *once* what occurred *once*, they can narrate *x-times* what occurred *x-times*, *once* what occurred *x-times*, and *x-times* what occurred *once*. In this context, Genette speaks of singulative, repetitive, and iterative narratives.[37] In his analysis of time and especially repetition, Genette addresses issues that are of central importance to the exegesis of Hebrew narrative.

---

34. G. Genette, *Figures I–III* (Paris: Seuil, 1966–72); idem, *Nouveau discours du récit* (Paris: Seuil, 1983). His work was later translated into English (*Narrative Discourse Revisited* [Ithaca, NY: Cornell Univ. Press, 1988]) and German (*Die Erzählung* [Munich: Fink, 1994]).

35. See idem, *Erzählung*, 31–46.

36. Ibid., 62–63.

37. Ibid., 82–103.

Mieke Bal: Functional Events and Focalization

In the 1980s, another important contribution to the study of narrative poetics was presented by Mieke Bal, currently professor of theory of literature at the University of Amsterdam. In her book *Narratology*,[38] Bal builds on concepts found especially in Chatman and Genette, expanding them particularly in the area of point of view. Pursuing the question of the way that narratives are constructed in general, Bal sets out to develop a set of tools that readers can use to describe individual narrative texts. She defines narrative as "a series of logically and chronologically related events that are caused or experienced by actors"[39]—events that are then presented by a narrator from certain aspects, including sequence, narrative time, construction of character, and point of view.

Two areas are particularly noteworthy in Bal's discussion: the classification of events and the question of narrative perspective. Because events form a central part of any narrative, narrative poetics must be able to define what an event is. Going beyond Chatman's simple division of events into kernels and satellites, Bal suggests the following criteria for selecting and, more importantly, weighting the events of a narrative: (1) An essential function of any event is the transition from one state into another. Therefore, *change* becomes an important criterion in determining what narrative elements are events.[40] (2) *Choice* is a second important criterion, because an event opens various possibilities that lead to different possible conclusions. Bal speaks of a functional event when the choices opened by it become important later on in the narrative. (3) *Confrontation* is another criterion.[41] Bal suggests that actors appear in contrasting groups in virtually any narrative—constellations that can change over the course of the narrative. According to Bal, every functional event consists of a confrontation between two actors, or more precisely, "two actors, and one action."[42] By combining the questions of change, choice, and confrontation, the reader is able to classify the events of a narrative text according to their importance to the narrative structure.

---

38. M. Bal, *Narratology: Introduction to the Theory of Narrative* (Toronto: Univ. of Toronto Press, 1985). The book was originally published in Dutch as *De theorie van vertellen en verhalen* (Muiderberg, 1980).

39. Idem, *Narratology*, 5.

40. Thus "John is ill" does not constitute an event; "John falls ill," however, does (ibid., 14).

41. In this context, Bal refers back to W. Hendricks, "Methodology of Narrative Structural Analysis," *Semiotica* 7 (1973) 163–84.

42. Bal, *Narratology*, 17

Table 2.

The Reader	The Focalizer	Type of Suspense
does not know	does not know	riddle, detective narrative
does not know	knows	secret
knows	does not know	threat
knows	knows	no suspense

A second important area that Bal discusses is the question of narrative perspective. Taking a clear stance against previous discussions of perspective, Bal insists that we must distinguish between "the vision through which the elements are presented . . . and the identity of voice that is verbalizing that vision."[43] By introducing the term *focalization*, which she defines as "the relationship between the 'vision,' the agent that sees, and that which is seen,"[44] Bal hopes to sharpen this distinction and enhance the analysis of narrative structure. When analyzing the agent that sees, or in Bal's words the *focalizer*, an important distinction is made between character-bound or internal focalization and non-character-bound or external focalization. Having identified the focalizer, the interpreter can determine what the focalizer is focalizing on, what attitude he displays in this process, and whether the focalized object can be verified by a third party (here Bal distinguishes between perceptible and non-perceptible objects). Dismissing the distinction between a first-person and a third-person narrator as irrelevant (compare Bal's statement: " 'I' and 'He' are both 'I' "),[45] Bal proposes a classification of focalizer using the categories *external* versus *internal* and includes the question of the epistemological level of the narrator—that is, whether his or her knowledge of the event narrated is limited or not. A comparison between the epistemological level of the focalizer and that of the reader is an especially useful tool when one is analyzing how suspense is created in narrative. Bal argues that the epistemological levels of the focalizer and the reader determine suspense as summarized in table 2. As I will discuss below, the analysis of the epistemological levels made a strong impact on the study of the narrative poetics of Hebrew narrative, particularly in the work of Meir Sternberg.

---

43. Ibid., 101.
44. Ibid., 104.
45. Ibid., 121.

Narrative Poetics and Biblical Narrative

Erich Auerbach

Erich Auerbach made important contributions to the interpretation of Hebrew narrative that were motivated not by theological but by literary questions. His monumental work *Mimesis: Dargestellte Wirklichkeit in der abendländischen Literatur* takes biblical narrative as its starting point for a sweeping discussion of Western narrative tradition, especially in the area of what Auerbach refers to as "realistic narrative."[46]

In his discussion of Hebrew narrative, Auerbach discovers a stylistic peculiarity unique to these texts. Based on a style analysis of the Aqedah in Genesis 22, he marvels at the narrative minimalism that shapes these texts: "Ohne jede Einschaltung, in wenigen Hauptsätzen, deren syntaktische Verbindung miteinander äußerst arm ist, rollt die Erzählung ab."[47] Even though Auerbach has subsequently been criticized for his one-sided emphasis of this stylistic peculiarity, especially in proclaimed contrast to the work of Homer (see the contribution by I. de Jong in this volume), his description of Hebrew narrative minimalism has subsequently proven highly influential to the work of many exegetes. Auerbach is especially interested in the effect this narrative minimalism has on the reader. He claims that the text is deliberately cryptic and enigmatic and demands an increased effort on the part of each reader.[48] When facing Hebrew narrative, we are condemned to an act of intensive interpretation. Without resorting to the term, Auerbach thus anticipates what is subsequently described as *close reading*. In his claim, this close reading is always controlled by powerful parameters of norms and values put forward by the narrative world of the text.

---

46. E. Auerbach, *Mimesis: Darstellung der Realität in der abendländischen Literatur* (Bern: Francke, 1946). Realistic narrative, for Auerbach, is the portrayal of everyday life that shows this life in its human and social context and takes it seriously even in its tragic aspects (see especially pp. 426–33). The highpoints of realistic narrative are biblical narratives, Dante, and the 19th-century French novel (Stendhal, Balzac). Biblical narrative is thus the first to succeed in giving vivid expression to vivid experience in which the common, the realistic, even the ugly find their place. Hans Frei builds on this definition and adds to it by stating that realistic narrative is also determined by characters and settings that cohere with the narrative subject (see H. Frei, *The Eclipse of Biblical Narrative: A Study in Eighteenth and Nineteenth Century Hermeneutics* [New Haven: Yale Univ. Press, 1974] 11).

47. Auerbach, *Mimesis*, 17 ("The narrative takes its course without any interruption, with a few main clauses with the most minimal syntactic connections").

48. Ibid., 18–19.

Zvi Adar

Zvi Adar's book *The Biblical Narrative*[49] appeared in 1959 and thus predates the appearance of most major works dealing with an analysis of Hebrew narrative by more than 20 years. Even though many of Adar's conclusions can now be criticized as too general, he anticipated many of the central concerns that were later to inform a poetics of biblical narrative.

Adar claims that Hebrew narratives are highly artistic renditions of popular folktales. This artistry is found not primarily in their subject matter but in the compositional skill and narrative strategies employed by the authors. Adar distinguishes between isolated stories, long stories, and narrative books and assumes a stylistic unity common to all of these categories. Each biblical narrative, regardless of length is "typical" for the style of biblical narrative in general.[50] This assumption allows him to analyze individual narratives and draw conclusions, which he then applies to the whole of biblical narration. Adar does not doubt that the final text is an outcome of textual growth, yet he understands the growth of biblical literature from small narrative units to large compositions as being the result of great artistic skill. For Adar, a diachronic examination of biblical narratives entails a composition-critical examination of the artful principles behind the gathering of individual narrative units.[51]

Adar echoes Auerbach in his description of the concise and economic narrative style exemplified by Hebrew narrative. These stories avoid verbosity or lengthy descriptions void of function for the narrative plot. Narrative expositions are very short and include only what is absolutely necessary for the story. The central aspects of the story appear without any digression.[52] The density of biblical narrative presents a challenge to the reader who needs to "read intensively"[53] in order to gain information on the internal motives of the characters because the text does not provide these directly.

---

49. Z. Adar, *The Biblical Narrative* (Jerusalem: Dept. of Education, 1959).

50. Ibid., 8.

51. Ibid., 199–200.

52. "Once the narrator has opened the subject itself he does not stray either to the right or the left, and only occasionally introduces an incidental remark in so far as it is required for the understanding of what is happening. In the course of the plot itself, each detail is subordinate to the aim; every sentence and every word fulfill the function that is reserved for them in the inner life of the chapter; and from this point of view the Biblical story is a classic example of an organic unity, a true artistic creation" (ibid., 55).

53. Ibid., 56.

The treatment of character is, in Adar's view, the greatest strength of biblical narrative. Even though he assumes that most biblical characters are historical figures or character types taken from folk tales, Adar assumes that each character is an individual artistic creation, based on, but not limited by, historical or typological models.[54] A central aspect of biblical narrative style is thus the absence of stereotypes in the creation of biblical characters. This does not imply that certain personality traits are not preferred over others, such as practical cleverness and great faith.[55] Adar's final focus is theological: the main character of Hebrew narrative and thus the main focus of these texts is God. Each character study in Hebrew narrative is a stepping-stone toward understanding God.[56]

Luis Alonso Schökel

One of the first biblical exegetes to be influenced directly by Auerbach's work was L. Alonso Schökel. In his 1957 dissertation,[57] his focus still is primarily on the *poetics of lyrical texts* in the Hebrew Bible, especially in the prophetic books, the book of Psalms, and Job. In this context, Alonso Schökel develops tools for the description and stylistic analysis of Hebrew poetry. Although the work does contain a brief section on dialogue,[58] the analysis of narrative is not his main concern. This changes with his early article on narrative art in the book of Judges.[59] Here, he refers back to the style analyses presented by Auerbach while simultaneously lamenting the absence of a *poetics of Hebrew narrative*. Surveying the contemporary state of biblical research he states, "Eine grundsätzliche, systematische und abgerundete Darstel-

---

54. Ibid., 49–50.

55. Ibid., 52. Even subsidiary characters are not necessarily stereotyped. As Adar states: "These figures are outstanding in their simplicity, but it is possible that one reason for this is that they are described in one dimension only. . . . One central human value emerges from a single situation in the life a subsidiary hero, and thus we are accustomed to attach the concept of the Biblical figure to subsidiary figures like Naboth, Barilai and Hannah, which intensively convey a human value of a particular type, such as rootedness, fidelity or honesty; and this involves the danger of a narrow or superficial view of the Biblical type" (p. 131).

56. Ibid., 138–39.

57. Published as *Estudios de Poética Hebrea* (Barcelona, 1963). A condensed German translation appeared as *Das Alte Testament als literarisches Kunstwerk* (trans. K. Bergner; Cologne, 1971). Together with A. Graffy, Alonso Schökel translated and adapted this material and published it in English as *A Manual of Hebrew Poetics* (Rome: Pontifical Biblical Institute, 1988).

58. Idem, *Manual of Hebrew Poetics*, 170–79.

59. Idem, "Erzählkunst im Buch der Richter," *Bib* 42 (1961) 143–72.

lung der alttestamentlichen Erzählung besitzen wir nicht. Mehr noch: sie wird kaum als ein Desiderat empfunden."[60] In his exegesis of narratives taken from the book of Judges, Alonso Schökel follows observations by Martin Buber and Franz Rosenzweig and emphasizes the use of leading motifs (*Leitwörter*), chronological order, and repetition.[61] He concludes that source criticism remains incomplete and inadequate if it is not supplemented by an examination of narrative art in the texts.[62]

In his subsequent work, Alonso Schökel continues to pursue the question whether poetic analysis could be an appropriate approach to Hebrew narrative texts. In his 1974 contribution,[63] he dissociates the literary study of Hebrew texts from any type of sterile formalism[64] and also from any reduction of Hebrew narratives to "pure literature"

---

60. Ibid., 147 ("We cannot lay claim to a basic systematic presentation of Old Testament narrative. Even more: there is hardly any desire to create such a presentation"). Alonso Schökel does refer to previous isolated comments on stylistic features of Hebrew narrative, none of which shows an interest in Hebrew narrative style for its own sake: A. Schulz, *Erzählkunst in den Samuelbüchern* (Münster, 1923); W. Baumgartner, "Ein Kapitel vom hebräischen Erzählungsstil," in *Eucharisterion: Studien zur Religion und Literatur des Alten und Neuen Testaments* (ed. H. Schmidt; Göttingen, 1923); H. Gunkel, *Einleitung in die Psalmen* (Göttingen, 1933); H. Eising, *Formgeschichtliche Untersuchungen zur Jakobserzählung* (Emsdetten, 1940); E. Täubler, *Biblische Studien II* (Tübingen, 1958).

61. On *motifs*, see Alonso Schökel, "Erzählkunst," 149. Compare M. Buber, "Leitwortstil in der Erzählung des Pentateuchs," in *Die Schrift und ihre Verdeutschung* (ed. M. Buber and F. Rosenzweig; Berlin: Schocken, 1936) 211–38; F. Rosenzweig, "Das Formgeheimnis der biblischen Erzählungen, " in ibid., 239–61; M. Buber, "Das Leitwort und der Formtypus der Rede," in ibid., 262–75. An English translation of these texts is found in *Scripture and Translation: Martin Buber and Franz Rosenzweig* (trans. L. Rosenblatt; Bloomington: Indiana Univ. Press, 1994).

On *chronological order* and *repetition*, see Alonso Schökel, "Erzählkunst," 154–57.

62. Ibid., 169.

63. Idem, "Hermeneutical Problems of a Literary Study of the Bible," in *Congress Volume: Edinburgh, 1974* (VTSup 28; Leiden: Brill, 1975) 1–15.

64. He clearly distances himself from Russian formalism (see, e.g., Propp, *Morphology of the Folktale*) and structuralism. The influence of structuralism on biblical studies created a separate school of biblical exegesis that cannot be dealt with adequately in this context. For an introduction to this area, see R. Barthes et al., *Structural Analysis and Biblical Exegesis* (trans. A. Johnson; Pittsburgh: Pickwick, 1974); H. White, "French Structuralism and OT Narrative Analysis: Roland Barthes," *Semeia* 3 (1975) 99–127; D. Patte, *What Is Structural Exegesis?* (Philadelphia: Fortress, 1976); R. Polzin, *Biblical Structuralism: Method and Subjectivity in the Study of Ancient Texts* (Philadelphia: Fortress, 1977); D. Patte and A. Patte, *Structural Exegesis: From Theory to Practice* (Philadelphia: Fortress, 1978); D. Jobling, *The Sense of Biblical Narrative: Structural Analyses in the Hebrew Bible I + II* (JSOTSup 7, 39; Sheffield: JSOT Press, 1978–86). In practice, a structural analysis and a narrative-critical analysis will show many points of contact. See, for example, J. Fokkelman, *Reading Biblical Narrative: A Practical Guide* (Leiden: Deo, 1995).

that is studied solely for the purpose of esthetic pleasure. Alonso Schökel argues that form neither detracts from the meaning of the text nor remains extrinsic to meaning; instead, "form is meaningful. . . . There is no realized and perfect meaning before it takes verbal form. The perfect separation between form and content is, in fact, impossible. In literature the meaning exists in and through form."[65] Each interpreter of Hebrew narrative must thus pay attention to the content of a text as well as the narrative configuration through which this content is communicated.[66]

Samuel Sandmel and Meir Weiss

Apart from the strong influences generated from literary studies in general, narrative criticism of biblical texts was also shaped to a large degree by Jewish scholars who were able to bring their knowledge of the rich heritage of rabbinic scholarship to bear on the questions posed by a poetic approach.[67] Other than the above-mentioned Zvi Adar, two early Jewish scholars who influenced and shaped the development of Hebrew narrative poetics were Samuel Sandmel and Meir Weiss. In his 1961 article "The Haggadah within Scripture,"[68] Sandmel describes the situation of biblical scholarship, not without irony, as follows:

> I confess to becoming weary of a typical Ph.D. exercise: the discovery of the sources alleged to exist in documents. Stated absurdly, the premise behind such studies, now that scientific biblical scholarship is at least 160 years old, seems to be that nobody ever wrote anything: he only copied sources. There has been a spate of studies embracing source and derivation: what Philo tells, he got from the rabbis; what Jesus taught, he got from the rabbis; what Paul taught, he got from the rabbis (or the Wisdom of Solomon). What the NT teaches is derived from the Dead Sea Scrolls. It is certainly legitimate to ask, are there discernable sources behind this document. But the issue is prejudiced when the question is put, What are the sources behind the document? And when the searcher for the

---

65. Alonso Schökel, "Hermeneutical Problems," 7.

66. A wide range of terminology is used to describe this distinction between content and narrative configuration: story–plot (Forster, *Aspects of the Novel*), Stoff–Erzählung (Kayser, *Sprachliche Kunstwerk*), fabula–sujet (T. Todorov, *Théorie de la littérature: Textes des formalistes russes* [Paris: Seuil, 1965]), story–discourse (Chatman, *Story and Discourse*), source–discourse (M. Sternberg, *The Poetics of Biblical Narrative: Ideological Literature and the Drama of Reading* [Bloomington: Indiana Univ. Press, 1985]), histoire–récit (Genette, *Nouveau discours*).

67. Compare K. P. Bland, "The Rabbinic Method and Literary Criticism," in *Literary Interpretations of Biblical Narratives* (ed. K. R. R. Gros Louis et al.; Nashville: Abingdon, 1974) 16–23.

68. S. Sandmel, "The Haggadah within Scripture," *JBL* 80 (1961) 105–22.

sources forgets the particular document allegedly containing a source, the student has embarked on an egregious tangent! An *oblivion to the text itself seems to me the greatest defect in present-day biblical scholarship.*[69]

Sandmel argues that scholars must pay more attention to what is now known as *innerbiblical interpretation*.[70] While he does understand biblical narrative as literature that grew by accretion,[71] he likens biblical narrative—"the fanciful *retelling* of tales"—to Haggadah.[72] Here, too, a switch takes place from a focus on the hypothetical growth of a text to the description of this "fanciful retelling"; in other words, from the historical context of the source(s) to the narrative strategies employed in the creation of the discourse.

Taking a stance highly critical of "form criticism" as developed by Hermann Gunkel, Meir Weiss argues for the use of internal instead of external approaches in biblical interpretation.[73] Instead of discussing whether a certain text conforms to prior conceptions of genre or poetic convention, the interpreter should develop poetic criteria developed intrinsically from each individual text. He refers to this approach as "total interpretation":

> The basic principle of "Total Interpretation" . . . is that the interpretation of poetry is not concerned with external aspects, e.g., genre, *Sitz im Leben*, *Sitz im Kultus*, or pattern, not with what a particular idiom or motif *generally* signifies. The interpreter of poetry must concern himself only with internal aspects, i.e., with what the poet has made of the raw material in the particular poem under consideration.[74]

---

69. Ibid., 108 (emphasis mine).

70. The large body of work in this area cannot be presented adequately in this context. As an introduction to innerbiblical exegesis, see B. Childs, "Psalm Titles and Midrashic Exegesis," *JSS* 16 (1971) 137–50; P. Ackroyd, "The Chronicler as Exegete," *JSOT* 2 (1977) 2–32; D. Carson and H. Williamson, eds., *It Is Written: Scripture Citing Scripture. Essays in Honour of Barnabas Lindars* (Cambridge: Cambridge Univ. Press, 1988); M. Fishbane, *Biblical Interpretation in Ancient Israel* (Oxford: Clarendon, 1985); S. Harris, *Proverbs 1–9: A Study of Inner-Biblical Interpretation* (SBLDS 150; Atlanta: Scholars Press, 1995); K. Schmid, "Ausgelegte Schrift als Schrift: Innerbiblische Schriftauslegung und die Frage nach der theologischen Qualität der biblischen Texte," in *Die Kunst des Auslegens: Zur Hermeneutik des Christentums in der Kultur der Gegenwart* (ed. R. Anselm et al.; Frankfurt a.M.: Peter Lang, 1999) 115–29.

71. Sandmel, "Haggadah within Scripture," 122.

72. Ibid., 110.

73. M. Weiss, *The Bible from Within: The Method of Total Interpretation* (Jerusalem: Magnes, 1984). Originally published in Hebrew in slightly abbreviated form as *HaMiqra Kidemuto* (Jerusalem, 1962).

74. Idem, *Bible from Within*, 63; Weiss refers back to Martin Buber's thoughts in (Buber) "Die Sprache der Botschaft," *Die Schrift und ihre Verdeutschung* (Berlin: Schocken, 1936) 1095–96: "Nirgendwo . . . ist aus den biblischen Erzgüssen ein 'Inhalt' auszuschmelzen,

Even though a biblical text is "at the same time a linguistic document and an historical source," it "must be apprehended *first of all* as an artistic creation, on the basis of an interpretation which illuminates it from within, as poetic form."[75]

Whereas Weiss is initially interested in prophetic and lyrical texts, he moves to narrative texts in subsequent publications.[76] In accordance with his program of "total interpretation," Weiss insists that the analysis of basic principles of narrative strategy must become a part of the exegesis of Hebrew narrative texts as supplement and corrective to historical-critical approaches.[77] This focus on the various narrative strategies employed in the text differs from the focus of historical-critical exegesis as it centers, not on the question "Where does the material contained in the text come from?" but rather, "How is this material formed, interconnected, and shaped to produce a particular text?" Weiss is quite aware that the tools for analyzing these narrative strategies were developed much later than the text itself but dismisses this concern as irrelevant:

> Es lässt sich wohl darüber streiten, ob eine biblische Erzählung Märchen oder Sage ist, ob sie als Legende oder Mythos aufzufassen sei, ob sie dieser oder jener Gattung angehört. . . . Hingegen aber ist es eindeutig feststellbar, ob in einer Erzählung, der Erzähler selbst spricht, oder ob er einer der handelnden Personen das Wort lässt, ob die Zeitfolge geradlinig vorwärts schreitet oder rückwärts gewandt ist. Diese Fragen werden von jedem epischen Text—orientalischen oder occidentalischen, antiken oder modernen—gestellt, und ihre Beantwortung trifft in das Herz der Erzählung.[78]

---

sondern ein jeder besteht in seiner einheitlichen, unauflöslichen Gestalt—unauflöslicher noch als die des echten Gedichts; nirgends kann hier auf ein ursprüngliches Was zurückgegangen werden, das dieses Wie empfangen habe, aber auch ein anderes vertrüge."

75. Weiss, *Bible from Within*, 66. Weiss readily acknowledges the various scholars that shaped his approach, such as E. Auerbach, W. Kayser, E. Staiger, M. Wehrli, and L. Alonso Schökel. For a very detailed overview of the background to Weiss's approach, see ibid., 1–46.

76. Idem, "Einiges über die Bauformen des Erzählens in der Bibel," *VT* 13 (1963) 456–75; idem, "Weiteres über die Bauformen des Erzählens in der Bibel," *Bib* 46 (1965) 181–206.

77. Idem, "Einiges über die Bauformen," 457.

78. Idem, "Weiteres über die Bauformen," 205: "We can certainly debate whether a biblical narrative is fairytale or saga, legend or myth, this or that genre. . . . It is, however, a matter of clear observation whether in a narrative the narrator speaks himself or whether he gives voice to one of the acting characters, whether time proceeds linearly or with flashbacks. These questions are asked of any epic text—oriental or occidental, ancient or modern—and the answer strikes at the heart of the narrative."

By using the term *Herz der Erzählung* ('heart of the narrative'), Weiss is clearly shifting from the intention of the real author to the intention of the implied author (*intentio operis*) without using this terminology.[79]

In Weiss's 1963 article, the focus is on *erlebte Rede* ('free indirect discourse'),[80] that is, the presentation of the subjective point of view of a specific character without the use of direct speech. According to Weiss, the most important technique in this regard is the use of the Hebrew word הנה. His analysis of respective passages is complemented by an accumulation of rabbinic sources in which the issue of implied speech is already discussed. His 1965 article focuses on chronological order in narrative, especially where linear chronology is abandoned in favor of retrospectives. Drawing on early comments by Gunkel, Weiss analyses these retrospectives in regard to their function for the communicative design of the narrative. By emphasizing the variations in content between the narrator's description of an event and the retrospective report of that same event in the voice of a character, Weiss anticipates the work by Robert Alter, Meir Sternberg, and especially George Savran.

Kenneth Gros Louis:
Literary Interpretations of Biblical Narratives

Published independently of the work by Alonso Schökel and Weiss, a volume of literary readings of biblical narratives was compiled in 1974 in response to a series of summer institutes for secondary school teachers of English concerned with teaching Bible in their literature classes.[81] Following the 1963 decision by the U.S. Supreme Court to ban the devotional reading of Bible in public schools, interest in teaching the Bible *in* literature (that is, discussing literature that alludes to biblical texts) and teaching the Bible *as* literature had strongly increased in the American educational system. The various essays gathered in *Literary Interpretations of Biblical Narratives* meet this interest. Although there are three studies on New Testament texts, the first volume mainly compiles literary analyses of Old Testament passages from Genesis, Exodus, the books of Judges and Ruth, the characters of Elijah, Elisha, and Jonah, as well as a study of the books of Isaiah, Job, and Ecclesiastes.

This volume understood itself to be a pioneering venture into relatively uncharted territories, because the study of the Bible as literature

---

79. Compare Booth, *Rhetoric of Fiction*, 70–75.
80. Thus the English equivalent suggested by Sternberg, *Poetics of Biblical Narrative*, 52–53.
81. K. R. R. Gros Louis, J. Ackerman, and T. Washaw, eds., *Literary Interpretations of Biblical Narratives*, vol. 1 (Nashville: Abingdon, 1974).

had not yet produced a significant body of scholarship.[82] The con-
tributors to these volumes, the majority of whom belonged to English
departments, understood their work as a decisive shift away from
what they saw to be the major preoccupation of biblical scholars: the
quest for the historical reality behind the biblical text. Instead of playing the biblical texts against a supposed underlying historical reality,
these authors affirmed that the text itself posits a reality to be understood and interpreted in its own right, primarily in terms of its literary
craftsmanship.[83]

This paradigm shift was exemplified by the term *literary criticism*.
Whereas in biblical scholarship, this term was used in analogy with the
German *Literarkritik* to describe the search for the original writings, including their date of origin, their textual growth, and the historical
context of their authors, to students of literature in general this term
referred to the analysis and interpretation of a text that presented
human experience in artistic form.[84] Underlying this paradigm shift
was the conviction that the biblical texts were indeed suffused with a
high degree of literary artistry that had to be understood in order to be
appreciated fully. Although the various essays in *Literary Interpretations*
are applications of a "literary approach" to biblical texts, the methodological suppositions underlying such a "literary approach" are not
laid out in systematic detail. This leaves many questions unanswered,
including (1) the issues connected with reading the text solely in an
English translation and (2) the relationship that exists between the semantics and syntax of the original Hebrew and its literary artistry.[85]

---

82. As the work by Adar, Weiss, and Alonso Schökel shows, this assessment of the
status quo was not entirely correct.

83. K. R. R. Gros Louis, "Introduction," in *Literary Interpretations of Biblical Narratives*,
vol. 1 (ed. K. R. R. Gros Louis, J. Ackerman, and T. Washaw; Nashville: Abingdon, 1974)
1:10–12.

84. Leland Ryken, "Literary Criticism of the Bible: Some Fallacies," in ibid., 25.

85. The detailed analysis of Hebrew narrative syntax has long shown that no interpretation can neglect the Hebrew language without severe consequences for the quality
of the interpretive endeavor. Among many excellent contributions, see E. Talstra, "Text
Grammar and Hebrew Bible II: Syntax and Semantics," *BiOr* 39 (1982) 36–38; R. E. Long-
acre, *Joseph: A Story of Divine Providence — A Text Theoretical and Textlinguistic Analysis of
Genesis 37 and 39–48* (Winona Lake, IN: Eisenbrauns, 1989 [2nd ed., 2003]); A. Niccacci,
The Syntax of the Verb in Classical Hebrew Prose (trans. W. G. E. Watson; JSOTSup 86;
Sheffield: JSOT Press, 1990); S. Meier, *Speaking of Speaking: Marking Direct Discourse in the
Hebrew Bible* (Leiden: Brill, 1992); and C. L. Miller, *The Representation of Speech in Biblical
Hebrew Narrative: A Linguistic Analysis* (HSM 55; Atlanta: Scholars Press, 1996).

David Robertson

Given the gradual melding of general literary studies with biblical studies, it was no surprise that the status of biblical narratives became an issue. Were these texts literature, history, or theology, and how could these seemingly competing claims be reconciled? In his 1977 book *The Old Testament and the Literary Critic*,[86] David Robertson opts for a radical paradigm shift in biblical studies. His interaction with the biblical texts starts with the premise that these narratives should be studied as pure literature, read solely for the purpose of esthetic pleasure.[87] This paradigm shift entails the following assumptions:

- The text to be interpreted is a whole, and every part is of equal importance.
- Interpretation must be governed by the principle that any part of the text is a reflection of the whole text.
- The text is a self-referential, autonomous, imaginative universe.
- The context in which a text is read depends on the arbitrary choice of the reader. Creating new and interesting contexts pays handsome dividends for literary study.
- The "truth" of a narrative depends only on whether the parts of the narrative are "true" to the whole and thus contribute to its beauty.
- The value of literature lies in its imitation of reality. It allows the reader to "play" or observe a "play" as an existential exercise.[88]

Another premise, not made explicit by Robertson, also seems to be the choice to read the text in translation (Robertson uses the RSV), because the book does not contain a single reference to the biblical text behind the English translation. In accordance with his basic principles, Robertson compares Exodus 1–15 to the *Bacchae* by Euripides and Psalm 90 to the "Hymn to Intellectual Beauty" by Percy Shelley. He concludes that many biblical texts do not have the same esthetic rank as other masterpieces of the Western literary tradition.[89] While Robertson's

---

86. D. Robertson, *The Old Testament and the Literary Critic* (Philadelphia: Fortress, 1977).

87. "We assume that the entire Bible is imaginative literature and study it accordingly" (ibid., 3).

88. Ibid., 7–11.

89. The idea that biblical narrative is inferior from a purely artistic point of view is by no means a new attitude. In the 18th century, Bishop Lowth protested against condescending attitudes toward biblical texts that arose from "criticizing it according to foreign and improper rules [that] would make that composition appear lame and imperfect" (R. Lowth, *Lectures on the Sacred Poetry of the Hebrews* [trans. G. Gregory; London, 1787] 403). An attitude that combines an esthetic approach to biblical literature with a condescending attitude toward it may be one reason why "reading the Bible as literature" has met with a great deal of skepticism, especially among theologians.

radical position remains on the fringe of narrative studies in biblical scholarship,[90] the issue of the relation among Bible-as-literature, Bible-as-theology, and Bible-as-history continues to be a central concern of subsequent scholars.

Robert Alter

Robert Alter is Professor of Hebrew and Comparative Literature at the University of California, Berkeley. With this combination of training in both Hebrew language and comparative literature, Alter combined in person the two areas of scholarship that were coming together in the study of Hebrew narrative poetics.[91] In 1981, he published *The Art of Biblical Narrative*, a book that received wide recognition not only among biblical scholars but also from the general public.[92] This popularity was witness to the fact that studies in biblical narrative art could also excite a lay readership and create widespread interest in biblical storytelling. The book was the culmination of a series of previous articles and essays, published from 1975 to 1978.[93] Alter defends the appropriateness of analyzing the biblical narratives by methods normally used for the study of modern fiction. Following the assumptions that governed the work of Weiss, Alonso Schökel, and others,[94] he posits that the shape of narrative is inseparable from the meaning of these narratives and that biblical exegesis must include analysis and evaluation of this narrative shape. For Alter, literary art is inseparably connected to the religious purpose of Hebrew narrative. Unlike Robertson, however, he does not completely turn his back on historical scholarship, recognizing that it may be of great benefit to recognize how a final redactor carefully com-

---

90. See the critique of biblical narratives as "pure literature" in Alonso Schökel, "Hermeneutical Problems"; as well as Sternberg's devastating criticism of Robertson (Sternberg, *Poetics of Biblical Narrative*, 4–5).

91. Alter's nonbiblical works include *Partial Magic: The Novel as Self-Conscious Genre* (Berkeley: Univ. of California Press, 1975); *Modern Hebrew Literature* (New York: Behrman, 1975); *A Lion for Love: A Critical Biography of Stendhal* (with collaboration of Carol Cosman; New York: Basic Books, 1979). The area of biblical narrative and general literary studies are directly combined in *The Invention of Hebrew Prose: Modern Fiction and the Language of Realism* (Seattle: Univ. of Washington Press, 1988).

92. Idem, *The Art of Biblical Narrative* (New York: Basic Books, 1981). The book was awarded the National Jewish Book Award by the Jewish Book Council in 1982.

93. Idem, "A Literary Approach to the Bible," *Commentary* 60 (1975) 70–77; "Biblical Narrative," *Commentary* 61 (1976) 61–67; "Biblical Type-Scenes and the Uses of Convention," *Critical Inquiry* 5 (1978) 355–68; "Character in the Bible," *Commentary* 66 (1978) 58–65.

94. Alter himself mentions Auerbach's and Sternberg's early work.

posed the text.[95] In practice however, Alter readily dismisses most results of historical scholarship as unhelpful.[96]

Addressing the question whether it is appropriate to use an approach developed for fictional narrative texts when reading biblical narrative, Alter resorts to the term *historicized prose fiction*.[97] With this term, he attempts to describe the nature of biblical narrative between creative discourse and the historical events that may or may not lie behind this discourse. In his view, the source, or the story of biblical narrative is firmly rooted in history, but the shaping of this source into the narrative discourse employs a wide range of narrative strategies also found in fictional literature. By resorting to narrative prose as the vehicle to transport historical content, ancient Israel displayed a marked shift away from the mythical texts of its surrounding neighbors.[98] Alter argues for a connection between Israel's narrative art and its world view. Clarifying his position in a later article, Alter states, "Categories for thinking about the world are an untidy bundle . . . even more untidy is the relation between this bundle and the forms of artistic expression that evolve within a culture."[99] He nevertheless maintains that such a relation exists and must be taken into consideration when dealing with the text.

The various chapters of his book deal with the use of type scenes, dialogue, and repetition in biblical narrative. Most of his examples are taken from Genesis and the books of Samuel;[100] they exemplify Alter's interpretive virtuosity and provide the reader with interesting observations on minute narrative details. In his discussion of what he refers to as "type scenes," Alter compares the betrothal scenes[101] in Genesis 24, 29; Exodus 2; and 1 Samuel 9. By contrasting the differences between otherwise similar narrative patterns, he sharpens the profile of each individual text. In his discussion of dialogue, Alter recognizes

---

95. Alter, *Art of Biblical Narrative*, 19–20.

96. Alter does seem to assume that Genesis–2 Kings is basically preexilic and that the narratives on David were created a few decades later than Genesis (see Alter 1983, 148) and refer to the Genesis text in its final form (see also idem, "A Response to Critics," *JSOT* 27 [1981] 113–17, esp. p. 114).

97. Alter takes this term from H. Schneidau, *Sacred Discontent* (Baton Rouge: Louisiana State Univ. Press, 1977) 215.

98. Alter, *Art of Biblical Narrative*, 26–32.

99. Idem, "Response to Critics," 113.

100. Alter is, however, convinced that his observations will yield fruit in all other Hebrew narratives as well (ibid., 117).

101. Idem, *Art of Biblical Narrative*, 52.

that the stylization of dialogue by the narrator is a large part of characterization.[102] Narrative characters reveal their personalities in the structure of their direct speech. In his discussion of repetition and composite artistry, Alter attacks two classic criteria of diachronic exegesis by claiming that repeated information and seeming contradictions are not indications of breaks in the text and thus traces of textual growth but clues to the narrator's intention that should be evaluated in the context of the communicational design of the narrative.

In 1982, Gros Louis and Ackerman published a followup volume to their literary interpretations.[103] It reflects on the studies on biblical narratives written by David Robertson, David Gunn, and Robert Alter, among others, and recognizes them as especially valuable because "these scholars were trained in both biblical studies and literary criticism."[104] As a result, Gros Louis summarizes 11 basic assumptions supposedly shared by scholars who approach the Bible as literature:

1. Not everything in the Bible is literary in nature.
2. Literary analyses of the literary aspects of the Bible are virtually nonexistent.
3. What has been called "literary criticism" of the Bible is not the kind of literary criticism teachers of literature do.
4. In fact, the biblical scholar's definition of "literary criticism" is virtually opposite of the literary critic's definition.
5. Teachers of literature are *primarily* interested in the literary reality of a text and not its historical reality.
6. The literary reality of the Bible can be studied with the methods of literary criticism employed in any other text.
7. Approaching the Bible as literature, then, means placing emphasis on the text itself—not on its historical and textual backgrounds, not on the circumstances that brought the text into its present form, not on its religious and cultural foundations.
8. The literary critic assumes unity in the text. To quote Northrop Frye, "A purely literary criticism . . . would see the Bible, not as a scrapbook of corruptions, glosses, reductions, insertions, conflations, misplacings, and misunderstandings."
9. The literary critic assumes conscious artistry in the text.

---

102. Ibid., 63ff.

103. K. R. R. Gros Louis and J. Ackerman, eds., *Literary Interpretations of Biblical Narratives*, vol. 2 (Nashville: Abingdon, 1982).

104. Robertson, *Old Testament and Literary Critic*. D. Gunn, *The Story of King David* (JSOTSup 6; Sheffield: University of Sheffield, 1978); idem, *The Fate of King Saul* (JSOTSup 14; Sheffield: JSOT Press, 1980). Alter, *Art of Biblical Narrative*. Gros Louis, *Literary Interpretations of Biblical Narratives*, 2:8.

10. The literary critic, then, explores such topics as narrative structure, scene placement, selection and ordering of episodes, plot conflicts, image patterns, thematic emphasis, character development, and so on.
11. Literary criticism of the Bible is not biblical scholarship; it is literary criticism. The two are complementary.[105]

As subsequent publications show, neither these individual points nor the list as a unit was able to uphold the claim to universality that was envisioned by the authors.[106]

Adele Berlin

Although Alter's *Art of Biblical Narrative* has become the most widely received book on narrative criticism,[107] it is by no means the only major contribution that appeared in the 1980s. Two years after the appearance of Alter's *Art of Biblical Narrative*, Adele Berlin published *Poetics and Interpretation of Biblical Narrative*.[108] Berlin builds upon the work of Todorov, Alter, and Chatman in an attempt to discover general poetic principles that govern the shaping of Hebrew narrative.[109] In line with her predecessors, Berlin argues vehemently that narrative is above all a form of representation. As she states, "Abraham in Genesis is not a real person any more than a painting of an apple is a real fruit."[110] Narrative poetics must concern itself with an analysis of how this representation is constructed. While acknowledging that the text may have grown and changed over time, Berlin's analysis proceeds from an encounter with the text in its final form; moreover, she places the burden of proof on any who argue that this final form is synthetic and use this claim to determine the age and growth of a text.[111]

---

105. Idem, "Some Methodological Considerations," in *Literary Interpretations of Biblical Narratives* (ed. K. R. R. Gros Louis and J. Ackerman; Nashville: Abingdon, 1982) 2:14–15.

106. See, for example, Sternberg, *Poetics of Biblical Narrative*, 7.

107. Alter's book is still the most common monograph cited, if a text deals with narrative criticism at all, often leading to the impression that all of narrative criticism begins and ends with this book. Compare diverse texts such as Porter, ed., *Dictionary of Biblical Criticism*, 237; and C. Westermann, *Erzählungen in den Schriften des Alten Testaments* (Stuttgart: Calwer, 1998).

108. A. Berlin, *Poetics and Interpretation of Biblical Narrative* (Bible and Literature 9; Sheffield: Almond, 1983; repr. Winona Lake, IN: Eisenbrauns, 1994). See also the article leading up to this book: idem, "Characterization in Biblical Narrative: David's Wives," *JSOT* 23 (1982) 69–85.

109. "If the same things are said, and said in the same way, often enough, then some general conclusions can be drawn, some poetic principles discovered" (idem, *Poetics and Interpretation*, 20).

110. Ibid., 13.

111. Berlin states: "At the very least [narrative poetics] can prevent historical criticism from mistaking as proof of earlier sources those features which can be better explained

In her search for general poetic principles, Berlin focuses on two areas: characterization and point of view. When analyzing biblical characters, she distinguishes between full-fledged characters, types, and agents. Agents are figures that have no distinguishing features at all and merely serve as plot functions. Types are characters that embody a single character trait (for example, Nabal the fool in 1 Samuel 25). Full-fledged characters display a certain degree of complexity and are capable of development and change. They are shaped by many different strategies, including external description, presentation of the inner life of a character, stylized dialogue, and contrast with other characters.[112] As examples of these different character types, Berlin lists David's wives Michal, Bathsheba, and Abigail.

All of the information conveyed to a reader by means of narrative is shaped by the point of view mediating this information—that is, by the narrator. Berlin states, "The reader is shown only what the author wishes to show. Never can the reader step behind the story to know a character other than in the way the narrative presents him."[113] The implied narrator's point of view becomes visible to the reader through many devices, including relational modifiers; the description of a character's inner life, thoughts, and emotions; and through circumstantial clauses, often with a shift in tense to indicate a shift in perspective. In a reading of the book of Ruth, Berlin illustrates the poetic principles described earlier. The book concludes with thoughts on the relationship between poetic interpretation and historical-critical methods.

Peter Miscall

Peter Miscall's *Workings of Old Testament Narrative*, published the same year as the above-mentioned book by Berlin,[114] was written during a sabbatical year that the author spent at the English Department

---

as compositional or rhetorical features of the present text" (ibid., 112). The line between indications of earlier sources and rhetorical features is not easily drawn. Even a literary critic such as Robert Alter may confuse the two, as Berlin rightly points out: "Alter can have his midrash without calling it an allusion. By referring to the second story as an allusion to the first, Alter, the arch-opponent of historical criticism, is, irony of ironies, using the supposedly literary approach to learn diachronic lessons about the relative dating of the texts" (A. Berlin, "Literary Exegesis of Biblical Narrative," in *Not in Heaven: Coherence and Complexity in Biblical Narrative* [ed. J. Rosenblatt; Bloomington: Indiana Univ. Press, 1991] 120–28).

112. Idem, *Poetics and Interpretation*, 40ff.

113. Ibid., 43. With this definition, Berlin creates much simpler categories than those associated with Mieke Bal's concept of focalizer.

114. P. Miscall, *The Workings of Old Testament Narrative* (Philadelphia: Fortress, 1983).

of the University of Denver. Once again, an attempt is made to combine insights from general literary studies and the interpretation of Old Testament narrative, although his book is less of a theoretical reflection than an interaction with various narrative texts taken from Genesis 12 and 1 Samuel 16–22. Miscall assumes that interpretation of Old Testament narratives implies a *close reading*[115] that traces the "workings" of a narrative matrix. Without postulating a correct and purposeful communication from the author to the reader, Miscall operates under the assumption that any text is a structure in and of itself and that reading consists of describing this structure. In the encounter with the text, the reader faces many blanks that remain ambiguous and is thus unable to decide what the "correct" reading may be. Instead of insisting on a "correct" reading, the reader should interpret by relating passages to each other "in order to enrich the reading of one part and of the entire corpus."[116] The idea of "enriching" the text becomes central to Miscall's concept of *close reading*, a concept that stands diametrically opposed to the search for a "correct" reading. As he states:

> The reactions to the biblical text with its manifold difficulties, inconsistencies, and even contradictions, have been to suppress the text itself in some fashion in favor of a univocal reading or interpretation, usually historical or theological, or to rend the text into sources, fragments, "genres," etc., which can then supposedly support definitive meaning."[117]

In opposition to this sort of reductionism, Miscall advocates emphasizing the indeterminacy of the text in a way that "leaves the reader free to play."[118]

Meir Sternberg

With his more than 500-page-long magnum opus *The Poetics of Biblical Narrative: Ideological Literature and the Drama of Reading*,[119] Meir Sternberg has written the most extensive hermeneutical reflection on the study of biblical narrative to date. Already his 1978 volume *Expositional Modes and Temporal Ordering*[120] laid much of the theoretical groundwork for his later interaction with biblical narrative. In *Poetics*,

---

115. This is the first occurrence of this term that I have encountered.

116. Ibid., 3.

117. Ibid., 4.

118. Ibid., 11. For an application of Miscall's approach to a large body of text, see idem, *1 Samuel: A Literary Reading* (Bloomington: Indiana University Press, 1993).

119. Sternberg, *The Poetics of Biblical Narrative*.

120. M. Sternberg, *Expositional Modes and Temporal Ordering* (Baltimore: Johns Hopkins Univ. Press, 1978).

Sternberg postulates that authors cannot and do not assume that their readers bring prior knowledge to the reading of a narrative text. Instead, the narrator must supply this knowledge in expositional segments.[121] The reader does not need any information for understanding the narrative beyond what the narrator includes in his or her exposition.[122] The exposition thus becomes an important means of reader guidance. Expositional material can stand at the beginning of a narrative (initial exposition) or be conveyed to the reader over the course of the narrative (delayed or distributed exposition). In all cases, expositional material can be delineated from its surroundings by its use of time.[123]

A series of articles published in Hebrew led up to the creation of Sternberg's 1985 book.[124] Sternberg posits that any reading of a narrative text must deal with the functional structures of narrative used by an author to communicate with his readers. In his words, "[O]ur primary business as readers is to make purposive sense of [the narrative], so as to explain the *what's* and the *how's* in terms of the *why's* of communication."[125] This "primary business" is the business of poetics. Again Sternberg:

---

121. This is even the case when a narrative continues a story thread already told; see ibid., 4.

122. "[The information in the exposition] is all you need keep in mind for the purposes of the present narrative. If you are possessed of more information than that, all the better, but . . . do not drag [all this information] into the novel or you will throw the latter novel out of focus" (ibid.). Compare Shimeon Bar-Efrat, *Narrative Art in the Bible* (JSOTSup 70; Sheffield: Almond, 1989) 113–21; and earlier (1959), Adar, *Biblical Narrative*, 55.

123. Already in his 1978 work, Sternberg illustrated this distinction between scenic and expositional texture with a biblical text, Job 1:1–5:

> The reader is thus led to conclude that verses 1–5 are expositional by a combination of three complementary indicators—two textural and one chronological. The pronounced quantitative difference in specificity, produced by the manipulation of time-ratios, draws the reader's attention to the secondary position occupied by the opening part within the context of Job's story. And so at the same time does the qualitative difference in concreteness, since the "real kernel" of a narrative must necessarily consist of a concrete action, while the deconcretized opening might equally have paved way for any number of stories about Job. (Sternberg, *Expositional Modes*, 25)

124. M. Perry and M. Sternberg, "The King through Ironic Eyes: The Narrator's Devices in the Story of David and Bathsheba and Two Excursuses on the Theory of the Narrative Text," *Hasifrut* 1 (1968) 263–92; idem, "Caution: A Literary Text!" *Hasifrut* 2 (1970) 608–63; M. Sternberg, "Repetition Structure in Biblical Narrative: Strategies of Informational Redundancy," *Hasifrut* 25 (1977) 109–50; idem, "The Truth vs. All the Truth: The Rendering of Inner Life in Biblical Narrative," *Hasifrut* 29 (1979) 110–46.

125. Idem, *Poetics of Biblical Narrative*, 1.

Poetics is the systematic working or study of literature as such. Hence, to offer a poetics of biblical narrative is to claim that biblical narrative is a work of literature. Not just an artful work; not a work marked by some aesthetic property; not a work resorting to so-called literary devices; not a work that the interpreter may choose (or refuse) to consider from a literary viewpoint or, in that unlovely piece of jargon, as literature; but a literary work.[126]

Such poetics has little to do with the list of assumptions proposed by Gros Louis, which are supposedly shared by all who approach the Bible "as literature."[127] Examining the workings of narrative does not imply that narrative is ahistoric or nonideological. Instead, a poetics of biblical narrative clarifies the various relationships between discourse and source in terms of the communicational matrix of the text. A "literary approach" is nothing more or less than a "discourse-oriented approach"[128] that focuses on temporal ordering, chronological breaks, analogical design (parallelisms, variations, repetitions, symmetry, and chiasm), point of view, representational proportions (scene and summary), informational gapping, and strategies of characterization, to name a few aspects.

Building on insights of the "New Critics" as well as Wayne Booth, Sternberg speaks of the intention of a text not as an author's psychological state embodied in words but the interaction between the observable structure of a narrative and the thus-conditioned effects on the reader. Even though there can be much debate on whether the effect of a text is more due to the text's inherent structure or each reader's presuppositions, it is clear that both elements play a role in the process of reading. Narrative criticism uncovers and evaluates this structure, or "narrative code."[129]

The focus on narrative code does not imply that narrative analysis is not interested in history or that texts analyzed for their narrative code must by definition be ahistorical. Here Sternberg takes issue with Alter's concept of sacred prose fiction. Alter overlooks a basic ambiguity inherent in the terms *history* and *fiction*. History refers to what actually happened, fiction to what is imagined and invented—but not exclusively. History and fiction not only refer to different classes of source, they also refer to different types of discourse: "history to re-creative and

---

126. Ibid., 2.
127. See above, pp. 42–43.
128. Sternberg, *Poetics of Biblical Narrative*, 23.
129. Ibid., 11.

fiction to creative discourse."[130] The nature of the discourse is not solely determined by the nature of the source. Historical discourse can be based on fictional sources, just as fictional discourse can be based on historical sources. Regardless of the historicity of the *source*, the determination of a narrative as either fictional *discourse* or historical *discourse* is, in Sternberg's view, a silent, often unconscious agreement between the author and the reader because there is no clear stylistic difference between the two. In line with Auerbach, Sternberg concludes that biblical narrative is not only historical discourse but *the* historical discourse, "the one and only truth that, like God himself, brooks no rival."[131] To approach biblical narrative either as inferior history or as superior fiction misses this point entirely.

Sternberg also rejects the claim that literary study must assume that its object of study is nonideological. The claim that any student of the bible "as literature" must reject the text's claim to sacredness is utter nonsense. Instead, biblical narratives interweave history, esthetics, and ideology in a mode of discourse that can be analyzed and explained according to the strategies that shape this discourse. Poetic analysis thus rejects neither historical nor ideological aspects of the narrative but asks how the communicational matrix of the discourse presents these aspects to the reader.

In lengthy chapters, Sternberg examines the relationship between ideology, esthetics, and history within the parameters of biblical narrative. He comes to the conclusion that epistemological limitation is a central driving force that binds these aspects together.[132] The particular stylistic features of biblical narrative combine continually to emphasize the reader's lack of knowledge. Among these are (a) the narrator's omniscience, (b) the narrator's extreme minimalism and selectivity, (c) repetition between narration and dialogue. Dialogue is compared with narration and vice versa, often highlighting grave dif-

---

130. Ibid., 24.

If the title to history-writing hinged on the correspondence to the truth—the historicity of the things written about—then a historical text would automatically forfeit or change its status on the discovery that it contained errors or imbalances or guesses and fabrications passed off as verities. . . . If fiction contrasts with fact, it contrasts even more sharply with fallacy and falsity, which are value judgments passable on factual reporting along. Falling between fallacy and falsity, therefore, *bad* historiography is bad *historiography*: no more, no less. (Ibid., 25)

131. Ibid., 32.

132. Sternberg points to Genesis 4, Num 11:4–18, and 1 Kgs 8:38–39 as texts that clearly outline the emphasis on the epistemological limitation of human beings.

ferences between the voice of the narrator and the voice of a single character.[133] These and other features result in a multitude of gaps and ambiguities in the text that turn the reading of biblical narrative into a tentative process of inference. With a narrative that is constructed like an obstacle course,

> reading turns into a drama of understanding—conflict between inferences, seesawing, reversal, discovery, and all. It is by a sustained effort alone that the reader can attain at the end to something of the vision that God has possessed all along: to make sense of the discourse is to gain sense of being human.[134]

The ambiguity of biblical texts is balanced by what Sternberg refers to as "foolproof composition":

> By foolproof composition, I mean that the Bible is difficult to read, easy to underread and overread and even misread, but virtually impossible to, so to speak, counterread. . . . The essentials are made transparent to all comers: the story line, the world order, the value system.[135]

Thus a maneuvering between "the truth and the whole truth"[136] becomes a central poetic principle in biblical narrative. Besides many short passages used to illustrate his arguments, Sternberg illustrates his hermeneutical reflection with interpretations of Genesis 24, 2 Samuel 11, Genesis 37ff., and 1 Samuel 15.

Shimeon Bar-Efrat

Shimeon Bar-Efrat's monograph on narrative criticism was first published in Hebrew by *Sifriat Poalim* in 1979, with a second edition in 1984. Although it was known to Hebrew speakers and referred to by

---

133. In continuation of Sternberg's work, George Savran made this aspect the central focus of his excellent monograph *Telling and Retelling: Quotation in Biblical Narrative* (Bloomington: Indiana Univ. Press, 1988). In four chapters, he presents a comprehensive overview of repetition between narration and dialogue in biblical narrative: (1) Repetition and Quotation in Biblical Narrative; (2) Formal Aspects of Quoted Direct Speech; (3) The Function of the Quotation: Story Analysis; (4) The Function of the Quotation: Discourse Analysis.

134. Sternberg, *Poetics of Biblical Narrative*, 47. Sternberg brilliantly illustrates this drama of reading in an analysis of 2 Samuel 11 by asking the questions: Did Uriah know what David had done? Did David know whether Uriah knew? Did Joab know? In comparing what the character might know with what the reader can know, Sternberg applies Bal's ideas to biblical narrative (see above).

135. Ibid., 50. It is easy to recognize common assumptions between Sternberg's "foolproof composition" and Auerbach's "tyrannical text."

136. Sternberg, ibid., 56 (see also pp. 230–63).

Alter,[137] it only became available to the English-speaking audience after 1989 when it was published by Almond Press under the title *Narrative Art in the Bible*.[138] The book's chapter headings read as a summary of the basic interests that motivate narrative criticism of biblical narratives: the narrator, the characters, plot, time and space, and style. Bar-Efrat concludes with an in-depth analysis of the narrative of Amnon and Tamar in 2 Samuel 13.

This book gathers an unparalleled collection of wonderful examples of biblical narrative art, conveniently arranged according to topic and linked to an index of biblical reference for easy perusal. Thus, it is perfectly suited to introducing readers to the various nuances of biblical storytelling. His discussion of plot is especially enlightening at the point where he uses the basic unit of dialogue between two characters (which he refers to as a "scene") as a means to determine plot structure. He shows convincingly that many biblical plots are artfully constructed, using repetition and variation, chiasm, and symmetry.[139]

In comparison with the differentiated theoretical work presented by Booth, Chatman, Sternberg, and others, Bar-Efrat spends little time discussing the theoretical background of his approach. Thus, when he writes in his preface that he aims at "presenting a way of reading which is based on the employment of tools and principles current in the study of literature,"[140] he unfortunately does not explain why these tools are current or what justifies their use or where an interested student could turn in order to learn more about the topic.[141]

Jean-Louis Ska

Ska understands that his book *Our Fathers Have Told Us*, published in 1990,[142] was a latecomer to the wealth of studies on biblical narrative that appeared in the 1980s. He recognizes that his short volume builds on the work by Alter, Sternberg, Berlin, and the others and intends to offer readers "a kind of introduction to the major works

---

137. Alter, *Art of Biblical Narrative*, 16.

138. Bar-Efrat, *Narrative Art in the Bible*. The book was recently translated into German: *Wie die Bibel erzählt: Alttestamentliche Texte als literarische Kunstwerke verstehen* (Gütersloh: Gütersloher Verlag, 2006).

139. Ibid. (1989), 95–111.

140. Ibid., 8.

141. Bar-Efrat does conclude his book with a short bibliography; however, the works cited here have little direct interaction with the book itself because Bar-Efrat dispenses almost entirely with footnotes.

142. Jean-Louis Ska, *Our Fathers Have Told Us: Introduction to the Analysis of Hebrew Narrative* (Rome: Pontifical Biblical Institute, 1990).

published in the field of narrative analysis of Biblical texts,"[143] while presenting his own perspective on various topics.

Ska begins by defining narrative as a type of text shaped by a narrator (a voice) and a plot.

> The narrator is the "mediator" between the world of the narrative and the world of the audience. He presents or summarizes the events, gives the pace of the narration, introduces the characters and decides to let them speak for themselves or not, etc. . . . Plot distinguishes a narrative from a poem (lyric art) or from philosophical writings, for instance, in that its structure is at the same time chronological and logical (cf. the basic principle *post hoc, propter hoc*). In a plot, the development rests upon an idea of temporal succession. There is a "before" and an "after."[144]

The unity of a narrative is achieved through the unity of the narrated action. Once the action comes to an end, the narrative reaches its conclusion.[145] Ska distinguishes between plots of resolution, where the question "what will happen" provides the driving force, and plots of revelation, where the action becomes secondary to other factors, such as character development.[146]

In his discussion of the narrator, Ska provides an excellent summary of the discussion on the difference between the "real" and "implied" author and its counterpart the "real" or "implied" reader. He also recognizes that the boundary between narrator and character is not insurmountable, as many characters themselves turn into narrators in the course of a plot. In this context, Ska also discusses the unreliable narrator by pointing to 1 Kgs 3:16–28, where Solomon must show his intellectual prowess and distinguish between a reliable and an unreliable narrator, who confront him with different versions of the same tale.[147]

This separation between various narrators and narrative levels leads Ska to a differentiated account of point of view. Because the characters do not all give voice to the narrator's point of view, the statements they make must be read as a polyphony of contrasting and often conflicting

---

143. Ibid., v.

144. Ibid., 2.

145. Ska refers here to J. Culler, "Defining Narrative Units," in *Style and Structure in Literature* (ed. R. Fowler; Oxford: Blackwell, 1975) 123–42.

146. It can be argued that Ska's definition of plot is reductionistic. As Bar-Efrat's many examples show, plot is more that a mere succession of actions; plot is also the entire structure of a narrative unit. A single event in a plot can be fully understood only in relation to the entire plot structure.

147. Ska, *Our Fathers Have Told Us*, 45.

perspectives.[148] Because of this polyphonic structure, evaluating characters and understanding the motivation behind their statements and
actions become important tasks for the narrative critic. Ska states,
"What does the study of Biblical characters aim at? . . . Critics . . .
endeavor to specify the function of the characters with regard to the
plot."[149] In his discussion of characters and characterization, however,
Ska unfortunately falls short of Chatman's excellent observations and
attempts (much like Adele Berlin) to classify biblical characters as
"dynamic" or "static," and "round" or "flat." I doubt that these binary
oppositions are able adequately to describe the multitude of biblical
characters.

In his discussion, Ska comes to the important conclusion that the
analysis of biblical narrative is a creative endeavor. He states, "The
active participation of the reader is an essential part of the act of reading. A text is like a score of music. The music remains dead unless
somebody plays or sings what is written in the score. A Biblical text
remains dead unless the reader interprets it."[150]

David Gunn and Danna Fewell

The 1993 book *Narrative in the Hebrew Bible*, written by David Gunn
and Danna Fewell,[151] attempts to address a wider range of narrative
features than had been discussed previously, while building on a different set of hermeneutical assumptions. With much greater emphasis
than the books discussed above, Gunn and Fewell insist that the interpretation of narrative hinges

> crucially upon the reader, and not just in terms of a reader's compe-
> tence. Meaning is not something out there in the text waiting to be dis-
> covered. Meaning is always, in the last analysis, the reader's creation,
> and readers, like texts come in an infinite variety. No amount of learn-
> ing to read biblical narrative correctly will lead inexorably through the
> given poetics of the text to the correct interpretation.[152]

---

148. Ska points to 1 Samuel 8–12 as an example and states, "The narrator's voice
should not be confused with Samuel's. Samuel is not the 'official spokesman' for the narrator who may hold different views" (ibid., 80).

149. Ibid., 83.

150. Ibid., 63.

151. D. Gunn and D. Fewell, *Narrative in the Hebrew Bible* (Oxford: Oxford Univ.
Press, 1993).

152. Ibid., xi. As this quotation shows, it is not constructive to draw hard lines between narrative criticism and reader-response criticism. Although the two do focus on
different sides of the interaction between text and reader, there is a great deal of overlap
between them.

The authors take issue with older definitions of *Gattung*, such as 'legend', 'saga', 'novella', and 'etiology', because these labels always convey a preconceived notion of the relation between discourse and historical fact. They boldly proclaim: "We could argue that there is no such thing as what actually happened; there are only stories (or histories) of what happened, always relative to the perspective of the storyteller (historian)."[153] Along with the question of historicity, the authors also dismiss the question of the "correct" reading of a narrative text. They argue that the quest for this correct reading granted the interpreter a privileged status while destroying the text that most people actually read.[154] In opposition to this development, the authors state, "We are not offering the correct way of reading the Bible. Rather we are suggesting lines of interpretation and a reading method for people of our own times who share something of our own culture. Our hope is to provoke enlivening engagement with biblical stories."[155]

Gunn and Fewell present readings of Genesis 4, 38; Judges 10–12; 2 Samuel 21–24; the book of Jonah; and Daniel 3. Much of their attention is focused on the issue of characterization. In contrast to Berlin and Ska and with strong ties to the work of Seymour Chatman, they argue against any notion of type in the formation of biblical characters. It is a mistake to assume that biblical narrative is primitive, simply because it is old. Instead, readers should recognize the open construction of biblical characters and "allow the Bible the kind of complexity that we find in other kinds of literature."[156] The most challenging task in this regard is coming to some kind of understanding of the character of YHWH.[157]

The authors never tire of arguing that narrator and the real author are entirely different concepts. They even go so far as to state, "[T]he narrator is a character who tells the story while other characters enact it."[158]

---

153. Ibid., 6.

154. One sure effect of this tradition of biblical criticism was to take the possibility of serious initiative in interpretation out of the hands of laypersons and keep it firmly in the hands of scholars. Scholars alone could conduct the arcane arguments about sources and redaction. They then could *tell* others the results of their research. To read the Bible one had to be constantly reading the scholars. (Ibid., 8)

155. Ibid., 33.

156. Compare Chatman, *Story and Discourse*, 119. Quotation from Gunn and Fewell, *Narrative in the Hebrew Bible*, 49.

157. Ibid., 89. These statements come very close to what Zvi Adar had already presented in 1959.

158. Gunn and Fewell, ibid., 52.

Whereas Sternberg and most other narrative critics view the biblical narrator as fully reliable at all times, Gunn and Fewell challenge this notion: "We cannot ignore the possibility that a narrator attuned to deploying irony against characters might deploy it against readers, for example, by intruding ironic as well as straightforward evaluative comment."[159] By allowing the possibility of a deliberately ironic and thus, in a certain sense, unreliable narrator, the authors make a unique contribution to the discussion of biblical narrative poetics. They cite the example of 1 Samuel 17 compared with 2 Samuel 21, where the presentation of conflicting information on the question "who killed Goliath?" may be a deliberate attempt by the narrator to destabilize a reader's security.[160]

In a later chapter, Gunn and Fewell deal with the "lure of language," including the use of repetition, multivalence and metaphor, allusion and intertextuality. This discussion is one of the great strengths of their book, although their presentation is not as comprehensive as the work of George Savran.[161] The authors posit that ancient Hebrew prose enjoys repetition, not only in poetry, but also in prose texts. Combined with slight variations in the repeated material, the repetition "can equate and contrast events or characters or even whole other texts through association, inviting the reader to consider the significance of similarities and dissimilarities."[162] Just as repetition invites the reader to consider certain narratives in light of others, intertextuality and allusion also produce dialogue between texts. They clearly define intertextuality as a matter of the reader's creativity, as readers make connections between texts not the "texts themselves."

Gunn and Fewell conclude their discussion by turning to what they refer to as the ethics of interpretation. Even though the implied narrator may lead the reader in a certain direction, the reader may choose to oppose this direction. Because "texts are not objective representations of reality, but of particular value systems," readers may choose to rebel against this value system if they find reasons to oppose it.[163] They

---

159. Ibid., 56.

160. This idea of deliberate destabilization also affects redaction criticism. The authors state: "We could conceive of the story as a story told by various narrators, now the one, now another, intruding without warning—none wholly reliable because always subject to subversion by another" (ibid.).

161. See above, n. 133 (p. 49).

162. Gunn and Fewell, *Narrative in the Hebrew Bible*, 148.

163. Ibid., 191 (quotation). B. Long ("The 'New' Biblical Poetics of Alter and Sternberg," *JSOT* 51 [1991] 71–84) criticizes Sternberg and Alter for repressing the reader in his

maintain that this challenge to the "foolproof composition" of a text is already implied in the composition of the biblical canon, in which voices from the margins challenge the dominant voices in the center. By deliberately reading the text, for example, as Canaanites, not as Israelites, as women, not as men, readers can challenge the ideology of the implied author and expose its limitations. In doing so, readers may be uncovering a world in need of redemption and healing and a world view much in need of change. This is the kind of reading that can transform us. If we realize that the world of the Bible is a broken world, that its people are human and therefore limited, that its social system is flawed, then we might start to see more clearly our own broken world, our own human limitations, our own defective social systems.[164]

Yairah Amit

A recent publication on narrative criticism[165] is an adaptation of a series of lectures delivered on the Israeli Broadcast University of Galei Tzahal by Yairah Amit. She introduces her topic by comparing the discourse shapes of the story of Samson's escape from Gaza as told by Josephus, Pseudo-Philo, and the Masoretic Text (Judg 16:1–3). This comparison clearly communicates the difference between source and discourse and the need to look at the shape of the discourse when interpreting narrative texts.[166] Her book *Reading Biblical Narrative*

---

freedom to choose his reading position: "Alter and Sternberg move aggressively toward universalizing, if not virtually absolutizing, their own practice" (p. 74). Long denies that the intention of the implied author is "out there" for all to see (p. 78) and warns against supplanting one oppressive hermeneutic with another (p. 84).

164. Gunn and Fewell, *Narrative in the Hebrew Bible*, 205. These thoughts are continued in J. Collins, *The Bible after Babel: Historical Criticism in a Postmodern Age* (Grand Rapids, MI: Eerdmans, 2005).

165. Y. Amit, *Reading Biblical Narratives: Literary Criticism and the Hebrew Bible* (Minneapolis: Fortress, 2001). Amit is no "newcomer" to the studies of biblical narrative poetics. See Y. Amit, "The Story of Amnon and Tamar: Reservoir of Sympathy for Absalom," *Hasifrut* 32 (1983) 80–87 [Hebrew]; "The Function of Topographical Indications in the Biblical Story," *Shnaton* 9 (1985–87) 15–30 [Hebrew]; "The Dual Causality Principle and Its Effects on Biblical Literature," *VT* 37 (1987) 385–400; "The Multi-Purpose 'Leading Word' and the Problems of Its Usage," *Proof* 9 (1989) 99–114; *The Book of Judges: The Art of Editing* (trans. J. Chipman; Leiden: Brill, 1999); *Hidden Polemics in Biblical Narrative* (trans. J. Chipman; Leiden: Brill, 2000).

166. For further comparisons of these three discourse types, see also my essay in this volume: "Samuel's 'Farewell Speech': Theme and Variation in 1 Samuel 12, Josephus, and Pseudo-Philo"; as well as my *Narrative Art and Reader Creativity: A Comparative Reading of 1 Samuel 9:1–10:16* (Theological Research Exchange Network, 1999 [http://www .tren.com/e-docs/search_w_preview.cfm?p048-0245]).

summarizes many insights of previous narrative critics. She speaks about beginnings and endings, building on the work of Bar-Efrat and Sternberg. In her discussion of plot, she proposes two ways of analyzing plot: the pediment structure (based on the fivefold sequence consisting of exposition, complication, change, unraveling, and ending) and the scenic structure, which analyzes plots through the particular sequence of dialogues that follow upon each other.[167] Her presentation of plot patterns is based on Alter's definition of "type scenes," and her discussion of characterization takes up the distinction among agents, types, and full characters proposed by Adele Berlin.[168]

Amit makes her own contributions to the field of narrative poetics particularly in the following areas: the use of place-names in biblical narrative, the demarcation of the literary unit, the interaction between historical-critical scholarship and narrative poetics, and the reliability of the narrator. Amit suggests that the uses of many place-names in the Hebrew Bible are not historical reference but poetic devices. Whereas most narrative critics maintain that the minimalism of biblical narrative excludes information given purely to create the illusion of reality,[169] Amit suggests that many vague geographical references only serve to create the impression of historical writing and must thus be seen as an indication of fictional discourse.[170] In other cases, place-names can contribute to shaping narrative characters and can function as intertextual links.

Amit recognizes that any analysis of the shape of the discourse is highly dependent on the demarcation of the literary unit. Because biblical narrative is void of clear outlines, the reader or commentator must decide where to draw the lines of a narrative unit. These lines are not static. Quoting Perry and Sternberg, she states, "The boundaries of a literary unit are dynamic; they are not defined in advance, once and for all, but are redefined and reorganized anew, according to the ques-

---

167. Amit, *Reading Biblical Narratives*, 47. Surprisingly, Amit seems to believe that all expositional material is located at the outset of a narrative, thus ignoring the distinction, made by Sternberg, between initial exposition and delayed or distributed exposition (see Sternberg, *Expositional Modes*, 20–21). Compare Bar-Efrat, *Narrative Art in the Bible*, 95–111.

168. See Alter, *Art of Biblical Narrative*, 52. Berlin, *Poetics and Interpretation*, 40. Amit includes an interesting reflection on whether God in biblical narrative should be seen as an agent, a type, or a full-fledged character (Amit, *Reading Biblical Narratives*, 74).

169. See R. Barthes, "L'effet de réel," *Littérature et Réalité* (Paris: Seuil, 1997) 81–90.

170. Amit, *Reading Biblical Narratives*, 120. She refers to Judg 3:19, 4:6–11; and Job 1–2.

tion one seeks to answer."[171] Several criteria are important in making this decision: thematic unity, structural observations such as symmetry and inclusio, considerations of time and plot unity, and matters of poetics and style such as the use of key words. Thus, the demarcation of literary units is not entirely arbitrary, but it is important to realize that the "outline of a story is dynamically determined . . . the reader of biblical stories has an unusually active role, in the absence of clear boundaries and titles. The reader who defines the subject determines its scope."[172]

In complete contrast to the paradigm suggested by D. Robertson, K. Gros Louis, and others, Amit maintains that biblical narrative poetics must in all cases take the findings of historical criticism into consideration. This begins with textual criticism[173] but also includes literary criticism—that is, *Literarkritik*. She illustrates her thoughts by pointing to Judg 8:24–27 and asking whether the text's criticism of the creation of an ephod by Gideon is a later insertion by an overzealous editor or not. The shape of the discourse changes dramatically, depending on whether this evaluation is included or not. She concludes:

> It has been shown that the biblical literature underwent editorial processes over time; ignoring this possibility leads to a kind of scholarly one-sidedness that relies on rigid assumptions and seeks elaborate ways to justify the singularity of the received text, while ignoring the literary artistry of the biblical world, as well as the writers' intellectual world. This is not to say that one must invariably adopt the conclusions of Bible criticism, but that it is best to take them into account.[174]

The narrative critic and the historical-critical scholar meet in their observations on the text and do well to consider each other's evaluations of these observations critically.

The chapter "Whom to Believe?" addresses the reliability of the biblical narrator. Amit does maintain, unlike Gunn and Fewell, that the narrator, on a par with God, is reliable in all cases, but she also emphasizes that reliable narrators of different texts can convey quite different world views. A comparison of these contrasting narrators is not an issue of unreliability but of competing claims to truth. Comparing Chronicles to 1–2 Samuel, she states, "The author of Chronicles, with

---

171. Ibid., 15.
172. Ibid., 21.
173. Amit refers to the examples of Judg 16:2, 1 Sam 1:24, and 2 Sam 13:21–22, where neglect of textual criticism would lead a narrative critic to analyze a text incorrectly.
174. Amit, *Reading Biblical Narratives*, 31.

his rhetorical approach, chooses the effective poetic option of a reliable and authoritative narrator for the world of the story for which he is responsible."[175] The reader, however, is thus presented with a choice between two story worlds, effectively granting him the freedom to rebel against the guidance of one reliable narrator!

Narrative Poetics in Germany

German biblical scholarship, traditionally a stronghold of historical-critical scholarship, has been slow to admit narratological approaches to exegesis. Instead of interacting with narrative poetics in a differentiated manner, scholars have often bundled various types of literary readings together under the title "synchronic exegesis," rejecting readings of this sort with sweeping generalizations.[176] Nevertheless, interest in narrative poetics has increased during the last ten years.[177]

I would like to highlight three recent publications that attempt to build a bridge between the historical-critical methods and narrative poetics. The first is a textbook on Old Testament exegesis written by Helmut Utzschneider and Stefan Ark Nitsche. Their *Arbeitsbuch literaturwissenschaftliche Bibelauslegung* was published in 2001.[178] It combines linguistic, narratological, and historical-critical tools in a wide-ranging approach to interpreting Old Testament texts. The order in which they present these tools is striking. Following guidelines on how to make a rough translation and a chapter on textual criticism, the authors move to a text-pragmatic analysis of the text's surface structure. In this context, they make a clear distinction between the real authors and the implied author and posit that a knowledge of the real

---

175. Ibid., 99.

176. This attitude continues up to the present. See T. Naumann, "Zum Verhältnis von Sychronie und Diachronie in der Samuelexegese," in *David und Saul im Widerstreit* (ed. W. Dietrich; OBO 206; Fribourg: Academic Press / Göttingen: Vandenhoeck & Ruprecht, 2004) 51–65, esp. pp. 58–59.

177. See the discussions in G. Schunack, "Neuere literaturkritische Interpretationsverfahren in der anglo-amerikanischen Exegese," *Verkündigung und Forschung* 41 (1996) 28–55; K. Koenen, "Prolepsen in alttestamentlichen Erzählungen: Eine Skizze," *VT* 47 (1997) 456–77; C. Westermann, *Erzählungen in den Schriften des Alten Testaments* (Stuttgart: Calwer, 1998); M. Oeming, *Biblische Hermeneutik: Eine Einführung* (Darmstadt: Primus, 1998) 70–75; M. Oeming and A. Pregla, "New Literary Criticism," *ThR* 66 (2001) 1–23; H. Utzschneider and E. Blum, eds., *Lesarten der Bibel: Untersuchungen zu einer Theorie der Exegese des Alten Testaments* (Stuttgart: Kohlhammer, 2006); I. Müllner, "Zeit, Raum, Figuren, Blick: Hermeneutische und methodische Grundlagen der Analyse biblischer Erzähltexte," *Protokolle zur Bibel* 15 (2006) 1–24.

178. H. Utzschneider and S. Nitsche, *Arbeitsbuch literaturwissenschaftliche Bibelauslegung: Eine Methodenlehre zur Exegese des Alten Testaments* (Gütersloh: Gütersloher Verlag, 2001).

author and his intention is not in all cases necessary for understanding a piece of literature.[179] The text itself can be regarded as a literary-esthetic subject. Following a detailed discussion of text analysis on its semantic, syntactic, and structural levels, the authors direct their attention to the question of genre in Old Testament literature. Of the various examples listed, the genre dealt with in greatest detail is narrative. Chapter 5 refers back to the work of Bar-Efrat, Berlin, Genette, Lämmert, Ska, Sternberg, and others and sketches the basic outline of biblical narrative poetics. The most striking aspect of this presentation is the fact that it precedes the discussion of the classic historical-critical methods (discussed in this order: tradition criticism, source criticism, redaction criticism). Students who follow the exegetical guidelines laid out by Utzschneider and Nitsche will first interact with the text on all sorts of levels *before* moving on to historical-critical methodology. This sequence of exegetical steps is a radical shift away from classic German textbooks on exegesis that would only focus on the text in its final form *after* having worked through all aspects of historical criticism.

Realizing that a concise presentation of narrative poetics and biblical narrative was lacking in German, my dissertation (published in 2005)[180] combines a methodological discussion of narrative poetics with a close reading of 1 Samuel 8–12. This combination first situates a narratological approach to biblical narrative within the context of general narrative poetics and then places this hermeneutical paradigm within the context of historical-critical work on the early interaction between Saul and Samuel. It discusses the various methodological presuppositions and tools used in the study of narrative poetics in order to evaluate possible interactions between historical criticism and narrative poetics on a methodological level. In a discussion of 1 Samuel 8–12, I emphasize the distinction between the characters' voice and the narrator's perspective as an important consideration when determining source-critical criteria that justify the assumption of a disjunct text.

---

179. Auch für moderne literarische Texte gilt, dass die Kenntnis ihres realen Autors und dessen Intention für das Verständnis des Werkes nicht unbedingt erforderlich ist. . . . Das bedeutet, dass die Texte der Hebräischen Bibel auch für sich selbst sprechen könenn und müssen. Ihre Texthaftigkeit ist nicht notwendig und unbedingt an ihre realen Autoren oder Autorinnen und deren Intentionen gebunden. (Ibid., 64)

180. J. Vette, *Samuel and Saul: Ein Beitrag zur narrativen Poetik des Samuelbuches* (Münster: LIT, 2005).

Building on previous observations by Alonso Schökel[181] and Meir
Sternberg, the book concludes that mutual condemnation, polite noncommunication, and even the peaceful division of labor between historical criticism and narrative poetics do not help us to understand
biblical narrative. Instead, exegetes will have to join forces in gathering
detailed observations on the text and then consider in each individual
case whether noticeable features of biblical narrative are signs of fissures in the diachronic makeup of the text or can be better explained as
compositional elements of its discourse structure. Any sweeping preference for one over the other fails to do justice to the text.

The most recent monograph on narrative poetics in German is *Poetik
in der ezählenden Literatur im Alten Testament* by Klaus Seybold.[182] Seybold particularly deals with the work of Sternberg and Alonso Schökel
in greater detail than previously common in German Old Testament
publications. The great strength of this book is its desire to use the
insights of narrative poetics to enrich and expand historical-critical
exegesis. It is thus surprising that at the outset of his discussion he
maintains that any poetic analysis can only happen *after* the text has
been submitted to a source-critical analysis, which serves to protect
the exegete against arbitrary decisions in the demarcation of literary
units.[183] This is a reading of Sternberg that is foreign to much of what
Sternberg states in his *Poetics of Biblical Narrative.* It also takes the exact
opposite order of the exegetical steps suggested by Utzschneider and
Nitsche. The same unquestioned superiority of the historical-critical
approach is also evident when Seybold uses the classic *Gattungen* of
Old Testament narrative (myth, fairy tale, saga, legend, historical report, novella, epic verse, and historiography) to structure his book,
without critically interacting with Sternberg's reflection on the relationship between history and fiction on the levels of source and discourse that call these very *Gattungen* into question. Seybold does not
discuss the distinction between source and discourse (which is basic to
narrative poetics) in any explicit fashion, and thus his presentation of

---

181. Especially L. Alonso Schökel, "Of Methods and Models," in *Congress Volume:
Salamanca, 1983* (VTSup 36; Leiden: Brill, 1985) 3–13.

182. K. Seybold, *Poetik der erzählenden Literatur im Alten Testament* (Stuttgart: Kohlhammer, 2006); note also the 2006 translation of Bar-Efrat's volume into German, *Wie die
Bibelerzählt.*

183. Seybold, *Poetik,* 17. Against Amit, Seybold seems to assume that all dynamic de-
marcations of literary units are completely subjective except for those that use the tools
of historical-critical scholarship.

various narratives becomes a somewhat formalistic discussion of narratives primarily grouped together according to length.

Outlook

Even if we take Forster and Lubbock as a starting point, interest in the poetics of narrative, especially of biblical narrative, is not yet very old. This is particularly true in the German context. Even though many of its basic paradigms have now been presented by various authors, it still remains to be seen what position this approach will occupy in the canon of exegetical methods. The friction between different interpretive paradigms will continually point us to important issues such as stylistic norms against which a text should be measured, the role of reader subjectivity and creativity in the exegetical process, and the relation between the text as an artifact and the factual history against which it is supposedly set. These questions are important to all readers of biblical texts, and any constructive controversy on these questions will be beneficial. As Sternberg states, this controversy "will not make life easier for anybody . . . but the study of the Bible will be the gainer." [184]

---

184. Sternberg, *Poetics of Biblical Narrative*, 23.

Is There a Universal Genre of "Drama"?

Conjectures on the Basis of "Dramatic" Texts in Old Testament Prophecy, Attic Tragedy, and Egyptian Cult Plays

HELMUT UTZSCHNEIDER

Augustana Neuendettelsau

The scholarly interpretation of ancient texts is a cross-cultural undertaking from both a synchronic and a diachronic perspective. The texts of the ancient world must be considered synchronically; however, they are written in different languages and originate from different cultural areas. Diachronically, the texts must be interpreted in a manner that is appropriate to their origin but is meaningful to modern readers. Thus, concepts of genre have a crucial function.

In literary research, modern concepts of genre are often applied to ancient texts. For instance, in OT studies in Germany, the biblical Joseph story and the book of Jonah are sometimes called *novelles* (which should not to be confused with the English *novel*). In German literary terminology, a *novella* tells "an event that could happen in reality and that claims to be new."[1] A mere transmission of this definition to biblical texts or texts of other ancient literature seems hardly adequate.

Therefore, concepts of genre in a cross-cultural application must be constructed in a very careful manner. They must span great expanses of time, they must be meaningful for texts and readers from different cultures, and last but not least, in doing so, they must correspond to the general needs and ideas of human communication or behavior. I would like to call these concepts *universal*.

Author's note: A more detailed and expanded German version of this essay, "Ist das Drama eine universale Gattung? Erwägungen zu den 'dramatischen' Texten in der alt. Prophetie, der attischen Tragödie und im ägyptischen Kultspiel," is published in my *Gottes Vorstellung: Untersuchungen zur literarischen Ästhetik und ästhetischen Theologie des Alten Testaments* (BWANT 9/15; Stuttgart: Kohlhammer, 2007).

1. G. Schweickle and I. Schweickle, eds., *Metzler Literaturlexikon: Begriffe und Definitionen* (2nd ed.; Stuttgart: Metzler, 1990) 329. My translation.

Under modern conditions and based on recent discourse, this may sound strange. Poststructuralist literary studies maintain a skeptical attitude toward general concepts as such, toward concepts of genre in particular, and even more toward the assumption that there could be suprahistorical, human, or even metaphysical ideas that influence the production or reception of texts. Suspicion of essentialism lurks everywhere. Therefore, some recent scholars advise renouncing the concept of *genre* as such, as do some representatives of historical criticism of the OT. Nevertheless, modern literary studies as a whole have not bidden farewell to genres, because they function as a system of communication. Authors and readers refer to genres. Genres are, according to the definition of a modern literary scholar, "historical facts" that exist "in the form of real literary works and as nonobligatory rules or usages embodied in texts or drafted by contemporary literary theory."[2]

I personally do not see any contradiction between a concept of genre that is historically constructed and faithful to the texts on the one hand and related to anthropological essentials or ideas on the other. Thus, my concept of a universal genre will be somewhat essentialistic.

In the following, I want to present a set of ancient texts that are called "dramatic" or "drama" in each respective discipline—that is, in Egyptology, classical studies, and in OT studies. These texts will be the basis for examining whether there is a "universal" concept of genre that can be called *dramatic* or *drama* that is appropriate to the texts and meaningful for modern readers. It is assumed that the presence of a speech is the basic criterion for labeling a work a *drama* or *dramatic*, whereas nonverbal elements such as music and dance are concomitant elements.

In the first section below, I will give a short introduction and characterize the texts. In the second section, I will demonstrate two literary criteria that are crucial for understanding texts as being "dramatic." Third, I will point out two central social and intellectual functions of dramatic texts. And finally, I will return to the question of the universality of the concept *dramatic/drama*.

The Texts

The texts taken into consideration here originate from the Old Testament, from Egypt, and from Athens. They stand not only for

---

2. U. Suerbaum, "Text, Gattung, Intertextualität," in *Ein anglistischer Grundkurs: Einführung in die Literaturwissenschaft* (ed. B. Fabian; Berlin: Schmidt, 2004) 82–125, esp. p. 97. My translation.

themselves but also for other similar texts, even considerable corpuses of texts in each area of provenience. The texts are the following:

- Speeches in the books of Micah and Hosea that are representative of the speeches of the OT prophets
- Texts and images from the reliefs in the Temple of Horus in Edfu in Middle Egypt, the so-called "Play of Horus,"[3] representing the old Egyptian cult plays as transmitted in the "Dramatic Ramesseum Papyrus" or in the "Mamisi" of the Temple of Isis in Philae[4]
- Passages in Sophocles' *Oedipus at Colonus*[5] as an example of Classical Attic tragedy

These three texts and the corpuses that they represent are quite near each other in time of origin.

In the prophetic corpus of the Hebrew Bible, or the OT, there are few passages going back to the times of the earlier, "classical" prophets, Amos, Hosea, Micah, or Isaiah, in the late 8th or early 7th century B.C.E. Most prophetic speeches as well as the structures and plots of the prophetic Scriptures must be traced back to the literary work of the transmitters and redactors in the 6th to 4th centuries B.C.E.

The Attic tragedies were written exclusively in the 5th century in Athens. Sophocles' *Oedipus at Colonus* is the most recent of all of them; Sophocles probably finished it in 406, the year of his death. It may have been staged for the first time in 401, after the siege of Athens by the Spartans.

For the Egyptian texts that can be interpreted as cult plays, a much longer span of time must be taken into consideration. The "Dramatic Ramesseum Papyrus" includes a "Play in Honour of Sesostris I," a king of the Twelfth Dynasty, approximately 1950 B.C.E. In contrast, the texts and pictures of the temple reliefs in Edfu and Philae are Ptolemaic; that is, they stem from the 4th to 1st centuries B.C.E. Our example, the Edfu "Play of Horus," was finished in approximately 110 B.C.E., during the reign of Ptolemaeus IX Soter II. The subject of the play, The Myth of Horus, is much older, of course.

Altogether it can be said that most of our texts stem from the second half of the first millenium B.C.E., but some Egyptian texts are

---

3. A. M. Blackman and H. W. Fairman, "The Myth of Horus at Edfu—II: The Triumph of Horus over His Enemies—A Sacred Drama," *JEA* 28 (1942) 32–38; *JEA* 29 (1943) 2–36; *JEA* 30 (1944) 5–22. Idem, *The Triumph of Horus: An Ancient Egyptian Sacred Drama* (London: Batsford, 1974).

4. See J. C. Goyon, "Dramatische Texte," *LÄ* 1:1140–44.

5. Text according to Sophocles, *Dramen: Griechisch und deutsch* (ed. W. Willige; 3rd ed.; Zurich: Artemis, 1995). www.gutenberg.org/files/31/31-h/31-h/htm#colonus.

considerably older. The texts all come from the same cultural area, the eastern Mediterranean region. Nevertheless, they differ in many respects, and it is difficult to discover any literary dependence, even though some scholars assume this sort of connection between the prophetic speeches and the Greek tragedies.

It is beyond dispute that the Attic tragedies of the three great Athenian poets Aeschylus, Sophocles, and Euripides should be considered "dramatic." They were written for the annual theater contest during the festival of the Great Urban Dionysia in March and April. They normally were put on stage by their authors in the Theater of Dionysus in Athens. The theater's construction and equipment as well as its ensemble are known to some degree. The ensemble consisted of two to three actors and the choir. We also are generally informed regarding the conventions of the performances, such as the masks, painting, dances, and music. Attic tragedy is the archetype of Western European dramatic and stage traditions, and it is mainly responsible for the close connection between drama and stage. We will question this close connection in this essay, especially the question whether acting and performance are essential elements of a dramatic text. As is well known, this question has been discussed since the *Poetics* of Aristotle.

Whether the Egyptian texts that are interpreted as "dramatic" were ever put on stage is much less certain than regarding the Attic tragedies. H. W. Fairman, an editor of the "Play of Horus," concluded that it was "a . . . religious drama acted annually at Edfu during the festival of victory."[6] It was Fairman's edition of the play, not the play itself that was performed in 1974 by the drama department of a British university college. It is very possible that a priestly lecturer declaimed the text of the play (see below, pp. 77–78). For the actual readers, the dramatic character of the play depends exclusively on its texts and on the relief paintings.

Admittedly, only a minority of OT scholars share the interpretation of the Hebrew prophetic speeches as dramatic texts. In the German-speaking context, this minority is represented, for example, by Klaus Baltzer and, most recently, by Stefan A. Nitsche—apart from myself, of course. Klaus Baltzer interprets Deutero-Isaiah as a "liturgical drama" that was performed during the Festival of Unleavened Bread, most likely in the outer court of the temple in Jerusalem.[7] In Baltzer's opinion,

---

6. Fairman, *The Triumph of Horus: An Ancient Egyptian Sacred Drama*, 19.
7. K. Baltzer, *Deutero-Jesaja* (KAT 10/2; Gütersloh: Gütersloher Verlag, 1999) 29–38. See also the English version of this commentary published in in the Hermeneia series.

Deutero-Isaiah was written in the second half of the 5th century; this means that it was contemporary with the Attic tragedies. Accordingly, Baltzer points out several corresponding features in the Greek texts and in Deutero-Isaiah, such as the so-called hymns of Deutero-Isaiah (for example, Isa 42:10–13; 44:2–32), which he compares with the chorus in the Attic tragedies. S. A. Nitsche interpreted the so-called Apocalypse of Isaiah (Isaiah 24–27) as a dramatic text—initially on the basis of mere literary criteria. In a second assessment, based on the *Isaiah Scroll* (1QIsaᵃ) from Qumran, he showed that the poetic layout of the scroll— that is, its *spatia* and *paragraphoi*—support this interpretation.[8] My own work in this field is mainly a literary analysis of the books of Micah and Hosea.[9] In the opinion of the above-mentioned exegetes, including myself, the literary form of the text is decisive for its dramatic character, as I will show.

Literary Criteria of Dramatic Texts

As demonstrated in detail in my work on Micah, there are primarily two literary criteria by which texts are characterized as "dramatic": (1) by means of direct speeches and addresses, changing speakers, themes, and perspectives, they evoke the impression of actors' entrances; (2) the speeches visualize the scene of the entrances—in other words, they stage the location and other visual circumstances embodied in the speeches. Both criteria will now be demonstrated.

Speech as Scenic Entrance

Onstage, an entrance, which is "the appearance or exit of at least one person,"[10] is the smallest unit of acting. In dramatic texts as we know them, entrances are denoted and delimited by stage directions that announce by name the next person speaking. In prophetic texts, there are no stage directions of this sort.[11] This is why the texts are not identifiable as dramatic texts at first glance. Nevertheless, entrances give structure to the prophetic speeches. These structured entrances

---

8. S. A. Nitsche, *Jesaja 24–27: Ein dramatischer Text. Die Frage nach den Genres prophetischer Literatur des Alten Testaments und die Textgraphik der großen Jesajarolle aus Qumran* (BWANT 166; Stuttgart: Kohlhammer, 2006) passim.

9. H. Utzschneider, *Micha* (ZBKAT 24/1; Zurich: Theologischer Verlag, 2005) passim; idem, "Situation und Szene: Überlegungen zum Verhältnis historischer und literarischer Deutung prophetischer Texte am Beispiel von Hos 5,8–6,6," *ZAW* 114 (2002) 80–105.

10. B. Asmuth, *Einführung in die Dramenanalyse* (Stuttgart: Metzler, 1994) 41.

11. By the way, as far as we know the earliest manuscripts of Greek dramatic texts did not announce the next speaker by name but with poetic alignment or paragraphs set off with spaces, as S. A. Nitsche found in the Qumran manuscripts.

are identifiable by mere textual signals, especially by change of speaker or addressed persons, who are indicated by the personal pronouns "you," "I," or "we"; or by announcing the next speaker by his or her name or function. Entrances are also emphasized by other textual or structural signals, such as by a change of theme or perspective. This may be demonstrated by considering the Prologue of the book of Micah (Mic 1:2–7) as an example:

2 Listen, peoples, all of you!
  Pay attention, Earth and her fullness.
  The lord, YHWH, is against you as a witness,
  The lord, YHWH, from his holy palace.

3 Yea, behold, YHWH is setting out from his place,
  He is descending and trampling upon the heights of the earth.
4 The mountains are melting beneath him,
  valleys are splitting open [meanwhile],
  like wax in the presence of fire,
  like water cascading down a sluice.

5 All of these are because of Jacob's misconduct
  and because of the sins of the house of Israel.
  What is Jacob's misconduct?
  Is it not Samaria?
  What is the height of Judah?
  Is it not Jerusalem?
6 And so I will make Samaria into stones for vineyards.
  And I will pour her stones into the valley.
  And her foundations I will lay bare.
7 And all her carved images will be scattered,
  all her gifts will be burned by fire,
  and all her idols I will make a desolation.
  For from the fee of a prostitute she gathered them,
  and a fee of a prostitute they shall become.

Verse 2 begins with an imperative, that is, with direct speech, but the speaker is not mentioned. Nevertheless, the entrance of this speaker is implied. He or she cannot be God, because God is mentioned in the third colon of the verse in third person. The speech is addressed to "the peoples, all of you." Their presence is presupposed—in whatever form.

Verses 3 and 4 represent the second entrance. They are separated from the preceding entrance by the Hebrew *ki*, a formative signal; in the English translation, this is rendered "Yea." Moreover, there is a change of theme, and the speech has a new direction. The peoples are no longer the addressees. A spectacular advent of God, a theophany, is depicted. The character of the text as direct speech is indicated by the Hebrew particle *hinnēh*. Connected with a participle, it forms a *futurum instans*–construction. This construction presupposes the presence of a speaker. We are reminded of the so-called *teichoscopia*, with the prophet as speaker.

The last entrance is separated from the preceding by the textual signals in v. 5: the connecting phrase "all of these" is a back-reference; the questions open a new speech. In v. 6, it is clear that the speaker represented by the pronoun "I" is God. The destruction of the city of Samaria is depicted as in the preceding theophany in vv. 3–4.

As a whole, the scene consists of three entrances. In the first entrance, the people are addressed by an unknown speaker, probably the prophet; in the second entrance, the prophet depicts a theophany; and in the third, YHWH himself is the speaker. The theophany and the speech by God point at the temple as the location of the scene.

Speech as Performance

Dramatic texts and theater are closely connected. I want to make the case in this essay that dramatic texts in themselves are theatrical in the sense of the Greek word θεάομαι, which means 'to look at, to behold'. Dramatic texts are inherently (audio-)visual without being staged. What do the speaking or addressed persons look like? How are they dressed? What is their facial expression? In which environment do they move? Which noises accompany the performance of the actors? By implicitly answering these questions, the texts themselves are "synaesthetic."

I want to demonstrate this by considering some passages in Sophocles' *Oedipus at Colonus*. Especially in the prologue and the *parodos*, Sophocles sketches an outline of the location of the whole play. As a stranger and a suppliant (ἱκέτης; see below) looking for a resting place, the blind Oedipus, guided by his daughter Antigone arrives at a region that Antigone describes as an idyllic place near Athens. There are laurels and olives, and a nightingale is singing (lines 16–19). This short description of the Attic landscape is repeated and amplified in a famous chorus later in the play (lines 668–94).

Not only is the background of the scenery depicted in speeches, so are the visual elements of the story and the persons themselves. Antigone asks her father to sit down on an unhewn stone (line 19). An inhabitant of Colonus who happens to be passing by wants to drive Oedipus from his resting place: "The spot thou treadest on is holy ground!" (line 39). But Oedipus refuses to leave, and so the man from

Colonus departs to ask his fellow-citizens for advice. Meanwhile, Oedipus and Antigone hide themselves in a grove, waiting for the decision of the citizens of Colonus. It arrives in the shape of the chorus; Oedipus appears and terrifies the men of Colonus with his appearance and his voice: "O dread to see and dread to hear!" (line 140). But they call him to come closer, guided by Antigone. Oedipus's steps out of the grove are depicted by repeated exchanges, which illustrate the burdensome walk of the old and blind man:

> "Thy hand then!"
> > "Here, O father, is my hand."
>
> . . .
>
> "Shall I go further?"
> > "Aye."
>
> "What, further still?"
>
> . . .
> > "Follow with blind steps, father, as I lead." (lines 170–83)

So, the speech's content imagines the location and the actions carried out by the characters. The German technical term *Wortkulisse*[12] refers to scenery included in texts. Of course, these textual *Wortkulissen* need to be supported by the readers' imaginations, and gaps must be filled in by means of intertextual knowledge. For instance, the horror evoked by the appearance of Oedipus is illustrated in the audience's memory of the fact that Oedipus blinded himself with his own hand in Sophocles' *Oedipus the King* (line 1268). In a way, the reader is like the blind Oedipus: "Ears to the blind, they say, are eyes" (line 138), or in the translation of Ernst Buschor: *Mein Auge ist das Ohr. Ich sehe die Rede* ('My eye is my ear. I see the speech'). This is exactly what is meant by *Wortkulisse*.

It would be interesting to compare this performance in the imagination of readers and listeners with our knowledge of the staging of *Oedipus at Colonus* in Athens in the 6th century B.C.E. I suppose that acting the play on a real stage needs the cooperation of the audience to the same extent that reader cooperation is necessary in a *Wortkulisse*. And both—the real stage with its scenery and the *Wortkulisse*—depend on the dramatic text. I think that Aristotle was right when he insisted that both 'imagination' (ὄψις) and 'performance' (ἀγών) are based on the textual capacities of the drama, such as the plot (μῦθος), the persons, and the speech (λέξις; see Aristotle, *Poetics* 1450b).

---

12. Asmuth, *Einführung in die Dramenanalyse*, 52.

Functions of Dramatic Texts

The Imagining of Mythological and
Historical Narratives in Dramatic Texts

It is common in the OT prophetic literature for speeches to be embedded in narratives and vice versa. The extensive narratives in the book of Jeremiah are well known in this regard. In the Hebrew version, the narratives (Jeremiah 26–45) appear within a framework of speeches (Jeremiah 2–25/46–51). In the Minor Prophets, there are also narratives embedded in speeches—for instance, at the beginning of Hosea.

The book of Micah is one of The Twelve works that is without (or nearly without) any narrative. Nevertheless, clear connections with the historical narratives of the OT can easily be found. My first example is the word of doom against Zion in Mic 3:12:

> Therefore on account of you Zion will be ploughed like a field
> And Jerusalem will become a rubble heap
> And the mountain of the house (will become) heights of the forest.[13]

The prophetic word is found once more as a quotation in narrative in the book of Jeremiah (Jer 26:18–19). This narrative flashes back to the time of Jeremiah from the end of the 7th century to the end of the 8th century B.C.E. It deals with the conflict between the prophet Micah and the representatives of the Jerusalem kingdom and Hezekiah himself. If one relates the narrative and the word of Micah to the Assyrian conquest of Israel and Judah, Micah's word of prophecy appears to be holding Jerusalem responsible. According to the narrative, Hezekiah repented his sins and therefore Jerusalem was not captured. However, in the time of Jer 26:18–19, Jerusalem is being threatened by the Babylonians. Jeremiah warns and requires repentance. But Jehoiakim refuses to repent and Jeremiah is threatened with the death penalty. So in Jeremiah 26, Micah's oracle and the obedience of Hezekiah function as a contrast with the disobedience and misconduct of Jehoiakim. In the book of Micah itself, the prophetic word is clearly connected with the capture of Jerusalem by the Babylonians (see Mic 4:8–10).

Another example of the relationship between a prophetic speech and the traditions of the Assyrian conquest appears in Mic 1:10–16. In this poem, the scene of the Assyrian campaign of 701 B.C.E. is reproduced. In some sort of flashlight-teichoscopia, the speaker shows the

---

13. Translation according to F. I. Andersen and D. N. Freedman, *Micah: A New Translation with Introduction and Commmentary* (AB 24E; New York: Doubleday, 2000) 378.

destruction of towns and villages surrounding Jerusalem, whereas the undamaged city, which in v. 16 is depicted as "mother," is requested to be in mourning for her children.

> 10 In Gath don't report it,
>   don't weep at all!
>   In Beth-leaphrah
>   roll yourselves in the dust!
> 11 Pass on your way,
>   inhabitants of Shapir,
>   in nakedness and shame.
>   . . .
>   (to the mother Jerusalem:)
> 16 Make yourself bald and cut off your hair
>   for the children of your delight!
>   Make yourself as bald as the eagle,
>   for they have gone from you into exile.

In the OT, a number of narratives can be found that deal with this memorable situation (2 Kgs 18–20; Isaiah 20). The narratives show that the experience of the destruction of Judah and the salvation of Jerusalem has been made paradigmatic of the official political theology in the Jerusalem kingdom in the 7th and 6th centuries B.C.E. The dramatization of this narrative tradition in prophetic speeches not only transported the experiences of the past into the present for the listeners but also updated these experiences with new interpretations. The speeches allowed the listeners to take part in these events and at the same time showed them in a new light for each new generation of listeners. So the speeches are both: a renewal and a generalization of the traditions.

A quite similar type of intertextuality can be found in the relationship between the Attic tragedies and the narrative traditions of old Greek myths and epics. "The material of tragedy is myth,"[14] says Hellmut Flashar, a well-known German interpreter of Sophocles. Apart from oral traditions and vase paintings, poetry, especially epic poetry is the most important source for the tragedies. They imagine, interpret, and generalize the traditions of the past, just as the prophetic speeches do. Once more, Hellmut Flashar states, "The present is reflected in the past and becomes available for generalization."[15]

Quite striking is the intertextuality between the "Play of Horus" and a narrative version of the Horus myth called the "Myth of the

---

14. H. Flashar, *Sophokles: Dichter im demokratischen Athen* (Munich: Beck, 2000) 18 (translations mine).

15. Ibid.

Winged Disk."[16] This myth is depicted in the register above the play on the same wall in the Edfu temple precinct. The contents of the myth and the play are closely related, for example, in the use of the hippopotamuses as images of mythical and political enemies and in harpooning as the method of destroying them. Possibly both texts were read, though at different feasts.

Thus, in the Egyptian cult plays, the same connection between imagining and generalization of mythical and epic traditions can be detected as in the dramatic texts from Israel and Greece. J. P. Sørensen points out the transparency of the mythical Horus to the present king, which is imagined and performed in the play:

> primeval and present are dramatically juxtaposed and made to mirror each other as the stages in a redundant mythical process. Although the drama delineates a descent from primeval to present level, from hippopotamus to human enemy, from Horus to Ptolemy IX, it does not in a historical sense narrate the story of how the present condition came to be. Rather it recasts the present in its mythical form and shows it, idealized in terms of royal ideology, as variation on a mythical theme.[17]

Consequently, it can be said that the intertextuality between dramatic speeches and historical epic played an important role in the three cultural realms. In dramatic texts, significant traditions of the past were imagined, interpreted, and generalized.

Drama as Reflected Ritual

The cultural anthropologist Victor Turner pointed out that there could be a mutual, perhaps even a dialectical relation between social dramas and cultural performances. Life is both an imitation of art and vice versa.[18] Doris Bachman-Medick has carried on this approach. Social rituals and stage dramas are both concerned with situations of liminality that are faced by societies as well as by individuals. Birth, marriage, and death are some of these situations, which are important motifs in social life and in literary dramas. However, literary dramas

---

16. See A. Egberts, "Mythos und Fest: Überlegungen zur Dekoration der westlichen Innenseite der Umfassungsmauer im Tempel von Edfu," in *4. Ägyptische Tempeltagung: Feste im Tempel* (ed. R. Gundlach and M. Rochholz; Ägypten und Altes Testament 33/2; Wiesbaden: Harrassowitz, 1998) 17–29. D. Kurth, *Treffpunkt der Götter: Inschriften aus dem Tempel des Horus* (Zurich: Artemis, 1994) 217.

17. J. P. Sørensen, "Three Varieties of Ritual Drama," *Temenos* 22 (1986) 79–92, esp. p. 83.

18. See V. Turner, *From Ritual to Theatre: The Human Seriousness of Play* (New York: Performing Arts Journal, 1982).

are not simply reproductions of social dramas. Dramas are reflections of rituals; that is, rituals can be justified, distanced, criticized by literary dramas, and even led *ad absurdum*. A good example in modern theater of a reflected ritual is Bertolt Brecht's play *Kleinbürgerhochzeit*.[19] I am convinced that this approach is also appropriate for our ancient dramatic texts and is able to shed new light on them. In all these texts, rituals are present in one way or another. I turn to examples.

The second part (or "scene," as I see it) of Micah (Mic 1:8–2:6) is full of references to mourning rituals: the nakedness and crying of the prophet (Mic 1:8, 10), the forbidden weeping of the people of Gath (Mic 1:10), the rolling in the dust (1:10), the baldness of Mother Jerusalem (Mic 1:16), and last but not least, the Woe speech of the prophet in Mic 2:1–2 as the climax:

> 1 Woe—planners of iniquity and doers of evil on their beds
>   In the light of the morning they do it,
>   Because they are mighty
> 2 When they covet fields,
>   then they seize [them]
>   and houses
>   they steel them.[20]

The Woe speech intrinsically belongs to the mourning ritual for a deceased individual. In the normal course of the ritual, it introduces the obituary for the deceased. In this speech, the mourners imagine the bereavement they suffer. In Mic 2:1, the Woe speech is definitely not used for this function. It is intentionally distanced and used to point out the consequences of the evil done by the mourned ones. Of course, these doers of evil are quite alive, but their deeds are lethal to their victims and, in the long run, to themselves. Christof Hardmeier called these Woe speeches *Trauermetaphorik* 'metaphors of mourning' and stressed their rhetorical function. He is quite right—but that is not all. The citations of rituals portray those who cite them in a role. By citing a ritual out of context with its intrinsic function, the prophet becomes an actor and the ritual a drama.

A very interesting case of a reflected ritual appears in Hos 6:1–6. The poem in Hos 6:1–3 is usually understood as a "community lament"

---

19. See D. Bachman-Medick, "Kulturelle Spielräume: Drama und Theater im Licht ethnologischer Ritualforschung," in *Kultur als Text: Die anthropologische Wende in der Literaturwissenschaft* (ed. D. Bachmann-Medick; 2nd ed.; Tübingen: Francke, 2004) 98–121, esp. p. 102.

20. Translation by Andersen and Freedman, *Micah*, 257 (revised slightly).

or a part of it. In the ritual itself, a common lament is normally followed by an oracle from God, who responds to the lament; of course, an oracle of salvation is expected. Indeed, in Hos 6:4–5 God becomes the speaker. But with this oracle, the structure of the lament is both maintained and broken.

The lament of the people:

> 1 Come, let us return to YHWH!
>   Although he tore us apart, he will heal us.
>   Although he smashed us, he will bandage us.
> 2 He will revive us after two days,
>   and on the third day he will raise us up.
>   We will live in his presence so that we know him.
> 3 We will pursue knowledge of YHWH.
>   His utterance is as certain as sunrise.
>   He will come like rain for us.
>   Like spring rain, he will water the earth.

This is followed by a speech of YHWH addressed to the people:

> 4 How shall I deal with you, Ephraim?
>   How shall I deal with you, Judah?
>   Your mercy passes away like a morning cloud,
>   and like early dew, it passes away.

In the lament, the people assure themselves of the certitude of God's salvation and expect a positive oracle. In the following oracle, God doubts the truthfulness of the people and denies their expectations. There is a negative correspondence between God's own reliability and the people's loyalty. In my opinion, this means that the dramatic text is criticizing and rejecting the ritual of public lament, because it has lost its foundation. And it does so by using the forms and language of the ritual. But this is not the end. In the last part of his speech, YHWH introduces a new theological perspective on his relation to Israel, a relationship that is not founded on rituals but on *ḥesed* (which means 'mercy' or 'loyalty', or even 'love') and knowledge.

> 6 For I desire mercy rather than sacrifice
>   and knowledge rather than offerings.

Finally, OT rituals are used to structure a prophetic book or parts of it. The second part of the book of Micah (Micah 6–7), for instance, is structured as a *rîb* 'lawsuit', including all parts of it such as the hearing of evidence, accusation, sentence, and act of grace.

The relation between ritual and drama that we have illustrated with OT dramatic texts can also be supported by Greek tragedies. F. Zeitlin has shown in detail that the tragedies contain the whole ritual world of ancient Greece: rites of purification and expiation, suppliant and apotropaic ritual, rituals of celebration, and mantic rituals, not forgetting the *rites de passage* surrounding birth, marriage, and death.[21]

Similar to prophetic books, tragedies can be constructed around rituals. In particular, the ritual of ἱκετεία ('supplication') has lent its structures and themes to classical tragedies. The ἱκετεία is a ritual by which strangers ritually plead for the right to settle among other ethnic groups. Aeschylus and Euripides wrote plays entitled Ἱκετίδες 'suppliants'. And also our example, Sophocles' *Oedipus at Colonus*, is on the whole designed as a ἱκετεία. Oedipus and his daughter plead for permission to stay in Colonus. But there are obstacles: the citizens of Colonus reject their supplication at first. Creon and Polyneices try to force them to return to Thebes. It is Theseus, the ruler of Athens, who ensures that Oedipus and Antigone can remain in Colonus. Ultimately, however, Oedipus dies and finds asylum and rest in a tomb in the holy grove of Colonus. Against this background and based on the ritual of ἱκετεία, the aged Sophocles was facing death and was probably reflecting his own life and, in doing so, the fate of humankind.

A highly sophisticated use of rituals can be seen in Sophocles' *Antigone*. By contrasting the rituals of power and mourning, Sophocles designs the two antagonistic characters of his play: Creon and Antigone. Antigone resists the rituals of power by performing the rituals of mourning to an excessive extent. This may be understood as a critical attitude toward ritual as such; a new perspective on the motives of human behavior is winning the upper hand over the ritual layer. Antigone expresses this perspective in her famous words: "Love and not hatred is the part for me" (line 524).

The relationship to ritual seems to me to be rather close both for the dramatic texts of the Hebrew Bible and for the Greek tragedies. In both, rituals are reflected, distanced, and criticized. This may merely be a poetic device for constructing plots or developing characters. But to me it appears more and more to be a way to open up new theological or anthropological perspectives.

Let us now have a short look at the world of Egyptian cult plays.

In the "Play of Horus," a bridge is built between the dramatic text and performance, on the one hand, and the ritual itself, on the other,

---

21. See F. I. Zeitlin, *The Ritual World of Greek Tragedy* (Ph.D. diss., Colombia University, 1970) passim.

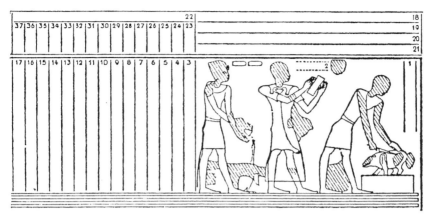

Fig. 1. Scene from Edfu showing a scene from the "Play of Horus." First published by Émile Chassinat, Le Temple d'Edfou, vol. 10, fasc. 2 (Cairo: Institut Française d'Archéologie orientale, 1960), pl. 146. Copyright © IFAO.

especially in the last scene of the play.[22] Figure 1 shows a butcher slaughtering a Hippopotamus, a priest reading a papyrus scroll (probably the play itself), and the king feeding a goose with corn. The dramatic text on the left side of the image opens with a description of the victorious king:

> The King of Upper and Lower Egypt
> Son of Re
> (Ptolemaeus-may-he-live-for-ever-Beloved of Ptah)
> is triumphant in the broad hall,
> he has overthrown the *Mnryw* of all the countries of Asia.
> Lo he is triumphant in the broad hall,
> he has suppressed his enemies,
> he has taken hold of his back,
> he has clutched the foes by their forelocks.

What follows are "stage directions" that repeat the image in words and introduce the concluding hymn:

> Bringing in the Hippopotamus in form of a cake before
>   him-with-the-uplifted-arm.
> Dismembering by the butcher.

22. Blackman and Fairman, "The Myth of Horus at Edfu—II," *JEA* 30 (1944) 13–15. Fairman, *The Triumph of Horus*, 113 (fig. 1).

Recital of this Book against him by the chief lector on the twenty-first
   day of the second month of Proyet.
To be spoken by the prophets, the fathers of the god, and the priests: . . .[23]

In this last scene of the play, characters act in sacral roles but in human
ways. In addition to the chorus and the king, mainly Gods—Horus,
Isis, Seth—have been speaking and acting in the preceding scenes. The
hippopotamus, which represented Seth and was harpooned by the God
Horus in the preceding scenes, is now present in the form of a cake,
which must be divided. My assumption is that the last scene of the
"Play of Horus" represents the interface between ritual and drama. The
preceding mythological scenes or speeches of the drama aim toward
the ritual depicted in the last scene. Or seen the other way around, the
ritual, which is celebrated every year, is the last part of a mythical act
that recurs in a dramatic performance. We may imagine this performance as a "real" play on stage, as declaimed by a priest, or simply as a
mute relief on the western wall of the temple precinct.

The connection between drama and ritual is a crucial moment for
the dramatic texts of antiquity (and presumably, not only in antiquity).
However, this connection appears in quite different shapes. In Egypt,
the connection is very close. There is as far I can see no intellectual gap
between drama and ritual; on the basis of myth, they are intertwined.
Thus, drama reflects ritual in that drama gives the mythological reason
for the ritual. In Greece and in Israel, however, we observe a more complicated and distant relationship. The function of justifying ritual disappears. The citation of ritual can be a poetic device. The alienation
from rituals can be seen as a means of characterizing or criticizing the
participants in the rituals. Even the rituals themselves can be put into
question.

Drama as a Universal Genre?

It was the aim of our examination to construct a concept of dramatic
genre that might be called "universal" because it spans great cultural
distances from both a synchronic and a diachronic perspective and because it is linked to basic human needs and ideas. On a broad basis of
ancient Mediterranean texts, it can be demonstrated that speeches that
form an actor's "entrance" (pp. 67–69) and that educe scenic imagery
(pp. 69–70) meet the basic literary criteria for being considered dra-

---

23. Text according to Blackman and Fairman, "The Myth of Horus at Edfu—II," *JEA*
30 (1944) 13.

matic texts. These criteria can be applied not only to texts in the classical and modern theatrical tradition but also to texts that have been declaimed or have been transmitted and read only in written and illustrated form. As basically dramatic texts, they also can be shown to fulfill certain social and intellectual functions. They imagine and renew historical and mythical traditions of their society by interpreting and generalizing them (pp. 71–73). However, they can also reflect the ritual texts of their society by justifying, distancing, or criticizing the rituals (pp. 73–78).

Regardless of many differences, the texts compared above are similar enough to subsume them in a genre called *dramatic texts*. The functions of these dramatic texts are not confined to antiquity: (1) renewing and interpreting fundamental traditions by transmitting them in "great narratives" and (2) reflecting social or religious rituals are basic needs and ideas that are part of human communication and behavior. Therefore, this genre can rightly be called *universal*.

Narratology and the Classics:
The Proof of the Pudding . . .

IRENE J. F. DE JONG
University of Amsterdam

This essay consists of three parts: first, a brief historical overview of the way that the discipline of classics came to adopt modern literary theories; then, an introduction to two practical applications of one literary theory, narratology, to classical texts; and finally, an example of the way that the introduction of modern theory may lead to new areas of research.

Classics and Literary Theory:
A Historical Overview

The best soccer player of Holland, Johan Cruyff, coined a saying that quickly became proverbial: "every advantage has its disadvantage." This saying was very appropriate to the situation in classical studies at the end of the 1960s. Armed since antiquity with an impressive arsenal of terms and concepts with which to analyze and interpret texts, scholars of the classics did not feel the need to catch up with the developments of modern literary theory; indeed they had begun, in the words of Professor of Latin and Comparative Literature in Konstanz, Manfred Fuhrmann, to "fence [themselves] off from" developments in other disciplines. In his *Antrittsvorlesung* in 1968, Fuhrmann put his finger directly on the problem: classical philology, once the incontestable leader of the field of literary interpretation, had become isolated and withdrawn within the confines of its own discipline. Scholars were suffering from a *Modernitätsdefizit*.[1]

But, as in so many other respects, the 1960s initiated major changes in classical studies. The subject of ancient texts and modern criticism was addressed with some regularity in articles and books. The titles of

---

1. M. Fuhrmann, *Die Antike und ihr Vermittler: Bemerkungen zur gegenwärtigen Situation der klassischen Philologie* (Konstanz: Unversitätsverlag, 1969) 21.

these studies speak volumes: "Ancient Texts and Modern Literary Criticism," *Post-Structuralist Classics*, *Innovations of Antiquity*, and *Modern Critical Theory and Classical Literature*.[2]

Most introductory sections in these works asked the question why classical studies have been slow in adopting modern theory. According to Fuhrmann in 1968, it was the dominant legacy of the classical period of German classical philology—the time of Friedrich August Wolf, Lessing, Goethe, Winckelmann, and Humbold with their idealization and *Klassizismus*—that held classics in its firm grip. Segal, also in 1968, came up with another analysis:

> When we come to consider specific methods of criticism, it is clear that classical critics have not of late been pioneers or innovators of new approaches, as they were in the early part of the century. No new critical theories have arisen from classical studies per se. We cannot today claim a Nietzsche, a Frazer, a Cornford, or even a Gilbert Murray, nor do we have a critic of the theoretical scope or synthetic imagination of a Northrop Frye. The reason for this is perhaps that classical studies have grown more cautious about generalization. Critics prefer to work in the securer, more manageable areas of a single author or work.[3]

In other words, the tradition of slow, close reading prevented classical scholars from coming up with large, sweeping literary theories. In 1977, in a special issue of the journal *Arethusa* devoted to Classical Literature and Contemporary Literary Theory, Carl Rubino pointed out another relevant fact: the structuralist theories of the 1960s, which were mainly developed by French thinkers, were simply very hard reading. However, urged Rubino, "[T]here is no substitute for reading the structuralist texts themselves, difficult though that may be."[4]

And indeed, modern theories were slowly adopted by classical scholars. Thus in the mid-1990s, two volumes appeared that offered a

---

2. C. Segal, "Ancient Texts and Modern Literary Criticism," *Arethusa* 1 (1968) 1–25; C. Rubino, "'Lectio difficilior praeferenda est': Some Remarks on Contemporary French Thought and the Study of Classical Literature," *Arethusa* 10 (1977) 63–83; A. Benjamin, ed., *Post-Structuralist Classics* (London: Routledge, 1988); R. Hexter and P. Selden, eds., *Innovations of Antiquity* (New York: Routledge, 1992); I. J. F. de Jong and J. P. Sullivan, eds., *Modern Critical Theory and Classical Literature* (Leiden: Brill, 1994); C. P. Segal, "Introduction: Retrospection on Classical Literary Criticism," in *Contextualizing Classics: Ideology, Performance, Dialogue—Essays in Honor of John J. Peradotto* (ed. T. M. Falkner, N. Felson, and D. Konstan; Lanham, MD: Rowman & Littlefield, 1999) 1–15; S. J. Harrison, ed., *Texts, Ideas, and the Classics: Scholarship, Theory, and Classical Literature* (Oxford: Oxford University Press, 2001).

3. Segal, "Ancient Texts," 10.

4. Rubino, "Lectio difficilior praeferenda est," 66.

sample of modern approaches to ancient texts. Both acknowledged that gradually modern theory was entering the field of the classics. Thus, the volume edited by Sullivan and me in 1994 opens as follows, perhaps somewhat overoptimistically:

> In recent decades the study and teaching of literature in Europe and the Americas have been radically influenced by modern critical theory in its various forms. Although the influence and the leading exponents of these various theories and approaches have been most noticeable in the study of modern literatures and culture, there has also been a perceptible impact of these theories in the study of Greco-Latin literature.[5]

The introduction of Hexter and Selden in 1992 was more open about the tensions that the introduction of modern theory created within classics:

> [T]o judge from recent conferences, convention sessions, courses, books, and journals, critical appreciation of Greco-Roman literature is itself in a state of significant transition. Partly under the influence of intellectual energy drawn from neighbouring fields . . . the received forms of linguistic and historical positivism are undergoing transformation. For some the critical right has condemned this development as a degeneration of science . . . into speculation, while the critical left has hailed the trend as the belated displacement of a moribund philology by an ethically more conscientious hermeneutics.[6]

Indeed, an address by the president of the English Classical Association in 1995 had the title "Cast Out Theory: Horace *Odes* 1.4 and 4.7."[7] It was in reaction to these tensions that the introduction to the volume edited by Harrison in 2001 was given the conciliatory title "Working Together." The volume set out "to promote a simple idea: that, in the contemporary context of the study and interpretation of classical literature at universities, conventional classical scholarship and modern theoretical ideas need to work with each other in the common task of the interpretation of texts." More specifically, the editor hoped "that this volume will encourage skeptically inclined literary classics to believe that the application of literary (and other) theory can provide new and enriching resources for their traditional scholarship, and remind the more theoretically inclined that they need and rely on traditional

---

5. De Jong and Sullivan, *Modern Critical Theory and Classical Literature*, 1.

6. Hexter and Selden, *Innovations of Antiquity*, xii.

7. D. West, "Cast Out Theory: Horace *Odes* 1.4 and 4.7," Classical Association Presidential Address, Oxford 1995.

scholarship."[8] As the second and third part of this essay will show, I wholly subscribe to this last point: modern theoretical approaches should not replace traditional approaches but build on their solid foundation, enriching and complementing them.

So far I have only paid attention to books and articles that specifically addressed the academic question whether modern theory can be applied to classical texts. But of course, in the meantime, from the 1970s onward, studies also appeared that simply *used* these modern theories. To present these studies here would go beyond the scope of this paper. Fortunately, since 2002, an excellent overview by Schmitz has been available: *Moderne Literaturtheorie und antike Texte*. In a series of 12 chapters, he first introduces, both historically and systematically, the branch of modern literary theory that ranges from formalism and structuralism via narratology and intertextuality to deconstruction, psycho-analytic, and feminist theory; and then he gives an overview of applications of this branch to classical texts. When we compare his title with that of the first study on the subject, by Segal in 1968, "Ancient Texts and Modern Literary Criticism," we note the self-confident reversal of the order: first theory, then texts.

In his introduction, Schmitz gives a clear and helpful discussion of all the old classical prejudices against modern theory and ends up with a passionate plea for the intelligent, creative, and eclectic use of the good things that modern theory has to offer the classical scholar. One remark of his seems to me to be a fitting conclusion to my introductory section:

> In Deutschland mehr noch als in anderen Ländern hat die Klassische Philologie die Anregungen und Herausforderungen der modernen Literaturtheorie mit einer gewissen Verzögerung aufgenommen . . . , zugleich ist diese Verspätung jedoch auch ein Vorteil. Die Betriebsamkeit ist fort, aber die . . . großen Fragen, die die Literaturtheorie aufgeworfen hat, sind geblieben . . . Für uns aber ergibt sich die Gelegenheit, in sicherer Entfernung vom Kampfgeschrei der frühen Jahre diese Fragen und Probleme ruhiger ins Auge zu fassen.[9]

What Schmitz says here about German classical scholars and modern theory, in my view also applies to classics and modern theory as a whole: the disadvantage of the slow adoption of modern theory by classical scholars has also proven an advantage. The hectic preoccupa-

---

8. Harrison, ed., *Texts, Ideas, and the Classics*, 1 and 17.
9. T. A. Schmitz, *Moderne Literaturtheorie und antike Texte: Eine Einführung* (Darmstadt: Wissenschaftliche Buchgeselschaft, 2002) 15.

tion with theory that characterized the 1970s and 80s has ebbed away. The dust has settled, and what remains are the theoretical concepts that have proven their value in actual interpretation. In the next two sections, I will offer examples of one of these lasting and fruitful theories.

Narratology and the Classics, Example 1: A Narratological Commentary on the Odyssey

In this part of my essay, I will present two examples of what the application of modern theory to ancient texts can produce that derive from my own research of the past and the present. Ever since my dissertation in 1987, I have worked with concepts from narratology, or *Erzählforschung* in my analysis and interpretation of ancient texts: mainly Homer, Herodotus, and (parts of) tragedy.[10] The term *narratology* was coined in 1969 by Todorov, but in fact many central concepts, such as the distinction between *mimesis* and *dihegesis* or *speech* versus *narrator text*, go back to antiquity.[11] In modern times, novelists such as Henry James or Flaubert began to reflect on aspects of the art of the novel. Then the Russian formalists contributed central concepts such as *fabula* versus *sjuzet*. But the real heyday of narratology was the 1960s and 70s, when important models were developed by Stanzel, Booth, Genette, Bal, and Chatman.[12] For historical overviews of the

---

10. Some of my key publications: *Narrators and Focalizers: The Presentation of the Story in the Iliad* (Amsterdam: Grüner, 1987; 2nd ed., London: Duckworth, 2004); *Narrative in Drama: The Art of the Euripidean Messenger-Speech* (Leiden: Brill, 1991); "Narratology and Oral Poetry: The Case of Homer," *Poetics Today* 12 (1991) 405–23; "The Origins of Figural Narration in Antiquity," in *New Perspectives on Narrative Perspective* (ed. W. van Peer and S. Chatman; New York: State University of New York Press, 2001) 67–81; "The Anachronical Structure of Herodotus' Histories," in *Texts, Ideas, and the Classics* (ed. S. J. Harrison; Oxford: Oxford University Press, 2001) 93–116; (with R. Nünlist), "From Bird's Eye View to Close Up: The Standpoint of the Narrator in the Homeric Epics," in *Antike Literatur in neuer Deutung* (ed. A. Bierl, A. Schmidt, and A. Willi; Leipzig: Saur, 2004) 63–83; "Narratologia e storiografia: Il racconto di Atys e Adrasto in Erodoto 1.34–45," *QUCC* 80 (2005) 87–96; "Where Narratology Meets Stylistics: The Seven Versions of Ajax' Madness," in *Sophocles and the Greek Language: Aspects of Diction, Syntax, and Pragmatics* (ed. I. J. F. de Jong and A. Rijksbaron; Leiden: Brill, 2006) 73–93.

11. For another example, see R. Nünlist, "The Homeric Scholia on Focalization," *Mnemosyne* 56 (2003) 61–71; idem, *The Ancient Critic at Work: Terms and Concepts of Literary Criticism in Greek Scholia* (Cambridge: Cambridge University Press, 2009).

12. M. Bal, *Narratology: Introduction to the Theory of Narrative* (2nd ed.; Toronto: University of Toronto Press, 1997); W. Booth, *The Rhetoric of Fiction* (2nd ed.; Chicago: University of Chicago Press, 1983); S. Chatman, *Story and Discourse: Narrative Structure in Fiction and Film* (Ithaca, NY: Cornell University Press, 1987); G. Genette, *Narrative Discourse: An Essay in Method* (trans. J. E. Lewin; Ithaca, NY: Cornell University Press, 1980);

development of narratology, I refer to the studies by Martin, Herman, and Vervaeck, while an encyclopedic overview is found in the recently published *Routledge Encyclopedia of Narrative Theory*.[13]

Taken together, these theories have offered us a precise, refined set of tools with which to analyze the role of the narrator and narratee, and aspects of time, setting, description, and characterization. These tools have proven to apply well also to ancient texts. Indeed, "[T]he application of narratology to classical texts has been a success story."[14] Thus, the recent decades have brought us narratological studies on Homer, Hesiod, Thucydides, Sophocles, Euripides, Apollonius Rhodius, Virgil, Ovid, and Apuleius.[15] My explanation for the success of narratology in the field of classics is that it largely resembles rhetoric, which was the framework of old within which both ancients and moderns analyzed ancient literary texts. The French narratologist Genette, particularly in introducing neologistic terms, leans heavily on ancient rhetoric: of the series analepsis, prolepsis, paralepsis, paralipsis, and metalepsis, three have ancient roots (prolepsis, paralepsis, and metalepsis), and the others have been newly formed on the basis of an easily understood logic.

By way of a first example of what modern theory can bring to ancient texts, I want to adduce the *Narratological Commentary on the*

---

idem, *Narrative Discourse Revisited* (trans. J. E. Lewin; Ithaca, NY: Cornell University Press, 1988); F. Stanzel, *A Theory of Narrative* (trans. C. Goedsche; Cambridge: Cambridge University Press, 1984).

13. W. Martin, *Recent Theories of Narrative* (Ithaca, NY: Cornell University Press, 1986); L. Herman and B. Vervaeck, *Handbook of Narrative Analysis* (Lincoln: University of Nebraska Press, 2001); D. Herman, A. Jahn, and M.-L. Ryan, eds., *The Routledge Encyclopedia of Narrative Theory* (London: Routledge, 2005).

14. Harrison, ed., *Texts, Ideas, and the Classics*, 13. Cf. Schmitz, *Moderne Literaturtheorie*, 54: "Mit der Narratologie betreten wir ein Gebiet, auf dem strukturalistischen Ansätze ungemein fruchtbar geworden sind."

15. D. Fowler, "Deviant focalisation in Virgil's Aeneid," *PCPS* 36 (1990) 42–63; M. Fusillo, *Il tempo delle Argonautiche: Un analisi del racconto in Apollonio Rodio* (Rome: Edizione dell'Ateneo, 1985); idem, *Naissance du roman* (Paris: Seuil, 1991); J. Grethlein, *Das Geschichtsbild der Ilias: Eine Untersuchung aus phänomenologischer und narratologischer Perspektive* (Göttingen: Vandenhoeck & Ruprecht, 2006); A. Markantonatos, *Tragic Narrative: A Narratological Study of Sophocles' Oedipus at Colonus* (Berlin: de Gruyter, 2002); S. Richardson, *The Homeric Narrator* (Nashville: Vanderbilt University Press, 1990); T. Rood, *Thucydides: Narrative and Explanation* (Oxford: Oxford University Press, 1998); K. Stoddard, *The Narrative Voice in the Theogony of Hesiod* (Leiden: Brill, 2004); S. M. Wheeler, *A Discourse of Wonders: Audience and Performance in Ovid's Metamorphoses* (Philadelphia: University of Pennsylvania Press, 1999); J. J. Winkler, *Auctor and Actor: A Narratological Reading of Apuleius' Golden Ass* (Berkeley: University of California Press, 1985). And see n. 10 above.

Odyssey that I published in 2001. Commentaries are an extremely important, widespread, age-old tool in the study of classics (as in many other disciplines or philologies).[16] What is a narratological commentary?[17] In order to make this clear, I will first describe briefly the traditional form of classical commentaries. Commentaries summarize scholarship on a text in the form of line-by-line lemmata. As such they are: (1) problem solving, (2) comprehensive, and (3) microtextual.

Commentaries are problem solving in that they are aimed primarily at explaining difficulties: they elucidate problematic grammatical constructions or obscure words, provide the historical or archaeological background information needed to understand what is said, and summarize interpretations of puzzling passages.[18] Commentaries are comprehensive in that they offer their users summaries of all that has been said about the problems in the text in question. Thus we find, side by side, philological, linguistic, historical, metrical, and literary comments. Commentaries usually proceed word by word, or at most, line by line.

These three main characteristics of commentaries should be seen in light of their ancient predecessors: the *zetemata* (monographs on 'problems'), the *hypomnemata* (line-by-line explanations of the text), and finally the *scholia*, which offer excerpts of all this material in the form of word-by-word or line-by-line lemmata.

This traditional format has proven its worth, and to this very day commentaries are being published and widely used. However, disadvantages also cling to the commentary. Because a commentary concentrates on specific problems, the text being discussed is handled with selectivity. Often a commentator is so distracted by the need to deal with a problem in line x that he or she may miss an interesting point in the next line. This selectivity is reinforced by the authoritative nature of classical scholarship:[19] once a scholar of name has stamped a word or passage as being problematic, all later scholars feel obliged to respond. Because of commentaries' comprehensive nature,

---

16. The phenomenon of the commentary has recently been the topic of two collections of papers, the first also dealing with commentaries from outside the world of classics: G. W. Most, ed., *Commentaries – Kommentare* (Aporemata: Kritische Studien zur Philologiegeschichte 4; Göttingen: Vandenhoeck & Ruprecht, 1999); R. K. Gibson and C. S. Kraus, eds., *The Classical Commentary: Histories, Practices, Theory* (Leiden: Brill, 2002).

17. For a fuller and more technical discussion, see my "Narratological Commentary on the Odyssey: Principles and Problems," in ibid., 49–66.

18. See also Most, *Commentaries – Kommentare*, xiii.

19. See also ibid., xii.

a mass of heterogeneous scholarship is included. Often the relation or relevance to the text under discussion is lost, and we end up with scholarship for the sake of scholarship.[20] Because of commentaries' word-by-word nature, the meso- and macro-levels of a text are largely left unexplored.[21]

These disadvantages are all the more regrettable in the case of a narrative masterpiece such as the *Odyssey*. I therefore devised the concept of a *narratological commentary*, which means a commentary that is not comprehensive (and therefore not heterogeneous), but instead concentrates on one, admittedly large aspect of the text: its narrativity. Thus, narratological commentary is interested in the role of the narrator and narratees, methods of characterization, the handling of time (anticipations and retroversions, retardations and summaries, *in medias res* technique, etc.), and the role of place (descriptions of scenery). While more restricted in its scope, it is at the same time fuller in that it is interested in the text as a whole, not just the words or passages that in the past have been deemed problematic.

Finally, this sort of commentary is interested in scenes rather than words, although words may be commented upon. In the spirit of what I said at the end of the introductory section, I would like to stress that of course in this commentary I have also used and applied insights from the vast quantity of nonnarratological Homeric scholarship available, notably the important work on type-scenes, speeches, paradigmatic narratives, and so on. In my view, the introduction of narratology in classics should not take the form of a radical *çhange* of paradigm but of an *expansion* of the analytical apparatus.

With these methodological preliminaries in mind, we proceed with an illustration. For this purpose, I have chosen a passage from the *Odyssey*, book 5. Odysseus has been living for seven years with the nymph Calypso, who wants him to stay with her forever and promises him immortality. Our hero, however, longs to go home but has no ship

---

20. This danger has become even greater with the advent of the computer in humanities studies. Secondary literature or parallel passages are now readily available with one press of the button. For a principal defence of the *copia* or abundance of commentaries, see H. U. Gumbrecht, "Fill Up Your Margins! About Commentary and Copia," in *Commentaries – Kommentare* (ed. G. W. Most; Aporemata 4; Göttingen: Vandenhoeck & Ruprecht, 1999) 443–53.

21. Here it should be noted that there is a recent trend toward the insertion of essay-like sections in commentaries; see C. S. Kraus, "Reading Commentaries/Commentaries as Reading," in *Classical Commentary* (ed. R. K. Gibson and C. S. Kraus; Leiden: Brill, 2002) 3.

and is marooned on her island. Finally, the gods decide it is time for him to go home, and they send Hermes to Calypso, who, conversing with the goddess alone, orders her to let her lover go. Calypso reacts with anger at this male interference in her private life but is once more instructed by Hermes that Odysseus's departure is Zeus's will (and, we may add, the traditional course of the plot). After Hermes has left, Calypso fetches Odysseus from the beach and announces that she will help him build a raft to go home, but soon she tries again to persuade him to stay with her. At this point we read the following lines (194–99):

> They made their way, the man and the god, to the hollow cavern,
> and he seated himself upon the chair from which Hermes lately
> had risen, while the nymph set all manner of food before him
> to eat and drink, such things as mortal men feed upon.
> She herself sat across the table from godlike Odysseus,
> and her serving maids set nectar and ambrosia before her.

In a recent, traditional *Odyssey* commentary by Hainsworth,[22] we are given three comments on line 194 and one on line 197—all dealing with one word. Of these four comments, three concern linguistic matters and one pertains to metrical matters. In my narratological commentary, all lines are covered:

195–96: An instance of the 'he sat down on the seat from which he had risen' motif; cf. 18.157; 21.139, 166, 243, 392; 23.164; and *Il.* 24.597. Here it is given a subtle twist: Odysseus sat down on the seat from which *Hermes*—note the emphatic runover position—had risen. Odysseus does not know about Hermes' visit, but the narratees do and they are reminded of it just prior to the moment when Calypso tries to wriggle out of Zeus' order conveyed by him.

196–201: Before launching her final attack, Calypso dines Odysseus. Noting explicitly that he is served mortal food, while she is served immortal food, the narrator subtly makes clear, even before Odysseus' final rejection of immortality, the unbridgeable gap between 'man and god' (cf. the telling periphrastic denominations in 194).

198: The fact that Calypso seats herself opposite Odysseus indicates that she will address him; a significant seating arrangement.

This one short example must suffice to give an impression of the way in which a focus on narrative aspects of a text may lead to other observations and hence to another organization and use of the age-old classical tool, the commentary.

---

22. A. Heubeck, S. West, and J. B. Hainsworth, *A Commentary on Homer's Odyssey,* vol. 1 (Oxford: Oxford University Press, 1988).

Narratology and the Classics, Example 2:
A Narratological History of Greek Literature

Some ten years ago, I hit upon the idea that it is strange that someone interested in the history of ancient Greek literature has at his/her disposal a large number of literary histories; that someone interested more specifically in the development of Greek drama, historiography, rhetoric, or literary criticism can also consult a series of handbooks; but that someone interested in the forerunners of the most popular literary genre of our own times, the novel, stands empty handed in that no literary history of ancient Greek narrative exists. I decided that the time had come to write such a literary history, and once again called on narratology to provide the framework. Rather than focusing on a man, his works, and his readers, this narratological history discusses the narrator and his narratees, aspects of time such as prolepsis and analepsis, characterization, point of view, and so on. Of course, the number of narrative texts in Greek literature is far too great to be mastered by one person, so I have collected a team of some 12 scholars to write this multivolume history (called *Studies in Ancient Greek Narrative*). In 2004, the first volume appeared, which deals with the narrator and his narratees—from Homer via historiography, drama, philosophy, and rhetoric to the ancient novel. In 2007, the second volume, which deals with aspects of time, was published.[23]

The ambitions of the project are twofold. In the first place, it aims at offering a series of narratological studies of ancient Greek narrative texts. In section 2, I listed the Greek authors who have received narratological attention: Homer, Hesiod, Thucydides, Sophocles, Euripides, and Apollonius Rhodius. But for many more texts, no such analysis is available, and the *Studies in Ancient Greek Narrative* is the first pioneering work. In the second place, this literary history sets out to describe how narrative devices function within different genres and how they develop over the course of time at the hands of different authors. What has already become clear after one volume is that this focus on narrative devices brings to light interesting new continuities and discontinuities in the history of ancient Greek literature.

Let me provide one example. One of the outcomes of the first volume, which dealt with narrators and narratees, was that, though

---

23. I. J. F. de Jong, R. Nünlist, and A. Bowie, *Narrators, Narratees and Narratives in Ancient Greek Literature* (Studies in Ancient Greek Narrative 1; Leiden: Brill, 2004); I. J. F. de Jong and R. Nünlist, *Time in Ancient Greek Literature* (Studies in Ancient Greek Narrative 2; Leiden: Brill, 2007).

the Homeric epics are without doubt the single most influential literary text of ancient literature, the model of the Homeric narrator has
not been equally influential. The Homeric narrator is (1) external—that
is, he does not himself play a role in the story; and (2) covert—that is,
he does not openly comment on his story. Now while Greek literature
abounds with external narrators, most of these are not covert but
overt—that is, they do comment and show their feelings. Thus the two
epics of Homer and Apollonius Rhodius, which on the surface closely
resemble each other and have always been analyzed in terms of *imitatio*
and *aemulatio*, on this point markedly differ from each other. A comparison of two passages may illustrate my point. The first, from the
Iliad, concerns our first meeting with Helen, the woman who, because
of love, left her husband and city and thereby caused the Trojan War
(3.125–28):

> Iris found Helen in her room, working at a great web of purple cloth for
> a double cloak, and in it she was weaving many scenes of the conflict be-
> tween the horse-taming Trojans and the bronze-clad Achaeans, which
> they were enduring for her sake at the hands of Ares.

This is vintage Homer: no explicit word of criticism or emotion but
merely a description of Helen's weaving. Contrast with this the way in
which Apollonius in his *Argonautica* refers to the heroine of his story,
Medea, the woman who (also because of love) leaves her father and
country (4.1–4):

> You yourself, goddess, tell of the suffering and thoughts of the Colchian
> girl [Medea], you, Muse, child of Zeus; within me my mind whirls in
> silent helplessness, as I ponder whether I should call it the mad sickening
> burden of desire or a shameful panic which caused her to abandon the
> tribes of the Colchians.[24]

Of course, it would be wrong to conclude that a covert narrator such as
Homer does not have emotions or opinions; he is able to express them
indirectly, for example, by having Helen weave a guilt-ridden web
about the Trojan War that she caused.[25] My point is that the model of

---

24. R. Hunter, trans., *Apollonius of Rhodes: Jason and the Golden Fleece (The Argonautica)*
(Oxford: Clarendon, 1993).

25. For more examples of Homer's subtle and implicit ways of guiding the perception and emotions of his readers, see J. Griffin, *Homer on Life and Death* (Oxford: Oxford
University Press, 1980); and my *Narrators and Focalizers*. For more on the narrator of the
Argonautica, see M. P. Cuypers, "Apollonius Rhodius," in *Narrators, Narratees, and Narratives* (ed. I. J. F. de Jong, R. Nünlist, and A. Bowie; Leiden: Brill, 2004) 43–62.

the Homeric narrator—the covert narrator—has not found many followers, an observation that leads us to modify our picture of Homer as the fountain of all Greek literature.[26]

The primary aim of the narratological history of Greek literature just sketched is to benefit classical scholarship. But there is an additional reason for this project, which is interest in narratology itself. In a 2003 article, leading narratologist Fludernik urgently argued for "the diachronization of narratology"—that is, a scholarly interest in the history of narrative forms and functions that, she noted, was largely lacking.[27] She mentions as possible research topics: "whether the medieval romance finds its continuation in the early modern verse epic," "how much reader address occurs across the centuries and whether these formulas have specific functions that remain constant, or whether they alternate between a number of functions," "when were certain techniques or constellations first used, or when did they become current and, even later, predominant?" and whether "certain features and techniques acquire a different function at crucial points of the restructuring process of the narrative paradigm." The second half of her article is an analysis of the developments in methods of scene-shifting in a corpus of British texts ranging from the late medieval times to the early 20th century.

The narratological history of Greek literature turns out to ask exactly the kind of historical questions about the introduction, use, adaptation, and reuse of narrative techniques that Fludernik sketches and to offer exactly the kind of diachronical use of narratology that she proposes. As I phrase it in the general introduction to vol. 1:

> [T]he aim of this enterprise is to combine the synchronic and the diachronic, to offer not only analyses of the handling of a specific narrative device by individual authors, but also a larger historical perspective on the manner in which techniques change over time, are put to different uses and achieve different effects in the hands of different authors, writing in different genres, and handling different material.

Having so far written in this essay about the many ways in which classical scholarship has benefited from an "injection" of modern literary theory, I consider it to be an exciting idea that classical scholarship has

---

26. Aristotle already noted Homer's unique (in relation to other epic poets) penchant for "showing" rather than "telling"; see my "Aristotle on the Homeric Narrator," *Classical Quarterly* 55 (2005) 616–21.

27. M. Fludernik, "The Diachronization of Narratology," *Narrative* 11 (2003) 331–48.

something important to offer modern theory in return: one of the first systematic, longitudinal, narratological studies of the development of narratives devices in a large and important corpus.

Prospects: Narrative Authority in
(Early and Classical) Greek Literature

In this last part of my essay, I will show how the introduction of modern theory may lead to new research questions by way of an example. While editing the chapters of the first volume of the narratological history of Greek literature, I was struck by the fact that this question was hardly discussed: what strategies does a narrator have with which to construct a reliable persona for him/herself and to make him/herself a speaker whose words are deemed both relevant and reliable? The reason seems to be that the question of narrative authority, as I call it, so far has not been the object of any systematic narratological discussion.

Narratology has provided us with a set of criteria with the help of which we may distinguish all kinds of narrators: external and internal narrators, overt and covert narrators, primary and secondary narrators, to mention the most important.[28] But little systematic theoretical attention has been paid to the question of the authority of a narrator: where does the story she tells come from, what are her sources, why does she tell her narrative? The narratologist Friedman in 1955 introduced the notion of the omniscient narrator; Booth in 1963 discussed the figure of the unreliable narrator; and Stanzel briefly spoke about "the motivation of the act of narration" or why a narrator narrates.[29] These stray remarks are all we have, but they do not cover the many forms that the establishment of narrative authority can take, by a long shot.

Here Greek literature offers a rich and interesting corpus: because it was largely a public affair, involving important societal or ideological values, its narrators had all the more reason to invest themselves with

---

28. For a discussion of these types of narrators and secondary sources, see my "Introduction: Narratological Theory in Narrators, Narratees, and Narratives," in *Narrators, Narratees, and Narratives* (ed. I. J. F. de Jong, R. Nünlist, and A. Bowie; Leiden: Brill, 2004) 1–24.

29. N. Friedman, "Point of View in Fiction: The Development of a Critical Concept," *PMLA* 70 (1955) 1160–84; Booth, *The Rhetoric of Fiction*, 158–59; Stanzel, *Theory of Narrative*, 93.

authority. I have just begun my research into narrative authority and
can therefore only present a few preliminary results.[30]

One well-known strategy for establishing narrative authority is to
invoke the Muses, as happens in the opening of the *Iliad* (1.1–7):

> The wrath of Peleus's son Achilles sing, goddess,
> the disastrous one, who brought the Greeks countless sorrows
> and hurled down to Hades many mighty souls
> of heroes, making their bodies prey to dogs
> and all the birds' feasting—and this was the working of Zeus's will—
> starting with the moment they first stood apart in quarrel,
> leader of men Agamemnon and godlike Achilles.

It has long been fashionable to interpret these lines as implying that
the narrator sees himself as a mere passive agent, a mouthpiece of the
Muse. In my view, however, we must understand the relationship
between narrator and Muse in terms of the well-known archaic principle of double motivation: both god (Muse) and mortal (narrator) are
involved at the same time. A good example of double motivation is the
double claim of the singer Phemius both that he is *autodidaktos* 'self-
taught' and that a god "planted various paths of song in his mind"
(*Od.* 22.347–48). Acknowledging the help of a god does not detract
from but enhances the worth of a mortal: the gods only help those who
deserve to be helped. Invoking the Muses at the opening of his narrative, therefore, is a powerful means for the Homeric narrator to establish his authority. His is not going to be just any narrative about the
past but a divinely authorized tale.[31]

At another place in his narrative, the narrator makes clear how
exactly the help of the Muses authorizes his story (*Iliad* 2.484–47):

> Tell me now, you Muses, who have your homes on Olympus—
> for you are goddesses, are present, and know all things by direct
>   perception,
> and we hear only stories and have no first-hand knowledge—
> who were the leaders and lords of the Greeks.

Again, this passage is often misunderstood, scholars translating line
486 as 'we only hear stories and know nothing' and suggesting that the

---

30. There already exist some studies that address the question of authority; see
J. Marincola, *Authority and Tradition in Ancient Historiography* (Cambridge: Cambridge
University Press, 1997); S. Goldhill, *The Poet's Voice: Essays on Poetics and Greek Literature*
(Cambridge: Cambridge University Press, 1991); and C. Segal, "Tragic Beginnings: Nar-
ration, Voice, and Authority in the Prologues of Greek Drama," *YCS* 29 (1992) 85–112.

31. See my *Narrators and Focalizers*, 45–53, and literature on the Muses there.

narrator is totally dependent on the Muses. However, the Greek verb *idmen*, from *oida*, is related to *video* 'see' and here clearly still carries the force of its original meaning of 'know by personal perception'. What the narrator is here placing in opposition are the hearsay knowledge of the past that mortals have and the eyewitness knowledge that the Muses have. The narrator seeks the collaboration of the Muses, because they are divine eyewitnesses of history. In Greek culture (before philosophers such as Plato, who began to undermine the value of perception to gain knowledge), eyewitness knowledge was considered the most reliable source of information. This becomes clear from the following compliment that Odysseus pays the singer of the Phaeacians, Demodocus, who has just been singing about an episode from the Trojan War (*Odyssey* 8.489–92):

> (Demodocus, you must have been taught by the Muse and Apollo)
> for it is absolutely right that you sing of the Achaeans'
> venture, all they did and had done to them, all the sufferings
> of those Achaeans, as if you had been there yourself or heard it
> from one who had been.

This compliment, coming as it does from a person who himself "had been there," indeed was one of the protagonists of the war, is all the more forceful.[32]

When we turn from the Homeric narrator and professional singers such as Demodocus to Homeric characters acting as (secondary) narrators, we note that they never call on the Muses but have other means of establishing their authority. In the first place, they may recount what they themselves have done, experienced, or witnessed in the past. Thus the old hero Nestor time and again refers to events from his youth (*Iliad* 11.670–76):

> If only I were young now, and the power was still in me,
> as when a quarrel arose between us and the Eleans
> over a cattle raid, when I myself killed Itymoneus,
> the brave son of Hypeirochus, who lived in Elis.
> I was driving off his herds in reprisal, and he was fighting
> for his cattle at the head of his men when he was hit by a spear from
>   my hand,
> and fell to the ground, and his country troop scattered.

---

32. I note in passing that this passage again confirms the conception (and importance) of the Muses as eyewitnesses to history: because Demodocus speaks as if he had been there, Odysseus concludes that he must have been taught by the Muses.

When they have not participated in the events themselves, Homeric characters may turn to "hearsay" to authorize their story, as when Tlepolemus tells about the exploits of his famous father Heracles (*Iliad* 5.638–42):

> [Sarpedon], you are inferior to those men
> who were born to Zeus in earlier times.
> But such a man, they say, was the mighty Heracles,
> my own father, of daring spirit, with the heart of a lion.
> He once came here for the sake of Laomedon's horses,
> and with only six ships and fewer men than these he sacked the city
>   of Ilion
> and widowed her streets.

Tlepolemus did not watch his father in action at Troy but has recourse to what others say about him. I note in passing that the same tag, 'they say' (Gr. *phasi*), is used very sporadically (*Iliad* 2.783; 17.674; *Odyssey* 6.42) by the primary narrator as well and then has a somewhat different effect: temporarily giving up his divine omniscience, he presents his information—about the monster Typhoeus lying in Arima and about Mount Olympus as the seat of the gods—as mere hearsay.

And finally, Homeric characters may simply tell a story without indicating how they know it (*Iliad* 6.130–42):

> I [Diomedes] will not fight against any god from heaven
> since even the son of Dryas, Lycurgus, the powerful did
> not live long; he who tried to fight with the gods of the bright sky,
> who once chased the nurses of wild Dionysus
> down from the sacred moutain Nysa. They all scattered
> their holy wands on the ground, under the blows of murdering
>   Lycurgus's
> ox-goad. And Dionysus in terror
> dived into the sea's swell, and Thetis took him to her breast,
> fearful and trembling hard at the man's threat.
> Then the gods who live at ease became angry with Lycurgus,
> and Zeus struck him blind: and he did not live long
> after that, hated as he was by all the immortal gods.

It appears that this story, which belongs to a more remote past, is presented without authorization because it has become common knowledge.[33]

---

33. This last form of storytelling may be an instance of what Assmann has coined *kulturelles Gedächtnis*, while the first three forms of storytelling are instances of *kommunikatives Gedächtnis*; see J. Assmann, *Das kulturelle Gedächtnis: Schrift, Erinnerung und poli-*

Thus, the Homeric epics present four strategies of narrative authorization:

1. Muse invocation (divine eyewitness)
2. narrator's own experience (either as protagonist or as eyewitness)
3. hearsay ("they say," "it is said," "I have heard")
4. 0 = common knowledge

Beginning with this base, we must ask ourselves whether these four strategies remain constant in later literature, whether their functions change, and whether new strategies develop. In the remainder of this essay, I will discuss two later authors.

In the first half of the 5th century B.C., the poet Pindar wrote a series of victory odes, poems commissioned by aristocrats who won victories at athletic games, such as the Olympics. These victory odes consist of praise for the victor, his family, and his home city but also usually contain a mythic narrative that, by recounting the exploits of heroes from the past, aims at depicting the victorious aristocrats of the present as the direct successors of these mythical heroes. Interestingly enough, the Pindaric narrator uses the same authorizing strategies that we came across in Homer, but he uses them *all at the same time*; for example, in *Olympian* 9.41–55 + 80–81:

> [The narrator addresses himself] apply your speech to Protogenea's city [Opus], where [0], by decree of Zeus of the bright thunderbolt, Pyrrha and Deucalion came down from Parnassus and first established their home, and, without coupling, founded one folk, an offspring of stone. . . . Indeed *they tell* that mighty waters had flooded over the dark earth, but through Zeus's contriving, an ebb tide suddenly drained the floodwater. From them [Deucalion and Pyrrha] came your [Epharmostus of Opus, the victor and addressee of the ode] ancestors. . . . May I find the right words and fittingly drive forward in the chariot of the *Muses*.

What we see is that the Pindaric narrator on the one hand tells the story of Deucalion and Pyrrha without authorization, as an instance of common knowledge; but he also refers to hearsay and the Muses. Rather than taking this as contradictory, I interpret it as abundance: "pushing" all the well-established "buttons" of authorization, the Pindaric

---

tische Identität in frühen Hochkulturen (Munich: Beck, 1992), esp. pp. 49–59. However, his claim that cultural memory is the domain of a special, professional group of spokesmen does not work here: as we saw, cultural memory can also be told by random speakers, here Diomedes, while conversely, a professional storyteller such as Phemius may also narrate about the recent past, the communicative memory (cf. *Odyssey* 1.325–27).

narrator aims at the highest degree of reliability and authority (and hence praise).[34]

The Pindaric narrator not only (re)uses the Homeric forms of authorization but also adds a new type: reference to (named or anonymous) predecessors. An example is found in *Nemean* 6.50–54:

> Upon them [Ethiopians] fell a heavy opponent, Achilles, after stepping down from his chariot onto the ground, when he slew the son of shining Dawn with the point of his raging spear. The older poets found in such deeds as these a highway of song, and I myself follow along, making it my concern.

Indeed, the Pindaric narrator is even famous for the way in which he critizes older versions of myths and replaces them with his own (for example, in *Olympian* 1). A final, highly intriguing variant of the authority ploy is using predecessors for what in fact is probably his own invention, as for example, in *Nemean* 3.43–53:

> But fair-haired Achilles, . . . even as a child at play would perform great deeds; often did he brandish in his hands his short, iron-tipped javelin and, swiftly as the winds, deal death in battle to wild lions and kill boars. He would bring their gasping bodies to the Centaur, Cronus's son, beginning at age six and for all time thereafter. Artemis and bold Athena marveled to see him slaying deer without dogs or deceitful nets, for he overtook them on foot. This story I have from older poets.[35]

This story about Achilles' miraculous exploits as a boy is not known before Pindar, and though we can never be absolutely sure, it is certainly possible that the narrator is here merely pretending to be telling a story he has received from older poets. This device of passing off one's own invention as something found in the books of others was to have a great future in European literature, where many a novel has been presented as though it were a manuscript found.

I turn to the playwright Euripides, who worked in the second half of the 5th century B.C. The big difference between an epic and a vic-

---

34. This analysis of the strategies of authorization complements other studies of Pindaric self-reflexiveness, which mainly focus on the poetic "I," references to "praise" and "blame," and the role of poetry as a safeguard of *kleos* 'fame'. See H. Maehler, *Die Auffasung des Dichterberufs im frühen Griechentums bis zur Zeit Pindars* (Munich: Vandenhoeck & Ruprecht, 1963); H. Gundert, *Pindar und sein Dichterberuf* (Utrecht: Hes, 1978); and Goldhill, *Poet's Voice*, 128–66.

35. The suggestion that the *proteroi* 'older poets' disguises Pindaric invention is from I. L. Pfeijffer (*Three Aeginetan Odes of Pindar: A Commentary on Nemean V, Nemean III, and Pythian VIII* [Leiden: Brill, 1999]), who on pp. 351–52 and 490–91 discusses Pindar's handling of older poets.

tory ode is of course that in the case of drama we are dealing not with narratives *about* the past but enactments *of* the past. The spectators are (as it were) watching scenes directly from the past; they themselves become eyewitnesses. This phenomenon compensates for the fact that drama lacks a primary narrator who can call on a Muse or use other authorizing strategies to vouch for the reliability of his version of the past. Seeing becomes believing or at least leads to a willing suspense of disbelief. When dramatic characters tell stories, however, they use the same authorizing strategies as Homer and Pindar. However, in contrast to Pindar, a clear division is visible. The "eyewitness" strategy is invariably used by calling for a messenger, who appears in every play to recount its bloody climax; for example, in *Supplices* 651–53:

> (Messenger) I posted myself at the Electra gate *as a spectator,* on a *tower that offers a good view.* And *I see. . . .*

When the chorus acts as narrator, they may use the "hearsay" strategy, as in *Electra* 432–57, where the chorus, consisting of Argive women, tells about the Trojan War:

> Glorious ships, which once went Troyward on those countless oars . . . and brought the son of Thetis, Achilles, light springing in his step, with Agamemnon to the shores of Simois by Troy. . . . From a man of Troy sojourning at Nauplia harbor I heard, O son of Thetis, that on the circle of your famous shield. . . .

Prologue-speakers, before the action proper begins, inform the spectators about the prehistory of the plot, mostly using the common-knowledge strategy, as in *Electra* 1–10:

> [a Myceneaean farmer, husband of Electra, is speaking] Streams of Inachus that water the land of the Pelasgians! It was from you that [0] King Agamemnon set forth for war with a thousand ships and sailed to the land of Troy. When he had killed Priam, Troy's ruler, and captured the glorious city of Dardanus, he returned here to Argos.

What is interesting here is that, for the prologue-speaker, there are no events from the remote past, only recent events, and yet we find no references to witnessing or hearsay. It seems that the prologue-speaker is here adopting the time frame of the spectators in the theater, for whom the events do belong to the remote past and hence are common knowledge. Or we may even go one step farther and, in line with what was said above about Pindar's using predecessors to mask his own inventions, assume that the common-knowledge strategy was likewise chosen by Euripides in his prologues to authorize his own alterations of traditional myths, for which he was famous. It should be understood, however, that in so doing, he was no longer presenting his stories as true or reliable (the purpose of Homer and presumably Pindar) but as plausible.

The examples of authorizing strategies in Homer, Pindar, and Euripides must suffice to demonstrate what an investigation into the authority of the narrator might look like—a topic that could also be fruitfully pursued for modern novels. I conclude that the field of classics has successfully overcome its backlog in adopting and applying modern theory and that the narratological work that is done by classicists renews age-old scholarly instruments such as commentaries and literary histories and leads to new roads of scholarly research that are relevant to both classical and modern literary scholarship.

PART 2

The Identity of Authors and Readers

Ancient Writers, Modern Readers, and King Ashurnasirpal's Political Problems: An Exploration of the Possibility of Reading Ancient Texts

Barbara N. Porter

Casco Bay Assyriological Institute

Assyriology is a young, emerging field that until recently has often been unsophisticated in its approach to the analysis of texts. This is perhaps not entirely surprising. While scholars in fields such as classics and biblical studies have had most of their important texts firmly in hand and reasonably well translated for decades, or even centuries, and have long been equipped with reasonably reliable dictionaries and grammars of the ancient languages they work with, leaving them free to wrestle with the complexities of text interpretation, Assyriologists in contrast have spent the last 150 years reconstructing the forgotten Akkadian language in which Assyrian and Babylonian texts were written, learning to decipher the cuneiform sign system in which it was recorded, piecing together its often fragmented texts, reassembling scattered archives, and developing increasingly reliable dictionaries, grammars, and studies of the varying dialects and sign-lists used in different regions, periods, and specialized professional fields. To add to the complexity confronting them, Assyriologists are still digging up clay tablets and dusting them off. But we are making much progress. Increasingly sophisticated grammars and more accurate text editions appear every year, and after generations of work, the publication of the Chicago Assyrian Dictionary is almost completed. With the initial hurdles largely overcome, Assyriologists are free at last to focus more attention on the problems of interpretation of texts; we are now in hot pursuit of our methodologically advanced colleagues in other ancient fields, increasingly able to analyze our texts with sophistication (or to despair of the possibility of reading) with the best of them.

As an example of the helpfulness of modern literary-critical methods in deepening our understanding of ancient Akkadian texts and of the problems we sometimes encounter in trying to apply modern analytical techniques to these ancient documents, I will focus on the genre of Neo-Assyrian royal inscriptions—texts that were commissioned by the rulers of the Neo-Assyrian Empire to give an account of their qualities as a ruler and of the major events of their reign. Although these texts have often been taken as essentially objective records of the major events of each reign (if such a thing were possible), it is clear from even a cursory reading that they are instead carefully shaped and highly selective presentations of the king's successes and fine qualities, designed for different selected audiences and settings.

As my example, I will consider the case of two royal inscriptions commissioned by the ninth-century Assyrian king Ashurnasirpal II (883–859 B.C.E.). These two texts, known to Assyriologists as Ashurnasirpal's Annals and his Standard Inscription, were among the first Assyrian royal inscriptions to be discovered, translated, and published, and they have had a powerful role in shaping our assessment of Assyria and Assyrian culture ever since, contributing in particular to the ancient Assyrians' enduring reputation for rule primarily by violence and intimidation.

I will argue that this response to the two texts rests on a misunderstanding of their functions and intended impact and, as a consequence, of the king who commissioned them. Although Ashurnasirpal's conquests, by his own account, were often violent and must have been highly intimidating to those who bore the brunt of them or feared similar treatment, Ashurnasirpal took considerable pains under other circumstances to present a positive public persona to his subjects, vassals, and potential allies, encouraging their acceptance of his rule for the benefits it promised to bring them. A close reading of the Standard Inscription, as we will see later, suggests it to be one component of this sort of positive public relations effort, while a close reading of the Annals Text suggests that its often violent descriptions of war and punishment were not designed to intimidate outsiders or potential rebels, as has usually been supposed, but were instead written for the war-god Ninurta and his priests, an audience that was likely to have found its detailed accounts of the king's military successes and ruthless punishment of rebels a pleasing confirmation of the king's skill and piety.

The two texts were first discovered and commented upon in the middle of the nineteenth century by the pioneering British archeologist Sir Austen Henry Layard. Layard found both texts during excava-

tions that he conducted between 1845 and 1851 at Nimrud, site of the
ruins of ancient Kalḫu, a city constructed by Ashurnasirpal as his royal
residence and as the new seat of government for his rapidly expanding
empire.[1]

Layard found the relatively short Standard Inscription carved into
the stone of more than 400 large stone slabs that lined the walls of
Ashurnasirpal's new palace. In a temple just north of the palace, dedicated to the war-god Ninurta, Layard discovered the much longer text
now known to us as Ashurnasirpal's Annals. Layard reports finding
this inscription in one of the innermost chambers of the Ninurta
Temple, engraved, he reports, on "one enormous alabaster slab 21' ×
16'7" × 1'1" thick." The slab's surface and the side facing the room "was
occupied with one inscription, 325 lines in length," arranged in 2 parallel columns that broke off mid-sentence. On the underside of the
same slab, Layard found a second copy of this text, this time in 3 columns. According to Layard, this version of the text repeated "all the
historical details of that on the opposite side" as well as giving "the
records of two or three more years."[2] Layard himself published cuneiform copies of the texts that he discovered in his first seasons of excavation at Nimrud, but in the case of texts found in his later seasons,
including the Annals, he sent wet-paper squeezes as well as his hand
copies of many texts back to London for subsequent publication by
others.[3]

The Annals Text remains one of the longest Assyrian royal inscriptions known to us, providing detailed accounts of military campaigns
and some other events of the first 18 years of Ashurnasirpal's reign. Its
descriptions of military campaigns and of the punishments imposed
on cities that resisted the Assyrians are notorious for their unflinching
violence. This passage, describing the conquest and subjection of a city
that had refused to surrender to the Assyrians, is typical of the text:

> In strife and conflict I besieged (and) conquered the city. I felled 3,000 of
> their fighting men with the sword. I carried off prisoners, possessions,

---

1. For an up-to-date introduction to Nimrud, its ancient builder, and its excavation,
see Joan Oates and David Oates, *Nimrud: An Assyrian Imperial City Revealed* (London:
British School of Archaeology in Iraq, 2001).

2. Austen Henry Layard, *Discoveries among the Ruins of Nineveh and Babylon* (New
York: Harper, 1853) 304–5.

3. On the complicated history of the publication of the Ninurta Temple texts, see
Julian E. Reade, "The Ziggurat and Temples of Nimrud," *Iraq* 64 (2002) 135–216, esp.
pp. 186–91 and 201–10.

oxen, (and) cattle from them. I burnt many captives from them. I captured many troops alive: from some I cut off their arms (and) hands, from others I cut off their noses, ears, (and) extremities (?). I gouged out the eyes of many troops. I made one pile of the living (and) one of heads. I hung their heads on trees around the city. I burnt their adolescent boys and girls. I razed, destroyed, burnt, (and) consumed the city.[4]

Taking the Standard Inscription from the palace to be essentially a briefer version of this text's account, Layard summed up Ashurnasirpal and his reign in one brisk, disparaging sentence: "His expeditions seem to have been attended by great cruelties and sacrifice of human life, and he celebrates the burning of innumerable women and children."[5] Layard later went on to say of Assyrian historical inscriptions as a whole, "The Assyrian records are nothing but a dry narrative, or rather register, of military campaigns, spoliations, and cruelties."[6] Understanding Assyrian royal inscriptions as historically accurate accounts, Layard condemned Ashurnasirpal, and the Assyrians in general, as merciless rulers who governed primarily by means of violence—an assessment that greatly underestimates their political skills and complexity.

Later commentators suggested that Ashurnasirpal's texts should be seen as vehicles of propaganda designed to intimidate potential rebels and enemies, rather than as simple statements of fact, but these commentators nevertheless followed Layard in focusing on the violence of the Annals' accounts and concluding that it was typical of the king and his texts. Albert T. E. Olmstead, for example, in a classic history of the Assyrians published in 1923, called his chapter on Ashurnasirpal, "The Calculated Frightfulness of Assurnasirpal."[7] Today, handbooks of Assyrian history continue to assert that violence and intimidation were the hallmarks both of Ashurnasirpal's actions (which is to some extent correct, even by his own account) and also of Ashurnasirpal's public texts and imagery (a statement that, as I hope to show, our texts belie). Georges Roux, for example, refers to "the sadistic refinements" of Ashurnasirpal's "policy of terror" that were "duly recorded and dis-

---

4. From the edition of the Annals by A. Kirk Grayson, *Assyrian Rulers of the Early First Millennium bc I (114–859 bc)* (RIMA 2; Toronto: University of Toronto Press, 1991) text A.0.101.1, p. 201: col. i 118–ii 1.

5. See Layard, *Discoveries*, 307–8; for his comment that "the inscriptions across the sculptured slabs [in the Ninurta Temple] are nearly the same as the standard inscription in the northwest palace," see p. 309.

6. Ibid., 539.

7. Olmstead, *History of Assyria* (Chicago: University of Chicago Press, 1923; repr. 1975) 81.

played in writing and pictures," adding that they were "no doubt necessary to inspire respect and enforce obedience."[8] H. W. F. Saggs comments on the "frankness and apparent relish with which he relates the brutalities he inflicted on the conquered," and W. W. Hallo remarks that the "'calculated frightfulness' of Assurnasirpal is documented not only in his inscriptions but even more graphically in the monumental reliefs with which he decorated his palaces."[9]

In making this assessment of the king, however, scholars appear to have overlooked the genres represented by the two texts under consideration here, the quite different tone of their accounts, the settings in which they were displayed, and the different audiences for which these texts appear to have been intended. When we submit the Annals Text and later the Standard Inscription to a close reading in the manner of New Criticism or of modern French criticism's technique of *explication de texte*, however, focusing our attention as much on how things are said as on what is said, a quite different picture emerges of the king and of the public images that he presented.[10]

Before we can undertake a close reading of the Annals Text, however, we must first confront the difficulty of establishing a reliable version of that text to submit to analysis. Although establishing an accurate version of a modern text sometimes also presents problems, the case of the Annals Text illustrates the particularly daunting difficulties that may arise in dealing with texts that must first be excavated, pieced together from often damaged originals, and accurately published before they can be read and analyzed. Although a first edition of the Annals Text was promptly published by Edwin Norris in 1861, shortly after its excavation,[11] ambiguities were already apparent in his edition about the number of copies of the Annals Text found by Layard and subsequent early excavators; about the degree to which the various copies of the text that Norris's edition is based on were exact duplicates of one another; and about the locations in which the various exemplars of the text that Norris used in creating his edition

---

8. Roux, *Ancient Iraq* (Harmondsworth: Penguin, 1966) 263.

9. Saggs, *The Greatness That Was Babylon* (New York: New American Library, 1962) 107; W. W. Hallo and W. K. Simpson, *The Ancient Near East: A History* (New York: Harcourt Brace Jovanovich, 1971) 125.

10. See E. Badalì et al., "Studies on the Annals of Aššurnasirpal II: I. Morphological Analysis" (*Vicino Oriente* 5 [1982] 13–73), for an earlier close reading that focuses on the form of campaign accounts in the text.

11. In H. C. Rawlinson, *The Cuneiform Inscriptions of Western Asia* (London: British Museum, 1861) pls. 17–26.

had been discovered. Layard, as the reader may remember, reported discovering the Annals Text in two copies engraved on a single "enormous alabaster slab" found on the floor deep within the Ninurta Temple.

H. C. Rawlinson's introduction to the volume in which Norris' edition was published, however, mentions that variants to the text that are published there were drawn from "other copies of the same inscription."[12] The implication is that Rawlinson, who had excavated in the temple area shortly after Layard's departure but never published his results, was aware of the discovery of additional copies of the Annals inscription. The introduction to the cuneiform copy of the text complicates matters further by identifying the "Standard Copies" on which Norris based his Annals Text as coming from "the Pavement Slabs, engraved on both sides, which were found at the entrance of the Temple" (not in the temple's interior rooms, where Layard had reported finding his inscribed pavement slab, and inscribed on "slabs" rather than, like Layard's, on a single large stone).[13] In addition, Norris reports that some of the variants to his standard copies of the text are taken from "a series of slabs containing the same Inscription which were excavated from the Nimrud Pyramid," slabs the excavation of which in the ziggurat area has never been reported and the identity of which remains unclear.[14]

It appears that the text or texts that Norris used as the main source for the Annals Text in his edition are not the same exemplars of the Annals Text as the two copies found by Layard on a single, large stone and that Norris's text or texts were supplemented by the evidence of other, slightly different texts found in the ziggurat area. The identity of the various sources used by Norris in preparing the first edition of Ashurnasirpal's Annals and the extent to which they agreed with the text of Layard's inscriptions on the massive slab in the interior room of the temple remain unclear.

Later, L. W. King and Y. le Gac drew on Norris's edition, supplementing it with information from other texts and squeezes that they considered to duplicate the Annals or to contain parallel passages, to create two more editions of the Annals Text, differing slightly from one another and from Norris's text.[15] Layard's squeezes were eventually de-

---

12. Ibid., 4.
13. Ibid., pl. 17.
14. Ibid.
15. Y. le Gac, *Les inscriptions d'Aššur-naṣir-pal III* (Paris, 1907) 1–122.

stroyed after the early publications of the Annals were completed; his original slab, reburied at Nimrud because of its massive size, is now more water-damaged and increasingly illegible; and many of the other sources used as the basis of the early publications of the text cannot be identified with any certainty, as we have seen. As a result, it is no longer possible to return to the original sources to establish a single reliable text, or several closely related texts, for the Annals. A. Kirk Grayson, however, noting that the three initial publications agree to a large extent, has recently compared and reevaluated them to construct a modern edition and translation of the Annals which, despite the irreducible uncertainties, probably represents a fairly reliable version of Ashurnasirpal's original Annals Text or texts; it will serve as the basis of my analysis of the Annals Text here.[16]

When we submit this text to a close reading, it quickly becomes clear, as I have suggested, that the Annals Text was neither an objective historical record of Ashurnasirpal's reign, as Layard had assumed, nor a piece of frightening propaganda intended to encourage submission from conquered enemies or rebels, as later commentators have suggested, but a text with an altogether different audience and function.

This is strongly implied as early as the opening lines of the text, which begins with this invocation: "To the god Ninurta, the strong, the almighty, the exalted, and foremost among the gods, the splendid [and] perfect warrior whose attack in battle is unequalled" (i 1). The text, in other words, is explicitly a prayer, and the opening line identifies the prayer's intended recipient to be the god Ninurta. The next lines (i 1b–9a) introduce the god, characterizing him particularly as a god of storm and battle; his epithets here refer to him, for example, as "the swift, the ferocious," "king of battle," "the angry [and] merciless whose attack is a deluge, the one who overwhelms enemy lands [and] fells the wicked," "annihilator of the evil, subduer of the insubmissive, destroyer of enemies." While Ninurta emerges here as a fierce warrior god, these lines indicate that the effect of his violent battling is good: it destroys the wicked, imposing order on an unruly world. The passage

---

16. For Grayson's edition and his comments on the difficulties of establishing a reliable text for the Annals (with further bibliography), see Grayson, *Assyrian Rulers,* 190–223. For an evaluation of Layard and subsequent excavator's excavation reports, field notes, and letters, published and unpublished, and a thoughtful effort to resolve the problem of where various copies of the Annals Text were originally found, see Reade, "Ziggurat and Temples," esp. the discussion of the "dais" slab (M 27 on his plans), pp. 207–8. Reade (p. 208) is convinced that the entrance slabs that Norris refers to are in fact Layard's massive slab M 27 from the temple's interior.

ends by recalling his kindness, calling him "bestower of life, the compassionate god." Ninurta is cast here as ferocious but beneficent; in the eyes of this writer, the two qualities are not mutually exclusive but complementary. The text then names Ninurta as "the one who dwells in Calah, great lord, my lord," identifying him further as an important patron deity of Ashurnasirpal's new capital and thus of the king himself.

This line also provides the identity of the speaker who delivers the prayer; it is Ashurnasirpal himself, speaking in the first person to the war-god Ninurta, whom he here addresses as "my lord." The text now proceeds to describe Ashurnasirpal to his god. The passage (i 9b–17a), appropriately for a prayer, first emphasizes the king's closeness to the gods and his services to them: he is the "chosen of the gods Enlil and Ninurta, beloved of the gods Anu and Dagan, destructive weapon of the great gods," "the pious, beloved of your [that is, Ninurta's] heart," the king "whose priesthood is pleasing to your great divinity." It next characterizes him (like Ninurta) as a fierce and relentlessly successful warrior, beginning by calling him "marvelous shepherd, fearless in battle"; by introducing the images of a battling king that follow with this image of the king as a shepherd, the text implies that, like his god, Ashurnasirpal is fierce but that his very ferocity is an expression of his benevolence, because he provides a shepherd's protection for the weak against violent enemies. As we have seen, several of the epithets used to describe Ashurnasirpal echo those just used for Ninurta himself; like Ninurta, who represents the power of both storm and war, the king is a "mighty flood-tide," and like Ninurta, who is the "subduer of the insubmissive," Ashurnasirpal is "the king who subdues those insubmissive to him." This shared imagery seems intended to suggest that the king in many ways acts as Ninurta's embodiment on earth; the subduing attributed to Ninurta takes place in Ashurnasirpal's actions.

The line that follows (i 17b–18a) makes it clear that the royal activities described in both the first and second parts of the previous passage are religious in nature; like assuming the duties of a pious priest, waging war mercilessly is a central part of the Assyrian king's fundamental duty, to serve the gods. The line expresses this concept by describing Ashurnasirpal's call to become king: "When Assur [the chief god of Assyria], the lord who called my name (and) makes my sovereignty supreme, placed his merciless weapon in my lordly arms. . . ." The king's call to become king of Assyria is here followed immediately by Assur's gift of his own "merciless weapon." As Assyrian king, Ashurnasirpal's job will be to use this weapon and, in a sense, become it, being himself the "destructive weapon of the gods." This text is in fact a mandate for war as the king's religious obligation and a celebration of war as the fulfillment of the gods' commands and their good intentions for creating a well-ordered world.

Another list of royal epithets repeats the message that Ashurnasirpal is called by the gods to be priest, temple administrator, and, once again, "destructive weapon of the great gods." The king then breaks into a paen of self-praise as a warrior ("I am king . . . I am magnificent . . . I am a warrior, I am a lion"; i 31b–38a), after which the text repeats its account of the fact that a merciless weapon was the gods' first gift to the new king (i 40b–43a). Having now driven home the point that waging war is a royal religious obligation, the text has set the stage for the remainder of its account: a detailed and often remarkably gory narrative of the reign, characterized principally as 18 years of successful warfare.

The king's military activities are now described at great length in two accounts of each year's military campaigning, the first covering the campaigns of Ashurnasirpal's accession year and first 5 years of reign (i 43–ii 124), and the second describing the battles, punishments, and tribute-gathering that took place during his 6th to 18th regnal years (iii 1–112). As the passage quoted earlier suggests, these military narratives consist largely of accounts of conquests, city by city, of the slaughter that this involved in each case, and finally of the violent punishment of the cities or individuals who had resisted. For example, "I approached the city Udu . . . I besieged the city (and) conquered it by means of tunnels, siege-towers, (and) battering rams. I felled with the sword 1,400 . . . of their [fighting] men. I captured 780 soldiers alive. I brought out 3,000 captives from them. I impaled the live soldiers on stakes around his city," and so on (iii 110b–112). As this passage illustrates, the text is less concerned with reporting the details of fighting than with listing the numbers of the dead and captured.

In other cases, the text also provides a tally of the booty or tribute taken from each city or group. The text's two military accounts are separated by what appears to be a short independent inscription of the display type[17] (ii 125b–131a), which abruptly introduces the king yet again with already familiar titles and epithets, continues with a brief geographical summary of the lands conquered by the king, and then describes how the king built a statue and temple for Ninurta and

---

17. A term used by Assyriologists to describe royal inscriptions that group events geographically rather than reporting them year by year.

established festivals for him in Calah, while building shrines there for other gods as well. After itemizing these favors done for Ninurta and his divine colleagues at Calah, the Annals Text simply drops its discussion of royal building and launches into its second catalog of battles and tribute gathering, which continues for another 113 lines. The text concludes by attaching another independent display-type text, which introduces the king yet again with titles and epithets, summarizes again the regions he has conquered, and, after one more set of royal epithets, finally celebrates the completion of the new capital, populated with people captured in the king's campaigns and planted with fruitful orchards watered by irrigation canals, implying it to be a microcosm of the orderly and fruitful empire that Ashurnasirpal has created.

As this description implies, the Annals are an oddly awkward literary construction, combining repeated lists of royal epithets with two long military narratives strung together from annual accounts of campaigns, with these military accounts framed by short building inscriptions placed before and after them. The assorted texts joined together to form the Annals, in some cases duplicates of inscriptions used elsewhere, appear to be simply juxtaposed, with no effort to avoid duplication or make a transition between them, as Grayson notes.[18]

In light of the opening lines, the Annals, despite their detailed accounts of conquest, clearly are in fact a lengthy prayer. The god Ninurta whom they address is a god of war, and the text presented to him here is evidently structurally awkward because it is a compiled report to the god of the king's activities. Its authors have combined texts of different types, both annalistic war reports and short building inscriptions, to provide the god with an accounting, rendered in daunting detail, of the king's efficient fulfillment of the commission that the gods gave him when they named him king. He has indeed become their "destructive weapon," and this text is designed to provide the evidence and celebrate the happy result. Its detailed body counts and lists of booty culminate in a report on the completion of the new capital, which serves as evidence of the new imperial order that the king's battling has created. When the text is seen in this light, its accounts of the dismemberment of soldiers and the burning of adolescent boys and girls can no longer be understood as designed to intimidate enemies; they are instead integral parts of a detailed accounting of Ashurnasirpal's years of conscientious service to the war-god Ninurta. Ashurnasirpal's Annals

18. Grayson, *Assyrian Rulers*, 191.

are a religious text, designed to please one of the soldier-king's most important divine supporters.

The discovery of the text within the Ninurta Temple and its precincts gives further support to this conclusion. Access to the interior of temples in the Assyrian period was restricted. The people who were permitted to enter a temple included its religious functionaries, such as priests, cultic singers, temple scribes and administrators; its craftsmen, such as butchers, bakers, goldsmiths, weavers, and cooks; as well as the individuals labeled as *ērib bēti* 'enterer of the temple', prebendaries who were responsible in turn for the performance of certain services in a given temple on specified days. The existence of a group called "temple enterers" emphasizes the restricted nature of temples. The Assyrian king also had access to temples to perform certain rituals during the cultic year, probably accompanied by his guards and perhaps by high officials and members of the royal family. While more ordinary Assyrians may have had access to temple courtyards so that they could present gifts to the god at certain festivals, access to a temple's inner rooms appears to have been reserved for a restricted, elite group.[19]

What this means is that the Ninurta Temple's Annals inscription, displayed on the walls and floors of the temple's inner rooms and perhaps in the area of its ziggurat, was not accessible to outsiders at all. It is highly unlikely that foreigners, vassals, or even governors of Assyrian provinces ever saw it. This suggests that its intended audience was indeed the god whom it explicitly addresses, whose support Assyrians considered essential to the king's continued military success and longevity. In addition, its intended audience probably included the rich and powerful priests of the Ninurta Temple, who had constant access to the text and were in many cases literate, as well as the king himself, and perhaps some of his courtiers and family. Despite its overt violence, its setting makes it clear the Annals Text was not intended to intimidate but, rather, to present a highly positive

---

19. W. G. Lambert comments, "Though publicly supported, these temples were not places of public worship. Only the priests and, within limits, the ruling family and highest officers of states would be allowed to enter and participate in their worship," in *Ritual and Sacrifice in the Ancient Near East* (ed. J. Quaegebeur; Leuven: Peeters and Departement Orientalistiek, 1993) 193. For references to "temple enterers," see *CAD* E 290–92; and John McGinnis's "Review of A. C. V. M. Bongenaar, *The Neo-Babylonian Ebabbar Temple at Sippar: Its Administration and Prosopography*," in *JAOS* 120 (2000) 63–65. On Assyrian temples and their personnel, see Brigitte Menzel, *Assyrische Tempel*, vol. 1: *Untersuchungen zu Kult, Administration und Personal* (Rome: Pontifical Biblical Institute, 1981).

image of the conscientious king to Ninurta and his priests, who presumably would have been delighted by it.

If the Annals inscription of Ashurnasirpal has now proven to be
neither an objective account of the reign nor a piece of intimidating
propaganda directed at Ashurnasirpal's subjects, vassals, and allies,
what kind of a text was the Standard Inscription? Here again, a close
reading of the text helps to clarify its tone and message, and a consideration of its physical setting helps to identify the audiences for which
it was intended.

In the case of the Standard Inscription, there is no difficulty in establishing a reliable text to analyze, because more than 400 copies of the
Standard Inscription have been discovered, carved into the large stone
slabs that lined the walls and floors of the public rooms of Ashurnasirpal's Northwest Palace.[20] Arranged in a broad band of repeated copies
that encircled the palace's throne room, the Standard Inscription
would have been seen not only by the Assyrian king, his court, and
presumably his gods, but also by a broad range of visitors to the king
coming from across the empire, including Assyrian petitioners, foreign
vassals, allies, ambassadors, and the representatives of tributary states,
when they presented their annual tribute to the king.[21]

Ashurnasirpal's inscriptions report, in addition, that when the
palace was dedicated, the king invited 47,074 men and women from
across Assyria to Calah, as well as 5,000 foreign dignitaries, 16,000
people from the city itself, and 1,500 functionaries from other palaces.
This group, totaling 69,574 people, assembled in the palace for ten days
of celebration, during which they feasted; the prominently displayed
and much repeated Standard Inscription seems likely to have been
read aloud and if necessary translated for the benefit of this crowd of
visitors during the palace's dedication ceremonies.[22] Unlike the Annals
inscription, the Standard Inscription was made widely available to
Assyrians, other subjects of the empire, and foreigners.

---

20. The edition used here is Grayson's Ashurnasirpal text no. A.0.101.23, in *Assyrian
Rulers*, 268–76. Grayson lists the 406 exemplars of the text known to him on pp. 268–74,
with their places of publication. For their placement in the palace, see the entries in the
bibliography (p. 268) marked "objects." For the few significant variants and for the reason
that some copies were left incomplete, see p. 268.

21. For evidence about who had access to Assyrian throne rooms, see J. M. Russell,
Sennacherib's Palace without Rival at Nineveh (Chicago: University of Chicago Press, 1991)
223–40.

22. Described in the text known as Ashurnasirpal's Banquet Stele, Grayson's Ashurnasirpal text A.0.101.30, in *Assyrian Rulers*, 288–93.

The Standard Inscription, arranged in a maximum of 22 lines of text in its various copies, is much briefer than the Annals Text, and in contrast to that inscription, it is so bland as to be boring. As in the case of the Annals, its opening lines are an indication of its intended function. It begins with the words, "Palace of Ashurnasirpal," suggesting that the text, which was carved repeatedly in stone, was meant to identify permanently the palace and its illustrious builder to visitors and residents, reminding them again and again of the king's remarkable accomplishments.[23] An abbreviated version of the text was carved on the backs of the slabs as well, suggesting that the Standard Inscription was meant, not only for contemporary audiences, but also for kings who might find it in the distant future—an intended audience often explicitly referred to in Assyrian royal inscriptions.

Having named Ashurnasirpal as the king to whom the palace belongs, the text goes on to identify him (1–5a), first establishing his legitimacy as a king chosen and beloved of several great gods and as the descendant of earlier Assyrian kings. Like the Annals, these opening lines describe him as "destructive weapon of the great gods" and emphasize that he is an unbeatable warrior, calling him "marvelous shepherd, fearless in battle, mighty flood-tide which has no opponent . . . trampler of all enemies." The section ends by summing him up as "victorious over all countries" and recalling the gift of a "merciless weapon" that has marked his call to rule.

Having emphasized that he is above all an effective warrior for the gods, the text now itemizes Ashurnasirpal's military achievements. At this point, the difference in tone between this text and the Annals becomes abundantly clear. In contrast to the Annals' frequent and detailed descriptions of slaughters and flayings, the Standard Inscription provides a broad, generalized account of Ashurnasirpal's warfare: "I felled with the sword the extensive troops of the Lullumu in battle. With the help of the gods . . . I thundered like the god Adad, the devastator, against the troops of the lands Nairi, Ḫabḫu, the . . . Shubaru, and the land Nirbu." The vivid images of a battling king attacking the troops of a particular city have been replaced here by a reference to defeating the Lullumu, a generic term for obstreperous mountain people, and the Annals' accounts of the king with his bloody sword leading a charge against one city after another have been replaced by a vague,

---

23. Grayson's interpolation of the words "property of" at the beginning of the text is confusing; the text is not a property label but an identification of the ruler responsible for the palace's construction.

metaphoric description of the king as thundering like a storm against
a list of territories and peoples.

This is followed by a bland summary of regions and peoples
conquered by Ashurnasirpal: "The king who subdued (the territory
stretching) from the opposite bank of the Tigris to Mount Lebanon
and the Great Sea, the entire land Laqû (and) the land Suḫu including
the city Rapiqu; he conquered from the source of the River Subnat to
the land Urartu." The first phrase compresses all of Ashurnasirpal's
western campaigns into one reference to the area stretching west from
the Assyrian homeland to the Mediterranean; the second summarizes
the fall of the Middle Euphrates Valley; and the third covers the
northern campaigns.[24] The text continues this brisk and colorless geographical summary for another two and one-half lines and then sums
up the outcome of these campaigns, not with a description of punishments allotted, but with the comment that in each case the king had
appointed governors and made the peoples of these lands enter his
service. Every aspect of this account of Ashurnasirpal's campaigns
serves to distance the reader from their painful and violent aspects
and to reduce their description to a bland and matter-of-fact account
of imposing order. Violence is indeed still implied in this account, but
references to it are so oblique as to minimize its presence almost to the
point of elimination.

The epithets that follow are balanced, characterizing the king as
warlike and frightening but at the same time as the benevolent source
of the order now imposed on "the obstinate." He is simultaneously a
"ferocious dragon" and the "protection of the (four) quarters" of the
world. This section ends with a final justification of his use of violent
warfare: "his lordly conflict has brought under one authority ferocious
(and) merciless kings from east to west."

The text concludes with an eight-line description of the building of
the new capital and of the palace that is its crowning glory. Once again
we find a list of conquered peoples, but now they are being settled
peacefully in the city, their new home. The palace itself is then lovingly
described, a place full of exotic and beautiful woods that the king will
use for "my royal residence (and) for my lordly leisure for all eternity."

---

24. On the regions and campaigns represented by each phrase in this summary, see
Mario Liverani, *Studies on the Annals of Ashurnasirpal II. 2: Topographical Analysis* (Università de Roma "La Sapienza," Dipartimento de Scienze storiche, archeologiche e antropo-
logiche dell' Antichità, Quadereni de Geografica Storica 4; Rome: Università di Roma,
1992) 121–22 and fig. 16.

Adorned with sculptures of the wonderful creatures of the mountains and seas that the king now rules, the palace is filled with "booty from the lands over which I gained dominion." With these words, the text ends its picture of the new city and its palace as a microcosm of the newly ordered empire.[25]

This is the text that was made widely available to foreigners and Assyrians alike, and its contrast to the Annals Text is striking: in its brief account of the reign, not a drop of blood is mentioned, no one is flayed, and Ashurnasirpal protects the world, shaping a new order for the empire's fortunate people. Although the threat to potential rebels remains implied, it is carefully muted, so that the text's message to its wide audience is not of intimidation but of praise for a king who has fought valiantly against resistance to a new order that will benefit all the peoples of the empire.

To understand the full impact of the Standard Inscription, however, it is necessary to consider it in context, as ancient visitors to the palace would have experienced it. The art historian I. J. Winter has argued persuasively that the Standard Inscription, as it appeared in the throne room area, was only one element in a carefully integrated verbal, visual, and architectural construction.[26] The cuneiform text, repeated again and again in a broad belt of writing that encircled the throne room, was framed by a band of narrative visual images carved in the stone above and below the writing, or was carved across the figures of images that occupied the entire height of the stone slab. Although the repeated inscription is not a caption for any one of these varied images of the king— at war; engaged in the hunt; or flanked by gods and strange, stylized tree images—each visual image in the throne room, Winter argues, illustrates one of the epithets assigned him in the Standard Inscription.[27] In the throne room, text and images are combined to represent Ashurnasirpal as a fearful but benevolent ruler maintaining order and abundance in the world with the help of the gods.

Together, text and images provided a carefully choreographed experience, projecting a predominantly positive image of the king to the

---

25. Grayson, *Assyrian Rulers*, text no. A.0.101.23, pp. 268–76.

26. Irene J. Winter, "Royal Rhetoric and the Development of Historical Narrative in Neo-Assyrian Reliefs," *Studies in Visual Communication* 7/2 (1981) 2–38; idem, "The Program of the Throneroom of Assurnasirpal II," in *Essays on Near Eastern Art and Archaeology in Honor of Charles Kyrle Wilkinson* (ed. P. O. Harper and H. Pittman; New York: Metropolitan Museum, 1983) 15–32.

27. Idem, "Royal Rhetoric," 21–22.

people who came into his presence in the throne room.[28] As visitors approached the throne room from the outer courtyard, they found themselves flanked by massive carved images of powerful but friendly-looking winged bulls and lions, protective divinities that guarded the doorway. As they drew closer to the door, they were presented with the carved image of a long procession of foreigners like themselves pre-senting their tribute to the king, who lifts two arrows toward them in his hand in a gesture expressive of both dominance and greeting.

Across the carved figures in this largely encouraging tableau were engraved copies of the Standard Inscription, in large, easily readable cuneiform signs placed at eye level. It seems likely that the text was at this point read and explained to visitors, either by their own scribe-translators or by Assyrian escorts accompanying each embassy through the palace, to set the stage for their imminent confrontation with the great king himself.

As they moved into the throne room, however, visitors were now confronted with carved narrative scenes that showed Ashurnasirpal and his soldiers attacking enemy cities, their chariots thundering over the bodies of fallen enemies, or herding prisoners and booty toward the waiting monarch. These scenes would surely have been intimidat-ing to any potential rebel or recently conquered subject; their grim re-minders of the violence of recent campaigns would have provided a threatening balance to the blandly reassuring generalizations of the accompanying Standard Inscription texts. As the visitor continued down the long room toward the enthroned king, however, his atten-tion would have been drawn away from these scenes of warfare to a much larger, prominently elevated scene displayed near the center of the room that showed images of the king flanked by winged divinities and facing a strange, stylized date palm tree, over which hovered the figure of a god in a winged disk. As the visitor continued on down the long room to greet the king, he saw the same scene repeated on a raised slab behind the enthroned king himself, as if framing him.

The meaning of this enigmatic scene and of its central tree, which were repeated at the room's four corners and throughout the palace, has been long debated. Their prominent placement, however, their repetition, and their intimate association with the king strongly sug-

---

28. For the original placement of the now dispersed carved images in the throne room, with drawings, see Janusz Meuszyński, *Die Rekonstrucktion der Reliefdarstellungen und Ihrer Anordnung im Nordwestpalast von Kalḫu (Nimrūd)* (Mainz am Rhein: von Zabern, 1981), tables 1–2 (Raum B).

gest that the repeated tree scenes were central to the message of the throne room. As I have argued elsewhere,[29] I am convinced that the central image in the scene, a stylized date palm tree linked by wavy lines to an arch of surrounding palmettes, is an emblem representing the Assyrian Empire as a date palm orchard and that the flanking divinities, who reach out toward the king with objects that resemble male date palm flower clusters, are symbolically hand-fertilizing this empire (an agricultural process necessary in the mundane world for producing an ample crop of dates). The king, who stands between them, raising his hand toward the tree image and the god who hovers over it, appears here as the conduit through whom the gods' blessings reach the empire and bring it abundance. The tree scene, which serves as the climax of the throne room's visual program, is thus a powerful image of the king's beneficence and of his essential role in bringing the blessings of the gods to the world.

After the visitor made his obeisance to the enthroned king and re-treated respectfully down the long room, he returned to the courtyard through a doorway flanked by benevolent images of another winged guardian, this time raising a palm branch toward the exiting visitor as if to confer blessings on him, as well.

The cumulative impact of this visual and verbal experience was de-signed to be positive. Although the visitor as he entered the throne room was initially confronted with intimidating images of warfare, architectural clues had led the visitor past the violent images to focus on the prominently displayed images of king and gods working to-gether to bless the empire. The repetition of this scene at the end of the room, framing the king as the visitor at last reached him, makes it clear that the idea of Ashurnasirpal as the carrier of blessings to the world that he ruled was intended to dominate the visitor's experience, shaping his final vision of the enthroned king himself. As he passed out into the sunlight from the imposing throne room, the visitor had been shown a message in which elements of carrot and stick were carefully balanced, but the Standard Inscription that encircled the room, together with the throne room's visual images, had ultimately emphasized the benefits of cooperation with this dauntingly powerful but nevertheless beneficent king.

Just as a close reading of the Annals has made it clear that this text was not designed to intimidate subjects or foreigners but to please a

---

29. Barbara N. Porter, "Sacred Trees, Date Palms, and the Royal Persona of Ashurna-sirpal II," *JNES* 52 (1993) 129–39.

god and his priests, a close reading of the Standard Inscription makes it clear that this text was designed to minimize the intimidating aspects of Ashurnasirpal's rule, focusing instead on the happy results of his warfare. Meanwhile, the visual images that surrounded the text in the throne room were designed to reinforce its basically positive message, encouraging the visitor more through friendly persuasion than through terror and intimidation to remain a loyal subject of Assyria's high king.

The Achilles Heel of
Reader-Response Criticism and the
Concept of Reading Hermeneutics of Caution

Christof Hardmeier
University of Greifswald

"What methodological requirements need to be considered in the application of modern literary approaches to ancient literary texts?" This was the central question of the Heidelberg interdisciplinary conference, and it needs to be asked especially with regard to literary approaches, such as pragmalinguistics, reader-response criticism, and deconstructionism. In the following pages, I will approach this question primarily from the perspective of the Achilles heel of reader-response criticism. This Achilles heel consists of these dangers: (1) leaving the meaning of texts entirely to the reader's creativity without corroborating them with reliable criteria for their examination, and (2) uncritically submitting them to the prevailing trends and needs of reader response in specific interpretive communities.[1] To avoid misunderstanding, I need to state that I do not aim at debasing these approaches. On the contrary: the common approaches of reader-response criticism, to my mind, do not go far enough, and the conventional reception of speech-act theory within literary studies cannot simply confine itself to identifying specific speech acts or speech-act sequences *in* the texts.[2]

---

1. See, for example, D. J. A. Clines and J. C. Exum, "The New Literary Criticism," in *The New Literary Criticism and the Hebrew Bible* (ed. D. J. A. Clines and J. C. Exum; JSOTSup 143; Sheffield: JSOT Press, 1993) 11–25. In the eyes of Clines and Exum, "reader-response criticism regards meaning as coming into being at the meeting point of text and reader— or, in a more extreme form, as being created by readers in the act of reading" (p. 19). As "an obvious implicate" they state that "a text means whatever it means to its readers, no matter how strange or unacceptable some meanings may seem to other readers" (ibid.). Thus, they answer "the question of validity in interpretation" as follows: "if the author or the text cannot give validation to meanings, the only source for validity in interpretation has to lie in 'interpretative communities'—groups that authorize certain meanings and disallow others" (ibid.).

2. See, for example, A. Wagner, *Sprechakte und Sprechaktanalyse im Alten Testament: Untersuchungen an der Nahtstelle zwischen Handlungsebene und Grammatik* (BZAW 253; Berlin: de Gruyter, 1997).

Texts *as a whole* must be appreciated as linguistic scores of acts, which now must be explained in more detail.

In this context, there is also no doubt about the admissibility of modern questions of literary studies, for how can we analyze and understand the literary tradition at all if not with *our* methods and *our* knowledge about and experience with texts? Moreover, no one, not even the academically best educated or most highly qualified interpreter of literature can ever escape being the reader of the texts that he or she reads and interprets. Thus, the creative reading activity is an irrefutable and indispensable constituent of each text's understanding. And, of course, I totally agree with the principle of reader-response criticism that meaning must be regarded "as coming into being at the meeting point of text and reader—or, in a more extreme form, as being created by readers in the act of reading."[3] The crucial methodological point is therefore not which approaches to literary studies are more suitable and which are less. The question is, rather, whether these approaches are appropriate with respect to two main questions. First, has the material factuality of texts (ancient or modern) been considered adequately? Second, how have the approaches taken into account the fact that the meaning of texts is (beyond the dichotomy of fact or fiction) always and only constituted and reconstituted in reception processes? Furthermore, have they done this without falling victim to the Achilles heel of reader-response criticism, whether it be the arbitrariness of text interpretation or the presuppositions and preconceptions of interpretive communities? Both questions shall now be looked into in more detail.

The endeavor to find an appropriate and object-related way of looking at texts must begin with the universal but often-ignored elementary conditions of textual communication. These are axiomatic aspects of text communication that are determined by cultural anthropology and tied to elementary conditions of communication. They can be regarded as invariant factors of the human practice of communicating by means of linguistic signals that go beyond cultures and epochs in determining (past and present) the generating process of texts. From this point, we are able to derive an understanding of texts that is based on communication pragmatics. From this understanding, we can form elementary guidelines for an empirical approach to texts and possibly form a methodological basis for more than one academic discipline. Siegfried J. Schmidt has summarized these communication factors in

---

3. Clines and Exum, *New Literary Criticism*, 19.

the *kommunikatives Handlungsspiel* ('pragmatic play of communication') concept, which has become the basic issue of his text theory.[4] From this model is derived the following draft of (1) an understanding of texts based on communication pragmatics and (2) the sharpening of the recipient's consciousness in dealing with texts.

The Understanding of Texts Based on Communication Pragmatics: Texts as Artifacts of Linguistic Communication

An understanding of texts based on communication pragmatics is focused on the material basis of linguistic communication—that is, on the (cultural) remains and artifacts that, as objectifiable items, have come out of communication processes and have always come out of them involuntarily. According to this perspective, texts are material substrata of communication processes. These alone are accessible to (scientific) observation and description, and only from them are we able to infer the processes of understanding and sense-making that were performed on these texts and that should be (re)-performed anew in every process of reception. This way of looking at texts takes the following elementary facts into account:

1. The production and the reception of texts are—outside epochs and cultures—performative activities. Texts are therefore *performativa*. This understanding of texts extends the analysis of linguistic performance and individual speech acts within the texts to the texture of communication pragmatics and its components that shape the texts as a whole—that is, to the entire network of linguistic signals that guide text communication.[5]

2. Texts are intentionally produced (and thus, artificial) media of communication. As such, they are vehicles of meanings, that is to say,

---

4. See S. J. Schmidt, *Texttheorie: Probleme einer Linguistik der sprachlichen Kommunikation* (Uni-Taschenbücher für Wissenschaft 202; Munich: Schoeningh, 1973); and my *Textwelten der Bibel entdecken: Grundlagen und Verfahren einer textpragmatischen Literaturwissenschaft der Bibel* (Textpragmatische Studien zur Literatur- und Kulturgeschichte der Hebräischen Bibel 1/1–1/2; Gütersloh: Gütersloher Verlag, 2003–4) 1/1:47–161; 1/2:24–120, 177–87; furthermore, idem, "Literaturwissenschaft, biblisch," *RGG* (4th ed.) 5:426–29; idem, "Text, IV: Bibelwissenschaftlich," *RGG* 8:198–99; C. Hardmeier and R. Hunziker-Rodewald, "Texttheorie und Texterschließung: Grundlagen einer empirisch-textpragmatischen Exegese," in *Lesarten der Bibel: Untersuchungen zu einer Theorie der Exegese des Alten Testaments* (ed. H. Utzschneider and E. Blum; Stuttgart: Kohlhammer, 2006) 13–44; and M. Köhlmoos, "Drei neue Bücher zur Methodik alttestamentlicher Exegese," *ThR* 72 (2007) 493–500.

5. On the conception of texture and its components, see my *Textwelten*, 1/1:78–135; idem, "Literaturwissenschaft," 427–28.

linguistic sequences of instruction that are designed with reception in mind. In this way, language- and symbol-bound processes of sense-making and meaning constitution are programmed with each production of text or, rather, with regard to its reception.

3. Texts are physically grasp-able communication presenters that are produced in view of potential recipients. The textual communication proposal itself is a grammatically structured cluster of procedural instructions to be followed and must be understood as a score for sense-making. In this context, the category of sense (*Sinn*) functions as a purely descriptive category without qualitative connotations, particularly because the meaning of textual communication may also consist of the production of nonsense. As scores, texts are comparable to musical notations, which can only evoke people's emotions when they are played.

4. In texts as communication presenters, we can only observe the inherent multidimensional potential of locution and illocution in the form of the texture and its components. This is why we cannot directly see their essential aspects of meaning, sense, and function—because essential dimensions of textual meaning and sense, by following their linguistic and communication pragmatic instructions, are only realized in the course of the reception process and, furthermore, are inevitably determined by text-external factors such as presuppositions, situational conditions, world views, and so on. Thus, texts are, in terms of semantics, basically under-determined and open to a great extent.

5. Bearing these restrictions in mind, we need to see texts as tracks of signs that point to past performative communication processes like footprints in the snow. Thus, the reproductive or reconstructive act of text reception (methodically controlled, of course) must, like the reading of a musical score, follow the textual track, which is bound to linguistic items. The first task of academics dealing with texts, therefore (as methodologically [hermeneutically and philologically] trained recipients), is to process accurately the linguistic sequences of instruction that an author has designed as a textual form and communication presenter.

6. If one follows this track by reading or listening, the instruction sequences will ideally guide the receptive process of communication as far as the recipient allows him/herself to be led by this track of linguistic items and, in doing so, feels bound by the ethics of a *Lese- und Rezeptions-Hermeneutik der Behutsamkeit* 'reading hermeneutics of caution'.[6]

---

6. See my *Textwelten*, 1/1:36–45.

Of course, recipients always have the freedom to read texts differently in whatever way they like or even to read entirely against them.

7. Texts as artifacts of symbolic interaction and communication must be strictly distinguished from the double-sided performative activities in which textual meaning is constituted by the author as well as the reader. Communication proposals only gain importance "for us" in, with, and through the productive activity of authors and in the course of reading or listening by recipients. Each reception process in which the textually conditioned sense of a communication proposal must be reproduced anew stands autonomously facing the production process. This autonomy of each reception process implies (to stay with the image of the track) that the existing textual track does not fully determine one's own steps of "following the track," nor does it make them superfluous.

8. This is why texts must be understood, like musical notations, as vehicles of instruction for the reperformance of communication processes but by no means as direct semantic representations of contents, functions, and *Sinn* 'sense'. Rather, they only "make sense" insofar and as soon as they are replayed as procedures, that is, reconstructed in the course of the reception process and realized in this communication pragmatic way. Only by receptive activities does textual sense-making become external reality or become effective in practical contexts of life.

9. The empirical *text* pragmatic procedures must therefore be limited to the procedural and pragmatic aspects of text reception, inasmuch as they are implemented as instruction signals and sequences (texture components) in the texture.[7] Questions that go beyond text-internal observations include nonlinguistic—that is, text-external—situation-bound, mental and psychological, sociocommunicative, and other factors that strongly shape the communication process within the framework of the pragmatic play of communication (*kommunikatives Handlungsspiel*). This model of factors especially includes material forms of records (monumental inscriptions) and the social-use contexts of script-based texts (for example, expert literature or letters) that help establish the function and the sense of texts beyond their purely linguistic constituents.

10. Accordingly, the language-bound sense-making capability of texts must be limited to the text-inherent signals and their effects in the reception process—not only the propositional contents and the text-external, object-related references belong to this capability, but

---

7. On the conception of texture, see n. 5.

first and foremost the illocutionary effects of communication pragmatics. In these using effects, (1) spatial, temporal, and personal orientation is realized, (2) the author-addressee relation is implicitly and
explicitly guided, and (3) the illocutionary modes of textually designed
sequences of speech acts take effect.

In summary, one can say that, in each process of reading and listening, the sense, the function, and the meaning of texts can only be reconstructed through receptive activities. In this way only, they gain a new
and independent relevance within the contexts of the recipient's life.
This process of acquiring meaning presupposes the knowledge of linguistic means—that is, familiarity with the toolbox of linguistic signals
and guiding means (= dictionary, morphology, syntax, for example, of
Old Hebrew). These signals and means once were in principle at an author's disposal in the course of the production of communication proposals and are handed down in the texts specifically composed to be
read and listened to later. However, one must also have a comprehensive knowledge of the text-external horizons of knowledge and experiences in which these text productions were embedded, to which they
were implicitly related, and of which they were once an integral part.
Thus, the reception process as such is of utmost importance, particularly in a scientific manner of empirical reading and self-critical analysis of texts from the oldest known literate cultures. This key position
will now be examined in more detail.

The Act of Text Reading and Listening and Its Dangers:
A Reading Hermeneutics of Caution

It is well known that reading is a demanding exercise that requires
a great deal of experience and practical skill.[8] In the confines of this
space, I cannot mention all possible reasons why the reading and understanding of texts, particularly texts from early literate cultures, so
frequently derails and fails. However, I can point out the conditions of
behavioral anthropology by which each act of text reading or listening
is determined. On the one hand, the reader must be made aware of the
fickleness that is bound up with each act of text reception; on the other
hand, methodological guidelines need to be developed for taking these
dangers into account and not falling victim to them too easily.

---

8. See n. 6. This section is based on a paper that I presented at the Dutch Bible Society
on 25 April 2005, on the occasion of the presentation of the Stuttgart Electronic Study
Bible (ed. C. Hardmeier, E. Talstra, and A. Groves; *SESB 2.0: Stuttgart Electronic Study
Bible* [Stuttgart: German Bible Society / Haarlem: Netherlands Bible Society, 2006]), at
the Vrije Universiteit Amsterdam.

We may begin with the findings of neurobiology that misunderstanding is the normal case. The neurobiologist Gerhard Roth has drawn attention to this fact: "Das eine ist, was ich meine, wenn ich etwas sage; ein anderes ist, was das Gehirn meines Kommunikationspartners an Bedeutungen erzeugt, wenn die Sprachlaute an sein Ohr dringen"[9] ('It is one thing what I *mean* while saying something; it is yet another thing what the brain of my communication partner produces as meanings, when the sounds of language reach his ear'). He concludes: "Missverstehen ist das Normale, Verstehen die Ausnahme"[10] ('Misunderstanding is the normal case, understanding the exception'). For biblical and literary studies, the details of the reception process are especially important—that is, what our brains produce as meaning while reading pictograms, sequences of letters, syllables, and sequences of linguistic items.

According to Roth, another source of mutual misunderstanding, even in everyday communication, is the speaker's side: whatever I say or write is in the course of linguistic performance from the outset being torn "from the context that is predominant in myself," in which it "makes sense."[11] With the production of texts, one always and inevitably expresses much less than one has in mind. Therefore, the fickleness of understanding and the risk of misunderstanding will be doubled, for what has been said or written (in a reduced form) is probably meeting an entirely different inner context belonging to the communication partner, for whom the utterance often makes no or a completely different sense.[12] Misunderstanding is therefore the normal case for two reasons: first, because every linguistic utterance begins as a reduction of what the speaker intended to say or what the author has meant; second, because textual utterances usually meet quite different contexts of understanding when their sense is reproduced in the process of listening or reading.

Against this background, biblical texts in their handed-down linguistic form gain a unique importance. On the one hand, they are only very faint traces and fragile components of past communication

---

9. G. Roth, *Fühlen, Denken, Handeln: Wie das Gehirn unser Verhalten steuert* (Frankfurt am Main: Suhrkamp, 2001) 367.

10. Ibid.

11. Ibid., in the original German version: "Wenn ich meine Argumente vorbringe, so reiße ich sie aus dem in mir herrschenden Kontext heraus, in dem sie Sinn machen."

12. Ibid., in the original German version: "Sie (sc. die Argumente) dringen bei meinem Gesprächspartner in einen wahrscheinlich ganz anderen Kontext, in dem sie keinen oder einen ganz anderen Sinn ergeben."

processes. On the other hand, we can only observe these performances of communication in their linguistic form at this point in time. Thus, these texts form the only direct though very narrow bridge back to the biblical generations and also to the way those people have had their lives remembered, interpreted, and communicated face to face with God. Furthermore, when we read these texts today and try to understand them, we find ourselves in the position of recipients. This is why the question of the neurobiologist regarding script-based texts needs to be put more precisely as follows: what does our brain produce as meaning when the sequences of letters in biblical texts meet the retina of our eyes during the reading process?

Of course, reader-response criticism has already made the act of reading central to the understanding of a text. Regardless of what has been written and handed down, only we as readers are making sense out of the handed-down characters or are trying to wrest sense from historical documents against the background of our world of understanding. Because all understanding of texts irrefutably emerges from current reception activities, we have to say goodbye to the illusion that we will ever understand texts verbatim or without presuppositions. As yet, however, in biblical and literary studies (provided that they are oriented toward hermeneutics and reader-response criticism at all), we still have only concentrated on the first part of the question:[13] what is the meaning produced in our heads? Some have sought out the preconceptions and interests that determine and perhaps involuntarily distort the reconstruction of the text sense. Some have also—like the radical theorists of reader-response criticism—claimed that text sense can only be a joint creation of text and reader, without taking the far weaker partner, *text*, sufficiently into account.

The Sense-Making Function of Linguistic Items in the Reading Process: Core Questions of a New Philology Based on Communication Pragmatics

The second and much more elementary aspect of the question has, however, scarcely ever been taken into consideration: how does the sense of a text form in our brain when we are scanning the sequences of characters in biblical texts with our eyes? Whatever appears immediately to make sense in the process of listening to or reading communication proposals must then be related to the linguistic trace of the

---

13. For an examination of the concept of reader-response criticism, see my *Text-welten*, 1/1:25–27.

text. What is each linguistic item—that is, lexemes and morphemes of, for example, the Greek or Hebrew language—in the reading process contributing to the sense of handed-down texts within the context of phrases, sentences, and sequences of sentences? This is the core question of the new philology and lexicology that would need to be designed and constituted anew in accordance with communication pragmatics.

With regard to semantics, lexemes and morphemes are vehicles of instruction that do not have meaning of their own, as such. They do not represent realities behind the language. Only a certain extent of instruction is linked to their phonetic form, based on conventions. This is a small stimulus of instruction that is only put into effect in usage—but in a two-sided manner. On the one hand, elementary linguistic signals only make sense in connection with other elementary items. It is only in the way that an author links these items according to morphosyntactic rules with more-complex phonetic sequences of words, phrases, and sentences in texts that these elementary signals really make a specific contribution to the sense-making capability of a text. On the other hand, this sense will only be decoded during the reception process. Only if the instructional sequences are observed and followed precisely in the course of reading or listening does the sense of the texts form in recipients' heads approximately as the author has intended it. Thus the elementary items of a language are, on the one hand, semantic vehicles of instruction that only make sense in the context of the words, phrases, and sequences of the sentences in the text. On the other hand, recipients are not simply being led in the reading process only to realize the instructional content of these items. They also must be able to recognize the specific functions of the words, sentences, and text on the syntactical level in order to comprehend the full multidimensional sense of a text.

What a philological and textual analysis based on communication pragmatics must take into consideration can, in conclusion, only be mentioned briefly in terms of the basic types of narrative and rhetorical texts. The sense-making capability of narrative texts with regard to communication pragmatics may first of all be observable in the linguistic signals of speech that steer the formation of a narrated world in the reception process.[14] These are—apart from metacommunicative

---

14. On the characteristics of narrative communication and texts, see ibid., 1/1:64–75; 1/2:177–239.

signals of organizing such as, for example, headlines and metanarrative remarks or introductions to direct speech in embedded levels of communication—primarily the groups of signals that (1) organize the narrated horizon of time (for example, temporal marks), (2) highlight the scenic localizations (marks of locality), and (3) indicate a change in the constellations or roles of the protagonists involved in the narrated events and actions. Such a change can be observed, for example, when a protagonist is no longer being indicated only by pronouns (that is, pronominalization) but is later referred to in the narrated course of events by a role or function noun or by his/her name (that is, renaming or renominalization). In this case, he/she is not onstage for a certain time within the narrated world, and therefore the constellation of the remaining protagonists onstage has changed, and when he/she appears anew on the stage, this mostly will be indicated by renaming or renominalization.

The sense of narrative texts can only be inferred from the manner in which these temporal, local, and personal signals are linguistically organizing and shaping the narrated world. Furthermore, we must observe systematically how these partial structures of shaping are opened, detailed, or condensed, and above all how they will be closed,[15] in order to grasp the communication pragmatic sense of a narrative text in correlation with the logic of the narrated course of actions and events. Observations of phraseological or stylistic peculiarities, ring structures, and other ornamental aspects of the linguistic form are also important for the verification and falsification of insights in the texture and the sense-making capability of narrative texts.

Regarding rhetorical texts, their communication-pragmatic sense-making capability may primarily be observable in the linguistic signals that steer the course of speech and the sequence of argumentation.[16] Basically, these are the groups of signals that organize the interaction between speaker and audience in the process of speaking (above all, the pronouns and forms conjugated in first and second person); signals that also indicate the focusing of the speech toward the speaker-origo

---

15. On this basic concept of the narrator's responsibility to open and close as well as to detail and condense every kind of partial narrative structure, see ibid., 1/1:68–69; 1/2:200–215 and 232–39.

16. On the characteristics and linguistic means of face-to-face communication in texts, see ibid., 1/1:61–64.

of the "I"-"Now"-"Here" face to face a "You";[17] and third, signals that indicate the illocutive mode of the speech acts in the course of speaking (for example, asking, ordering, giving reasons, reporting, describing, etc.). Within this framework of communication pragmatics, we also must look at the inner logic of the topics mentioned as well as the way they are presented, in order to comprehend the full sense and the function of a speech sequence or of an entire direct speech.

In this way, the Torah speech of Moses in Deuteronomy 1–30 can be reconstructed in its integrated unity as a masterpiece of written orality within a narrative frame of headlines and speech introductions.[18] As script-assisted orality, it is intended to be performed repeatedly by reading it aloud and by listening. Another example is the book of Ruth and especially the dialogues between Ruth and her mother-in-law. It proves to be a theological model narrative, in that, on the one hand, YHWH's goodness emerges against all Naomi's expectations and proves her orthodox Torah-belief wrong. And, on the other hand, Ruth's YHWH-trust as a Moabite and Boaz's lived Torah-belief lead to the continuation of the migrant family of Elimelech—precisely what Naomi had in principle never expected to happen. Furthermore, one could also demonstrate the validity of such a text-phenomenological approach based on communication pragmatics in a fundamentally new understanding of the Aqeda story in Genesis 22—the story deals with neither a command to offer the son nor an abysmal test of Abraham's obedience to God.[19] The same is true for the reconstruction of prophetic narratives in Numbers and Kings, of narratives about King Josiah, of prophetic

---

17. On the speaker-origo and the origo-relatedness of verbal communication, see ibid., 1/1:62–63, 102–5; 1/2:66–67.

18. On written orality, see my "Bible Reading and Critical Thinking," in *Critical Thinking and the Bible in the Age of New Media* (ed. C. M. Ess; Lanham, MD: University Press of America, 2004) 77–94 = C. Hardmeier, *Erzähldiskurs und Redepragmatik im Alten Testament: Unterwegs zu einer performativen Theologie der Bibel* (FAT 46; Tübingen: Mohr Siebeck, 2005) 355–69; idem, "Das Sch^ema^c Jisra^ɔel in Dtn 6,4 im Rahmen der Beziehungstheologie der deuteronomistischen Tora (2000)," in ibid., 123–54; on the narrative frame of headlines and speech introductions, see idem, "Die textpragmatische Kohärenz in der Tora-Rede (Dtn 1–30) im narrativen Rahmen des Deuteronomiums: Texte als Artefakte der Kommunikation und Gegenstaende der Wissenschaft," in *Was ist ein Text? Ägyptologische, altorientalische, alttestamentliche und judaistische Perspektiven* (ed. L. Morenz and S. Schorch; BZAW 362; Berlin: de Gruyter, 2007) 207–57.

19. See idem, "Die Bindung Isaaks—ein Ver-Sehen (Gen 22): Wahrnehmungsfähigkeit und Offenheit zu Gott auf dem Prüfstand," *Realitätssinn und Gottesbezug: Geschichtstheologische und erkenntnisanthropologische Studien zu Genesis 22 und Jeremia 2–6* (Biblisch-Theologische Studien 79; Neukirchen-Vluyn: Neukirchener Verlag, 2006) 1–88.

discourses in Isaiah, Zephaniah, and Jeremiah, of the basic narratological structures of the Deuteronomistic History, of the book of Job, and of the narrative framework of the Holiness Code.[20]

---

20. On Numbers, see U. Weise, *Vom Segnen Israels: Eine textpragmatische Untersuchung der Bileam-Erzählung Num 22–24* (Textpragmatische Studien zur Literatur- und Kulturgeschichte der Hebräischen Bibel 3; Gütersloh: Gütersloher Verlag, 2006); on Kings, see my *Prophetie im Streit vor dem Untergang Judas: Erzählkommunikative Studien zur Entstehungssituation der Jesaja- und Jeremiaerzählungen in II Reg 18–20 und Jer 37–40* (BZAW 187; Berlin: de Gruyter, 1990); on King Josiah, see idem, "King Josiah in the Climax of the Deuteronomic History (2 Kings 22–23) and the Pre-Deuteronomic Document of a Cult Reform at the Place of Residence (23.4–15*): Criticism of Sources, Reconstruction of Literary Pre-Stages and the Theology of History in 2 Kings 22–23*," in *Good Kings and Bad Kings* (ed. L. L. Grabbe; JSOTSup 393; London: T. & T. Clark, 2005) 123–63; and L. C. Jonker, *Reflections of King Josiah in Chronicles: Late Stages of the Josiah Reception in 2 Chr 34f.* (Textpragmatische Studien zur Literatur- und Kulturgeschichte der Hebräischen Bibel 2; Gütersloh: Gütersloher Verlag, 2003). On Isaiah, see my "Geschichtsblindheit und politischer Opportunismus in Jes 22,1–14: 'Lasst uns essen und trinken, denn morgen sind wir tot' (Jes 22,13)," in *Essen und Trinken in der Bibel: Ein literarisches Festmahl für Rainer Kessler zum 65. Geburtstag* (ed. M. Geiger, C. M. Maier, and U. Schmidt; Gütersloh: Gütersloher Verlag, 2009) 374–95; idem, "Geschichtsdivinatorik und Zukunftsheuristik im schriftprophetischen Diskurs (Jesaja 9,7–10,27): Eine exegetische sowie geschichts- und religionsphilosophisch reflektierte Studie zu den Jesajadiskursen in Jesaja 1–11" (not yet published); and idem, "Zwei spätvorexilische Diskurse in Zefanja 1,1–3,8: Jhwhs Schlachtopfertag (1,7) und der Tag seines Ingrimms (1,15.18)," in *Diasynchron: Beiträge zur Exegese, Theologie und Rezeption der Hebräischen Bibel: Walter Dietrich zum 65. Geburtstag* (ed. T. Neumann and R. Hunziker-Rodewald; Stuttgart: Kohlhammer, 2009) 139–83. On Jeremiah, see my "Zeitverständnis und Geschichtssinn in der Hebräischen Bibel: Geschichtstheologie und Gegenwartserhellung bei Jeremia," *Realitätssinn und Gottesbezug: Geschichtstheologische und erkenntnisanthropologische Studien zu Genesis 22 und Jeremia 2–6* (Biblisch-Theologische Studien 79; Neukirchen-Vluyn: Neukirchener Verlag, 2006) 89–124; idem "Wahrhaftigkeit und Fehlorientierung bei Jeremia: Jer 5,1 und die divinatorische Expertise Jer 2–6* im Kontext der zeitgenössischen Kontroversen um die politische Zukunft Jerusalems," ibid., 125–54; "Zur schriftgestützten Expertentätigkeit Jeremias im Milieu der Jerusalemer Führungseliten (Jeremia 36): Prophetische Literaturbildung und die Neuinterpretation älterer Expertisen in Jeremia 21–23," in *Die Textualisierung der Religion* (ed. J. Schaper; FAT 62; Tübingen: Mohr Siebeck, 2009) 105–49; and on the Deuteronomistic History, see my "King Josiah," 128–33, 141–42, and 151–53; idem, " 'Geschichten' und 'Geschichte' in der hebräischen Bibel: Zur Tora-Form der Geschichtstheologie im Kulturwissenschaftlichen Kontext," *Erzähldiskurs und Redepragmatik im Alten Testament: Unterwegs zu einer performativen Theologie der Bibel* (FAT 46; Tübingen: Mohr Siebeck, 2005) 98–121. On Job, see idem, "New Relations between = Systematic Theology and Exegesis and the Perspectives on Practical Theology and Ethics," in *Reconsidering the Boundaries between Theological Disciplines* (ed. M. Welker and F. Schweitzer; Muenster: LIT / New Brunswick: Transaction, 2005) 71–80, esp. pp. 74–76 = in *Erzähldiskurs und Redepragmatik im Alten Testament*, 371–81, esp. pp. 374–77; on the narrative framework of the Holiness Code, see A. Ruwe, *"Heiligkeitsgesetz" und "Priesterschrift": Literaturgeschichtliche und rechtssystematische Untersuchungen zu Leviticus 17,1–26,2* (FAT 26; Tübingen: Mohr Siebeck, 1999) 53–120.

In summary, we need a new philology and text analysis based on communication pragmatics within the frame of reading hermeneutics of caution because misunderstanding texts is the normal case. The basic problem in understanding texts is not all those linguistic items and structures that we observe or others have noticed in a text but all those linguistic and pragmatic aspects that we are involuntary losing sight of in the reading process without perceiving it. We easily overlook metacommunicative and metanarrative steering signals as well as illocutive, interactive, or deictic pointers. Within narrative texts, we overlook the temporal and locative signals that organize the time and space horizon of the narrated world. This is because we are involuntarily following in the tracks of all these instruction signals without becoming aware of them and instead are focusing on the personal names, nouns, and verbs that bear the basic information and propositional content in which we are primarily interested.

A methodological way to stop this missing out on basic sense-making aspects in the reading process is to list and highlight systematically all the different linguistic signals of communication pragmatics in a text that steers the reading process beyond the passing on of information. The basic tools to find and highlight these signals systematically by computer are provided by the Stuttgart Electronic Study Bible mentioned above (n. 8, p. 126). In this way we will on the one hand be forced to perceive consciously these steering signals in the text, and in the course of this perceiving process we gain subtly differentiated insights into its communication pragmatic sense-making capability that will have been effected by the visualized linguistic signals in the reading process. On the other hand, we will obtain something like a basic map, comparable to a site- or navigation-map, for becoming aware simultaneously of all communication pragmatic signals and steering instructions in the course of further reading and interpretive evaluations of the text. However, this small methodological sketch of the empirical analysis of texts can only give an incomplete impression of this new philological approach within the scope of reading hermeneutics of caution. Thus I can only point to the more or less extensive studies mentioned above.[21]

---

21. See nn. 18–20.

Tell Me Who I Am:
Reading the Alphabet of Ben Sira

DAGMAR BÖRNER-KLEIN
University of Düsseldorf

Hebrew texts that are written in consonants without vowels and punctuation marks present the reader with a field of possibilities including a multiplicity of different interpretations.[1] In the field of rabbinic literature, we have literary patterns and a formulaic, standardized use of language to reduce ambiguity. However, "[T]he less conventional forms of expression are, the more scope they allow for interpretation."[2] This is the case with the Alphabet of Ben Sira which Eliezer Segal called a notoriously problematic text designed to upset the sensibilities of traditional Jews.[3] However, for a long time, the Alphabet of Ben Sira must have been a well-known, even famous Jewish book. More than 100 Hebrew manuscripts of the Alphabet of Ben Sira attest its popularity. Eli Yassif classified the manuscripts into two different types, because content and composition differ extensively from each other.[4] Type A is found in manuscripts in northwestern Europe, type B in manuscripts from Italy and Spain. Manuscripts of type A consist of an introduction on Job 9:10 ("Who does great things without limit and wonders without number"), a story of Ben Sira's birth, a dialogue with his teacher with Hebrew proverbs in alphabetical order, a story of

---

1. D. Robeys, *Introduction to Umberto Eco: The Open Work* (Cambridge, MA, 1989) x.

2. Ibid., xi.

3. See http://www.lilithgallery.com/library/lilith/The-Bible-of-ben-Sira.html: Eliezer Segal, Looking for Lilith: "So shocking and abhorrent are some of the contents of 'the Alphabet of Ben-Sira' that modern scholars have been at a loss to explain why anyone would have written such a book."

4. E. Yassif, *The Tales of Ben Sira in the Middle Ages: A Critical Text and Literary Studies* (Jerusalem, 1984) 16–19 [Heb.]. S. Schechter, "A Further Fragment of Ben Sira," *JQR* 12 (1900) 460–61. J. Marcus, "The Fifth Manuscript of Ben Sira," *JQR* 21 (1931) 223–40. A. M. Habermann, "Alphabet of Ben Sira: Third Version," *Tarbiz* 27 (1957–58) 190–202 [Heb.]. S. Hopkins, *A Miscellany of Literary Pieces from the Cambridge Genizah Collections* (Cambridge, 1978) 57–60, 66, 78–85.

Ben Sira at the court of Nebuchadnezzar, and an Aramaic list of proverbs in alphabetical order. Type B includes a group of additional questions asked by Nebuchadnezzar, but the whole section of Aramaic
proverbs is missing. The most reliable textual witness of type B is MS
Parma 2456 (de Rossi 1090), a 14th-century manuscript from Italy.[5]
Similar to this manuscript is MS Kaufmann 59 of the Rabbinic Seminary in Budapest,[6] the only manuscript of type B that transmits the
collection of Aramaic proverbs in alphabetical order.

Eli Yassif analyzed the Alphabet as a collection of narratives that
consists of folkloristic material. Günter Stemberger pointed to the
"ironic criticism of religion" within the text.[7] Joseph Dan noted that
the Alphabet of Ben Sira is "a [. . .] *satyrical* work," a "heretical collection of narratives" including "bizarre, obscene" stories.[8] David Stern
stated that the Alphabet is "one of the earliest examples of clear-cut
literary *parody* in classical Jewish literature."[9] With regard to the
Alphabet of Ben Sira, we not only have a multiplicity of textual witnesses, we also have a "multiplicity of different interpretations."[10]

Moshe ha-Darshan, who lived in the 11th century, quoted the
Alphabet for the first time.[11] Therefore, the *terminus ad quem* of the
final redaction is the end of the 10th century.[12] The *terminus a quo* is
the 8th century, because motifs of the Arabic fox fable Kalila and
Dimna occur in the Alphabet of Ben Sira.[13] In the 7th century, Abdal-
lah ibn al-Muqaffa translated these tales from Persian into Arabic.[14]
However, we do not know who wrote or composed the work.

5. B. Richter, ed., *Hebrew Manuscripts in the Biblioteca Palatina in Parma: Catalogue,
Palaeographical and Codicological Descriptions* (M. Beit-Arieh; Jerusalem, 2001) 146.

6. D. Z. Friedmann and D. S. Löwinger, "Alphabet of Ben Sira," *Hazofeh* 10 (1926)
250–81 [Heb.].

7. G. Stemberger, *Introduction to the Talmud and Midrash* (Edinburgh, 1991) 372–73.

8. J. Dan, "Ben Sira, Alphabet of," English *EncJud* 4:548–49; idem, *The Heart and the
Fountain: An Anthology of Jewish Mystical Experiences* (Oxford, 2002) 290.

9. D. Stern, "The Alphabet of Ben Sira and the Early History of Parody in Jewish
Literature," in *The Idea of Biblical Interpretation: Essays in Honor of James L. Kugel* (ed.
H. Najman and J. H. Newman; Leiden, 2004) 423.

10. Robeys, *Introduction* to *Umberto Eco,* x.

11. C. Albeck, ed., *Midrash Bereshit Rabbati* (Jerusalem, 1940) 28.

12. Yassif, *The Tales of Ben Sira,* 22.

13. Ibid., 24.

14. See A. Marmorstein, "A Note on the Alphabet of Ben Sira," *JQR* 41 (1950–51)
303–6. J. Dan, "Hidat Alfa Beta de-Ben Sira," *Molad* 23 (1965–66) 490–96. J. P. Asmussen,
"Eine jüdisch-persische Übersetzung des Ben-Sira Alphabets," in *Ex orbe religionum* 1
(1972) 144–55. S. T. Lachs, "The Alphabet of Ben Sira: A Study in Folk Literature," *Gratz* 2
(1973) 9–28. J. Dan, *The Hebrew Narrative Literature in the Middle Ages* (Jerusalem, 1974)

The Alphabet of Ben Sira leads the reader to reveal his of her fantasies and imaginations about the text. Different reading levels correspond to the readers' interests and knowledge about literature and allow them to find allusions to biblical, rabbinic, and folk literature. A reader who is only interested in being exhilarated or amused by reading will find satisfaction; a reader who seeks a deeper sense will also be rewarded and pleased by the cunning presentation of a message.

In David Stern's anthology *Rabbinic Fantasies: Imaginative Narratives from Classical Hebrew Literature,* we find a translation of the Alphabet of Ben Sira that follows Steinschneider's edition of 1858.[15] The translation presents the Alphabet of Ben Sira as a collection of amusing stories like the following one about the daughter of King Nebuchadnezzar:[16]

> [T]he king said to Ben Sira, "I have a daughter who expels a thousand farts [ומתעטשת] every hour. Cure her!"
>
> Ben Sira replied, "Send her to me in the morning with her attendants, and I will heal her."
>
> The next morning, she came with her attendants. When Ben Sira saw her, he began to act as though he were very angry.
>
> "Why are you angry?" she asked him.
>
> "Your father decreed that I must expel one thousand farts in his presence tomorrow and the following day. I am afraid he may put me to death. He gave me an extension of three days, but I still do not know what to do."
>
> "Do not worry," she said. "I will go in your place and expel one thousand farts in front of him for both of us."
>
> "If that is the case," replied Ben Sira, "stay here with me for three days and don't break wind, so that the farts will be ready on the third day."
>
> Every time a fart was about to come, the king's daughter stood up on one foot and stretched her eyes wide, as Ben Sira told her to do, and she contained herself and closed her "mouth" slowly, until the breaking of wind stopped completely. After three days no farts came out from her behind.
>
> On that day Ben Sira took her to her father, saying, "Go and expel one thousand farts for your father." She stood before the king, but she was unable to break wind even once. The king stood up and kissed Ben Sira.

One word in the story demands the reader's decision. He has to make up his mind how he will interpret the verb ומתעטשת, which is the

---

68–78 [Heb.]. E. Yassif, *Sipure Ben Sira bi-yeme ha-benayim mahadura bikortit u-firke mehkar* (Jerusalem, 1984). J. Dan, *Foreword to the Alphabet of Ben Sira: The Facsimile of the Constantinople Edition of 1519* (Verona, 1997) 11–13.

15. D. Stern, ed., *Rabbinic Fantasies: Imaginative Narratives from Classical Hebrew Literature* (New Haven, 1990) 167–202.

16. Ibid., 184–85.

Nithpael of עטש. This verb is not used in the Hebrew Bible, but in Job
41:10 the hapax legomenon עטישה occurs, an apparently related word.
Jastrow's *Dictionary* offers three textual references to explain the Nithpael of עטש.[17] The first appears in *Yal. Job* §927, referring to Job 41:10:
"Therefore, one must offer thanks when one sneezes [כשמתעטש]." The
second reference is *Num. Rab.* 9:21, which deals with the effect of the
water of bitterness that a woman is forced to drink in case her husband thinks her guilty of being an adulteress. *Num. Rab.* 9:21 states:
"The water wrought various kinds of strange effects upon her. If she
was white, it turned her black; if red, it made her green; her mouth
would emit an evil odor; her neck would swell; her flesh would decay;
she would be afflicted with gonorrhea [זבה]; she would feel inflated
[מתעטשת] and languid [מתפרקת אברים]."[18] This translation follows Jastrow's suggestion[19] exactly but, according to *Sipre Zuta* on Num 5:24[20]
and *m. Nid.* 9:8, there is another plausible interpretation. It also makes
sense to translate מתעטשת 'she will yawn and "sneeze"'. *M. Nid.* 9:8
states that sneezing is a symptom of near menstruation, a warning
sign of becoming unclean. Sneezing, which definitely can be seen
when it happens, identifies the adulteress.

We find the third text to which Jastrow refers in *b. Ber.* 24a–b:[21]

> R. Hanina also said:
> I saw Rabbi [while saying the *Tefillah*] belch and yawn and sneeze
> [ונתעטש] and spit [24b] and adjust his garment, but he did not pull it over
> him; and when he belched, he would put his hand to his chin.
> The following objection was cited:
> 'One who says the *Tefillah* so that it can be heard is of the small of faith;
> he who raises his voice in praying is of the false prophets; he who belches
> and yawns is of the arrogant; if he sneezes [המתעטש] during his prayer it
> is a bad sign for him—some say, it shows that he is a low fellow; one who
> spits during his prayer is like one who spits before a king.'
> Now in regard to belching and yawing there is no difficulty; in the one
> case it is involuntary, in the other case deliberate.
> But the sneezing in Rabbi's case does seem to contradict the sneezing
> in the other?—

---

17. M. Jastrow, *A Dictionary of the Targumim, the Talmud Babli and Yerushalmi, and the
Midrashic Literature: With an Index of Scriptural Quotations* (New York, 1903) 1055.

18. Translation: Judah J. Slotki, *Midrash Rabbah Numbers* (3rd ed.; London, 1983) 279.

19. Jastrow, *Dictionary of the Targumim*, 1055. ·

20. D. Börner-Klein, *Sifre Zuta, Rabbinische Texte, Tannaitische Midraschim* (Stuttgart,
2002) 32.

21. Translation: M. Simon, *Berakoth: Translated into English with Notes, Glossary and
Indices* (The Babylonian Talmud, *Zeraim*; London, 1935) 146–47.

There is no contradiction between sneezing and sneezing either; in the one case it is above, in the other below.

For R. Zera said:

This dictum was casually imparted to me in the school of R. Hamnuna, and it is worth all the rest of my learning: If one sneezes in his prayer it is a good sign for him, that as they give him relief below [on earth] so they give him relief above [in heaven].

The story comes to an end when a teacher recites the following passage:[22]

If a man was standing saying the *Tefillah* and he broke wind [ונתעטש], he waits until the odor passes off and begins praying again.

Some say:

If he was standing saying the *Tefillah* and he wanted to break wind, he steps back four cubits and breaks wind and waits till the wind passes off and resumes his prayer [. . .]

He [Rab Yehuda] said:

Had I come only to hear this, it would have been worth my while.

Here, in *b. Ber.* 24a–b, נתעטש is combined with an 'odor', which is a translation of רוח that signifies 'wind', usually without a smell. Therefore, even in the last case, the reader can understand ונתעטש as sneezing, because the message can be: whoever sneezes in public should step back. He has to take care and not sneeze at others, because the breath from his nose can defile other peoples' garments.

In all three cases, נתעטש can be interpreted as 'sneezing'. As a result, I translate ומתעטשת in the story of the king's daughter (according to MS Kaufmann 59) as 'she sneezes':

Nebuchadnezzar said to him: "My son, I know that there is a book about healing in your hand. Now, I have a daughter and she sneezes all the time, more than a thousand times in an hour. All the labor [for only] having scratches! There is no medicine left in the world that has not been given to her; a lot of medicine! Many amulets have been written, but she has not been cured. When you cure her, there will be nobody like you in the world."

Ben Sira said to him: "Send her tomorrow, and with her, two eunuchs who will watch over her."

He sent her the next day and he sat with her the whole day, and she was not able to do anything but sneeze. The following day, Ben Sira went out to the market.

When he returned, he said to her: "Woe to me; I fear that from today until the third day there will not be left over one of all mankind."

---

22. Ibid.

She said to him: "Why?"

He said to her: "Because your father has announced today: 'The person who will not come within the next three days and sneeze before me less than 300 sneezes will be put to death by sword.'"

She said to him: "Don't be afraid; I can sneeze before him 300 times for me and 300 times for you."

He said to her: "That will be fine! Sit down and don't sneeze for three days. And when you go after those three days, everything will depend on you."

She said to him: "That will be fine!"

At once, she sat down and watched her breath and controlled it so that she did not let out any sneezes.

On the third day, he said to her: "Go now to your father and sneeze in his presence."

She went to him and could not do it in his presence—not a single time. Nebuchadnezzar arose on his feet, kissed Ben Sira on his head, and said to him: "Tell me, which medicine did you give her?"

And he explained to him what he had done to her.

The stories in Steinschneider's edition and in MS Kaufmann 58 are very similar. In translation, the story transforms into either an obscene text (in Stern's anthology) or a text that could be read as a case study on healing a severe dust allergy. The presentation of the story depends on the reader's attitude toward the text. Therefore, the translator should at least point out that he or she decided against other possible interpretations.

The Alphabet itself deals with the problem of an unperceptive attitude toward language in the following story which, like the story of the king's daughter, has more than one reading level:[23]

"Why does a donkey urinate in the urine of another donkey, and why does it smell its own excrement?"

Ben Sira answered: God created the first donkey and handed it over to Adam. The donkey noticed that he was the fittest animal for carrying a load. He prayed before God and said: "Lord of the world, when will I have a rest [ריוח]"? God said to him: "When your urine [the water of your feet] flows as rivers, and the millstones [ריחים] can be made thereby to run, and when your excrement smells [מריח ריח] up to the skies. At this time, he will give you a rest [ריוח]. (The only reason to answer like this was to prevent his semen from disappearing from the world.)

After the donkey had heard this, he was pacified. He came to his she-ass and she gave birth to children; to them he transmitted the sign. Because of this, whenever he sees a fellow urinating, he too urinates to

---

23. D. Börner-Klein, *Das Alphabet des Ben Sira: Hebräisch-deutsche Textausgabe mit einer Interpretation* (Wiesbaden, 2007) 92–97.

make a river flow. And they smell their excrement to smell whether it smells up to the skies.

The dialogue between the donkey and God is not a simple one. There are many wordplays and metaphors. All wordplays consist of a combination of the letters *resh, waw, ḥet*. The word רוח (*rawaḥ*) means 'to feel relief'.[24] The word רוח (*riwaḥ*) means 'to make space'. Another רוח (*rewaḥ*) means 'space; relief; profit; gain, interest'.[25] The word רחים means 'millstones; heavy burden'.[26] 'Making a millstone run' is a metaphor for "having intercourse." In the story, the metaphorical and plain meanings are combined and only in combination does the message makes sense. The plain meaning of the text leads to a stupid act that gives no answer and no relief: The donkey urinates to let a river flow. He does not understand that children can help him to carry his burden. He would have relief by sharing his load with them. We have proof that this interpretation is not arbitrary in Aesop's fable "Zeus and the Donkeys,"[27] where the moral of the story is given at the end of the text:

> The donkeys were tired of being burdened with burdens and laboring all the days of their lives, so they sent ambassadors to Zeus, asking him to release them from their toil. Zeus, wanting to show them that they had asked for something impossible, said that their suffering would come to an end on the day when they pissed a river. The donkeys took him seriously and to this day whenever donkeys see where another donkey has pissed, they come to a halt and piss in the same place.
> *The fable shows that a person cannot escape his allotted fate.*

In the retelling of Aesop's fable in the Alphabet of Ben Sira, the author slightly changed this moral. A person can escape his allotted fate. He can interpret words.

The Alphabet of Ben Sira is, as Eli Yassif has shown, a collection of narrations. Some of the stories can be found in different folkloristic environments. They are not particularly Jewish, as the donkey story shows. But all animal stories of the Alphabet of Ben Sira can be interpreted as fables that convey an implicit moral. Each animal symbolizes a character, a virtue, or a vice. Thus, the stories provide examples of how to behave and how to act. They claim to find the middle way by avoiding the extreme or to behave according to the Aristotelian ethical

---

24. R. Alcalay, *The Complete Hebrew-English Dictionary* (Jerusalem, 1990) 2416.
25. Ibid., 2417.
26. Ibid., 2436.
27. *Aesop's Fable: A New Translation by Laura Gibbs* (Oxford, 2002).

concept.[28] In later times, even in church, this concept of moral teaching became popular:[29]

> [B]y the thirteenth century, churchmen increasingly used examples drawn from fables, *Bestiaries* and beast epics to illustrate their sermons. It was customary for a preacher to conclude his sermon by reciting from one to five moralized exempla. Collections of appropriate stories (arranged alphabetically) that could be used to yield moral lessons to the faithful were compiled in the thirteenth century. In these collections of exempla, we can see the growing popularity of animals as human exemplar.

The Alphabet of Ben Sira does exactly the same. It presents alphabetically arranged stories to yield moral lessons. In addition, the Alphabet of Ben Sira constantly refers to rabbinic literature. Most of the stories of the Alphabet have a rabbinic subtext. These subtexts are famously problematic texts in rabbinic literature, and the Alphabet develops an alternative to a given rabbinic point of view referring to rabbinic exegesis and rabbinic hermeneutics. This leads to another reading level in the Alphabet of Ben Sira, as in the story of Lilith, the first wife of Adam:[30]

> Soon afterward the young son of the king took ill. Said Nebuchadnezzar, "Heal my son. If you don't, I will kill you." Ben Sira immediately sat down and wrote an amulet with the Holy Name, and he inscribed on it the angels in charge of medicine by their names, forms, and images, and by their wings, hands, and feet. Nebuchadnezzar looked at the amulet. "Who are these?"
> "The angels who are in charge of medicine; Snvi, Snsvi, and Smnglof. After God created Adam, who was alone, He said, 'It is not good for man to be alone' (Gen. 2:18). He then created a woman for Adam, from the earth, as He had created Adam himself, and called her Lilith. Adam and Lilith immediately began to fight. She said, 'I will not lie below,' and he said, 'I will not lie beneath you, but only on top. For you are fit only to be in the bottom position, while I am to be in the superior one.' Lilith responded, 'We are equal to each other inasmuch as we were both created from the earth.' But they would not listen to one another. When Lilith saw this, she pronounced the Ineffable Name and flew away into the air. Adam stood in prayer before his Creator: 'Sovereign of the universe!' he said, 'the woman you gave me has run away.' At once, the Holy One, blessed be He, sent these three angels to bring her back.
> "Said the Holy One to Adam, 'If she agrees to come back, fine. If not, she must permit one hundred of her children to die every day.' The

---

28. See my *Alphabet des Ben Sira*, 316–32.
29. J. E. Salesbury, *The Beast Within: Animals in the Middle Ages* (New York, 1994) 126.
30. Translation: Stern, ed., *Rabbinic Fantasies*, 183–84.

angels left God and pursued Lilith, whom they overtook in the midst of the sea, in the mighty waters wherein the Egyptians were destined to drown. They told her God's word, but she did not wish to return. The angels said, 'We shall drown you in the sea.'

" 'Leave me!' she said. 'I was created only to cause sickness to infants. If the infant is male, I have dominion over him for eight days after his birth, and if female, for twenty days.'

"When the angels heard Lilith's words, they insisted she go back. But she swore to them by the name of the living and eternal God: 'Whenever I see your names or your forms in an amulet, I will have no power over that infant.' She also agreed to have one hundred of her children die every day. Accordingly, every day one hundred demons perish, and for the same reason, we write the angels' names on the amulets of young children. When Lilith sees their names, she remembers her oath, and the child recovers."

We find the word *Lilith* in biblical literature only in Isa 34:14: "The wild beasts of the desert shall also meet with the wild beasts of the island, and the satyre shall cry to his fellow; the screech owl [לילית] also shall rest there, and find for herself a place of rest" (KJV). In 1914, I. Lévi pointed out that, because of the parallel structure of the verse, the word was understood as 'demon'.[31] Jerome (349/50–420) identified Lilith with Lamia, a lover of Zeus whose children, except one, killed Hera. Lamia avenged this by killing other peoples' children, by sleeping with young men, and by weakening them. She was imagined as a female demon wandering around as a phantom of the night. In allusion to this, Jerome translated *Lilit* in Isa 24:14 as 'Lamia': "Et occurrent daemonia onocentauris et pilosus clamabit alter ad alterum ibi cubavit *lamia* et invenit sibi requiem."

The Babylonian Talmud mentions *Lilit* as a demonic being in *b. Šabb.* 151b and *b. B. Bat.* 73b, but it is the Alphabet of Ben Sira that for the first time uses this word as a name for Adam's first wife, although in *Gen. Rab.* 24:2/22:17 and *Gen. Rab.* 17:4 an unnamed first wife of Adam is mentioned.

The story of Lilith, who preferred to fly away from Adam when he insisted on being superior to her, is rooted in Gen 2:23: "This time, it is bone of my bone and flesh of my flesh." "This time" implies the existence of a former time. *B. Yebam.* 63a explains: "This teaches that Adam slept with all animals, but he was not satisfied. Only when sleeping with Eve was he satisfied." The Alphabet of Ben Sira rejects this point of view: Adam was created in the image of God. How could he be

---

31. I. Lévi, "Lilit et Lilin," *Revue des Études Juives* 68 (1914) 15–21.

guilty of sodomy? The Alphabet draws the only acceptable conclusion: Eve was Adam's second wife.

The story of Lilith and Adam in the Alphabet of Ben Sira has two subtexts: Gen 2:23 and its interpretation in *b. Yebam.* 63a. Without mentioning this, once again the Alphabet of Ben Sira serves to satisfy the reader's expectation of a frivolous story. However, to a reader who takes into account that the Alphabet of Ben Sira is developing a narrative critique on *b. Yebam.* 63a, the work presents a highly sophisticated exegetical explanation for a theological problem that arose in the Babylonian Talmud.

The Bible does not always tell stories in detail. The rabbis often missed having detailed descriptions in the biblical narratives. To retell the stories, they needed more information about biblical characters and biblical events than were available at first glance. In lieu of other sources, they developed hermeneutical rules that enabled them to infer information. In most of the stories, the unknown author of the Alphabet of Ben Sira criticizes deductive inferences. The author of the Alphabet makes clear that even the application of hermeneutical rules can lead to unacceptable interpretations. His narrative performance aims to *reform* rabbinic exegesis and to point to the fact that people need stories to enlighten their lives. In his opinion, a good story is much more moving than a sermon without inspiration, and being sophisticated is much more attractive than merely being funny.

The Powers of a Lost Subject: Reinventing a Poet's Identity in Catullus's Carmen 8

MELANIE MÖLLER

University of Heidelberg

Introduction

Miser Catulle, desinas ineptire, the opening line of one of Catullus's most famous poems, has made no small contribution to the role this text has played in biographical and empathetic traditions of interpretation. *Carmen* 8 has often been misunderstood as a document of the disappointment felt by a poet unhappily in love; but here, desperation is merely a pose: this *Carmen* offers no less than the poetic development of a self-reflexive subject within the fiction—a subject that, in its autoreflexivity and epistemological power, appears modern but in its inability to emancipate itself or even to act is almost postmodern.

Can an ancient self really bear modern or postmodern traits? We have long been accustomed to obeying the historical dogma according to which anachronistic applications of notions and concepts to ancient texts are subject to an axiomatic reservation. Caution seems particularly necessary in the case of the subject and its possible identity: despite numerous studies that, for all their historical-methodological restraint, have achieved highly promising results,[1] quite a few scholars

---

Author's note: A modified version of this article has also been published in German (in *Vom Selbst-Verständnis: Notions of the Self in Antiquity and Beyond* [ed. A. Arweiler and M. Möller; Berlin: de Gruyter, 2008] 3–20). I want to thank Glenn Patten (Heidelberg/Santa Barbara) for translating it into English. My thanks are also due to the editors of this collection and organizers of the conference that preceded it. (Translator's note: All translations of quoted texts are my own except where otherwise stated.)

1. See, for example, A. Schmitt, *Selbständigkeit und Abhängigkeit menschlichen Handelns bei Homer: Hermeneutische Untersuchungen zur Psychologie Homers* (Abhandlungen der Geistes- und Sozialwissenschaftlichen Klasse 5; Stuttgart: Franz Steiner, 1990); idem, "Individualität als Faktum menschlicher Existenz oder als sittliche Aufgabe? Über eine Grunddifferenz im Individualitätsverständnis von Antike und Moderne," in *Die Aktualität der Antike: Das ethische Gedächtnis des Abendlandes* (ed. C. Gestrich; Berlin: Wichern, 2002) 105–28; K. Oehler, *Subjektivität und Selbstbewußtsein in der Antike* (Würzburg:

believe that it is impossible "to make use . . . of premodern forms of understanding and relating to the self" in modern thinking on this topic.[2] While ancient models of self-assessment (and the models derived from them) remain bound to a notion of the human being in general, the search for an essence of the (individual) human being independent of this general notion has become "one of the indispensable questions of modernity."[3] It might therefore seem that the subject understood as an ontological substrate (*hypokeimenon*) in ancient philosophy and the socially determined subject of rhetorical-political public life are only comparable in a very limited sense to the epistemological subject of modernity and its "subverted" successors.

It may therefore be more promising to turn away from philosophical axiomata and sociological dispositions. In hunting for "negotiations with the self," we soon discover poetry, especially lyric poetry to be the genre most interested in inwardness and subjectivity, in that all perspectives are transferred into a lyrical "I," and this "I" allows for no objects outside itself. Those who have gone looking for concepts of subjective identity in classical antiquity, however, have been repeatedly put in their place by genre-theoretical and socially determined factors that, unlike their modern counterparts, have allegedly defined ancient lyrical forms. Nevertheless, it seems to me that this area offers much potential for approaching the phenomena we are looking for by way of concepts *comparable* with more recent notions of the self and of subjectivity that can be described in modern terms. This is true because, to a great extent, they not only have developed the *subjective* point of view decisive for all theories of the genesis of the epistemological subject but they have also called it into question on the basis of its philosophical and psychological implications.[4]

Königshausen & Neumann, 1997); R. L. Fetz et al., eds., *Geschichte und Vorgeschichte der modernen Subjektivität* (2 vols.; Berlin: de Gruyter, 1998); P. von Moos, "Persönliche Identität und Identifikation vor der Moderne: Zum Wechselspiel von sozialer Zuschreibung und Selbstbeschreibung," in *Unverwechselbarkeit: Persönliche Identität und Identifikation in der vormodernen Gesellschaft* (ed. P. von Moos; Cologne: Böhlau, 2004) 1–42; C. Gill, *The Structured Self in Hellenistic and Roman Thought* (Oxford: Oxford University Press, 2006).

2. This is the conclusion drawn by P. Bürger (*Das Verschwinden des Subjekts: Eine Geschichte der Subjektivität von Montaigne bis Barthes* [Frankfurt am Main: Suhrkamp, 1998] 16) in discussing Michel Foucault's interpretation of the classical *cura sui* (*Histoire de la sexualité* [3 vols.; Paris: Gallimard, 1976–84]).

3. P. Geyer, *Die Entdeckung des modernen Subjekts: Anthropologie von Descartes bis Rousseau* (Tübingen: Max Niemeyer, 1997) 263.

4. On the history of this subjective point of view, see R. Hagenbüchle, "Subjektivität: Eine historisch-systematische Hinführung," in *Geschichte und Vorgeschichte* (ed. R. L. Fetz et al.; 2 vols.; Berlin: de Gruyter, 1998) 1–88, esp. p. 33.

Subjectivity means, first of all, the "autoreflexivity of imagination" and comprises the relationship of a knowing or perceiving entity to itself, a criterion the justification of which modern critics of the subject have never contested.[5] For all concepts of the subject, self-awareness remains a constitutive element: "the acts of such self-awareness consist in individuals' relationships which are for themselves transparent and reflexive to their own mental, dispositional, and physical attributes or conditions."[6] "I"-identity also means the reflexive ability to view oneself like another subject; awareness of one's own identity includes both continuities and processes of change.[7] Postmodern reservations, of course, take up instead the idealist notion of an autonomous or even unified self; from this autonomistic perspective, the modern subject for many theorists has long been just as "dead" as the ancient subject allegedly always was. Instead of an independent "I," we now have a self that comprises several (by no means always cooperating) selves, crucially determined by alienation (the unconscious and similar instances), and that has lost its self-certainty.

My thesis is that this notion of a subject that knows that its identity is in tension between self-awareness and dependency also forms the basis of Catullus's *Carmen* 8.[8] The related problem of autonomy

---

5. See M. Frank, "Subjekt, Individuum, Person," in *Individualität* (ed. M. Frank and A. Haverkamp; Poetik und Hermeneutik 13; Munich: Fink, 1988) 3–20, esp. p. 7.

6. M. Pauen, "Selbstbewußtsein: Ein metaphysisches Relikt? Philosophische und empirische Befunde zur Konstitution von Subjektivität," in *Selbst und Gehirn: Menschliches Selbstbewußtsein und seine neurobiologischen Grundlagen* (ed. K. Vogeley and A. Newen; Paderborn: Mentis, 2000) 101–21, esp. p. 106.

7. See O. Marquard and K. H. Stierle, *Identität* (Poetik und Hermeneutik 8; Munich: Fink, 1979) 12: identity is understood here as the "problematic, processual, broken and nevertheless maintained identity of a subject" and remains bound to a person's continuity across time and his or her perceptibility.

8. The exceptional significance of *Carmen* 8 in this respect is also recognized by W. R. Johnson, *The Idea of Lyric: Lyric Modes in Ancient and Modern Poetry* (Berkeley: University of California Press, 1982) 122; he nevertheless treats the poem as a mere complement to *Carmen* 76, which he considers to be more important for the question of the subject. Thus, what remains implicit in *Carmen* 8 is made visible in *Carmen* 76: "a disease that has devoured the personality" (p. 122). Similarly tentative proposals can be found in H. J. Tschiedel, "Erwachendes, aufbegehrendes und verstörtes Ich: Manifestationen des Subjektiven in der römischen Literatur," in *Geschichte und Vorgeschichte* (ed. R. L. Fetz et al.; Berlin: de Gruyter, 1998) 255–83, esp. p. 268; Tschiedel sees the function of a poem such as we have before us in *Carmen* 8 in the 'constant self-reassurance' (*ständige Selbstvergewisserung*) of the poet. The most extended analysis along the lines of the interpretation I am suggesting here is that of W. Fitzgerald (*Catullan Provocations: Lyric Poetry and the Drama of Position* [Berkeley: University of California Press, 1995] 120–23), who reads *Carmen* 8 as a borderline situation on the basis of Benedetto Croce's concept of a theatrical "naïveté," which Croce believed to be at work in all of Catullus's poetry (*Poesia antica e moderna* [Bari: Laterza, 1941] 68).

from a philosophical-sociological and "poetological" perspective even determines the form and topic of the poem. The self negotiated in the text goes through phases that are entirely comparable with the development of the modern subject since its alleged discovery. In this way, the Catullus of *Carmen* 8 lands in a linguistic dilemma that—so we are told—first became a problem in postmodern theory. To the extent that "modernity always already contained its own postmodernity,"[9] Catullus's subject could also be a conglomerate capable of modernity.

Perspectives: Self-(de)structurings

If we consider *Carmen* 8 as a whole, it is significant that the first thing we notice is the splitting of the self called Catullus that is encountered in the poem. Hans Peter Syndikus describes this splitting as follows: "Out of the traditional conflict between two different attitudes in a single person, a more complicated and confusing emotional mixture has emerged in Catullus' text."[10] The expression of this confusion is, from a narratological perspective, the change of persons used by the speaker in his subjective case description:

Miser Catulle, desinas ineptire,	1
et quod vides perisse, perditum ducas.	
fulsere quondam candidi tibi soles,	
cum ventitabas quo puella ducebat	
amata nobis quantum amabitur nulla.	5
ibi illa multa cum iocosa fiebant,	
quae tu volebas nec puella nolebat,	
fulsere vere candidi tibi soles.	
nunc iam illa non volt: tu quoque inpote⟨ns noli⟩,	
nec quae fugit sectare, nec miser vive,	10
sed obstinata mente perfer, obdura.	
vale, puella. iam Catullus obdurat,	
nec te requiret nec rogabit invitam.	
at tu dolebis, cum rogaberis nulla.	
scelesta, vae te, quae tibi manet vita?	15
quis nunc te adibit? cui videberis bella?	

---

9. Geyer, *Entdeckung*, 11. A postmodern approach to Catullus's lyric poetry is taken by D. Wray, *Catullus and the Poetics of Roman Manhood* (Cambridge: Cambridge University Press, 2001) 37: "I may as well here explicitly characterize my project as an attempt to approach a premodern and preromantic Catullus by reading a postmodern Catullus."

10. H. P. Syndikus, *Catull: Eine Interpretation* (3 vols.; Darmstadt: Wissenschaftliche Buchgesellschaft, 1984–90) 1:111. The tragic figures of Euripides are viewed as models κατ᾽ ἐξοχήν for inner conflict; the motif of the inwardly torn human being has belonged to the standard repertoire of love poetry since the Hellenistic period.

quem nunc amabis? cuius esse diceris?
quem basiabis? cui labella mordebis?
at tu, Catulle, destinatus obdura.[11]   19

Wretched Catullus, you should stop fooling.   1
And what you know you've lost admit losing.
The sun shone brilliantly for you, time was,
When you kept following where a girl led you,
Loved by us as we shall love no one.   5
There when those many amusing things happened
Which you wanted nor did the girl not want
The sun shone brilliantly for you, truly.
Now she's stopped wanting, you must stop, weakling.
Don't chase what runs away nor live wretched   10
But with a mind made up be firm, stand fast.
Goodbye, girl. Catullus now stands fast,
Won't ask or look for you who're not willing.
But you'll be sorry when you're not asked for.
Alas, what life awaits you now, devil?   15
Who'll find you pretty now? What type touch you?
Whom will you love and whose be called henceforth?
Whom will you kiss? and you will bite whose lips?
But you, Catullus, mind made up, stand fast.[12]   19

The two different voices or personas initially heard in the poem dramatize in a kind of inner monologue—or asymmetrical dialogue—the attempt to avoid the threatening loss of self-control.[13] The one voice represents the irrational lover whose lack of willpower seems to be becoming a problem,[14] the other the rational mediator in this conflict between reason and emotion; this disposition may be a variation on dualistic classical concepts of the subject and their literary adaptions,

---

11. The Latin text is quoted according to R. A. B. Mynors, ed., *C. Valerii Catulli Carmina* (Oxford: Clarendon, 1958).

12. The translation is by G. Lee, ed. and comm., *The Poems of Catullus* (Oxford: Clarendon, 1990).

13. The loss of Alfenus's friendship is presented as the threat of self-loss in *Carmen* 30; particularly dramatic in this respect, however, are *Carmen* 72 and 76. Ellen Greene, for example, sees in *Carmen* 76 the lover and the poet confronted with the plurality of his own voices, which he can describe but not overcome ("The Catullan Ego: Fragmentation and the Erotic Self," *AJP* 116 [1995] 77–93, esp. p. 91). She draws similar conclusions, wrongly, from *Carmen* 8.

14. Propertius sketches a similar situation in *Elegy* 2.5. It cannot be denied that this conflict represents a Hellenistic motif (see, for example, Syndikus, *Catull*, 1:104–6); J. Godwin's commentary goes beyond the mere observation: "far more important is the issue of how the narrator . . . distances himself both from the *puella* and also from his *persona* as lover-poet" (J. Godwin, ed., *Catullus: The Shorter Poems* [Warminster: Aris & Phillips, 1999] 123).

drawing particularly on tragedy and Hellenistic poetry. The lover is addressed in lines 1–11 and in the last line (19) in the second person and given the appropriate personal pronouns; he bears the name "Catullus." The verbs addressed to this self[15] go from moderate jussive (lines 1–2) to more-intense imperatives (lines 9–11 and 19).

An exceptional role is played by *nobis* in line 5, which combines the lover and the mediator and stands in for the one-dimensional *tibi* or *mihi*.[16] The speaker, concerned to be rational, distinguishes a third person from the second at the transition from line 11 to lines 12–13, the center of the poem; although this third person bears the same name, the change appears to objectify the text.[17] We can presumably speak here of an internal focalization[18] because the speaker, to the extent that he is also the narrator, appears to know just as much as the lover. Thus, whereas the "you" is neutralized by the third person, the "I" remains absent: a first-person singular appears nowhere in the poem. The *puella*, who remains nameless and is addressed and presented as the occasion of the conflict, is however—as the object of reference— personally absent.[19] In reverse analogy to the lover, she receives in

---

15. Whereas soliloquies in the Homeric epics are primarily addressed to the different parts of the soul (καρδίη, θυμός, etc.; see further B. Snell, "Die Auffassung vom Menschen bei Homer," in *Die Entdeckung des Geistes: Studien zur Entstehung des europäischen Denkens bei den Griechen* [ed. B. Snell; 6th ed.; Göttingen: Vandenhoeck & Ruprecht, 1986; 1st ed.: Hamburg: Claaszen & Govers, 1946, 13–29]): self-apostrophe in tragedy addresses itself increasingly to the name of the speaker (especially noticeable after Euripides; see, for example, *Med.* 400–401). After this, soliloquies to one's own name also become the typical procedure in comedy (as, for example, in *sermo meretricius*) and in lyric poetry (see, for example, Theocritus 11.72); in later lyrics, the self-apostrophes from (particularly new) comedy serve not uncommonly as foil (for example, in the *paraklausithyron*). For further self-apostrophe in Catullus, see especially *Carmen* 51.13, 52, 76, and 79.

16. Wilhelm Kroll considers this to be a 'faux pas' (*Entgleisung*) and refers to the similar one in *Prop.* 2.8.17 (W. Kroll, ed. and comm., *C. Valerius Catullus* [Leipzig: Teubner, 1923; 7th ed.; Stuttgart: Teubner, 1989] 17).

17. See Syndikus, *Catull*, 109.

18. See I. J. F. de Jong, *Narrators and Focalizers: The Presentation of the Story in the Iliad* (2nd ed.; London: Bristol Classical, 2004), esp. pp. 29–40 and 101–48.

19. This diagnosis is based on the terminology of the discourse of love, such as Roland Barthes has conceived of it (*Fragments d'un discours amoureux* [Paris: Seuil, 1977] 19): "*je*, toujours présent, ne se constitue qu'en face de *toi*, sans cesse absent. Dire l'absence, c'est d'emblée poser que la place du sujet et la place de l'autre ne peuvent permuter" (Barthes's italics); "l'autre est absent comme référent, présent comme allocutaire. De cette distorsion singulière, naît une sorte de présent insoutenable; je suis coincré, entre deux temps, le temps de la référence et le temps de l'allocution: tu es parti (de quoi je me plains), tu es là (puisque je m'adresse à toi), je sais alors ce que'est le présent, ce temps difficile: un pur morceau d'angoisse" (pp. 21–22; Barthes's parentheses). See also G. Williams, *Tradition*

lines 1–11 (or rather, 9) the third person and the corresponding personal pronouns, but from line 12 onward she can no longer escape the direct address "you": here she is only associated with the second person. In the last verse, the speaker falls back into a closing self-address.

This speaker views himself from outside. The metrical division within describes a tension from within (the state of the self) and without (the given circumstances). The possibility of knowing this tension and its attribution remains initially bound to the distinction of the perspectives (the second against the third person): both stand in a correlative relationship to one another that manifests itself in the "negative reference"[20] of the one perspective to the other and in this way levels out the absoluteness of the "I" that as a logical consequence is not named in the poem. Ellen Greene has interpreted the changes of person and mood in Catullus's poem as the result of a (painful) self-splitting but relates the strategies of persuasion used by the speaker with respect to the "you" only to excessive passion: the suffering lover and speaker fall apart, as a result of erotic (self-)fragmentation, into different voices.[21]

Before pursuing the analysis of these self-splittings, I turn to one feature of subjectivity that seems to me to affiliate classical and (post-) modern forms in a particular way and requires closer attention. Subjectivity presupposes, as we have seen, the ability to distinguish between "inside and outside,"[22] that is, between what is one's own and what is not. According to a modern definition, "mental states must be recognized as being one's own," and this is true both synchronically (at the moment in which they are experienced) and diachronically (states that in the future will belong to the past must also be accepted as being one's own). This or these "(re)identifications of one's own states of mind," which also operate with intuition, were what Franz Brentano and others were thinking of when they spoke of the "uncorrectability of self-attribution."[23] The modern subject attributes a characteristic to

---

and Originality in Roman Poetry (Oxford: Clarendon, 1968) 461; Greene, "The Catullan Ego," 81; and Syndikus, *Catull*, 106.

20. Pauen, "Selbstbewußtsein," 111.

21. Greene, *The Catullan Ego*, 78 and 80–81; discussing E. Adler, *Catullan Self-Revelation* (New York: Arno, 1981).

22. Pauen, "Selbstbewußtsein," 106.

23. All quotations are taken from ibid., 106–7 and 109. Franz Brentano develops his theory about the nature of self-attributions and inner acts in the context of his *Psychologie vom empirischen Standpunkt* (3 vols.; ed. O. Kraus; Leipzig: Meiner, 1924), esp. 1:195–201.

itself when it experiences it as particularly emphasized in comparison with others. In sociological terms, one might go so far as to say that individuals only experience their (partial) identity in the reaction of (social) others to their own actions.[24] In *Carmen* 8, we can recognize such self-attributions on the part of the speaker to the "you" being spoken to, and the reference to moments of happiness now past with the *puella* presupposes a social reaction—namely, hers. The "other" or "stranger"—the *puella*—also functions here as a mirror of the emotional world of the self being negotiated.[25]

The ability of the self to distinguish includes the dialectic of autonomy and heteronomy, identity and alterity. This dialectic means that subjects seek for things similar to themselves in others, or they instrumentalize other subjects in order to find themselves mirrored within them. This notion, in turn, is based on a concept of narcissism that, in the modern period, is particularly apparent in La Rochefoucauld's *amour-propre*.[26] We can however see that Catullus's (as also, for example, Sappho's) love poetry is determined by it. This is shown not only by *Carmen* 8 but also, for example, by the endless enjoyment of the other in *Carmen* 7 or the complex desire for eternity in *Carmen* 109.[27] The personal interplays and the vigilant presence of the third person in *Carmen* 8 call a loss of the self to the "other," the *puella*, into question.

---

24. This is the position of George Herbert Mead as reported by Alois Hahn, "Was wissen die Sozialwissenschaften vom Menschen?" in *Kennen Wissenschaften den Menschen?* (ed. Rabanus-Maurus-Akademie; Frankfurt am Main: Knecht, 1980) 57–83, esp. pp. 79–83; see also von Moos, "Persönliche Identität," 3–4. This is the corollary of a sociohermeneutical problem, which recalls the paradox formulated by Jürgen Habermas:

> The relationship between I, you (another I) and we (I and the other 'I's) is . . . first created by means of an analytically paradoxical achievement. The speakers identify themselves simultaneously with two incompatible dialogue-roles and thus guarantee their identity in terms of the I as well as in terms of the group. The one (I) maintains his absolute non-identity over against the other (you); at the same time, however, by acknowledging each other as irreplaceable (*unvertretbare*) individuals, they both recognize their identity, and what binds them together is again something they have in common (we), namely a group which itself maintains its own individuality over against other groups, so that on the level of the intersubjectively bound collective the same relationship is created as between the individuals. ("Der Universalitätsanspruch der Hermeneutik," in *Hermeneutik und Dialektik: Festschrift für Hans-Georg Gadamer zum 70. Geburtstag* [2 vols.; ed. R. Bubner et al.; Tübingen: Mohr, 1970] 1:73–103, esp. p. 89)

25. See Geyer, *Entdeckung*, 69.
26. See ibid.
27. In *Carmen* 7, the number of kisses demanded by the beloved is carried with the proverbial Libyan Desert sand to absurdity; in *Carmen* 109 the speaker imagines an *aeternum foedus* (line 6).

If we were to extend the Lacanian psychoanalytical results of Paul Alan Miller,[28] we might even identify a *je-est-un-autre* transformation of the subject in Catullus, inasmuch as the speaker's "own" desire becomes a desire for the desire of the other.

Interpretation: Deconstructing and Reconstructing Identity

To Wilhelm Kroll, the structure of the poem seemed relatively simple, because it uses "scarcely any poetical devices" for its emotional impact. Kevin Newman compares it, on account of its rather bare use of simple, everyday language, to a "reportage."[29] Richard Thomas observes how, in *Carmen* 8, emotional excitement turns into art and therefore into artificiality;[30] the formal transparency serves the multi-dimensional development of the poetically transformed subject.

On a linguistic level, *Carmen* 8 is reminiscent of a dramatic monologue in the (Attic) New Comedy.[31] The striking appellative tone of the poem is supported by the hard, choliambic rhythm and the lack of enjambment.[32] Here, the dramaturgy of the process of emancipation is already visible. Its mediation also takes place by means of the temporal and perspectival structure: in terms of discourse analysis, the subject described in the poem is conceived as the crystallization point of past developments, present feelings, and future visions.[33] In this way, it makes the uncorrectability of self-attributions plausible.[34]

---

28. P. A. Miller, "Why Difference Matters: Catullus and Contemporary Theory," *CW* 9 (2002) 425–31. On the separation between poet and *persona* and their different psychological attributability, see also J. Sarkissian, *Catullus 68: An Interpretation* (Leiden: Brill, 1983). Neither Miller nor Sarkissian, however, explicitly considers the affinity to the concept of "je est un autre."

29. Kroll, ed., *C. Valerius Catullus*, 16; and J. K. Newman, *Roman Catullus and the Modification of the Alexandrian Sensibility* (Hildesheim: Weidmann, 1990) 158: "Everything in 8 seems like simple reportage."

30. R. Thomas, "Menander and Catullus 8," *Rheinisches Museum* 127 (1984) 308–16, esp. p. 316: "It is quite simply that a poem, if it is to endure, will be a work of art, not an emotional outburst. . . . We may detect emotion behind it, and we may weep when we read it; if so, that will merely be additional testimony to the poem's artistry."

31. The literary models for self-adhortation are numerous; allusions to Menander have been discussed in detail by Thomas, ibid. Thomas especially points to the similar form of the self-adhortation of the old man Demeas in the *Samia* (line 311). On parallels of content between *Carmen* 8 and comedy, see above, n. 15.

32. Line 2 has the caesura in the fourth instead of the third foot, an unusual place for it in choliambs; see Kroll, *C. Valerius Catullus*, 17.

33. According to Geyer, *Entdeckung*, 7–8.

34. See above, n. 23.

Correspondingly, *Carmen* 8 can be divided according to three temporal perspectives. The harmony with the fictitious beloved is placed in the past; alongside this temporal placement, we also find a strongly emphasized local deixis (*quo*, line 4; *ibi*, line 6). The present and the future are characterized by strife. In lines 1–2, we see an inventory that also plays a proleptic function (present: "what is the case?"); in lines 3–8, an analeptic retrospective is developed (past: "what was the case?"). The repeated reference to the current situation in lines 9–12 (present: "what is the case? what should the case be?") is followed finally in lines 13–18 by a threatening vision of the future (future: "what will the case be?"). In the last line, 19, the speaker calls the Catullus within the poem back to the present.

The poem blurts its message out straight away and draws the reader immediately into the dramatic state of mind of the divided Catullus. The emphatically placed *miser* describes in rational language a relationship to the self shaped by emotional misfortune;[35] it is adjacent to the vocative *Catulle*, a word that seems to combine the object and subject of action in one. In *ineptire*, a verb-form that Catullus uses only here, the hopelessness of remaining in his present condition becomes apparent. The semantic spectrum of this term, which goes back to *apere* (or the intensified form *aptare*), is best described in its sociorhetorical diversity by Catullus's contemporary, Cicero (*De or.* 2.17):[36]

> *quem enim nos ineptum vocamus, is mihi videtur ab hoc nomen habere ductum, quod non sit aptus, idque in sermonis nostri consuetudine perlate patet; nam qui aut tempus quid postulet non videt aut plura loquitur aut se ostentat aut eorum, quibuscum est, vel dignitatis vel commodi rationem non habet aut denique in aliquo genere aut inconcinnus aut multus est, is ineptus esse dicitur.*

> Of course the man whom we call "tactless" seems to me to bear a title derived from his want of tact, and this is most amply illustrated in our ordinary conversation, inasmuch as whosoever fails to realize the demands of the occasion, or talks too much, or advertises himself, or ignores the prestige or convenience of those with whom he has to deal, or, in short, is in any way awkward or tedious, is described as "tactless."[37]

---

35. B. Arkins interprets this self-apostrophe as "romantic irony" (*An Interpretation of the Poems of Catullus* [Lewiston, NY: Edwin Mellen, 1999] 29).

36. *Ineptiae* are popular in comedy as a negative counterpart to *aptum* (although the verb *ineptire* is not common and first appears in Terence: *Phorm.* 420; *Ad.* 934). On the substantial meaning of *ineptire* in *Carmen* 8, see also Fitzgerald (*Catullan Provocations*, 122), who quotes B. Croce's *Poesia antica* on the *naïveté* appearing in *ineptire* as the "systematic prevention of . . . self-consciousness."

37. The Latin text is quoted according to K. Kumaniecki, ed., *M. Tullius Cicero*, fasc. 3: *De Oratore* (Leipzig: Teubner, 1969; trans. E. W. Sutton and H. Rackham; London: Loeb, 1988).

The impropriety can thus refer to different sociologically relevant behaviors: to lateness, for example, or to inconvenience, unreasonability, tastelessness, talkativeness, and so on. Even if Catullus in several passages in his poems develops a strategy of dissociation that challenges social standards and suggests his own exceptional status, this social aspect seems to be sublimated in *Carmen* 8: here, the word becomes the point of departure for the poetic process of self-discovery. *Desinere* and *perire* (or *perdere*) both express the envisaged closure of the past, but the jussive in *desinas* seems less binding than the resultative perfect *perisse*, which prepares for the integration of the past. The temporal distance is in itself sufficient to ensure that the reaction remains subject to the conditions created by the *puella*. The negative result (*perisse*) is in turn bound to a perception in the indicative (*vides*, line 2); the definitive end and unambiguity of the assessment are already suspended in the same line: *perditum ducas* connects the facts with an implicit attitude of denial; the positive and the normative are separated.

After this appraisal, the view of the observing self turns to the past. The *candidi soles* (lines 3 and 8) encompass in a ring-composition a narrated past that shows itself to be simultaneously closed and fabulous in *quondam*. The subjectivity of perception is expressed unmistakably in the dative *tibi*: we are dealing with the impression of a "you" dependent on the speaker; the impression of the *puella* appears to be irrelevant. In this sense, the (*illa . . . tum*) *iocosa* (line 6) long past are also described as "only" having 'happened' (*fiebant*), rather than as something that both parties mutually and actively enjoyed.

In this passage, which already accords the *puella* only a marginal role, the speaker describes his sexual dependence on her and illustrates this by the tangible duration in the intensive *ventitabat* and the indeterminacy of the point of time: he has followed her everywhere without choice or will (*quo* = *quocumque*). *Ducebat* (line 4; cf. also *sectare*, line 10) makes the distribution of roles explicit. In this way, a relationship of domination is hinted at that is formulated with even more emphasis in other poems and that will become typical for Roman elegy.[38] In the past evoked in *Carmen* 8, it is the *puella* and she,

---

38. Paul Allen Miller has shown that Catullus's *Carmen* 11 operates with an imaginative identity in the sense of Lacan and Foucault (*Subjecting Verses: Latin Love Elegy and the Emergence of the Real* [Princeton: Princeton University Press, 2004] 429–30): Catullus depends on his relationship to Lesbia, symbolically to roles, laws, codes, and so forth; Lesbia dominates Catullus; Caesar dominates the world, and so on. This relationship of power and domination, indeed the self-assessment of the *ego* as such is substantially revised in *Carmen* 11; Catullus constitutes a subject-position with the help of the dissociation between the imaginary and the symbolic. Miller's interpretation is based on Lacan's

above all, who appear to have constituted "Catullus" as a *subiectum*: attempts at emancipation were (at that stage) not an issue. A reversal of the situation starts to emerge at line 5: the emphatic *quantum amabitur nulla*,[39] which also occurs in other poems, indicates a unique (erotic) intensity referring to the *puella* as the object of desire, but also to the lover and his agency, which appears from behind *nobis*.[40] The future form looks toward the second half of the poem and suggests eternal duration.

In line 8, the closing line of the "historical report" and a variation on its introduction in line 3, *quondam* is replaced by *vere*, a word that, here, functions as an emphatic particle but also implies an assessment: the entire line refers again only to *tibi*—that is, to the Catullus addressed at the beginning of the poem—while the memory of the speaker functions as a witness for the remembering subject. The speaker in *Carmen 76* refers to a past mediated by *memoria* in a similar way.[41] One might think that Catullus lets subjectivity become the truth.[42] This impression is strengthened by the fact that we hear nothing in *Carmen 8* about possible reasons for the *puella*'s change of heart, as we do in some other poems. We may assume that such reasons here are meaningless.

From line 9 on, attention is drawn with a sober-sounding *nunc*[43] abruptly back to the present, and as at the beginning, the tone of the poem moves to the level of negative predication. In postmodern terms, even Catullus's work on the subject is negative to the extent that it consists primarily of the "dismantling of self-deceptions" (Lacan).[44] This dismantling of self-deceptions is put in concrete poetic terms in what

---

theory that the human being becomes a social subject by entering the symbolic order of language—only then is a symbolic identity of this kind possible (see p. 32). In the interplay of subject-positions between Catullus and Lesbia, the categories of the normative subject and personal identity no longer coincide; it comes to an alternation between gender and subject-positions (see p. 48).

39. See, for example, *Carmen* 5, 37, and 87.

40. The uniqueness of love is also the focus of other poems, for example, in *Carmen* 37, 52, 87, and 107. This exceptional status is connected to an ability to orient oneself toward the outside world and thus to an "anthropology of self-transcendence" in Rousseau's sense (see Geyer, *Entdeckung*, 269).

41. *Carmen* 76 also begins with a reference to the past (line 1: *priora*) which is mediated by *memoria* (*recordari*).

42. The equation of subjectivity and truth is carried out by Kierkegaard in a critical discussion of Hegel; see Hagenbüchle, "Subjektivität," 51. A similar connection between subjectivity and truth can be found in *Carmen* 11, esp. lines 11–20.

43. The transition from *quondam* (line 1) to *nunc* (line 5) in *Carmen* 72 is comparable.

44. See Bürger, *Verschwinden*, 11.

follows, where *nec* advances in lines 10–13 to become one of the most important words: it culminates in the reciprocal play on words *velle* and *nolle*, referring to both fictitious partners (lines 7 and 9).[45] Harmony and strife appear here as acts of the will that determine each other, although the *velle* on the part of the lover initially gives the litotes in the *puella's nec . . . nolle* an oddly passive or indifferent aspect. This is, however, immediately rescinded by the simple and unambiguous *non volt* (line 9).[46]

The break with the apparently delightful past is assigned to a coping strategy that combines reason and emotion. What we have already seen in the ambivalent use of *ducere* (in line 2 as a call to reflection, in line 4 as an indication of blind obedience) is continued in *obstinata mente perfer*.[47] The dramatic force of the conflict is also expressed in the intensification from passive patience (*perfer*) to emotional severity (in the double *obstinata . . . obdura*, an opposition in which the two terms perhaps level each other out; both are hapax legomena in the *corpus Catullianum*!). This dramatic force culminates in the self-address as *impotens*[48]—but this impotence is autoreferentially overcome in the moment of its being expressed in language.

The imperative *noli* (supplied in *V* by Avantius) would nevertheless emphasize that not wanting can also become a goal. The subject so described thus appears, at least theoretically, to be in a position to free himself from his own feelings. In *Carmen 8*, controlled emotionality appears in the juxtaposition of *obstinata, mente*, and *obdura* as a solution and possible regulatory principle.[49] The will of the subject here under

---

45. Compare with the resultative *invitam* in line 13.

46. It cannot, of course, be excluded that some of the verbs used here—alongside *velle* and *nolle*, we can also think of *rogare* (line 14)—have a secondary sexual meaning (see Syndikus, *Catull*, 1:109 with n. 29; and N. Holzberg, *Catull: Der Dichter und sein erotisches Werk* [3rd ed.; Munich: Beck, 2003] 89–90). This side effect, however, in no way detracts from the autoreflexive substance of the poem.

47. On the tension between emotion and reason, see esp. poems 85 and 76: in both, inward satisfaction is opposed to reflection (85: *nescio—sentire*, line 2; 76: *voluptas—cogitare*, lines 1–2); self-torment and steadfastness are also negotiated (85.2 and 76.10–11). In *Carmen 76*, however, the will of the gods (line 12) appears as an external authority: neither an externalization of this kind nor a focus on death, such as is introduced in *Carmen 76* for dramaturgic reasons, takes place in *Carmen 8*.

48. *Impotens* is a correction from codex *R*; the *Veronensis* offers the meaningless inpote (in *X* assimilated to *impote*).

49. Greene ("Catullan Ego," 83) interprets *obdurare* as a formula belonging to the gender-specific subdiscourse in the poem: Catullus, suffering in a "female" way, calls himself back to "male" hardness. On Descartes and the possibility of liberation from one's own emotionality, see in particular Geyer, *Entdeckung*, 54–58.

negotiation, presented as the practical concern to be free from suffering, cannot be separated from its emotional foundations. Here, too, the discovery of the self circles around a reconciliation of drive and reason.[50] In Catullus, the contradictory elements become apparent as essential parts of the imagination.[51] On this level, the conflict is occasionally won by reason, if we take the *iam obdurat* in line 12 seriously. The change to the perspective of the third person has, as we have seen, a descriptive-objectifying force here, and the poet's *iam* (line 12) overtakes the *iam* of the *puella* and overpowers her in a moment: not even the triumph of a small victory in the present will be allowed to her. For the present moment, the (in Hegel's terms) "objective world" *of the poem* has been successfully assimilated to the "subjective state of mind" *of the speaker.*[52] That this process as a whole has to do with the conception of a biography is already strongly suggested by the imperative (*nec miser*) *vive* (line 10).

The look into the future begins with line 13 and is characterized by another change of person and a sudden change of mood.[53] The opening call—*vale, puella*—bids the girl farewell for the last time into the world of insignificance, and she, uncompromising to the last (*invitam*, line 13), remains without anyone to relate to, although she requires a referent.

The *scelesta, vae te* that introduces line 15 is a variation on an archaic religious formula that serves to discredit the absent, present girl. This new tone shifts the topos of uniqueness from line 5 and leads by way of the familiar strategy of emphasis to a renewed "negation" of the *puella*: *cum rogaberis* <u>*nulla*</u> (line 14). Now, however, it emerges that he, Catullus-in-the-poem, in fact constitutes her: for the *puella*, no life without him ought to be thinkable. At this point, identity and alterity fall together completely. The risk that the subject developed in the

---

50. To this extent, one could draw here on the Cartesian categories of *res cogitans* and *res extensa*.

51. By "contradictory," I also mean the irrational, inasmuch as "the process of rationalisation means an alienation of the reflecting subject from his or her irrational other": this formulation from Geyer's critical presentation of the Descartes interpretations of Foucault and Derrida (*Entdeckung*, 46).

52. According to Hegel's genealogical model, the subject is "expressed most purely" in the lyrical. Friedrich Theodor Vischer aptly describes the Hegelian transformation of the objective world by the subjective soul in his *Ästhetik oder Wissenschaft des Schönen* (1847–57) as an 'isolated ignition of the world in the subject' (*punctuelle[s] Zünden der Welt im Subjecte*) (§886).

53. The duration of love and the suddenness with which it ceases are contrasted in a similar way in *Carmen* 76 within a single line (*longum . . . subito*: line 13).

poem appeared to have taken[54] has in fact turned out to be dangerous for the *puella* in that she has been forced to subject herself to perspectives, to allow herself to be objectified.[55] The interchangeability, indeed the trivialization of the beloved without referent is unsparingly displayed in the chain of pronouns in lines 16–18. The mockery consists in the fact that this interchangeable, indeterminately impersonal, even figurative "something" is declined through all the cases (except for the ablative—this last step toward objectification is not taken by Catullus): *quis, cuius, cui, quem.* Once more, an unspoken "I" stands in the poetic space that could take the place of this impersonal whatever—if it wanted to.[56] Here, the *puella* is radically robbed of every means of development: she will suffer loss of contact (*quis . . . adibit*), she will lose her subjective-esthetic effect on others (*cui videberis bella*), she will lose *nolens volens* her emotionality (*quem amabis*) and remain without social ties (*cuius esse diceris*). To her loss of individuality is added the loss of all collective relationships. In *diceris*, we can also see the loss of language itself: if she is named "nobody's," then no one speaks of her—and of course, there can be no talk of her own ability to speak.

The lack of an address for the kisses looks at first glance to be trivial alongside these losses, but because kissing and coquettish biting is the hallmark of her existence in Catullus's poetry and represents her power over him,[57] its loss is all the more threatening: he is her creator and can make her disappear.[58] This also explains why, in *Carmen* 8, we

---

54. Compare Miller's remarks on *Carmen* 11: Lesbia reveals herself there to be a kind of *monstrum* and thus a risk for the *ego* (*Subjecting Verses*, 427).

55. This strategy is even more subtly implemented in *Carmen* 76: the *puella* is presented as weak and obstinate and thus as a personality unable to change, a sharp contrast with the *amator* described there. An improvement of his situation appears possible only by virtue of his reflection on her: the poem ends, after all, with him and his perspectives for improvement (lines 25–26: *ipse valere opto et taetrum hunc deponere morbum / o di, reddite mi hoc pro pietate mea*). In essence, we are dealing in both cases (*Carmen* 8 and 76) with a specific kind of "womanufacture" in A. Sharrock's sense ("Womanufacture," *JRS* 81 [1991] 36–49, 49): "Love poetry creates its own object, calls her Woman, and falls in love with her—or rather, with the artist's own act of creating her. This is womanufacture."

56. Similar E. A. Schmidt's commentary on this passage (*Catull* [Heidelberg: Carl Winter, 1985] 114): he diagnoses a "shift from no-one to not-I."

57. The verb *mordere* occurs only twice in the *corpus Catullianum*; its use in *Carmen* 8 appears to be its first appearance (the second is in Carmen 68.127: *mordenti*); but analogous formulations can be found (for example, *acris solet incitare morsus*, in *Carmen* 2.4).

58. That is also the case for other figures and constellations of figures within the *corpus Catullianum*. In this sense, J. P. Schwindt comments on the esthetic-programmatic *Carmen* 16 ("'Autonomes Dichten' in Rom? Die *lex Catulli* und die Sprache der literarischen Phantasie," in *Klassische Philologie inter disciplinas: Aktuelle Konzepte zu Gegenstand und Methode*

encounter so many formulations from other poems relating to the (or a) *puella* that occur both in happy, laudatory contexts and unhappy, derogatory ones.[59] At the same time, the vision of the future has an effect on the past remembered in the poem: the *puella* loses her magic as part of the fictitious romantic relationship.

The whole poem is characterized by operations of transference:[60] the lover transfers his own performed pain to the beloved. If one wanted to look at the whole poem again from this perspective and assume—with Lacan's work-technical psychology—that "one's own voice is identical with the suppressed voice of the other," then the previously described pain of the lover would be nothing other than the pain of the fictitious beloved.[61] The self-attributions, at least, become correctable again in this vision: the *puella* was a part of *himself* designed by *himself*, but he had designated this part as "other" and gradually recognized it as an "enemy" who "annihilates freedom."[62] What follows is its disciplining because the possibilities of his specific poetically excessive creativity are being unfolded.

There remains only the real ending, line 19, which looks at first glance like a return to the position of line 11 and, thus, resignation. However, this apparent return takes place under quite different conditions, and it is a different Catullus again who is here being spoken to. The fall back into the second person in the last line documents a changed situation in that the neutral perspective of the third person returns to the tactics of self-address only after the quasi-linguistic-haptic

---

eines Grundlagenfaches [ed. J. P. Schwindt; Bibliothek der Klassischen Altertumswissenschaft 110; Heidelberg: Carl Winter, 2002] 73–92, 82): "Where a description of the subject which has been intersubjectively shifted (from the speaker to his or her addressees) continues to refer to the written replacement which is dependent on the subject, there can be no topic which would be independent of this authorial subjectivity and therefore no topic which would transcend the forms of expression and desires for representation of this dominating *persona*."

59. Examples: *miser*: *Carmen* 51.5; *perdere*: *Carmen* 51.16; *soles*: *Carmen* 5.4; *quantum amabitur nulla*: *Carmen* 87.1–2; *Carmen* 37.12 (see above, n. 40); *vive*: *Carmen* 5.1; *basiare*: *Carmen* 5, *Carmen* 7, and elsewhere.

60. See Syndikus, *Catull*, 110.

61. Quotation from Hagenbüchle, "Subjektivität," 65. "Nothing other than the pain of the fictitious beloved" is the approach adopted by Miller ("Difference," 48–49) in his analysis of the relationship between "Catullus" and "Lesbia," without, however, giving closer attention to *Carmen* 8.

62. This is the radical formulation of Jean-Paul Sartre; Emmanuel Lévinas interprets the *subiectum* similarly literally as that which is subjected to an other. See further W. Schulz, *Ich und Welt: Philosophie der Subjektivität* (Pfullingen: Neske, 1979) 32–33; Hagenbüchle, "Subjektivität," 12.

overpowering of the *puella*. Thus, the Catullus of the last line can be described—in a gesture reducing the attitude of opposition (the prefix *ob-* becomes *de-*)—as *destinatus*, and the implementation of self-conscious and emotional reflection can be confirmed. This Catullus has integrated into himself the suffering lover of the second person, his objectified counterpart, the Catullus of the third person, and the speaker working toward emancipation under the influence of the vision sketched above, without giving up the diversity of perspectives implied by this plurality. This is because the perspectives do not cancel each other out but are identified in "a complex set of interrelationships":[63] the one remains the complement of the other.

The subject, trying to hold onto its identity, is thus at a remove from an *ego* that would betray intimacy and weakness. The renewal of self-address is carried out in the form of a repetition that is intensified (by the strong adversative *at*) and at the same time manipulated; it thus continues the thrust of the whole poem to repeat lines, parts of lines, or single words with slight variations. By means of this repetition, which goes beyond mere changes of emphasis in content, and through the pronounced position at the end of the poem, the self-address becomes form; it encompasses the *puella*'s announced loss of existence from both temporal directions (in coming from the past, it places itself formally *behind* the future). In this way, this poem can point beyond itself: the process that finds its tentative conclusion in *Carmen* 8 has an open end with a view to further attempts at emancipation from the imaginary romantic relationship that repeatedly include apparent "relapses" such as the one we have seen here.[64]

Readers who suspect that in the continuation of the poem from line 12 onward we are primarily dealing with the result of a passion that cannot be brought under control thus miss the point. According to such a view, the lover's obsession remains, despite his announced severity.[65]

---

63. Greene, "Catullan Ego," 91: "Although Catullus does not reconcile those 'many selves' in his poetry, he identifies them in a complex set of interrelationships that defies reduction to any unitary discursive practice or experience of the self." Greene evaluates this kind of love beyond *Carmen* 8 as *taeter morbus* and thus fails to recognize the fundamental metaphorical aspect; the same is true of M. Skinner's remarks on *Carmen* 76 ("Disease Imagery in Catullus 76.17–26," *CP* 82 [1987] 230–33).

64. Franz Stoessl dates the poem on the grounds of his biographical method to the "Zeit dieses ersten Zerwürfnisses" (*C. Valerius Catullus: Mensch, Leben, Dichtung* [Meisenheim am Glan: Hain, 1977] 103).

65. So, for example, Don Fowler in his nonetheless subtle interpretation of *Carmen* 8 ("First Thoughts on Closure: Problems and Prospect," *MD* 22 [1989] 75–122, esp. p. 99).

But what is obsessive here is not his erotic passion but his formal art—which alone constitutes the subject.[66] The linguistic form thus becomes an active tool that first creates the self and the "other," including every capacity for feeling and action. In this linguistic-poetic way, a kind of *cura sui* takes place, the function of which both on the thematic and, especially, on the formal level of the poem creates itself.

Conclusion: The Inner Circle

With respect to the whole complex of Catullus's love poetry, this poet achieves his poetic identity precisely by transforming his love for the *puella* (*Lesbia*), disguised as autobiographical material, into poetry. *Carmen* 8 belongs (alongside *Carmen* 76) to the poems in which a poet tries to distance himself from the poetic substance that apparently constitutes his identity.

In *Carmen* 8, Catullus has written a poem about inner conflicts, tensions, and above all, fragmentations. We observe a reflexive process of emphatic self-care structured as a process of self-creation. The conflict between reason and feeling results in a complex form of subjectivity that does not require (or no longer requires) an explicit "I," to such an extent that the "other," which represents a danger to the "I," has been dismantled. The *puella* as the "other," constituting the part of his own inner-poetic existence that represents a diffuse outside, has begun to compete with the division of the self. This explains why the subject also focuses itself when the "other" is observed, assessed, or addressed. The overpowered *puella*, *outside* his linguistic-poetic cosmos, is even less amenable to determination than he himself. The alterity can only become a part of the self-designed world of the subject in the poem. This is ultimately shown by the fact that the *puella* in *Carmen* 8 is even robbed of her pseudonym, *Lesbia*, while the poet allows his "selves" to come onto the stage under the name of *Catullus* and thus at least suggests that identity is a coexistence of different, constant, or unsteady selves.[67]

---

66. In this sense presumably also Schmidt, *Catull*, 114 on *Carmen* 8: "The passion is the form of the poem, and the form is the passion."

67. Catullus thus touches on a fundamental problem of every definition of "personal identity," inasmuch as this is the result of the subjective processing of personal-biographical continuity and discontinuity. To the extent that this (possible) inward continuity and constancy can be thought of and described as a "relationship to oneself," it could only be communicated outside (of language). See especially D. Henrich, "'Identität': Begriffe, Probleme, Grenzen," in *Identität* (ed. O. Marquard and K. H. Stierle; Munich: Fink, 1979) 133–86, esp. pp. 175–82.

Is perhaps the love for the *puella* in the *corpus Catullianum* every-where a metaphor for attempts at emancipation on the part of the subject trying to construct identity? This emancipation is implicitly successful by means of the poetic transformation. The poetic subject (which in the poem has become text) has created a cosmos that, in an almost romantic fashion, it carries in itself and rules. This cosmos is represented by the tension between the "you" influenced in the fic-tion, its "neutralized" counterpart, and the speaker, who is presented as sovereign. Fragmentation and the view from outside are only pos-sible by means of becoming poetry. The entire "movement of reflection of self-consciousness takes place (even here) through [a comparatively unadorned] language," which already places itself *within the poem* as an "instance of mediation" between the self and the world and func-tions as an instrument of (self-)distancing.[68] For even if metalinguistic statements can scarcely be read out of *Carmen* 8, the battle of the "selves" who appear is nevertheless sparked off by a fictitious love affair, which is in turn part of the poetic cosmos and thus calls the whole process of self-discovery into linguistic-poetic question.

Within this cosmos, "Catullus" risks his life—a "Catullus" who only includes the author of the poem to the extent that (as Giorgio Agamben has said) "the author marks the point at which a life puts itself at risk in the work."[69] Nevertheless, we cannot go beyond the level of functional description; only on this level can a claim to uniqueness, to incompara-bility be raised: this is what the *quantum amabitur nulla* (not just consti-tutive for *Carmen* 8) tells us. For from this functional perspective, the unique love of the afflicted subject is transferable to the incomparability of the poet to the extent that he is its director and thus architect of his identity/ies. The formally simple but still demanding esthetic transfor-mation of feelings and of the possibilities that they offer of overcoming them rationally are similar to a narcissistic dandyism.

This brings me to the final paradox. This narcissistic claim to incom-parability can only be part of the linguistic-poetic cosmos, with the subjects capable of knowledge and emancipation implicated in it. The author who has entered the text by way of self-negotiation can point beyond the clutches of this cosmos but cannot overcome them. As if Catullus had known of this dilemma, he begins his poem with the words *miser Catulle, desinas ineptire*. The word *ineptire* could become the

---

68. Quoted according to Geyer, *Entdeckung*, 16 (the author's parentheses).

69. G. Agamben, *Profanazioni* (Rome: Nottetempo, 2005) 77: "L'autore segna il punto in cui una vita si è giocata nell'opera."

quintessence of this dilemma, a word that as a verb is a hapax legomenon[70] in Catullus and thus verbalizes an ability to act at the very moment in which it—taken literally and in its immediate context in this
poem—appears to deny it.

---

70. See above, n. 37.

PART 3

Fiction and Fact

Forms of Talk in Hebrew Biblical Narrative: Negotiations, Interaction, and Sociocultural Context

FRANK H. POLAK

Tel Aviv University

Biblical narrative is to a large extent dominated by the dialogue, that is, the spoken interaction of two or more characters addressing one another in turn.[1] Narrative analysis, then, must consider two basic questions. First, what is it that imparts such a weight to the dialogue? We will try to answer this question by means of an analysis of some problematic dialogues and intricate negotiation processes in the tales of Moses and of Abimelech. The second question goes further: what is the social framework in which dialogic narrative can assume such great importance? In order to adjust our perspective, we will take into account reports of ancient Near Eastern dialogues and negotiation procedures as reflected in texts from Mari.

Dialogue, Interaction, Negotiation

Even though in many tales almost half of the texture is covered by spoken discourse,[2] the importance of the dialogue can hardly be indicated by merely quantitative parameters. Many scholars have noted the

---

1. According to my definition, *spoken discourse* includes the utterances that are represented as appearing in the character's voice by way of quoted discourse ("direct speech"), in interaction with the utterances of other characters or with the action sequence as such, as a reaction to what has happened, is happening, or could happen, or as a starting point for action. Extensive discourses, such as Moses' speech in the Plains of Moab (Deut 1:6–28:68) are viewed as texts in their own right; see my article, "The Style of the Dialogue in Biblical Prose Narrative," *JANES* 28 (2001) 53–95, esp. pp. 53–54.

2. See, e.g., G. Rendsburg, *Diglossia in Ancient Hebrew* (New Haven, CT: American Oriental Society, 1990) 160–61. According to A. J. C. Verheij, the books of 1–2 Samuel consist of 43.33% quoted discourse (*Verbs and Numbers: A Study of the Frequencies of the Hebrew Verbal Tense Forms in the Books of Samuel, Kings and Chronicles* [Assen: Van Gorcum, 1990] 32–36). In Genesis, Y. T. Radday and H. Shore find 42.71% spoken discourse (*Genesis: An Authorship Study* [Rome: Pontifical Biblical Institute, 1985] 24–25).

vividness imparted by the spoken exchange, its mimetic dimensions, and the special use of the dialogue to intimate the inner life of the characters and to suggest the relationship between them.[3] The attention that the narrator pays to the stylization of the dialogue is demonstrated by the fact, pointed out by Robert Alter, that in many cases two characters in interaction are using two distinct, contrasting styles.[4] However, the emphasis on the psychological dimensions of spoken discourse hardly does justice to narratives in which a character is endeavoring to persuade the addressee; for example: Abraham's negotiations with the Hittites concerning the Machpelah cave (Genesis 23), or the debate between Jephthah and the representatives of the Gileadites (Judges 11).[5]

---

3. On *spoken exchange*, see R. M. Dorson, "Oral Styles of American Folk Narrators," in *Style in Language* (ed. T. A. Sebeok; Cambridge, MA: MIT Press, 1959) 27–51, esp. pp. 43, 46–51.

On *mimetic dimensions*, see J. Licht, *Storytelling in the Bible* (Jerusalem: Magnes, 1978) 10–11; G. Genette, *Narrative Discourse: An Essay in Method* (trans. J. Lewin; Ithaca, NY: Cornell University Press, 1980) 162–65.

On *dialogue and relationships between characters*: among many discussions, I mention S. Bar-Efrat, *Narrative Art in the Bible* (JSOTSup 70; Sheffield: Almond, 1989) 64–77; R. Alter, *The Art of Biblical Narrative* (New York: Basic Books, 1980) 65–69; A. Berlin, *Poetics and Interpretation of Biblical Narrative* (Bible and Literature Series 9; Sheffield: Almond, 1983) 38–39, 64–66; M. Sternberg, *The Poetics of Biblical Narrative: Ideological Literature and the Drama of Reading* (Bloomington, IN: Indiana University Press, 1985) 11–16; G. W. Savran, *Telling and Retelling: Quotation in Biblical Narrative* (Bloomington, IN: Indiana University Press, 1988); H. C. Brichto, *Toward a Grammar of Biblical Poetics: Tales of the Prophets* (New York: Oxford University Press, 1992) 10–13, 18; and recently, A. D. Baum, "Zu Funktion und Authentizitätsanspruch der *oratio recta*: Hebräische und griechische Geschichtsschreibung im Vergleich," *ZAW* 115 (2003) 586–607. One of the characteristic features of the dialogic style is the expression of thought by means of a spoken monologue, as discussed by M. Niehoff, "Do Biblical Characters Talk to Themselves? Narrative Modes of Representing Inner Speech in Early Biblical Fiction," *JBL* 111 (1992) 577–95. In addition, one notes the description of divine inspiration as discourse uttered by God, for example, in Isa 8:1, 3; Jer 1:7, 9; 13:6; Ezek 3:16, 22; Amos 7:8, 15; 8:2 (as against Neh 2:12, "what my God had put into my mind to do"). The expressions used in Isa 5:2 and 22:14 are more delicate in that they mention the prophet's ear rather than divine speech.

4. Alter, *The Art of Biblical Narrative*, 71–74. Alter (p. 71) also points to the rhythmic symmetry of quoted discourse, which is also discussed in my paper "On Prose and Poetry in the Book of Job," *JANES* 24 (1996) 61–97, esp. pp. 67–76.

5. These cases have been discussed by N. MacDonald, "Driving a Hard Bargain? Genesis 23 and Models of Economic Exchange," in *Anthropology and Biblical Studies: Avenues of Approach* (ed. L. J. Lawrence and M. I. Aguilar; Leiden: Deo, 2004) 79–96; M. Sternfeld, "Double Cave, Double Talk: The Indirections of Biblical Dialogue," in *Not in Heaven: Coherence and Complexity in Biblical Narrative* (ed. J. P. Rosenblatt and J. C. Sitterson; Bloomington, IN: Indiana University Press, 1991) 28–57; K. M. Craig Jr., "Bargaining in Tov (Judges 11,4–11): The Many Directions of So-called Direct Speech," *Bib* 79 (1998) 76–85; E. Sand, "Two Dialogue Documents in the Bible: Genesis Chapter 23:3–18 and 1 Kings

In these tales, the social aspects of the interaction are no less important than the psychological effects.

Dialogue and Negotiations in the Ancient Near East

The social aspects of the dialogue stand out when the exchange serves as the framework for settling disputes, acquiring rights and, in general, attaining goals vis-à-vis the other participant in the encounter. Thus the discourse of the characters aims at a transaction, and the various speech acts constitute moves in a negotiation process. Although this give and take in narrative must be viewed as narrated rather than as real interaction, the narrative imagination requires the analogue of real negotiation tactics.

A negotiation process can be defined as a spoken encounter of two or more participants (sides or parties) in which one party tries to convince the other side to agree to its own proposals and point of view, and if it is unable to do so, at least to minimize possible damages to its cause. In order to achieve these ends, the skilled negotiator builds his or her case by a complicated interplay of promises, pleas, and threats, open or veiled. He uses his own assets as much as possible, while covering his weak spots or compensating for them by other means. On the other hand, he makes as much as possible of the weak spots of the opposite side and attempts to neutralize its strong points.[6] The second party must respond to these moves, divert them in another reaction, or use them for its own good.

In the ancient Near East, the art of negotiating was well developed, both in daily life and in diplomatic contacts.[7] According to texts from

---

Chapter 5:15–25," *ZABR* 8 (2002) 88–130. See also N. MacDonald, "Listening to Abraham—Listening to Yhwh: Divine Justice and Mercy in Genesis 18:16–33," *CBQ* 66 (2004) 25–43; J. R. Lundbom, "Parataxis, Rhetorical Structure, and the Dialogue over Sodom in Genesis 18," in *The World of Genesis* (ed. P. R. Davies and D. J. A. Clines; JSOTSup 257; Sheffield: Sheffield Academic Press, 1998) 136–45.

6. Various aspects of the art of negotiation are discussed by A. Galin, *The Dynamics of Negotiating: From Theory to Practice* (Hebrew; Tel Aviv: Tel Aviv University Press, 1996); eadem, *Negotiation: The Hidden Dimension* (Hebrew; Tel Aviv: Tel Aviv University Press, 2005); M. A. Neale and M. H. Bazerman, *Cognition and Rationality in Negotiation* (New York: Free Press, 1991); I. G. Asherman and S. V. Asherman, eds., *The Negotiation Sourcebook* (Amherst, MA: Human Resource Development Press, 1990); D. G. Pruitt, *Negotiation Behavior* (New York: Academic Press, 1981). At the end of the sixteenth century (1597, 1612) Francis Bacon ("Of Negociating") provided an eloquent witness to the ancient roots of the art of negotiating; see Bacon's *Essays and Colours of Good and Evil* (ed. W. A. Wright; Freeport, NY: Books for Libraries, 1972) 195–97, 287–88.

7. Negotiations in Old Babylonian texts from daily life are discussed by O. Tammuz, "Do Me a Favor! The Art of Negotiating according to Old Babylonian Letters," in *Intellectual Life of the Ancient Near East: Papers Presented at the 43rd Rencontre assyriologique*

Mari, reporting on the talks between Hammurapi and Zimrī-Līm's ministers (1770, 1764 B.C.E.), several negotiation tricks were already in use. Reports on these talks enable us to follow the course of the negotiations in detail—at least as the envoys viewed the process—the moves involved, and the reactions to these moves.[8] In particular, one notes (a) the importance of setting and (b) the atmosphere of mutual trust and cooperation; (c) the crucial role of initiative; (d) the references to the common interest and positive reviews of bilateral relationships in the past as arguments in the negotiations; (d) promises of future concessions alternating with (e) veiled threats, as an incentive to concessions;[9] (f) the use of counterproposals to meet proposals of the second party.

Conversation Analysis

When the negotiations are conducted by spoken intercourse, the course of the interaction can be analyzed through the methods of "conversation analysis" (hereafter CA), the discipline that deals with the interaction between two (or more) people speaking one to another.[10]

---

internationale. Prague, July 1–5, 1996 (ed. J. Prosecký; Prague: Academy of Sciences of the Czech Republic, Oriental Institute, 1998) 379–88. On diplomatic negotiations, see in particular B. Lafont, "Rélations internationales, alliances et diplomatie au temps des royaumes amorrites: Essay de synthèse," in *Amurru 2. Mari, Ébla et les Hourrites: Dix ans de travaux. Deuxième partie* (ed. D. Charpin and J.-M. Durand; Paris: Éditions Recherche sur les Civilisations, 2001) 213–328; J.-G. Heintz, "Nouveaux traités d'époque babylonienne ancienne et formules d'alliance de la bible hébraique," in *Les rélations internationales: Actes du Colloque de Strasbourg 15–17 juin 1993* (ed. Ed. Frézouls and A. Jaquemin; Paris: Boccard, 1995) 69–94; D. Elgavish, *The Diplomatic Service in the Bible and Ancient Near Eastern Sources* (Hebrew; Jerusalem: Magnes, 1998).

    8. See my paper "Negotiating with Ḥammū-rāpi: A Case Study," in *Birkat Shalom: Studies in the Bible, Ancient Near Eastern Literature, and Postbiblical Judaism Presented to Shalom M. Paul* (ed. C. Cohen et al.; Winona Lake, IN: Eisenbrauns, 2008) 643–65.

    9. On threat and promise, see also T. C. Schelling, "An Essay on Bargaining," *The American Economic Review* 46 (1956) 281–306, esp. pp. 293–301.

    10. See in general, J. Gumperz, *Discourse Strategies* (Cambridge: Cambridge University Press, 1982); I. Hutchby and R. Wooffitt, *Conversation Analysis: Principles, Practices and Applications* (Cambridge: Polity, 1998). A critical discussion that views conversation as part of an interpersonal interaction, including "face work," gestures, and silence is offered by E. Goffman, *Forms of Talk* (Philadelphia: University of Pennsylvania Press, 1983) 5–54, 60–72. Dialogue structure in biblical narrative is discussed by C. L. Miller, *The Representation of Speech in Biblical Hebrew Narrative: A Linguistic Analysis* (HSM 55; Atlanta: Scholars Press, 1996) 235–43, 257–61; R. F. Person, *In Conversation with Jonah: Conversation Analysis, Literary Criticism, and the Book of Jonah* (JSOTSup 220; Sheffield: Sheffield Academic Press, 1996). A goal-oriented view of conversation, which by implication turns into a deal, as proposed by W. Edmondson (*Spoken Discourse: A Model for Analysis* [London: Longman, 1981] 75–87), is upheld in my papers "On Dialogue and Speaker Status in the Scroll of Ruth," *Beit Mikra* 46 (2000–2001) 193–218 (Hebrew with English summary);

While it is to be admitted that a literary dialogue lacks many of the characteristics of actual spoken interaction, the alternation of speaking turns, initiative and response, rejection and counterproposal is prolific in drama and literary dialogues and thus requires the insights gained by CA, even if in narrative it is the narrator who governs the entire encounter.[11] In biblical narrative one notes, for example, the alternation of question and response in the Goliath tale. When Saul asks, "Whose son is that boy, Abner?" and the latter answers, "By your life, Your Majesty, I do not know" (1 Sam 17:55), this is an instance of initiative and response.[12] Saul's reaction closes the exchange, "Then find out whose son that young fellow is" (v. 56). No less characteristic is the alternation of blessing and response as Boaz greets his harvesters, "The Lord be with you!" and they answer, "The Lord bless you!" (Ruth 2:4).

At the final stage of the conversation between Adonijah and Bathsheba, the prince entreats the queen mother: "Please ask King Solomon—for he won't refuse you—to give me Abishag the Shunammite

and "On Dialogue and Speaker Status in Biblical Narrative," *Beit Mikra* 48 (2002–3) 1–18, 97–119 (Hebrew with English summary); and, of late, V. H. Matthews, *More Than Meets the Ear: Discovering the Hidden Contexts of Old Testament Conversations* (Grand Rapids: Eerdmans, 2008).

11. The literary status of written dialogue is clarified by Kenneth M. Craig Jr., "In Conversation with 'In Conversation,'" *JHS* 1 (1996/97, article 2; http://www.arts.ualberta.ca/JHS/); and R. F. Person Jr., "Continuing the Conversation on Jonah: A Response to Miller and Craig," ibid. Remarkably, the Middle Assyrian *Tukulti-Ninurta Epic* reflects the diplomatic negotiations between the Assyrian king Tukulti-Ninurta I (1244–1208), and the king of Babylon Kashtiliash IV (1242–1235) through a literary prism; see P. Machinist, "Literature as Politics: The Tukulti-Ninurta Epic and the Bible," *CBQ* 38 (1976) 455–82; idem, *Before the Muses: An Anthology of Akkadian Literature* (2 vols.; 2nd ed.; ed. B. R. Foster; Bethesda, MD: CDL, 1995) 1:212–30, esp. ii 25′–v 30′.

Actually, an early systematic discussion of conversation structure in the novel is is presented by a literary scholar: E. Lämmert, *Bauformen des Erzählens* (Stuttgart: Metzler, 1955) 214–33. D. Burton applies the methods of conversation analysis to the structure of drama (*Dialogue and Discourse: A Sociolinguistic Approach to Modern Drama Dialogue and Naturally Occurring Conversation* [London: Routledge & Kegan Paul, 1980]); see also V. Herman, *Dramatic Discourse: Dialogue as Interaction in Plays* (London: Routledge, 1995); M. Toolan, *Language in Literature: An Introduction to Stylistics* (London: Arnold, 1998) 194–213; M. Coulthard, *An Introduction to Discourse Analysis* (2nd ed.; London: Longman, 1985) 180–92; Person, *In Conversation with Jonah*, 11; concerning antiquity: R. Müller, *Sprechen und Sprache: Dialoglinguistische Studien zu Terenz* (Heidelberg: Carl Winter, 1996) 15–64. Texts such as the letters by Zimrilim's ministers present an authentic report of the dialogue in the sense that it is formulated by one of the participants.

12. Or in the terms of conversation analysis, an adjacency pair (Hutchby and Wooffitt, *Conversation Analysis*, 39–43, 47–53); see also Miller, *Representation of Speech*, 235–43, 257–61; Person, *In Conversation with Jonah*, 16–22, 37–40, 44–50; Müller, *Sprechen und Sprache*, 17; Lämmert, *Bauformen des Erzählens*, 214–16.

as wife." She accepts his request: "Very well. I will speak to the king in your behalf" (1 Kgs 2:17–18).[13] These examples suffice to demonstrate the importance of CA for biblical narrative.

The latter examples of spoken interaction return us to the negotiation process, which is as well-known in biblical narrative as it is in antiquity, even though the tactics differ from modern methods in many respects. Accordingly, we must consider the tactics used by the different parties. A second, but no less important issue relates to the weight the narrator attaches to such negotiations, and to the sensitivity he expects from the audience/reading public. Finally, and most importantly, we must raise the question what kind of society it is in which narratives on negotiations play such a central role.

Narrative Codes and Norms

Because we are studying negotiation tactics of a different culture, as mediated through ancient narrative, we must expect to encounter structures other than the patterns to which we are accustomed. After all, the ways of narrative are to a large extent conditioned by cultural norms that are correlative with the societal framework. How strong this dependence is has been shown by the linguistic anthropologist S. B. Heath in her analysis of the narrative attitudes in two nearby American blue-collar communities, with a Caucasian and an Afro-American population, respectively.[14] In the former community, parents encouraged their children to give factually accurate accounts of what happened. By their parents' attitude and guiding questions ("What happened next?"), children learn to "report exactly how something is said, maintain a single consistent label for items and events, and render stories in absolute chronological order."[15] On the other hand, in the Afro-American community, children were asked to embroider on the themes they had touched upon and thus to embellish their narrative in order to capture attention, rather than to report the actual event.[16] Nar-

---

13. One also notes the subsequent conversation of Bathsheba and Solomon, who rejects his mother's request (1 Kgs 2:22–23); and, by the same token, the conversation between Joab and Benaiah (v. 30). A classic example of a game of initiative and response is encountered in the tale of the Tekoite woman (2 Sam 14:4–20).

14. S. B. Heath, *Ways with Words: Language, Life, and Work in Communities and Classrooms* (Cambridge: Cambridge University Press, 1983) 19–57.

15. Ibid., 157–66. Notably, this is not the way childen were taught in the nursery school (pp. 165–66).

16. Ibid., 166–84, 18; see also J. Maybin, "Language and Education," in *The Routledge Companion to Sociolinguistics* (ed. C. Llamas, L. Mullany, and P. Stockwell; London; Routledge, 2007) 158–629. Similar distinctions are made by J. P. Gee, "Two Styles of Narrative

rative traditions, then, are related to cultural norms and societal context.[17] The interpretation of quoted dialogue and negotiation tactics also involves this sort of culturally conditioned narrative codes. What, then, is the place of negotiations in biblical narrative?

The Tactics of a Negotiator

The bilateral relations between Israel under David and the post-Hittite kingdom of Hamath (2 Sam 8:8–10) entail a negotiation process. As shown by Mari texts, the presents Toi offered to David are an integral part of a diplomatic accord.[18] The exchange of messages between Hiram and Solomon (1 Kgs 5:15–24[1–10]) pretends to reflect diplomatic negotiations, even though the reponsibility for the literary form of these royal missives lies with the historian-redactor-narrator.[19]

Abimelech, Isaac, and Abraham

A characteristic negotiation situation presents itself in the short episode of the agreement reached by Isaac and Abimelech of Gerar (Gen 26:26–31). Because this tale ends with a sworn agreement, it concerns negotiations regarding the relationship between the two ethnic groups and thus parallels, in a sense, the international negotiations between Niqmaddu and Šuppiluliuma, or between Zimrī-Līm and Hammurapi.[20]

Construction and Their Linguistic and Educational Implications," *Discourse Processes* 12 (1989) 287–307. Hence the justification for criticizing the criteria of literary-historical criticism, as reflected by, e.g., R. W. L. Moberly, *At the Mountain of God: Story and Theology in Exodus 32–34* (JSOTSup 22; Sheffield: JSOT Press, 1983) 28–30; S. Niditch, *Oral World and Written Word: Ancient Israelite Literature* (Louisville: Westminster John Knox, 1996) 110–17.

17. See F. C. Bartlett, *Remembering: A Study in Experimental and Social Psychology* (Cambridge: Cambridge University Press, 1932) 63–94; idem, "Some Experiments on the Reproduction of Folk Stories," *Folklore* 31 (1920) 30–47; reprinted in *The Study of Folklore* (ed. A. Dundes; Englewood Cliffs, NJ: Prentice-Hall, 1965) 247–58, esp. pp. 251–56 (and the comments by Dundes on pp. 244–45).

18. See 1 Sam 18:3–4 and my paper, "The Covenant at Mount Sinai in the Light of Texts from Mari," in *Sefer Moshe: The Moshe Weinfeld Jubilee Volume—Studies in the Bible and the Ancient Near East, Qumran, and Postbiblical Judaism* (ed. C. Cohen, A. Hurvitz, and S. M. Paul; Winona Lake, IN: Eisenbrauns, 2004) 119–34, esp. pp. 131–32.

19. Recently this section has been discussed by Sand, "Two Dialogue Documents in the Bible."

On the historian-narrator, see, e.g., C. F. Burney, *Notes on the Hebrew Text of the Book of Kings* (Oxford: Clarendon, 1903) 53; J. A. Montgomery, *A Critical and Exegetical Commentary on the Books of Kings* (ed. H. S. Gehman; ICC; Edinburgh: T. & T. Clark, 1951) 133.

20. See my paper, "Negotiating with Ḥammu-rāpi"; Elgavish, *The Diplomatic Service in the Bible and Ancient Near Eastern Sources*, 62–73 [Hebrew].

The first step in our analysis is to consider the arrangement of the interaction between Isaac and Abimelech as an encounter of two participants speaking in turn, of which the one is the initiator, opening with a proffer, and the second is the respondent, who counters with a reply.[21] The reply can signify acceptance (the "preferred" response from the initiator's point of view) or rejection, refusal or refutation (a "dispreferred" response).[22] The respondent may also prefer dodging the question (which would be "dispreferred" as well); silence may indicate various different responses, dependent on the context.[23] In the following discussions, the speaking turns will be indicated as T1, T2, and so on. The initiator's turns will be indicated as *a*, the respondent's as *b*; thus we have T1 a, T1 b; T2 a, T2 b; and so on. This notation will include silent responses.

A second aspect of the negotiation process pertains to the interlocutors' moves—that is, any speech act by one of the parties that changes the situation in the interactional framework (including nonlinguistic acts).[24] Consider, for instance, the opening of the Isaac-Abimelech tale:

T1 a   Gen 26:6   ואבימלך הלך אליו מגרר ואחזת מרעהו ופיכל שר־צבאו

Abimelech's arrival at the scene could not be described as a speech act but does definitely constitute a move that opens the interaction, and thus the arrival itself is not an encounter.[25] Isaac meets the party from Gerar with a challenge:[26]

T1 b   v. 27   ויאמר אלהם יצחק מדוע באתם אלי ואתם שנאתם אתי ותשלחוני מאתכם

---

21. Hutchby and Wooffitt, *Conversation Analysis*, 38–69; Polak, "Dialogue and Speaker Status in Ruth," 194–96 ; idem, "Dialogue and Speaker Status in Biblical Narrative," 2–8.

22. In CA (Hutchby and Wooffitt, *Conversation Analysis*, 43–47) answers are classified as "preferred" / "dispreferred" responses, rather than as "positive" / "negative": if the preceding question was in the negative mood, "yes" may entail a negative answer, and "no" may indicate acceptance.

23. See C. L. Miller, "The Pragmatics of *waw* as a Discourse Marker in Biblical Hebrew Dialogue," *ZAH* 12 (1999) 165–91. See also pp. 185–86 below.

24. Goffman (*Forms of Talk*, 24) defines a "move" as "any full stretch of talk or of its substitutes [e.g., 'body language'] which has a distinctive unitary bearing on some set or other of circumstances in which the participants find themselves . . . such as a communication system, ritual constraints, economic negotiating, character contests . . . , or whatever."

25. See Edmondson, *Spoken Discourse*, 34–37. An additional category includes "paralinguistic" acts, such as laughing, weeping, or falling silent.

26. Because we are dealing with narrative in which the narrator allows the character to act as he sees fit, any reference to actions and spoken discourse by the characters must be understood as referring to acts in the narrative world as represented by the narrator.

How are we to understand Isaac's reaction? Is he simply expressing his resentment at his expulsion from Gerar (26:13–16)? The methods of CA enable us to interpret this move in light of the reaction of the other side, based on the way the move was received. Abimelech and his company seem eager to please the complainant:

T2 a   vv. 28–29

ויאמרו ראו ראינו כי־היה ה' עמך ונאמר תהי נא אלה בינותינו
בינינו ובינך ונכרתה ברית עמך: אם־תעשה עמנו רעה כאשר
לא נגענוך וכאשר עשינו עמך רק־טוב ונשלחך בשלום
אתה עתה ברוך ה'

In order to explain their position and intentions, Abimelech and his party shower praise on Isaac. This reaction goes far beyond the rebuttal implied in the asseveration, ". . . just as we have not molested you but have always dealt kindly with you and sent you away in peace."[27] Abimelech concludes, as he opened, with a blessing, "From now on, be you blessed of the Lord." In other words, even though Abimelech makes sure he dismisses Isaac's complaint, he goes a fair way to appease his neighbor. These concessions are the outcome of Isaac's aggressive reaction to the king's appearance at his encampment. This reaction, then, was a matter of tactics rather than mere anger. Isaac did not allow them time to state their case but took the initiative and almost by force extracted the concessions he needed. And indeed, now that he has attained his goal, he is ready to proceed with the covenant ceremony:

T2 b   v. 30

ויעש להם משתה ויאכלו וישתו

The next day, they can exchange oaths and bid one another farewell. Isaac's tactics have paid off.

A different story is told regarding the agreement between Abimelech and Abraham (Gen 21:22–30), which is generally considered a doublet of the Isaac tale.[28] This narrative likewise opens with the appearance of Abimelech and his party, but this time they take the initiative and propose a sworn alliance (vv. 22–23). Abraham's reaction is positive, אנכי אשבע (v. 24), expressing his readiness for an accord of this sort. Nevertheless, Abraham continues to raise problems and berates Abimelech about the wells he has dug (v. 25). Only when Abimelech

---

27. My English renderings follow the NJPSV unless indicated otherwise.

28. The reader may find a slightly more elaborate discussion of this passage in my paper, "Speaking of Kingship—The Institution of the Monarchy in Israel: Negotiations, Historical Memory and Social Drama," in *Religious Responses to Political Crises* (ed. H. Reventlow and Y. Hoffman; Library of Hebrew Bible/Old Testament Studies 444; London: T. & T. Clark, 2008) 1–15, esp. pp. 1–11.

assures him that he had no hand in the matter (v. 26) does Abraham
continue with the ceremony (v. 27).

One may wonder how Abraham could retreat that easily from his
positive response.[29] From a linguistic point of view, however, אשבע, as
a *yiqtol* form, should be construed as a volitive rather than as a simple
present or a future tense.[30] Abraham, then, does not reject Abimelech's
overtures but uses Abimelech's interest in normalizing the relationship to attain a satisfactory settlement on the question of the wells.
Thus, the expression of his readiness to accept the Philistine proposal
serves Abraham in preparation for the demands he intends to raise.
An aggressive reaction could have jeopardized the prospects opened
by Abimelech's interest in an agreement. In this respect, Abraham's
stance differs from Isaac's in that Isaac had already experienced much
Philistine hostility (26:13–16) and thus had nothing to lose.

Moses and Pharaoh

Another striking negotiation process is found in the narrative of the
appearance of Moses and Aaron before Pharaoh to convey the divine
demand to the king (Exod 5:1–5). The opening clause (5:1) introduces
the two brothers as the initiators of the exchange and Pharaoh as the addressee:[31] "Afterward Moses and Aaron came and said to Pharaoh":[32]

---

29. Gunkel, followed, in substance by, for example, Westermann, finds a contradiction here that indicates division into source E (vv. 23–24, 27) and J$_b$ (vv. 25–26);
H. Gunkel, *Genesis übersetzt und erklärt* (Handkommentar zum Alten Testament 1/1; 3rd
ed.; Göttingen: Vandenhoeck & Ruprecht, 1910) 233–35; C. Westermann, *Genesis* (3 vols.;
Biblischer Kommentar: Altes Testament 1; Neukirchen-Vluyn: Neukirchener Verlag,
1974–82) 2:425–26.

30. See Y. Endo, *The Verbal System of Classical Hebrew in the Joseph Story: An Approach
from Discourse Analysis* (Assen: Van Gorcum, 1996) 47–49, 59; B. K. Waltke and M. P.
O'Connor, *An Introduction to Biblical Hebrew Syntax* (Winona Lake, IN: Eisenbrauns,
1990) 506–10.
In an outright undertaking of the obligation "I will swear" as a performative, one
would expect the instantaneous perfect, as shown by S. R. Driver, *A Treatise on the Use of
the Tenses in Hebrew* (3rd ed.; Oxford: Clarendon, 1892) 15; Endo, *The Verbal System*, 58;
Waltke and O'Connor, *Introduction to Biblical Hebrew Syntax*, 488.

31. The opening of a dialogue customarily indicates both initiator and addressee
(e.g., Gen 3:1; 23:3; 25:29–30; 37:5–6; 1 Kgs 5:16[5:2]; Ruth 1:8; 2:2, 5, 8; 4:1) and appears
even when all participants have been mentioned before in the preceding exposition, for
example, Gen 25:29–30; 31:26, 36; see L. J. de Regt, *Participants in Old Testament Texts and
the Translator* (Assen: Van Gorcum, 1999) 18–19; Polak, "Dialogue and Speaker Status in
Biblical Narrative," 6–8.

32. Following Everett Fox, rendering MT ואחר באו. Modern versions, such as the
NJPSV or the NRSV render בָּאוּ as 'went'. But in the present verse, the Hebrew (followed
by the LXX, targums, Peshitta, and Vulgate) centers on the endpoint rather than on the
way toward it. See Everett Fox, *Now These Are the Names: A New English Rendition of the
Book of Exodus* (New York: Schocken, 1986) 34.

T1 a Exod 5:1   כה־אמר ה' אלהי ישראל שלח את־עמי ויחגו לי במדבר

Pharaoh's reply is outright rejection and blunt refusal to recognize the deity:

T1 b v. 2   ויאמר פרעה מי ה' אשר אשמע בקלו לשלח את־ישראל
             לא ידעתי את ה' וגם את־ישראל לא אשלח

This move is followed by a renewed demand by the two brothers:

T2 a v. 3   ויאמרו אלהי העברים נקרא עלינו נלכה נא דרך שלשת ימים במדבר
         ונזבחה לה' אלהינו פן־יפגענו בדבר או בחרב

On the face of it, this demand parallels the appeal in the opening of the tale and could thus be regarded as a doublet from a different source.[33] However, renewal of initiative is a normal move when the first proffer is rejected.[34] In the tale at hand, the renewal of the demand is underlined by a number of explanations and elaborations. In particular, one notes the menacing פן יפגענו בדבר או בחרב, which in view of the preceding nocturnal assault on Moses (4:24–26) should not be considered an empty threat: if Pharaoh will not comply, the work force will be smitten. The reference to אלהי העברים clarifies the identity of the deity in whose name the brothers are speaking, and the mention of the divine apparition (נקרא עלינו) heightens their authority. On the other hand, the elaboration of the goal of the journey, a three-day journey in order to sacrifice to God, must show that their demand is far from immoderate.[35]

Pharaoh's response is negative again:

---

33. For the attribution of 5:1–2 to E and of v. 3 to J, see B. Baentsch, *Exodus. Leviticus. Numeri* (Handkommentar zum Alten Testament; Göttingen: Vandenhoeck & Ruprecht, 1903) 37–38; S. R. Driver, *Exodus* (Cambridge Bible Commentary; Cambridge: Cambridge University Press, 1911) 34–35. H. Holzinger, however, views v. 1a as crucial for J and vv. 1b–2 as compatible with v. 3 (*Exodus* [Kurzer Hand-Commentar zum Alten Testament; Tübingen: Mohr-Siebeck, 1900] 17); followed by W. H. Schmidt, *Exodus*, vol. 1 (Biblischer Kommentar: Altes Testament 2; ; Neukirchen-Vluyn: Neukirchener Verlag, 1988) 246; W. H. C. Propp, *Exodus 1–18: A New Translation with Introduction and Commentary* (AB 2; New York: Doubleday, 1999) 249–50.

34. Edmondson, *Spoken Discourse*, 89–93; Lämmert, *Bausteine des Erzählens*, 215; in biblical narrative, one notes, for instance, the reassertion of the promise in Gen 18:14 in contrast to its first utterance in v. 10.

35. The motif of a three-day journey recalls the three-day journey in the desert until the Israelite trek reached Marah (Exod 15:22–23). This allusion is all the more significant because the Marah tale also contains covenant elements (15:25b–26); see my paper, "Water, Rock and Wood: Structure and Thought Pattern in the Exodus Narrative," *JANES* 25 (1997) 19–42, esp. pp. 21–22, 25–26. Accordingly, the demand of 5:3 could reflect an ancient tradition rather than a mere subterfuge.

T2 b   5:4   ויאמר אלהם מלך מצרים למה משה ואהרן תפריעו את־העם ממעשיו
                 לכו לסבלתיכם

This time, Pharaoh's refusal is underlined by the use of his title "king of Egypt." Thus the narrator highlights Pharaoh's authority,[36] contrasting it with the powerlessness of Moses and Aaron, whom he summarily returns to the labor force. The threat is dismissed in an additional comment:

v. 5   ויאמר פרעה הן־רבים עתה עם הארץ והשבתם אתם מסבלתם

Because in Pharaoh's opinion the main problem is the growth of the Israelite population ("the people of the land are already so numerous"), he is not impressed by the threat of divine affliction. This rebuttal deprives Moses and Aaron of any argument they may have had.

These segments show that some of the problems besetting the interpretation of biblical narrative are related to the way the narrator allows his characters to develop their negotiation tactics. Nowhere is the problematic of negotiation tactics more clear than in Moses' expostulation in the wake of the festivities of the Golden Calf.

Moses' Entreaties to God

The threat of catastrophic divine punishment in the wake of the dance around the Golden Calf urges Moses to intervene on behalf of his people. The Sinai narrative presents us with a series of intercessory prayers and actions on the part of Moses, as well as divine responses and decisions, but the order and coherence of the stages of both the events and the speeches remain problematic to such a degree that even a redactional hypothesis cannot be said to provide a solution.[37] Rather than more analysis, we need a different perspective. Text-immanent

---

36. The title "king of Egypt" is also used in the introduction of "the cupbearer and the baker of the king of Egypt" (Gen 40:1, 5), the authority bestowed on Joseph (41:46), and in the scene of the midwives who defied his authority (Exod 1:15–18). The status of authority is also at the center of Exod 3:18–19; 6:11, 13, 27; 14:8.

37. A review that highlights the extreme diversity in recent critical treatment of chaps. 32–34 ultimately indicates three problem fields (K. Schmid, "Israel am Sinai: Etappen der Forschungsgeschichte zu Ex 32–34 in seinen Kontexten," in *Gottes Volk am Sinai: Untersuchungen zu Ex 32–34 und Dtn 9–10* (ed. M. Köckert and E. Blum; Gütersloh: Chr. Kaiser, 2001) 9–40, esp. pp. 33–35. Detailed proposals of possible redactional stratification are offered by, for example, J. C. Gertz, "Beobachtungen zu Komposition und Redaktion in Exodus 32–34," in *Gottes Volk am Sinai*, 88–106; E. Aurelius, *Der Fürbitter Israels: Eine Studie zum Mosesbild im Alten Testament* (Coniectanea Biblica: Old Testament 27; Stockholm: Almqvist & Wiksell, 1988) 57–105; see also, e.g., Holzinger, *Exodus*, 108–10; Baentsch, *Exodus*, 268–85; Driver, *Exodus*, 346–63.

exegesis has indeed contributed much to the interpretation of this pericope,[38] but many details remain problematic; it has not been able to throw light on the norms underlying the narrative.

In these chapters, a series of entreaties and appeals by Moses with the aim of appeasing the divine fury (32:30–34; 33:12–23)[39] interacts with responses by God, who announces a radical and definitive penalty but grants mercy. Moses, on the other hand, takes harsh punitive steps but demands and eventually obtains forgiveness.[40] This sequence of appeals and responses indicates dialogue and negotiation[41] and thus should be viewed in the complex perspective of negotiation tactics.

Moses' Plea (Exodus 32:7–35)

The notion of negotiations between God and human agents necessarily is problematic, because mortals must always doubt their ability to prevail over the deity. The tale of Moses' call ends with the divine command to carry out the divine commission (Exod 4:14–16), in spite of Moses' objections. Moreover, the deity will always perceive human

---

38. Detailed rhetorical interpretations are proposed from a canonical perspective by M. Widmer, *Moses, God and the Dynamics of Intercessory Prayer* (FAT 8; Tübingen: Mohr Siebeck, 2004) 91–225; Moberly, *The Mountain of God*, 66–83, 182–88; E. G. Newing, "Up and down—in and out: Moses on Mount Sinai. The Literary Unity of Exodus 32–34," *Australian Biblical Review* 41 (1993) 18–34. On the views of Brichto and Irwin, see nn. 40–41 below. Redactional-authorial unity is proposed by B. S. Childs, *Exodus: A Commentary* (OTL; London: SCM, 1974) 557–58, 608–10; E. Blum, "Israël a la Montagner de Dieu: Remarques sur Ex 19–24; 32–34 et sur le contexte littéraire et historique de sa composition," in *Le Pentateuque en question: Les origines et la composition des cinq premiers livres de la Bible à la lumière des recherches récentes* (ed. A. de Pury and T. Römer; 3rd ed.; Geneva: Labor & Fides, 2002) 271–95, esp. pp. 279–82; C. Houtman, *Exodus* (3 vols.; Historical Commentary on the Old Testament; Kampen: Kok / Leuven: Peeters, 1993–2000) 3:605. M. Buber discusses two leading words in chaps. 32–33, עם and עלה ("Das Leitwort und der Formtypus der Rede," *Werke* [3 vols.; Heidelberg: Kösel & Schneider, 1964] 2:1150–58); see also idem, *Moses: The Revelation and the Covenant* (New York: Harper & Row, 1958) 147–56.

39. In the deuteronomic recast (on which, see Widmer, *Moses, God and the Dynamics of Intercessory Prayer*, 38–39, 99–90) only the latter thread remains (Deut 9:18–19), whereas the ordeal has disappeared, as the ashes of the calf were cast away (v. 21).

40. The interplay of these two movements has been highlighted by W. H. Irwin, "The Course of the Dialogue between Moses and Yhwh in Exodus 33:12–17," *CBQ* 59 (1997) 629–36, esp. pp. 630–31.

41. The interaction, intuitively but significantly developed in *Midr. Exod. Rab.* 42:1, 3, 10; and 43:1–7 is mentioned by Buber ("Leitwort," 1150, 1153, 1157), Childs (*Exodus*, 567, 572, 593), and Houtman (*Exodus*, 679) and highlighted by Widmer, *Intercessory Prayer*, 90, 94; Irwin, "Course of the Dialogue"; Y. Muffs, "Who Will Stand in the Breach? A Study of Prophetic Intercession," *Love and Joy: Law, Language and Religion in Ancient Israel* (New York: Jewish Theological Seminary, 1992) 9–48, esp. pp. 12–15; S. E. Balentine, *Prayer in the Hebrew Bible: The Drama of Divine-Human Dialogue* (Minneapolis: Fortress, 1991) 18–20, 136–39; H. C. Brichto, "The Worship of the Golden Calf," *HUCA* 54 (1983) 1–44, esp. pp. 24–28.

thought and intention, like Sarah's laughter (Gen 18:12), but no human is able to fathom the intentions behind divine utterances in full, to assess the goals behind them, and thus to adopt suitable tactics.[42] This problem must be taken into account when we analyze the moves of both intercessor and deity.

Did the "great sin" of calf worship leave room for negotiations with the deity?[43] How could Moses dare to defy God? An answer to this question is suggested by the comments transmitted by *Midr. Exod. Rab.* (42:10) on God's proclamations of his intention to destroy Israel, הניחה ל ויחר־אפי בהם ואכלם (Exod 32:10, 'let me be, that my anger may flare against them and I may destroy them', Everett Fox).[44] According to the anonymous exegete, the opening הניחה לי,[45] in its very redundancy, helped Moses to understand that God actually left the decisison to him and wanted him to serve as intercessor. This interpretation, adopted by Rashi and Radak,[46] was rejected by Abarbanel as midrashic but dovetails with the findings of pragmatics and speech-act theory, because it places the possibility of Moses' interference on the agenda.[47] But Moses,

---

42. The importance of the knowledge of the other side's intentions and limits is indicated by Schelling, "On Bargaining," 281–83. In the negotiations between Hammurapi and the king of Mari, one notes Asqudu's letter to Zimrilim concerning the intentions of the Babylonian king (*AEM* I/1, text 40, lines 6–14).

43. The critical status of vv. 9–10, introduced as they are by ויאמר ה׳, following וידבר ה׳ in v. 7, is problematic. Driver (*Exodus*, 351; unlike Baentsch, *Exodus*, 270) attributes vv. 9–10 to the redactor (R^JE), in contrast to vv. 7–8. But the repetition of the *inquit* in v. 9 is in accordance with the norms of biblical narrative and could indicate a pause in the divine speech, as shown on pp. 186–87 below.

44. Fox, *Now These Are the Names*, 180.

45. The midrash likens the position of Moses toward God to that of the *paedagogos* toward the father who took his son into the bedroom in order to chastise him but cried from within the room not to withold him from punishing his son. By these cries, the *paedagogos* understood that the decision was up to him. A similar explanation is presented in the Babylonian Talmud with regard to Deut 9:14 (*b. Ber.* 32a).

46. See also Widmer, *Intercessory Prayer*, 97–101; Balentine, *Prayer in the Hebrew Bible*, 136; Childs, *Exodus*, 567.

47. The notion of "raising the question" is introduced by J. R. Searle, *Speech Acts: An Essay in the Philosophy of Language* (Cambridge: Cambridge University Press, 1969) 124–25; the importance of indirect illocutionary acts is discussed by, for example, R. Carston, *Thoughts and Utterances: The Pragmatics of Explicit Communication* (Malden, MA: Blackwell, 2002) 15–49; D. M. Bell, "Innuendo," *Journal of Pragmatics* 27 (1997) 35–59. In this context, S. Hurvitz and I. M. Schlesinger speak of extrapolation ("Studying Implicit Messages: A Different Approach," *Journal of Pragmatics* 41 [2009] 738–52, esp. pp. 742, 744–45). S. Nicolle and B. Clark show that participants in their experiments "try to work out the overall communicative intention behind the utterance" ("Experimental Pragmatics and What Is Said: A Response to Gibbs and Moise," *Cognition* 69 [1999] 337–54, esp. p. 351).

virtually powerless in face of the divine ire, needs particular means to persuade his suzerain. The arguments he uses refer to acts of divine grace, the delivery from Egypt, and the promises to the patriarchs (vv. 11, 13). These are the values by which God motivates the initiation of the covenant with Israel, and now these values serve Moses as grounds for his plea against heavy punishment of the people.[48] Moreover, Moses argues that the Egyptians will revile God for the annihilation of the Israelites, thus offsetting the foreign recognition of his greatness (Exod 9:16; 10:2).[49] Moses, then, is represented as using the tactics of the weak in order to persuade God by means of divine values and aims.[50] The narrator notes that Moses has indeed succeeded in warding off immediate annihilation, because "the Lord renounced the punishment he had planned to bring upon his people" (v. 14),[51] but, most significantly, he refrains from expressing forgiveness. The issue has not yet been settled.[52]

Moses' next step is punishment by human means, as the Levites step forward to kill all transgressors (Exod 32:25–28).[53] If one follows the

---

48. See Widmer, *Intercessory Prayer*, 116–19; Balentine, *Prayer in the Hebrew Bible*, 138; Muffs, "Who Will Stand in the Breach?" 12–13; M. Greenberg, "Moses' Intercessory Prayer (Exod. 32,11–13, 31–32; Deut. 9,26–29)," in *Yearbook Ecumenical Institute for Advanced Theological Studies (Jerusalem) 1977–1978* (Jerusalem: Fransiscan Printing Press, 1978) 21–35, esp. pp. 28–31; Balentine, *Prayer in the Hebrew Bible*, 137–39; J. Muilenburg, "The Intercession of the Covenant Mediator (Exodus 33:1a,12–17)," in *Words and Meanings: Essays Presented to David Winton Thomas* (ed. P. R. Ackroyd and B. Lindars; Cambridge: Cambridge University Press, 1968) 159–81, esp. pp. 180–81.

49. This argumentation returns in Num 14:15–17 and also functions in Isa 48:11; Ezek 20:9, 14, 39, 44; 36:22–23, 32; the grounds for Moses' argumentation do not appear in the deuteronomic version of the Golden Calf (Deut 9:18–20), the dependence of which on Exodus 32 has been reaffirmed by Greenberg, "Moses' Prayer," 30–34; C. E. Hayes, "Golden Calf Stories: The Relationship of Exodus 32 and Deuteronomy 9–10," in *The Idea of Biblical Interpretation: Essays in Honor of James L. Kugel* (ed. H. Najman and J. H. Newman; Leiden: Brill, 2004) 45–93. Childs (*Exodus*, 586–87) points to the secondary development of the 40-days theme in Deut 9:18.

50. Such tactics are discussed by G. I. Nierenberg, *The Art of Negotiating* (repr.; New York: Cornerstone, 1980) 149–50; Galin, *The Dynamics of Negotiating*, 302. See also Widmer, *Intercessory Prayer*, 108–19.

51. So also Balentine, *Prayer in the Hebrew Bible*, 138. In Buber's view ("Das Leitwort," 1151–53), this note indicates the stages of the exchange. However, because Buber's discussion centers on the leading words עם and עלה, he does not follow the logic of the negotiation process.

52. Similarly Widmer, *Intercessory Prayer*, 122; W. H. C. Propp, *Exodus 19–40: A New Translation with Introduction and Commentary* (AB 2A; New York: Doubleday, 2006) 556.

53. The fragmentary remains could hardly reflect continuous narratives and do not provide enough context for reconstruction of the source. The poetic reminiscence of the role of the Levites in Deut 33:8–9 suggests a connection with Massah and Meribah (cf.

logic of punishment/forgivingness, it is difficult to account for these measures, because the threat of annihilation has already been removed (v. 14). Moreover, Moses' next step is to ascend to the mountain in order to try to appease the deity (v. 31). This sequence seems confusing. Is Moses exacting punishment or obtaining mercy? If he has been able to obtain mercy, what is the meaning of additional entreaties? And what is their significance if punishment has already been exacted?

The context of a negotiation process, however, enables us to follow Moses' moves without difficulty. The mediator has succeeded in averting immediate disaster, but he still must placate his divine overlord and thus still needs arguments. In the present context, this is the role of the slaughter brought about by the Levites. This punishment is to provide the backdrop to his appeal to absolve Israel's sins. When he ascends to God, Moses admits to the "great sin" but also presents an ultimatum:[54]

T1 a   v. 32   ועתה אם־תשא חטאתם ואם־אין מחני נא מספרך אשר כתבת

This ultimatum, however, is rejected:

T1 b   v. 33   מי אשר חטא־לי אמחנו מספרי

This divine riposte is followed by a counterinitiative:

v. 34   ועתה לך נחה את־העם אל אשר־דברתי לך
הנה מלאכי ילך לפניך וביום פקדי ופקדתי עליהם חטאתם

This proclamation modifies the agenda. God allows Moses a concession by ordering him to continue leading his people. But there is no remission of sins. The threat of an ultimate penalty is still impending over Israel.[55]

Exod 17:1–7; Ps 95:8–9). The thesis that this tradition preceded the linking of this theme to the Golden Calf narrative (Exod 32:26–29) has been advanced by S. E. Loewenstamm, "The Investiture of Levi," *From Babylon to Cana'an: Studies in the Bible and Its Oriental Background* (Jerusalem: Magnes, 1992) 55–65; idem, "The Death of Moses," ibid., 136–166, esp. pp. 137–45. This thesis reveals the need for a radical reanalysis of the Sinai narrative (cf. Ps 81:12–15).

54. In v. 32, the NJPSV solves the ellipse (GKC §§167a; 159dd) by inserting "well and good," reflecting Rashi's explanatory remark, מוטב. Driver (*Use of the Tenses*, 181–82), followed by the NAB, views the protasis as a wish, taking אם with the imperfect as לו with the perfect but thereby relinquishing the connection between the two contrasting 'if' clauses, similar to, for example, 1 Sam 12:14.

55. The divine plague (v. 35) has been viewed as the continuation of the ordeal (Holzinger, *Exodus*, 111; Baentsch, *Exodus*, 274). But Buber ("Leitwort," 1151), Brichto ("Worship," 19) and Houtman (*Exodus*, 606) view this verse as an aside concerning punishment at a later stage of the desert wanderings. Such connections, however, are not made explicit in Numbers 14–17.

Moses Obtains Concessions (Exodus 33:1–23)

The narrative continues with the divine instructions to Moses regarding the way he is to lead Israel to the land promised to the patriarchs (33:1–3). These instructions repeat the former promises, in particular in Moses' commission at the burning bush (Exod 3:6–8, 16–17) and in the Book of the Covenant (23:20–23), and thus indicate the renewal of these declarations. However, this proclamation also contains a restriction: because of the calf worship, God will not go up in the midst of Israel in order to prevent their annihilation when they sin again (33:3b). Instead, the people will be led by a "messenger of God." This restriction is a new element in the narrative, for in the former promise (23:20–23) the function of this "messenger" is not motivated by God's absence. In the present context, however, the function of the "messenger" carries overtones of divine punishment, even though Moses is enabled to carry on with the trek to Canaan.[56]

At this point the dialogue breaks off and is not taken up again (v. 12) until after a long interruption about the ensuing developments in the Israelite camp (vv. 4–11).[57] Following the removal of the ornaments (vv. 4–6) and the building of a tent "of meeting" outside the Israelite quarters (vv. 7–11), Moses once again turns to God in order to obtain clarifications regarding his role and his position vis-à-vis God.[58] Thus he takes up the earlier proclamation of the divine concessions:

T1 a   33:12–13

ויאמר משה אל ה' ראה אתה אמר אלי העל את־העם הזה
ואתה לא הודעתני את אשר־תשלח עמי
ואתה אמרת ידעתיך בשם וגם־מצאת חן בעיני

Moses' first move, emphatically underlined by presenting his case by using the verb ראה,[59] is raising the issue of God's accompaniment with him. But isn't his question incongruous after the explicit announcement

---

56. Consequently, I find it difficult to accept Muffs's comment ("Who Will Stand in the Breach?" 13) that Moses' audacity failed to prevail.

57. Because these episodes are a sidetrack with regard to the negotiation process, this is not the place to analyze them; Widmer (*Intercessory Prayer*, 143–44) highlights thematic continuity connected with the "face" of God; see Childs, *Exodus*, 588–93.

58. See Irwin, "Course of the Dialogue"; Moberly, *The Mountain of God*, 68–69, 74; F. H. Polak, "Theophany and Mediator: The Unfolding of a Theme in the Book of Exodus," in *Studies in the Book of Exodus: Redaction-Reception-Interpretation* (ed. M. Vervenne; BETL 126; Leuven: Leuven University Press, 1996) 117–47, esp. pp. 142–44.

59. This introductory verb, noted by Childs (*Exodus*, 593), returns as an inclusio in the last clause of Moses' speaking turn (v. 13b); see also, e.g., Gen 41:41; Exod 7:1; 31:2; Deut 1:8, 21; 4:5; 11:26; Josh 6:2; 1 Sam 24:12; 2 Sam 7:2; 15:3; Jer 1:10; Ezek 4:15; Zech 3:4; 6:8; Eccl 7:27, 29; 1 Chr 28:10.

that Israel will be guided by a "messenger" (33:2)? Is this lack of co-herence not indicative of the coalescence of different traditions?[60] The same problems are raised by Moses' next questions, until we get the impression that the text is in total disarray, in spite of the impressive threefold repetition of אתה (anaphora).[61]

These puzzling problems are but a symptom of the perplexities posed by the situation at hand. Moses must negotiate the presence of the divine guidance and the removal of the threat hovering over his people. Thus he must formulate his case very carefully vis-à-vis his divine interlocutor, who, moreover, has all power and can annihilate all opposition in the twinkling of an eye. When we follow the text in the light of this situation, we may be able to unveil the tactics behind Moses' perplexing way of speaking and the baffling order of the dialogue.

Moses' first complaint, ואתה לא הודעתני את אשר־תשלח עמי (v. 12aβ) does not just ask for a name. It is Moses' way of placing the "messenger" on the agenda again, without explicitly questioning the divine decision not to lead Israel himself.[62] The additional saying, ואתה אמרת ידעתיך בשם וגם מצאת חן בעיני (v. 12b), is a reminder of the status granted to him and a corroboration of his requests.[63]

Moses continues with a second petition, introduced by ועתה, and thus an operative request in the wake of his apparent complaint:

v. 13 ועתה אם־נא מצאתי חן בעיניך הודעני נא את־דרכך ואדעך
למען אמצא־חן בעיניך וראה כי עמך הגוי הזה

On the face of it, this request concerns the modes of divine guidance. But if that were the point, the closing motivation, וראה כי עמך הגוי הזה, would be purposeless. Hence, this saying actually is the key to Moses' argumentation, implying that he is requesting the deity not to disre-gard his reponsibility for "this people" and thus to continue to lead them. Once again, Moses underlines God's solidarity with his people.

---

60. Baentsch (*Exodus*, 274–75) attributes 33:2 to R^JE, whereas Driver (*Exodus*, 358–59) regards this verse as a gloss.

61. Gertz, "Komposition und Redaktion," 102–4; Baentsch, *Exodus*, 274–79. On the other hand, Driver (*Exodus*, 360–63) attributes vv. 12–23 in their entirety to J.

62. Similarly Muffs, "Who Will Stand in the Breach?" 14–15; Brichto, "Worship," 25–26; Houtman, *Exodus*, 679; following the 12th-century Jewish commentator from Orléans, Josef Bekhor Shor, *Commentary to the Pentateuch: A Facsimile Edition Based on Various Edi-tions* (3 vols.; Jerusalem: Makor, 1978) 1:152 (Hebrew; reprint of Jellinek's 1855 edition, Leipzig).

63. See Muilenburg, "Intercession," 178.

The boon implied in but not uttered explicitly in Moses' questions is granted by the divine response:[64]

T1 b v. 14 ויאמר פני ילכו והנחתי לך

In this response, the narrator indicates that God understood Moses' implicit request.[65] Now that the petition has been granted, the mediator can bring out its urgency:[66]

T2 a v. 15 ויאמר אליו אם־אין פניך הלכים אל־תעלנו מזה

Once again, Moses' request is underscored by additional arguments:

v. 16 ובמה יודע אפוא כי־מצאתי חן בעיניך אני ועמך הלוא בלכתך עמנו
ונפלינו אני ועמך מכל־העם אשר על־פני האדמה

Thus Moses closes his petition with a renewed reference to Israel's election, implying the continued validity of the covenant and the promise to the patriarchs. At this stage, the divine response raises a new issue:

T2 b v. 17 ויאמר ה' אל־משה גם את־הדבר הזה אשר דברת אעשה
כי־מצאת חן בעיני ואדעך בשם

This declaration grants Moses another boon that he had requested, "I will also do this thing that you have asked." However, the issue itself is not mentioned. Moses is given a cue by the motivation for this boon, "For you have truly gained my favor and I have singled you out by name," an allusion to his argumentation (33:12b, 13a). But apart from information regarding the divine guidance in their trek, Moses' only request was to know God's ways. At this juncture, Moses goes further and asks to view the divine presence:

T3 a v. 18 ויאמר הראני נא את־כבדך

Seemingly, this request is entirely unconnected to his former request to be instructed in God's ways.[67] However, the divine response to Moses' new petition takes his previous request into account:

---

64. Brichto ("Worship," 26) reads this verse as a counterquestion: "If I go in person, will that satisfy you?" One wonders whether this meaning for הניח is feasible. Moreover, the divine response actually annuls the divine threat of v. 2 and thus implies far more than just a counterquestion.

65. So also Houtman, *Exodus*, 679 ('God understands what Moses is after'). Irwin ("Course of the Dialogue," 633–34) views the divine responses to Moses' requests as a "delayed response," but in the present case God seems to anticipate Moses' explicit petition.

66. One could hypothesize that v. 15 should precede v. 14, but reordering of this sort still does not answer the questions raised by vv. 12–13.

67. This is the view of Childs, *Exodus*, 596. According to Houtman (*Exodus*, 679), Moses is now demanding complete clarity.

T3 b   v. 19   ויאמר אני אעביר כל־טובי על־פניך וקראתי בשם ה' לפניך
                           וחנתי את־אשר אחן ורחמתי את־אשר ארחם

On the face of it, this reponse opens with an alternative to Moses'
new wish—in a certain sense, a counterproposal: Moses will not perceive the divine presence but a lesser mode of appearance, טוב, which
is often used as a divine quality related to divine protection (Ps 31:20),
to צדקה (Ps 145:7), to חסד, and to רחמים (Isa 63:7; Ps 25:7).[68] This response,
then, falls short of Moses' request to be shown the divine presence but
nevertheless implies a concession. We must view the promises of divine
mercy in the second colon in this light, because they form a partial response to Moses' initial plea not to wipe out the people (32:11, 32–33).
Obtaining this pardon, then, seems to be the hidden intention that God
discerned behind Moses' request to perceive the divine presence. One
may, however, wonder what the connection could be among the ideas
of perceiving the divine presence (33:18), general pardon (v. 19b), God's
proclamation of his name (v. 19a), and the revelation of God's ways as
requested in Moses' first petition (v. 13). Does this conundrum permit
a solution, or are we dealing with an aggregate of different variants
within a general traditional framework? Here too, the cue is provided
by the progress of the negotiations.

At the next stage (v. 20), the promise to "make all my טוב pass before
you" (v. 19) is followed by the explanation that Moses is not allowed
visual perception of the deity. A second follow-up announces a safe
place for Moses to stand, as God passes by (vv. 21–23) and thus provides a compromise between the explanation of the adynaton (v. 20)
and Moses' demand (v. 18). Thus, this episode represents a logical progression rather than an indiscriminate aggregate of variant traditions.

This progression can be analyzed as a succession of stages in a negotiation process. It is a typical feature of Biblical Hebrew narrative that
a series of two or more different addresses (speaking turns) by the same
speaker may indicate an implicit turn of the second party, who met the
preceding address with silence or perhaps with a gesture indicating
consent or rejection (silent turn-taking).[69] In the present episode, the

---

68. See also Ps 25:13; 27:13; Hos 3:5; Jer 31:12, 14.

69. A systematic discussion of this phenomenon is offered by C. L. Miller, "Silence as
a Response in Biblical Hebrew Narrative: Strategies of Speakers and Narrators," *JNSL* 32
(2006) 23–43; see also Herman, *Dramatic Discourse*, 98–99; de Regt, *Participants in Old Testament Texts*, 13; further references are given in my papers "Dialogue and Speaker Status
in the Scroll of Ruth," 214 n. 56; "Dialogue and Speaker Status in Biblical Narrative," 14
n. 34. Pauses between different stages in the argumentation are common in human intercourse, as shown by, for example, Hutchby and Wooffitt, *Conversation Analysis*, 81.

divine proposal to let his טוב pass before Moses (T3 b, 33:19) meets with an icy silence:

T4 a   33:19   [Silence]

Moses' silence necessitates an explanation, which is once again met by silence:

T4 b   v. 20   ויאמר לא תוכל לראת את־פני כי לא־יראני האדם וחי

T5 a   [Silence]

This icy reaction elicits a compromise:

T5 b   v. 21   ויאמר ה' הנה מקום אתי ונצבת על־הצור
        v. 22   והיה בעבר כבדי ושמתיך בנקרת הצור ושכתי כפי עליך עד־עברי
        v. 23   והסרתי את־כפי וראית את־אחרי ופני לא יראו

Thus Moses has succeeded in pressing his demand to view the divine presence.[70] But he still persists in his silence:

T6 a   [Silence]

This reaction to the compromise leads to an additional concession:[71]

T6 b   34:1   ויאמר ה' אל־משה פסל־לך שני־לחת אבנים כראשנים וכתבתי
                    על־הלחת את־הדברים אשר היו על־הלחת הראשנים אשר שברת

In addition, Moses is ordered to ascend the mountain totally alone (34:2–3). Thus he has reached his goal, the reinstitution of the covenant after it was broken by the worship of the Golden Calf. Finally, then, Moses can comply with the divine orders, carving two tablets of stone and going up to Mount Sinai as commanded (v. 4).

See n. 43 above. M. Anbar discovers the doubling of the speaking formula in texts from Mari ("Formule d'introduction du discours direct au mileu du discours à Mari et dans la Bible," *VT* 47 [1997] 530–36).

70. The meaning of viewing God's back has been expounded by M. Oeming, "Gottes Offenbarung 'von hinten' (Ex 33,24): Erwägungen zu einem wenig beachteten Aspekt des alttestamentlichen Offenbarungsverständnisses," *Verstehen und Glauben: Exegetische Bausteine zu einer Theologie des Alten Testaments* (BBB 142; Berlin: Philo, 2003) 109–19; metaphorical use of "face" and "back" is indicated by Widmer, *Intercessory Prayer*, 166–67.

71. Even though the command in 34:1 signals a new stage, as indeed indicated by the mention of both parties, this is not an entirely new episode (as might be gathered from the chapter division), because the Masoretic section division (BHS; so also according to A. Dothan, ed., *Tora, Nevi'im, Ketubim* [Tel Aviv: Ady and the School of Jewish Studies of Tel Aviv University, 1973] 1120; see also *Westminster Leningrad Codex*, http://www.tanach .us/Tanach.xml) indicates a "closed" parasha boundary, rather than an "open" one, which doesn't appear until 34:26. The preceding open boundary sets 33:16 off from 33:17.

But how is this goal related to the revealing of the divine presence or the knowledge of God's ways? These question can only be answered in light of the ensuing theophany.

The Divine Revelation (Exodus 34:1–10)

As Moses stations himself at the designated place, God descends in a cloud and passing before him proclaims his name and titles:[72]

T7 a	34:6	ויעבר ה' על־פניו ויקרא ה' ה' אל רחום וחנון ארך אפים ורב־חסד ואמת
	v. 7	נצר חסד לאלפים נשא עון ופשע וחטאה ונקה לא ינקה פקד עון
		אבות על־בנים ועל־בני בנים על־שלשים ועל־רבעים

Moses' reaction includes prostration and a final petition:

T7 b	v. 8	וימהר משה ויקד ארצה וישתחו
	v. 9	ויאמר אם־נא מצאתי חן בעיניך אדני ילך־נא אדני בקרבנו
		כי עם־קשה־ערף הוא וסלחת לעוננו ולחטאתנו ונחלתנו

Moses' ultimate request, then, is the forgiveness of Israel's sins, the renewal of the divine guidance, a boon that had already been granted (33:13–14), and the institution of a נחלה relationship.[73] Thus all requests are united in one single petition, which finally meets divine approval as God proclaims:

T8 a	v. 10	ויאמר הנה אנכי כרת ברית
		נגד כל־עמך אעשה נפלאת אשר לא־נבראו בכל־הארץ ובכל־הגוים
		וראה כל־העם אשר־אתה בקרבו את־מעשה ה'
		כי־נורא הוא אשר אני עשה עמך

This declaration, then, proclaims the institution of the covenant. Indeed the reference to the divine wonders returns the tale to the themes of the theophany scene at Mount Sinai (Exod 19:15–19; 20:18–21).[74] The description of "wonders such as have not been created in all the earth, among all the nations"[75] corresponds with Moses' request to prove Israel's distinctness from all the nations of the earth (33:16). But this proclamation also includes outstanding key elements that do not appear in the divine self-introduction of the Decalogue.

---

72. Admittedly, because the use of the verb ויקרא does not define an explicit subject, the subject may be Moses, with an implicit change of subject. But in this case, the continuation with וימהר משה becomes quite problematic. The present interpretation tallies with 33:19.

73. The connection between these verses and chaps. 32–33 is elaborated by K. H. Walkenhorst, "Warum beeilte sich Mose niederzufallen? Zur literarischen Einheit von Ex 34,8f," *BZ* 28 (1984) 185–213.

74. Thereby the narrative is most likely addressing an alternative version of the theophany narrative, which, however, is not reproduced as an independent "source."

75. Fox, *Now These Are the Names*, 192.

The first attributes to be mentioned are

אל רחום וחנון ארך אפים ורב חסד ואמת

a God compassionate and gracious, slow to anger, abounding in kindness and faithfulness (34:6)

It is more than coincidence that this proclamation opens with the noun "El" and his description as "compassionate." In the Ugaritic epic, one of the prominent epithets of *Ilu* is *dpʾid*, related to Arabic *fuʾād* 'heart', which is rendered 'the beneficent' or 'the compassionate'.[76] The ensuing epithet, נצר חסד לאלפים נשא עון ופשע וחטאה ('extending kindness to the thousandth generation, forgiving iniquity, transgression, and sin') is not restricted to "those who love me and keep my commandments," as found in the Decalogue (20:6). Thus, in spite of the threat concluding the divine self-description, "by no means clearing the guilty, but visiting the iniquity of parents upon children and children's children" (34:6, NRSV), the salient idea is that of mercy, מידת הרחמים in rabbinic terminology.[77]

These considerations justify the conclusion that God's proclamation of the divine attributes dovetails with and responds to two of Moses' main requests, the reinstatement of the covenant (33:13b, 16) and the remission of sin (32:32). God's present declaration represents these mercies as emanating from intrinsic qualities of God's suzerainty and thus provides relief for Moses' fears. Because this proclamation was given by the divine presence passing by, it is guaranteed by God's כבוד itself, in accordance with Moses' request to view God's presence (33:18).[78] Indeed, this declaration provides the ground for Moses' entreaties on behalf of his people at Kadesh, following the Israelite disbelief in the possibility of entering Canaan (Num 14:17–19).

Viewed in this perspective, the tale of Moses' expostulation with God (Exodus 32–33) depicts an extremely delicate but ultimately successful negotiation process, in which Moses uses sophisticated negotiation

---

76. See e.g., S. B. Parker, ed., *Ugaritic Narrative Poetry* (SBLWAW 9; Atlanta: Scholars Press, 1997) 24 (CAT I.15 II 14, Greenstein: 'the Compassionate') 122 (CAT 1.4 II 10, M. Smith: 'the Beneficent') 63 (CAT 1.18 I 15: Parker: 'the Compassionate').

77. In *Sifre Deut.* 26:24 and *Midr. Exod. Rab.* 3:6 the connection between the Tetragrammaton and מידת הרחמים is motivated by reference to Exod 34:6; see also M. Kadushin, *The Rabbinic Mind* (New York: Jewish Theological Seminary, 1952) 215–17; Widmer, *Intercessory Prayer*, 183–89.

78. These issues are highlighted by Buber, "Leitwort," 1157–58; R. W. L. Moberly, "How May We Speak of God? A Reconsideration of the Nature of Biblical Theology," *TynBul* 53 (2002) 177–202, esp. pp. 199–200.

tactics in order to save his people from disaster. On the face of it, this tale looks like the typical product of a complicated redaction process, almost completely covering up all underlying narrative strata. However, these apparent complications in dialogue structure and narrative sequence are all related to Moses' stance in the negotiation process, his intricate weakness vis-à-vis the divine suzerain, and the frailty of his position after the Israelite sin, which leaves him without any arguments. If we follow the course of the negotiations, we see how Moses by subtle tactics obtains absolution of sins and renewal of the covenant in spite of the adverse circumstances.

The Social Context of Dialogic Narrative

These and numerous additional examples[79] show that the transactional dialogue, the spoken exchange that leads to a deal, and the negotiation process stand at the very heart of biblical Hebrew narrative. Furthermore, these tales demonstrate the high level of sophistication of the negotiation tactics as depicted by the narrators.

This conclusion raises a new question. How could these narrators assume that the audience would understand these tactics? That they would smile when hearing of Abraham's readiness to deliver the requested oath to Abimelech or of his answers to Ephron, and grin at Isaac's angry reproaches? That they would catch the subtlety in Moses' reply to Pharaoh and appreciate the sublime balance of his accomplished supplication to and bold demand from God? If the proclivity to transactional interaction were a singular feature in a few narratives, one could ascribe it to a personal preference of one or more individual narrators. However, because intercourse of this kind is very widespread in biblical narrative, it represents a prime cultural phenomenon with deep roots in the societal framework. Accordingly we cannot but assume that tales focusing on transactional dialogue and negotiation procedures reflect central societal processes. In other words, these tales are at home in a culture in which oral communication plays a central part and in which the noble art of give and take is highly developed among broad strata of society.[80]

---

79. Such as, e.g., Genesis 15; 16; 17; 18; 29–31; 33; 37; 40–45; 1 Samuel 16; 17; 20; 21:1–10; 24; 25; 26; 2 Samuel 15–16; 18; 19; 20; 1 Kings 2; 3.

80. The relationship between the work of art and the cultural capabilities of the public addressed has been discussed by Clifford Geertz, "Art as a Cultural System," *Local Knowledge: Further Essays in Interpretive Anthropology* (3rd ed.; New York: Basic Books, 2000) 94–120.

Oral Culture and Biblical Literature

Many data indicate that a culture of this type is presupposed by extensive strata of biblical literature. One notes the description of King Solomon as 'uttering three thousand proverbs' (1 Kgs 5:12: וידבר שלשת אלפים משל),[81] whereas the colophon of the Qoheleth scroll praises the "son of David, king in Jerusalem" for his endeavors to find out 'acceptable words, and that which was written uprightly, even words of truth' (ASV Eccl 12:10: דברי־חפץ וכתוב ישר דברי אמת).[82] By contrast, the eulogy of Solomon points to a milieu in which spoken discourse was considered a worthy medium for a wise king.[83] In such a context, the term "oral culture" does not imply low level or lack of sophistication.[84] The erudition attributed to Solomon, though not literate in the modern, alphabetic sense of the word, is no less developed than the education of a scribe composing a written collection of Proverbs.[85] Thus we must acknowledge the existence of a full-fledged oral erudition, paralleling literacy, and consequently to be recognized as "oracy," the erudition of an "orate" society.[86]

Oral narrative, then, is the narrative of an orate society, and as such it represents the ways of oral culture. What this means can be grasped through the Jacob-Laban tale. This story represents the agreements

81. This is the RSV rendering (1 Kgs 4:32). Significantly, the NJPSV and the NRSV render וידבר 'he composed', which conveys the meaning of the verse adequately in terms of our cultural presuppositions but glosses over the cultural context of the biblical description.

82. Additional references to writing or written documents in biblical Wisdom texts include Prov 3:3; 7:3; 22:20; Job 19:23; 31:35. This is but a weak indication of the connection between Wisdom literature and scribal education, as maintained by H. J. Hermisson, *Studien zur israelitischen Spruchweisheit* (WMANT 28; Neukirchen-Vluyn: Neukirchener Verlag, 1968); M. Weinfeld, *Deuteronomy and the Deuteronomic School* (Oxford: Clarendon, 1972; repr. Winona Lake, IN: Eisenbrauns, 1992) 158–71; a critical review of the evidence is offered by R. N. Whybray, "The Social World of the Wisdom Writers," in *The World of Ancient Israel* (ed. R. E. Clements; Cambridge: Cambridge University Press, 1989) 227–50, esp. pp. 230–35.

83. See S. Gandz, "Oral Tradition in the Bible," in *Jewish Studies in Memory of George A. Kohut* (ed. S. W. Baron and A. Marx; New York: Kohut Memorial Foundation, 1935) 248–69, esp. pp. 265–66.

84. See above all, P. Burke, *Popular Culture in Early Modern Europe* (2nd ed.; Aldershot Hants, UK: Wildwood, 1988) 23–29, 58–64.

85. Such as the well-known Egyptian Wisdom compositions or Sumerian gnomic literature, discussed by E. Gordon, *Sumerian Proverbs: Glimpses of Everyday Life in Ancient Mesopotamia* (Philadelphia: University Museum, 1959).

86. See my paper, "Sociolinguistics: A Key to the Typology and the Social Background of Biblical Hebrew," *Hebrew Studies* 47 (2006) 115–62, esp. pp. 153–57. The term *oracy* is widely used in pedagogical discussions to indicate speaking and listening skills; see, for instance, C. Hodgson, "Assessing Oracy: Storytelling," *Literacy Today* 53 (December 2007) 24–25.

between Laban and Jacob by verbal declarations (*solemnia verba*) rather than by written contracts,[87] even though the ceremony is described in much detail (Gen 31:44–51).[88] Agreements are memorialized by ceremonies with strong religious and social implications, such as a festive meal (Gen 26:30; 31:46, "on the mound"; Josh 9:11–15; 2 Sam 3:20),[89] the erection of a pillar (Gen 31:44, 51; or, alternatively, a mound of stones, which also merits name-giving and proclamation of a name, vv. 46–49) and the giving of presents (Gen 21:27–30; 1 Sam 18:3–4).[90]

Similar ceremonies are known from Upper Mesopotamia, in the realm of Mari, such as the agreement between Atamrum, the king of Andarig and Askur-Addu, king of Karanā, and other petty kings in the region: *ištu ṭēmšunu uštaddinū u riksā[tim irkus]ūma*, ^{anše}*ḫayarum iqqatil, aḫum aḫam nī[š] ilim*^{lim} *[u]šazkirma, ana kāsim ušbū, ištu iqrušū, kāsam ištū, aḫum ana aḫim qīštam iššīma* ('after they came to an agreement and concluded an accord, a donkey was slaughtered. They swore each to the other an oath on the life of the deity, and sat down to drink. After they had cut up [the meat] and drunk the goblet, each presented the other with a gift').[91]

---

87. On such rituals in Upper Mesopotamia (the realm of Mari), see B. Lafont, "Rélations internationales, alliances et diplomatie au temps des royaumes amorrites: Essay de synthèse," in *Amurru 2. Mari, Ébla et les Hourrites: Dix ans de travaux. Deuxième partie* (ed. D. Charpin and J.-M. Durand; Paris: Éditions Recherche sur les Civilisations, 2001) 213–328, esp. pp. 280–81; and my paper, "The Covenant at Mount Sinai in the Light of Texts from Mari," 126–28.

88. Gandz, "Oral Tradition in the Bible," 249–50; M. Haran, "The *Běrît* 'Covenant': Its Nature and Ceremonial Background," in *Tehillah le-Moshe: Biblical and Judaic Studies in Honor of Moshe Greenberg* (ed. M. Cogan, B. L. Eichler, and J. H. Tigay; Winona Lake, IN: Eisenbrauns, 1997) 203–19, esp. pp. 208–10. Lafont ("Rélations internationales," 280–81) points to agreements made with no written document in Upper Mesopotamia (the realm of Mari).

89. In the Old Babylonian period, even drinking alone may indicate a treaty relationship, as shown by Meptû's announcement: *aššur ekallātum u ešnunna ištū, inanna ana bītim ištēn itūrū* (A. 2459, lines 4–7: "Ashur, Ekallātum and Eshnunna have drunk, now they have turned into one house"), quoted according to D. Charpin and J.-M. Durand, "Aššur avant l'Assyrie," *MARI* 8 (1997) 367–91, esp. pp. 387–88. On ceremonies of this kind in a commercial context, see J.-M. Durand, "Sumérien et Akkadien en Pays Amorite," *MARI* 1 (1982) 79–89.

90. So also in the Mari realm, as indicated by *Archives Épistolaires de Mari 1/2* (ed. D. Charpin et al.; Paris: Éditions Recherches sur les Civilisation, 1988) text 404, line 64 (hereafter abbreviated as *AEM* 1/2).

91. *AEM* 1/2, text 404, lines 60–64; see my paper, "The Covenant at Mount Sinai," 131–32. F. Joannès (*AEM*, ibid.) reads *igrušū* in hendiadys with *ištū* 'after they went to drink the cup'. But because the verb *qarāšu* is attested with the meaning 'to cut up [meat]', the reading *iqrušū* seems preferable in this context.

In this sort of context, the giving of presents serves not only to create a sphere of communion[92] but also as a *memento* by which the occasion is remembered, as indeed indicated by Abraham's explanation to Abimelech (Gen 21:30).[93] In these narratives, writing is mainly mentioned as a divine activity (Exod 31:18; 32:15, 32; 34:1)[94] or in a more or less direct relation to the divine sphere (Exod 17:14; 24:4, 12; 34:27–28); in a human context it is rare and is fraught with danger (Judg 8:14; 2 Sam 11:15).[95] Significantly, Joshua declares that the stone that he had set "up there under the oak in the sanctuary of the Lord" will be a witness to the Shechem covenant, "for it has heard all the words of the Lord that he spoke to us" (Josh 24:26–27, NRSV). Accordingly this text centers on oral communication with animistic/dynamistic overtones. Because this proclamation pertains to an open-air tree sanctuary and thus is in flagrant violation of the explicit deuteronomic prohibition of sanctuaries of this sort (Deut 16:21–22), it precedes the Deuteronomistic version of the text of "the book of the law of God," written by Joshua (v. 26a, NRSV).[96] The latter note tallies with the presentation of the text of משנה תורת משה אשר כתב לפני בני ישראל

---

92. Earlier, A. van Gennep, *The Rites of Passage* (trans. M. B. Vizedom and G. L. Caffe; London: Routledge, 1960) 31–32; J. Pedersen, *Der Eid bei den Semiten in seinem Verhältnis zu verwandten Erscheinungen sowie die Stellung des Eides im Islam* (Strassburg: Trübner, 1914) 21–22, 25; see also my paper, "The Covenant at Mount Sinai," 130–31.

93. This theory of Gandz ("some objects employed as tangible aids to memory and as a primitive kind of record": "Oral Tradition in the Bible," 249) is confirmed by the brilliant discussion regarding a similar custom in Norman Britain, by M. T. Clanchy, *From Memory to Written Record: England 1066–1307* (2nd ed.; Oxford: Blackwell, 1993) 35–42.

94. See Niditch, *Oral World and Written Word*, 79–82; W. M. Schniedewind, *How the Bible Became a Book: The Textualization of Ancient Israel* (Cambridge: Cambridge University Press, 2004) 24–34; S. M. Paul, "Heavenly Tablets and the Book of Life," *JANES* 5 (1973) 345–53.

95. This category includes Samuel's writing of the law of the monarchy (1 Sam 10:25), in view of its connection to his previous negotiations with God.
See also Num 5:23; and T. Schaack, *Die Ungeduld des Papiers: Studien zum alttestamentlichen Verständnis des Schreibens anhand des Verbums* katab *im Kontext administrativer Vorgänge* (BZAW 262; Berlin: de Gruyter, 1998) 32–43, 55–64. This particular problem has been underrated by J. Schaper, "Exilic and Post-exilic Prophecy and the Orality/Literacy Problem," *VT* 55 (2005) 324–41.

96. J. A. Soggin, *Joshua* (London: SCM, 1972) 241; D. J. McCarthy, *Treaty and Covenant: A Study in Form in the Ancient Oriental Documents and in the Old Testament* (2nd ed.; AnBib 21A; Rome: Pontifical Biblical Institute, 1978) 221–24, 231–33, 241–42; S. D. Sperling, "Joshua 24 Reexamined," *HUCA* 58 (1987) 119–36; S. Aḥituv, *Joshua* (Hebrew; Jerusalem: Magnes / Tel Aviv: Am Oved, 1995) 366. Strangely, this issue has been disregarded by, for example, T. Römer, "Das doppelte Ende des Josuabuches," *ZAW* 118 (2006) 523–48, esp. p. 544; V. Fritz, *Das Buch Josua* (Tübingen: Mohr Siebeck, 1994) 236–37, 247–48;

(Josh 8:32, 'a copy of the Teaching that Moses had written for the Israelites', NJPSV), which Joshua wrote down on the stones of the altar at
Mount Ebal (8:30, 32).

Biblical Literature and the Culture of Writing

On the other hand, the description of the inscribed stones on Mount
Ebal corresponds with the status of writing in the books of Deuteronomy and 1–2 Kings, books in which writing occupies a central position. In Deuteronomy, the idea of writing the law stands at the center
of the ceremonies mentioned in chaps. 27 and 31,[97] while the the king
is supposed to "have a copy of this Teaching written for him on a scroll
by the levitical priests" (Deut 17:18). The book of Kings contains an
abundance of administrative detail, including the age of the Judean
king at his accession (e.g., 1 Kgs 22:42; 2 Kgs 12:1; 14:2, 21; 15:2, 33; 16:2;
18:2; 22:1; 23:31; 24:2, 18).[98] The redactional framework of this book not
only presupposes the royal administration but also consistently refers
to "the other events" during the king's reign and "all his actions" that
are 'recorded in the chronicles of the kings of Judah' (כתובים על־ספר דברי
הימים למלכי יהודה, e.g., 2 Kgs 12:20, NAB) or 'chronicles of the kings of Israel' (ספר דברי הימים למלכי ישראל, e.g., 2 Kgs 13:8, NAB).[99]

M. Anbar, *Josué et l'Alliance de Sichem: Josué 24:1–28* (Beiträge zur biblischen Exegese und
Theologie 25; Frankfurt a.M.: Peter Lang, 1992) 117–20, 136–37. The entire discussion is
critically reviewed by E. Noort, *Das Buch Josua: Forschungsgeschichte und Problemfelder* (Er-
träge der Forschung 292; Darmstadt: Wissenschaftliche Buchgesellschaft, 1998) 211–22.

Notably, the Deuteronomistic copy lacks the immediate contact with the divine
sphere that surrounds the writing down of words uttered directly by God (e.g., Exod
17:14) or following negotiations with God (1 Sam 10:25).

97. Note also, in an administrative context, Josh 18:4, 6, 8, 9; and in a religious context: 1:8 ("this Book of the Teaching"; and similarly 23:6; 24:26a). For ceremonies, see
Deut 27:3, 8; 31:9, 24; and in a legal context, Deut 24:1, 3. The "Song of Moses" (Deut
31:19ab) is to be written down as witness after its oral recitation (31:19b, 21a; note also
11:20). See Niditch, *Oral World and Written Word*, 79–80, 86–88; J. Schaper, "A Theology of
Writing: The Oral and the Written—God as Scribe and the Book of Deuteronomy," in
Anthropology and Biblical Studies (ed. L. J. Lawrence and M. I. Aguilar; Leiden: Deo, 2004)
97–119, esp. pp. 104–11.

98. Recently, L. Grabbe pointed again to the factual-administrative context of Kings
("Mighty Oaks from [Genetically Manipulated?] Acorns Grow: *The Chronicle of the Kings
of Judah* as a Source of the Deuteronomistic History," in *Reflection and Refraction: Studies
in Biblical Historiography in Honor of A. Graeme Auld* [ed. R. Rezetko, T. H. Lim, and W. B.
Aucker; VTSup 113; Leiden: Brill, 2007] 155–73).

99. See Niditch, *Oral World and Written Word*, 94–105; Schniedewind, *How the Bible Became a Book*, 110–13, 134–36; F. H. Polak, "Style is More Than the Person: Sociolinguistics,
Literary Culture and the Distinction between Written and Oral Narrative," in *Biblical Hebrew: Studies in Chronology and Typology* (ed. I. Young; JSOTSup 369; London: T. & T. Clark,
2003) 38–103, esp. pp. 52–55, 84–89; on prophetic texts, see Schaper, "Exilic and Post-exilic
Prophecy," 329–35.

The prose strata in the book of Jeremiah also attest to considerable administrative know-how, for instance, in the elaborate indications of dates (Jer 32:1; 36:9).[100] The scribal craft is paramount in the pericopes on the redemption of Hanamel's field (Jeremiah 32) and on the scroll on which Jeremiah's prophecies were written by Baruch (Jeremiah 36).[101] Thus, the literature representing the late Judean monarchy reflects a well-developed scribal culture.

Narrative in an Oral Culture

The scribal culture characteristic of deuteronomic literature and its congeners contrasts sharply with the orate culture implied in large sections of the narratives of the patriarchs, the exodus, and Israel's first kings, as indicated by the ways and customs of the world depicted in these narratives, and in addition, by their style that in many ways reflects a substratum of spontaneous spoken language.[102] In particular, it should be noted that an implicit pause in quoted discourse, indicated by the doubling of the *inquit* (ויאמר . . . ויאמר), matches the narrator's manner in the oral performance, in which the silent reaction of the addressee can be indicated by facial expression or gesture.[103] The social context presupposed by this type of narrative is the orate society, a society in which literacy is restricted to the royal administration and parts of the elite (including "a managerial ruling class"), and literary erudition is primarily that of oral poetry and narrative. Many data indicate that this description holds true for ancient Israelite society until the rise of the royal bureaucracy, possibly by the late eighth century B.C.E.[104]

It is the orate society which provides the social background for the focus on negotiation and the subtle negotiating art displayed in dialogical narrative.

---

100. The LXX includes the references to Nebuchadnezzar in Jer 46[26]:2 and 32[39]:1 but not in 25:1. The words in MT 25:1 from היא through בבל are not represented by the LXX.

101. In addition, mention is made of an exchange of letters with exiles in Babylonia (Jer 29:1, 25, 31). References of this sort to the scribal art appear likewise in Jeremianic poetry (Jer 8:8; 17:1, 13; 22:30). See Schaper, "Exilic and Post-exilic Prophecy."

102. The sociolinguistic aspects of the orate corpus have been discussed in my papers, "Style Is More than the Person," 55–75; and "Sociolinguistics, Typology and Periodization," 141–56.

103. See pp. 186–87 above. The importance of the narrator's gestures and facial expression and his histrionic capabilities in general is indicated by, for example, R. Finnegan, *Oral Literature in Africa* (Oxford Library of African Literature; Nairobi: Oxford University Press, 1976) 373–88; Antonio Scuderi, "Performance and Text in the Italian Carolingian Tradition," *Oral Tradition* 21 (2006) 68–89.

104. "Managerial ruling class" is the terminology of Z. Herzog and L. Singer-Avitz, "Redefining the Centre: The Emergence of State in Judah," *Tel Aviv* 31 (2004) 209–44, esp. p. 233. See also Schniedewind, *How the Bible Became a Book*, 63–90.

The Place of Narrative in the Orate Society

Thus an analysis of communication processes in biblical narrative indicates that dialogic narrative is the narrative of the ancient Israelite orate society. In this context, the concept of oral narrative is only partially comparable to that of "living narrative" of modern society, for the latter represents the casual intercourse of informal social networks.[105] This is, however, hardly the case in a predominantly oral society. In an orate culture, literary activity mainly takes place in the oral networks of communication[106] and thus is an integral part of the formal social networks, beginning with the royal court. In such a context, orate competence is an essential cultural value, fulfilling central societal functions.[107]

This conclusion is not based only on anthropological insights and innerbiblical analysis. The social and cultural status of narrative in a predominantly oral network is indicated by the royal correspondence from Mari (around 1770 B.C.E.), in which the reports of many official envoys and army commanders are formulated according to conventions that are very close to oral narrative.[108] Circumstantial detail is evidenced by the account of Yasīm-Il, Zimrilim's representative at the covenant ceremony of Atamrum and Askur-Addu (see above), describing how he witnessed the ceremony: *anāku marṣākūma, ina bilāni* 2 lú *ukalūninnīma, aššum ṣimdātim šemīm meḥret šarrī azzaz* ('I was ill, two men carried me on *stretchers* but I stood up before the kings to hear their agreement'; *AEM* 1/2, text 404, lines 21–22). Another report depicts the Babylonian king's rejoinder to the messengers of Išmē-Dagan, the king of Ekallātum: *ḥammu-rāpī kīam īpulšunūtīma umma šūma ana [mannim] ṣābam addin? qibē, qibē!* ('Hammurapi answered them thus, he said, to [whom] did I give troops? Tell me, tell me!'; *AEM* 1/2, text 384, lines 29'–31').

Dialogue structure is illustrated by the report by Yanṣib-Addu and his senior, probably, Išḥī-Dagan, concerning the negotiations with

---

105. E. Ochs and L. Capps, *Living Narrative: Creating Lives in Everyday Storytelling* (Cambridge: Harvard University Press, 2001) 1–33; N. R. Norrick, *Conversational Narrative: Storytelling in Everyday Talk* (Amsterdam: Benjamins, 2000) 1–17, 105–68; Livia Polyani, *Telling the American Story: A Structural and Cultural Analysis of Conversational Storytelling* (Norwood, NJ: Ablex, 1985) 30–83.

106. Characteristically, Heath (*Ways with Words*, 190–91, 197–201) shows that in the Afro-American community of Trackton, even adult reading was a social activity.

107. See also Schniedewind, *How the Bible Became a Book*, 52–56.

108. See my papers, "Sociolinguistics, Typology and Periodization," 157–58; "Negotiating with Ḥammū-rāpi."

Hammurapi. This report pretends to reflect the actual wording of the dialogues, suggesting even the tone of the exchange, and especially of the riposte (*AEM* 1/2, text 449, lines 22–25), culminating in a fast sequence of 'I said . . . he said' retorts (*umma anāku . . . umma šūma*; lines 56–67). The same report describes Hammurapi's attitude: *u pēšu ul īpuš adi ṭēmšu uqaṭṭû, mādiš uqīl* ('and he [the king] didn't start speaking until he [the envoy] had completed his message, he [the king] listened carefully'; *AEM* 1/2, text 449, lines 9–10; one notes the implied changes of subject). These envoys and ministers, then, knew how to tell a story and used their knowledge for politically and socially important purposes rather than for amusement only.[109]

The Mari documents demonstrate the cultural functions of narrative in an orate society and indicate that these functions are far wider and far more important than merely *belles-lettres*. In this respect, the situation evidenced by these documents underlines and even extends the picture in non-Western, orate societies as described by anthropologists such as B. Malinowski, R. Finnegan, and D. Ben-Amos.[110] Not only does narrative relate to the central concerns of the community, it is also of central importance for high-level forms of communication. Like proverbs, quotations of and references to narrative can play an important part in oratory and political deliberations,[111] as indeed indicated by Joab's suggestion that David might refer to the Abimelech tale in the king's possible reaction to the news of the Israelite counterattack at Rabbah of Ammon (2 Sam 11:21). Narrative competence is a basic cultural capability in an orate society: as indicated by the findings of Heath with regard to the Afro-American community at Trackton, in a

---

109. Note also the account by Itūr-Asdū of his discussions with the Babylonian minister; M. Guichard, "'La malédiction de cette tablette est très dure!': Sur l'ambassade d'Itûr-Asdû à Babylone en l'an 4 de Zimrī-Lim," *RA* 98 (2004) 13–32, esp. pp. 16–25 and lines 8–19; and also the reports by Risaya and Asqudu concerning the negotiations with the king of Ḫalab, Yarīm-Līm, about Zimrī-Līm's projected marriage to Yarīm-Līm's daughter, Šibtu (*AEM* 1/1, texts 10–11, and esp. text 11:34–40).

110. B. Malinowski, *Magic, Science and Religion and Other Essays* (Garden City, NY: Doubleday, 1954) 101–11; Finnegan, *Oral Literature in Africa*; D. Ben-Amos, *Sweet Words: Storytelling Events in Benin* (Philadelphia: Institute for the Study of Human Issues, 1975); S. Ó. Duilearga, "Irish Tales and Story-Tellers," in *International Folkloristics: Classic Contributions by the Founders of Folklore* (ed. A. Dundes; Lanham, MD: Rowman & Littlefield, 1999) 153–76.

111. The use of proverbs in diverse African communities is described by Finnegan, *Oral Literature in Africa*, 408–14, 444–56. In biblical quoted oratory, note the proverbs used by David (1 Sam 24:14–15) and Jehoash (2 Kgs 14:9), Samson's riddle (Judg 14:12–14), and Jotham's parable (Judg 9:8–15).

culture of this type, the art of oral story-telling forms an essential part of the basic education.[112]

Thus the central role of dialogue and negotiation tactics in biblical narrative tallies with the interests of the ancient Israelite adult community, in which the economic and political networks were dominated by oral communication. Both the narrator and the audience were acquainted with and interested in ways to carry on negotiations and the tricks used on these occasions. The prominence of negotiations and the subtlety of the tactics used indicate a vigorous culture of oral communication and oral narrative.

---

112. See n. 14 above (p. 172). It's difficult to believe that these cultural traits are restricted to Trackton only. On the contrary, the cursing contests mentioned by Heath (*Ways with Words*, 174–76) have been discovered in many other places, including a New York neighborhood (south-central Harlem) in which the youths provided W. Labov with a series of highly articulate narratives for sociolinguistic and narratological analysis (*Language in the Inner City: Studies in the Black English Vernacular* [Philadelphia: University of Pennsylvania Press, 1972] 306–44).

Of Mice and Men and Blood:
The Laws of Ritual Purity in the Hebrew Bible

HANNA LISS

Hochschule für Jüdische Studien, Heidelberg

When dealing with the Priestly material in the Hebrew Bible, one has to keep in mind that in the course of the last 2,500 years Jewish tradition has developed a sort of "Jewish reader response," having focused mainly on legal traditions encompassed in these texts, thereby sometimes even reading these texts as a guidebook for cultic practices. This might be the reason that—different from Homer's *Iliad* but also different from the stories in the book of Genesis or the book of Ruth—the question of the literary quality of ritual texts, that is, the perception of ritual texts as a literary work of art, is still at issue. As a first step of every textual investigation, therefore, we have to discuss the issue whether and in which way the text in question has *literary* qualities at all, because a text does not acquire literary quality automatically simply because its oral traditions were written down at a certain stage in history. With regard to the Priestly traditions in the Hebrew Bible, contemporary biblical scholars are in disagreement about whether these texts' literary disposition consists of a historical narrative more than a collection of (ancient) laws or whether the Priestly material more than all other biblical texts serves as *the* example of a biblical utopia.[1]

Author's note: An enlarged version of this paper is published as "Ritual Purity and the Construction of Identity: The Literary Function of the Laws of Purity in the Book of Leviticus," in *The Books of Leviticus and Numbers* (ed. Thomas Römer; Colloquium Biblicum Lovaniense 55; Leuven: Peeters, 2008) 329–54.

1. *On historical narrative*, see, for example, the discussion in N. Lohfink, "Die Priesterschrift und die Geschichte," *Studien zum Pentateuch* (Stuttgart: Katholisches Bibelwerk, 1988) 213–53. *On biblical utopia*, see the discussion in E. Blum, *Studien zur Komposition des Pentateuch* (Berlin: de Gruyter, 1990) 303–5, and n. 64; E. Zenger (*Einleitung in das Alte Testament* [3rd ed.; Stuttgart: Kohlhammer, 1998] 153) characterizes P as "a critical utopian contribution to the discussion about the temple that was not yet completed" [trans. H. L.]; see also K. Koch, "Die Eigenart der priesterschriftlichen Sinaigesetzgebung," in *ZTK* 55 (1958) 36–51, esp. p. 51; R. Albertz, *Religionsgeschichte Israels in alttestamentlicher Zeit*, vol. 2: *Vom Exil bis zu den Makkabäern* (2nd ed.; 2 vols.; Göttingen:

However, the methodological problem arising for exegetical analysis has not been discussed sufficiently—that is, the fact that a text thought to be a source for ancient Israelite laws of purity and their development (for example, Leviticus 1–16)[2] must be treated differently from a text understood as a programmatic outline for a future society. We should, therefore, keep in mind some basic, yet relevant questions for the Priestly texts: What is the literary quality of the texts at hand? How do these texts, as literary artifacts, convey their meaning? When, if ever, can Priestly texts on ritual purity be understood as fictional literature?[3]

The following topics are dealt with in the sections on ritual purity:

Parashat Shemini: Unclean animals (Lev 11:1–47)

- vv. 1–8 Quadrupeds/land animals // Deut 14:3–8
- vv. 9–12 Water animals // Deut 14:9–10
- vv. 13–19 Birds // Deut 14:11–21
- vv. 20–23 Flying insects
- vv. 29–38 Reptiles
- vv. 24–40 Purification procedures/reptiles (vv. 29–38)
- vv. 41–45, 46ff. Land swarmers

Parashat Tazria: Impurity after childbirth; scale disease (*zāraʿat*; Lev 12:1–13:59)

- Woman after childbirth (puerperal bleeding)
- Marks; scaly affection; boils; burns; scalls; tetters; baldness
- Mold disease in a fabric

Parashat Mezora: Purification after scale disease; genital discharges (Lev 14:1–15:33)

- Purification for a cured scale-diseased person
- Fungous houses
- Abnormal male discharges (pathological emission/gonorrheic discharges)[4]

Vandenhoeck & Ruprecht, 1996–97) 519 n. 105; I. Knohl, *The Sanctuary of Silence: The Priestly Torah and the Holiness School* (Minneapolis: Fortress, 1995) 156.

2. Compare B. Levine, *Leviticus: The Traditional Hebrew Text with the New JPS Translation* (Philadelphia: Jewish Publication Society, 1989): "Leviticus is an important source of information on the realistic functions of priesthood" (xxxv); see also p. xxxvii: "There is every reason to accept the cultic practice presented in Leviticus as essentially realistic."

3. Compare my "Imaginary Sanctuary: The Priestly Code as an example of fictional literature in the Hebrew Bible," in *Judah and the Judeans in the Persian Period* (ed. O. Lipschits and M. Oeming; Winona Lake, IN: Eisenbrauns, 2006) 663–89; idem, "Kanon und Fiktion: Zur literarischen Funktion biblischer Rechtstexte," in *BN* n.s. 121 (2004) 7–38.

4. Primary impurity—he himself: 7 days, sacrifice on the 8th day; secondary impurity: 1 day.

- Normal male discharges (nonpathological emission: semen)[5]
- Normal female discharges (nonpathological emission, e.g., menstrual discharges)[6]
- Abnormal female discharges (pathological emission)[7]

Parashat Chuqqat: The ash of the red heifer (Num 19:1–22:1)

- Production of the ash of the red heifer
- Purification after contamination with a human corpse

In the section on unclean animals, the text bans the eating of these animals but more importantly gives details on the prohibition of touching certain animals or carcasses and on purification rites for the persons and objects who came into contact with unclean and/or dead animals. The subsequent sections deal with impurity after childbirth and a variety of skin diseases and skin eruptions (*zāraʿat*; probably certain types of scale disease)[8] and their ritual purification, followed by a detailed description of ritual impurity caused by genital discharges (pathological as well as nonpathological) and their ritual purification. Any other kinds of bodily discharges like sweat, tears, spittle, urine, blood from wounds, nose bleeding, and so on are not dealt with at all. Within the system of ritual purity, they seem to be neutral. The section on bodily discharges focuses only on those related to the male and female reproductive organs. The section on the red heifer does not belong directly to this composition, yet its topics are related.

Those who are not familiar with Jewish lore and law might get the impression that we are dealing with texts portraying "a culture that is besotted with defilement."[9] We shall, therefore, start with a narrative from a later Midrash (ca. 5th or 6th century A.D.):

> A non-Jew questioned R. Yohanan ben Zakkai, saying: "The things you Jews do appear to be a kind of sorcery. A cow is brought, it is slaughtered, is burnt, is pounded into ash, and its ash is gathered up. Then, when one of you gets defiled by contact with a corpse, two or three drops of the ash mixed with water are sprinkled upon him, and he is told 'You are

---

5. Primary impurity—he himself: 1 day; secondary impurity: 1 day.

6. Primary impurity—she herself: 7 days; secondary impurity: 1 day / 7 days.

7. Primary impurity—she herself: 7 days, sacrifice on the 8th day; secondary impurity: 1 day.

8. Compare J. Milgrom, *Leviticus 1–16: A New Translation with Introduction and Commentary* (AB 3; New York: Doubleday, 1991) 774–76, 816–26; for the view of *zāraʿat* as a latent and persistent disease, compare N. Kiuchi, "A Paradox of the Skin Disease," *ZAW* 113 (2001) 505–14.

9. M. Douglas, "Poetic Structure in Leviticus," in *Pomegranates and Golden Bells: Studies in Biblical, Jewish, and Near Eastern Ritual, Law, and Literature in Honor of Jacob Milgrom* (ed. D. P. Wright, D. N. Freedman, and A. Hurvitz; Winona Lake, IN: Eisenbrauns, 1995) 239.

cleansed.'" R. Yohanan asked the heathen: ". . . Have you ever seen a man whom the spirit of madness has possessed?" The heathen replied: "Yes!" "And what do you do for such a man?" "Roots are brought, the smoke of their burning is made to rise about him, water is sprinkled upon him until the spirit of madness flees." R. Yohanan then said: ". . . It is the same with a man who is defiled by contact with a corpse—he, too, is possessed by a spirit, the spirit of uncleanness. . . ."

When (the non-Jew) left, R. Yohanan's disciples said: "Our Master! You shoved aside the heathen with a reed, but what answer will you give us?" R. Yohanan said: "By your lives (I swear): the corpse does not defile, nor does the (mixture of ash and) water cleanse! Rather, it [i.e., the purifying power of the red heifer] is the decree of the Holy One, saying . . . : 'I have decreed it as a decree. You are not permitted to transgress my decree: *This is the statute of the Torah* (Num 19:2).'"[10]

This text is fascinating in that a Jewish writer from the 5th or 6th century places a statement in the mouth of a famous rabbi from the 1st century that neither the ritual defilement nor the purification ritual as depicted in the text turns out to be "reality." Moreover, the *Pesiqta* conveys a kind of "reader-response evaluation." The "heathen view" of the text discerns a magical reality (defilement and purification) *behind* or even independent from the text at hand, thereby also limiting the meaning of the *text* to its surface: a corpse defiles something and the ritual of the ashes of the red heifer is needed for purification. The "Jewish perception" restricts the reality of defilement and purification in its textual expression to a divine order. Defiling and purifying take place on the textual level: a "reality" enclosed in the text. The Midrash thereby reveals an understanding of the entity "text" as consisting of the idea that a text itself creates its own world—the literary fiction being the realization of a man's impurity and his purification.

In the following, I shall ask whether Leviticus 11–15 in the Hebrew Bible, usually referred to as purity regulations, may also communicate signs of a fictional reality and how this could be revealed exegetically.

In recent years, biblical as well as rabbinic scholars have (re-)discovered the topic of ritual purity in biblical and later Jewish literature.[11]

---

10. *Pesiq. Rab Kah.* 4.7.

11. See among others J. Klawans, *Purity, Sacrifice, and the Temple: Symbolism and Supersessionism in the Study of Ancient Judaism* (Oxford: Oxford University Press, 2006); C. E. Fonrobert, *Menstrual Purity: Rabbinic and Christian Reconstructions of Biblical Gender* (Contraversions: Jews and Other Differences; Stanford: Stanford University Press, 2000); R. Wasserfall, ed., *Women and Water: Menstruation in Jewish Life and Law* (Brandeis Series on Jewish Women; Hanover: University Press of New England, 1999); S. Cohen, "Purity, Piety, and Polemic: Medieval Rabbinic Denunciations of 'Incorrect' Purification Practices," in ibid., 82–100.

However, classical literary-historical or form-critical exegesis has increasingly reached its limit in interpretation. In earlier times, the opinion prevailed that one could consider these ritual descriptions to be direct sources of historically or cultically significant information that could be extracted from the text without dealing with questions of their literary genre or other forms of literary representation. Others seemed to hold the view that one only needed to elucidate the cultic and social background of the text to reveal its meaning.[12]

With regard to the laws banning unclean animals, a couple of interpretations have been offered: Jacob Milgrom focused on the prohibition of eating blood (Lev 3:17; 17:10–12), thereby trying to find an "ethical system of diet laws."[13] However, the term *blood* used extensively in other sections on ritual purity is not even mentioned once in this context; neither is the prohibition of eating it. Some scholars brought forward the argument that the prohibited animals might have played a prominent role in the cultic life of Israel's neighbors and were, therefore, banned from Israel's altars and tables.[14] These attempts have turned out not to be very convincing because, for example, the pig was considered sacred to certain gods (such as Demeter) as well as being detested by others (for example, the Assyrians).[15] On the other hand, many of Israel's pure animals were deemed sacred in other cultures of the ancient Near East and Egypt as well; just note Hathor as a sacred cow or the bull as a symbol for Baal. Others even argue on the basis of the investigation of the social and cultural context of the dietary laws by archaeological finds (such as bone remnants), which provide evidence on dietary habits and cultic practice.[16] And last, but not least, much effort has been spent in source and literary criticism discussing the literary dependencies and variations of parts of this section on

---

12. For a survey of the main positions and issues, see C. Nihan, *From Priestly Torah to Pentateuch: A Study in the Composition of the Book of Leviticus* (Ph.D. Diss., Université de Lausanne, 2005) esp. pp. 1–41.

13. See J. Milgrom, "The Biblical Diet Laws as an Ethical System," *Int* 17 (1963) 288–301.

14. See, e.g., K. Elliger, *Leviticus* (HAT 1/4; Tübingen: Mohr, 1966) 150.

15. See the discussion in Milgrom, *Leviticus*, 649–53; see also J. Moskala, "Categorization and Evaluation of different kinds of Interpretation of the Laws of Clean and Unclean Animals in Leviticus 11," *BR* 46 (2001) 5–41. For a comprehensive survey of the theories on the classification of the animals in Leviticus 11, see Nihan, *From Priestly Torah to Pentateuch*, 325–42.

16. See W. J. Houston, "Towards an Integrated Reading of the Dietary Laws of Leviticus," in *The Book of Leviticus: Composition and Reception* (ed. R. Rendtorff and R. A. Kugler; VTSup 93; Leiden: Brill, 2003) 142–61; idem, *Purity and Monotheism: Clean and Unclean Animals in Biblical Law* (JSOTSup 140; Sheffield: JSOT Press, 1993) esp. pp. 124–80.

unclean animals; note, for example, the discussion about the list of unclean birds in Leviticus 11 / Deuteronomy 14. Interestingly enough, scholars focus almost exclusively on things banned from the table (man's as well as God's). In this, the matter of concern is reduced to the prohibition of "eating" certain animals.

Questions especially on the *literary* structure of Leviticus 11–15 as well as its intrinsic meaning are still an issue, although some work on this has already been done.[17] As Douglas in a couple of studies has illustrated,[18] these texts show an overarching structure that bears an extremely cerebral, closely argued statement based on a series of expanded analogies. One can set up a number of grammatical, phraseological and syntactical features as well as further rhetorical figures and stylistic devices as being characteristic of the style of these Priestly texts (for example, circular inclusio, chiasm, parallelismus membrorum, and reduplication). Therefore, recognizing the diegetic quality of the texts as well as their distinctive stereotypical language pattern should widen our understanding of the thematic scope of the text. The same holds true for the question of the literary genre of these texts, which is not at all easy to answer; however, as David Damrosch stated correctly: "Genre is the narrative covenant between author and reader, the framework of norms and expectations shaping both the composition and the reception of the text."[19]

In the book of Leviticus, the laws on ritual purity (Leviticus 11–15) are embedded in the narrative of Israel's stay at Mount Sinai (Exodus 19ff.), followed by the narrative of the manufacture and erection of the

---

17. Besides the form-critical studies (cf. R. Rendtorff, *Die Gesetze in der Priesterschrift: Eine gattungsgeschichtliche Untersuchung* [FRLANT 44/2; Göttingen: Vandenhoeck & Ruprecht, 1963]; K. Koch, *Die Priesterschrift: Von Exodus 25 bis Leviticus 16. Eine überlieferungsgeschichtliche und literarkritische Untersuchung* [FRLANT 53; Göttingen: Vandenhoeck & Ruprecht, 1959), see M. Paran, *Forms of the Priestly Style in the Pentateuch; Patterns, Linguistic Usages, Syntactic Structures* (Jerusalem: Magnes, 1989; Heb.), esp. pp. 47–136; J. W. Watts, "The Rhetoric of Ritual Instruction in Leviticus 1–7," in *The Book of Leviticus* (ed. R. Rendtorff and R. A. Kugler; Leiden: Brill, 2003) 79–100; for the studies by Mary Douglas, see n. 17.

18. See M. Douglas, "The Compassionate God of Leviticus and His Animal Creation," in *Borders, Boundaries and the Bible* (ed. Martin O'Kane; JSOTSup 313; London: Sheffield Academic Press, 2002) 61–73; idem, "Impurity of Land Animals," in *Purity and Holiness: The Heritage of Leviticus* (ed. M. J. Poorthuis and J. Schwartz; Jewish and Christian Perspectives 2; Leiden: Brill, 2000) 33–45; idem, *Leviticus as Literature* (Oxford: Oxford University Press, 1999).

19. D. Damrosch, *The Narrative Covenant: Transformations of Genre in the Growth of Biblical Literature* (San Francisco: Harper & Row, 1987) 85.

tabernacle and its equipment (Exodus 25–31, 35–40), the different types and the order of the sacrifices (Leviticus 1–7), the inauguration of the priests and the sacrifices of ordination (Leviticus 8–9), and the ceremony of the *Shabbat Shabbaton* ('Day of Atonement'; Leviticus 16). Already the rabbis had discovered that Leviticus 11 forms the exact center of the book: *b. Qiddušin* 30a notices that the letter *waw* in the word גחון (Lev 11:42) marks exactly the halfway point of the letters of the Torah.

Almost every section of these texts is introduced as divine speech: דבר אל בני ישראל לאמר . . . דבר אל בני ישראל לאמר ('And YHWH spoke to Moses [and Aaron], saying. . . .[20] Speak to the people of Israel, saying . . .')[21] and closed with the formula zō't hat-tôrâ . . . / zō't tôrat ha-. . . .[22] The literary frame portrays the whole textual sequence as divine speech. The divine speech forms the metacommunicative element between the lists of ritual instructions, thereby transforming each single ritual description into an integrated part of the whole narrative, notwithstanding the fact that literary-historical analysis might detect various Priestly manuals—*tôrôt*—the Sitz im Leben of which may have been in the temple library, where they were consulted and copied by the priests.[23]

Large parts of Leviticus 1–16, especially 11–15, are written in third-person narrative. It is, therefore, a *de*scription rather than a *pre*scription. Leviticus 11–15, therefore, forms an integral part of the narrative about the inauguration of Israel's cultic system and must be treated as such, not only with respect to its content but also regarding its literary expression.

This leads us to the question of the *stereotyped language pattern* and the *diegetic* quality of these texts. Scholars have often noticed in these sections a repetitive, sometimes even monotonous formula-and-ritual style as well as long-winded, detailed descriptions of even insignificant details. These author(s) use(s) them to create an atmospheric density and to overemphasize their claim to literary "reality." Obviously, the text's redundancy must be evaluated regarding its content.

The term 'touching'/'the touch' ($\sqrt{ng^\varsigma}$/*nega$^\varsigma$*) is the main element of repetition present in the description of the way impurity is transmitted

---

20. Lev 1:1; 4:1; 5:14, 20; 6:1, 12, 17; 7:22, 28; 8:1; 10:8; 11:1; 12:1; 13:1; 14:1, 33; 15:1; 16:1, et al. (36× between Lev 1:1 and 27:1).

21. Lev 1:2; 4:2; 6:18; 7:23; 7:29; 12:2; 16:2, et al.

22. Lev 6:2, 7, 18; 7:1, 7, 11, 37; 11:46; 12:7; 13:59; 14:2, 32, 54, 57; 15:32; 26:46.

23. See Nihan, *From Priestly Torah to Pentateuch*, 307.

and which persons and objects are susceptible to defilement. 'Touching' plays a prominent role not only with regard to the transmission of impurity and the defilement from unclean animals but also with regard to impurity due to scale disease and genital discharges. 'Touching'/'the touch' is used up to 74× times in Leviticus 11–15 and must, therefore, have a decisive function in the understanding of the subject matter. Syntactically, it is used mostly in the description of the consequences for each particular case of impurity.

The difference between Leviticus 11–15 and Deuteronomy 14 is quite remarkable. Even though near the beginning Deuteronomy 14 prohibits the touching of a carcass (v. 8), the chapter begins and ends with the prohibition of *eating* certain animals and even adds practical instruction about how to make money with carcasses of animals that are not slaughtered properly (v. 21). "Touching" is not an issue in itself, because selling an animal or its fur, bones, or other parts implies that a person must touch it.[24] This prohibition is, therefore, restricted to *dietary* habits, whereas Leviticus 11–15 thematically opens a distinctive semantic field ("touching").

With reference to the matter of touching, beginning with Lev 11:24, it is interesting that Leviticus 11–15 explicitly prohibits the touching of impure persons or objects only twice (Lev 11:8; 12:2). Usually the matter of touching is part of the consequences for each particular case of impurity. See, for example, Lev 15:19–24, the case of regular female discharge (menstrual discharge):[25]

> 19 When a woman has a discharge of blood that is her regular discharge from her body, she shall be in her impurity for seven days, and whoever touches her shall be unclean until the evening. . . . 21 Whoever touches her bed shall wash his clothes, and bathe in water, and be unclean until the evening. 22 Whoever touches anything upon which she sits shall wash his clothes, and bathe in water, and be unclean until the evening; 23 whether it is the bed or anything upon which she sits, when he touches it he shall be unclean until the evening. . . .

The case is brought up (primary impurity: *When a woman has a discharge of blood . . .*), and followed by the consequences (secondary impurity): What happens if person A (pure) touches an impure animal or an impure person B, or any contaminated object. In most cases, the de-

---

24. See *Sipra Shemini* 8:10, according to which only the touching of the flesh (not the bones, teeth, and talons) is prohibited; compare the commentary of R. Josef Bekhor Shor on Deut 14:8.

25. The same structure applies to Lev 11:24–39 and throughout Leviticus 15.

scription does not provide grounds for the stipulation or axiology. The divine speech, therefore, is connected primarily to the *definition* of a person's physical condition rather than to a legal plea. Moreover, the text insists that defilement causing impurity must be comprehended *only* with reference to the Sacred Space/the Holy, whether the *sancta* are explicitly mentioned, as in Lev 12:2, or not, as for example in Lev 11:24.

The status of impurity is the opposite of the status of purity. Both conditions are related only to the sanctuary and do not describe a physical condition as such. The sanctuary requires the status of purity. Therefore, male emission of semen and regular menstrual bleeding do not necessarily lead to a prohibition of touching another person, because this would result in a prohibition on sexual intercourse altogether; rather, they refer to a prohibition on approaching the sanctuary.[26]

A second topic is related to the impurity described so far: impurity is contagious by means of touching a person or objects. The same holds true for holiness. In transferring their state, holiness and impurity are *dynamic*,[27] whereas purity is static. This means that every area (the holy as well as the impure—both representing a particular space) tends to extend its spatial dimension. This guideline is established in the sections on the offerings and the portions for the priests; see, for example, Lev 6:18–21:

> Every male among the descendants of Aaron shall eat of it [= portion of my offerings] . . . anything that touches them shall become holy. . . . 19 The priest who offers it as a sin offering shall eat of it; it shall be eaten in a holy place, in the court of the tent of meeting. Whatever touches its [the sacrifice's] flesh shall become holy; and when any of its blood is spattered on a garment, you shall wash the bespattered part in a holy place.

Corresponding to contamination of the pure by contact with the impure, these sections describe the opposite: the (possible) transfer of the state of holiness from one object to another. However, as the unknown authors let us know, according to the divine decree, the Priestly task is it to prevent this situation from ever occurring. The sacrifices must be

---

26. The topic of forbidden sexual relations mentioned in Lev 18:19 and 20:18 (belonging to the Holiness Code) is embedded into a different literary and theological context. Likewise, the prohibition of sexual intercourse with a menstruating woman in later rabbinic literature was part of an erotic discourse rather than being an issue of ritual purity.

27. This expression was introduced into the subject by J. Milgrom, "The Dynamics of Purity in the Priestly System," in *Purity and Holiness* (ed. M. J. Poorthuis and J. Schwartz; Leiden: Brill, 2000) 29–32.

washed and eaten in a certain place—that is, a holy place (the outer court of the tent of meeting, which is still a holy area). Because the meat's and the blood's holiness is contagious, blood-defiled clothes must stay within the sacred area because, otherwise, the holiness would be extended. Objects belonging to the holy space are not to leave their spatial area, or else they will transfer their holiness to a space inappropriate for them. Thus, impurity and holiness turn out to be complementary entities. It is for this reason that the concept of the sanctification and consecration of the whole community[28] does not match the theological tenor of the texts at hand.

The starting point of the whole idea is God's holiness; he is *qādôš*. Unlike the created world, he is never subject to the categories 'impure' *tāmē* or 'pure' *tāhôr*. Both areas—the holy and the common—are strictly separated. And it is only with the concept of the tabernacle/the tent of meeting (*miškān*; *'ōhel mô'ēd*) that the area of holiness exceeds its limits. The categories 'impure' *tāmē* and 'pure' *tāhôr* had to be introduced to enable the holy to meet the common. Within this system of spatial categories, holiness cannot spread diffusely into common spaces, because this would mean the annulling of the whole system: holy space requires common space as its boundaries.

As a corollary, patterns of time and spatial dimensions are a central issue in the Priestly narrative.[29] As I have shown elsewhere,[30] the Priestly texts show an extensive use of idiomatic language of repetitive formulas and ritual-style patterns that present spatial and temporal categories (e.g., via an accumulation of deictic particles) to symbolize nonspatial relations. This is true in the larger narrative framework of the text at hand, from the creation story in Genesis 1 to the account of the erection of the tabernacle and the installation of the cult. The meeting between Israel and its God can take place only by means of Priestly mediation in the cult, its spatial area being the tent/tabernacle and Israel's camp around the tabernacle.

The concept of contamination and the transfer of impurity by means of touching persons or objects presupposes this pattern of spatial di-

---

28. See, for example, Exod 19:6.
29. With regard to the patterns of time compare, for example, only the topic of the eight-day scheme: In Gen 17:12, the eighth day is chosen for the circumcision (compare also Lev 12:3); in Lev 9:1, the eighth day is chosen for the dedication of the *miškān*; likewise, the sin of Nadab and Abihu took place on the eighth day; in Lev 14:10, 23 and 15:14, 29, the cleansed *mĕṣōrā'* as well as the *zāb* and *zābâ* bring their special *qorbanôt* on the eighth day.
30. See my "Imaginary Sanctuary," esp. pp. 676–82.

mensions. Within this system, *touching* turns out to be the key term. Primarily, touching denotes contact and subsequently the crossing of (bodily) boundaries. Touching conveys the moment of the formation or existence of spatial areas as well as the crossing of its respective boundaries. Thus, eating (referring to the section on unclean animals) turns out to be an intensifying spatial subcategory of touching. From this point, one can project the way that dietary instructions were developed by the Priestly authors. They formed a sort of reference room, either (1) extratextual, referring to sociocultural norms and traditions (dietary laws, laws of purity); or (2) with regard to the older literary traditions found in Deuteronomy, intertextual—that is, literary references stemming from an existing textual world (for example, the list of unclean birds). By means of fictionalizing, this element was taken from its reference systems and, simultaneously, a new reference system was established into which these decontextualized elements (dietary laws) were fit. This duplication of content forms the "ambiguity within the fictional text":[31]

Former context: e.g., dietary laws; social-cultural laws of purity	Lev 11–15	(One/a variety of) new reference system(s): e.g., the issue of spatial dimension

This sort of structuring is constitutive of fictional literature. In our context, it is all about the contact between one spatial area and another. Therefore, the sequence in Lev 11:29–38 concerning swarming creatures such as weasels, mice, or lizards is dealing particularly with the susceptibility of water or any other kind of liquid to contamination by these creatures, because liquids are most likely to exceed their boundaries and are hard to keep inside their spatial limits.[32]

---

31. Compare W. Iser, "Akte des Fingierens. Oder: Was ist das Fiktive im fiktionalen Text?" in *Funktionen des Fiktiven* (ed. D. Henrich and W. Iser; Munich: Wilhelm Fink, 1983) 121–51; idem, *Das Fiktive und das Imaginäre: Perspektiven literarischer Anthropologie* (Frankfurt/M.: Suhrkamp, 1991) 24–51; idem, *Der Akt des Lesens: Theorie ästhetischer Wirkung* (4th ed.; Munich: Wilhelm Fink, 1994) 155–61; G. Moers, *Fingierte Welten in der ägyptischen Literatur des 2. Jahrtausends v. Chr. Grenzüberschreitung, Reisemotiv und Fiktionalität* (Probleme der Ägyptologie 19; Leiden: Brill, 2001) 38–79.

32. In addition to water, *Sipra Shemini* 8:8 includes a variety of other liquids such as dew, wine, oil, honey, and milk. This topic is later taken up in Qumran and rabbinic literature as part of the issue called בכי יותן-texts—texts dealing with the problem of susceptibility of water/liquids; see, e.g., J. M. Baumgarten, "Liquids and Susceptibility to Defilement, in 4Q Fragments," in *The Eleventh World Congress of Jewish Studies*, division A

It is, therefore, not simply a question of edible and nonedible animals, genital discharges, and skin eruptions, even though an individual regulation on bodily purity may have formed the social-cultural or intertextual reference room for these texts. In this literary context, it is all about the categorization of spatial areas. The category of purity and impurity in correlation with touching unleashes another topical field ("space"). This topical field is not constructed simply as symbolic meaning that reaches beyond what is expressed in the text but is bound to the redundancy and stereotyped language pattern used in these sections: not a single spatial area that impurity may affect is left out. We see this clearly in Lev 15:1–12, 19–27, where a variety of "spaces" are mentioned ("every bed; any saddle; anything that was under him; everything upon which she lies; anything upon which she sits," and so on).

The body of a person with genital discharges and a scale-diseased person or a dead animal acquires a spatial quality: a spatial area of impurity is set up alongside the pure.[33] With regard to the case of *zāraʿat* ('scale-disease'), this becomes even more apparent because the term *zāraʿat* encompasses a variety of eruptions on the skin[34] that characteristically spread and thereby exceed their particular spatial limits. Interestingly enough, the text describes this problem as a disease (almost certainly not a specific disease) that affects the organ (skin) by which a person *touches* something else. *Zāraʿat* thus essentially needs to be placed in the category of the transfer of impurity. This is also the reason that a person is declared pure by the priest if the disease covers all his skin from head to foot (Lev 13:12–14):

> But if the disease breaks out in the skin, so that it covers all the skin of the diseased person from head to foot, so far as the priest can see, then the priest shall make an examination, and if the disease has covered all his body, he shall pronounce him clean of the disease; since it has all

(ed. A. Assaf; Jerusalem: World Union of Jewish Studies, 1994) 193–97; idem, "Liquids and Susceptibility to Defilement in New 4Q Texts," *JQR* (85) 1–2, 91–101; E. Ottenheijm, "Impurity between Intention and Deed: Purity Disputes in First Century Judaism and in the New Testament," in *Purity and Holiness* (ed. M. J. Poorthuis and J. Schwartz; Leiden: Brill, 2000) 129–47.

33. Milgrom (*Leviticus*, 44) points out rightly that Leviticus 15, therefore, determines fixed spatial areas and objects (e.g., bed, seat, saddle; underneath a person, at the place where the flow comes out) to be contaminated by genital discharge, etc. There is no diffusely contagious impurity floating in the room.

34. See Milgrom, ibid., 775–76, 816–26; J. Schwartz, "On Birds, Rabbis and Skin Disease," in *Purity and Holiness* (ed. M. J. Poorthuis and J. Schwartz; Leiden: Brill, 2000) 207–22, esp. pp. 207–8; J. Zias, "Death and Disease in Ancient Israel," *BA* 54 (1991) 146–59, esp. pp. 149–50.

turned white, he is clean. But if raw flesh ever appears on him, he shall be unclean.

The disease has spread to the bodily boundaries. Additional spreading of the rash is impossible, and the state of impurity has changed from dynamic to static, and impurity is therefore unable to transfer to another spatial area.[35] When declaring a person unclean, the priest fixes these boundaries. Impurity is the category that the priest determines on behalf of the divine. It is not a state of health as such.[36] As a corollary, the Priestly texts refer to these spatial areas and boundaries also in the descriptions of the purification and elimination rituals: the substance of ritual application (blood, oil) is placed on the lobe of a person's right ear, the thumb of the right hand, and the big toe of the right foot—either of the priest or of the person to be cleansed (blood: Exod 29:20; Lev 8:23–24; 14:14, 25; oil: Lev 14:17, 28). All the body parts mentioned symbolize the outer boundaries of a person's body.[37]

The texts, therefore, describe the categorization of Israel's world into a variety of spatial areas to be judged and determined by the priests. As a categorization within very closely fixed frames of time patterns, these texts are not primarily a practical manual for the priests to refer to when dealing with impure persons and objects. This also becomes apparent with regard to the "gaps" in the text, which one will notice as soon as (s)he tries to read the material as a guidebook for cultic practices.[38]

To conclude, the question arises why these stages and transmissions of purity and impurity are depicted in such great detail if, as suggested here, no practical conclusions are drawn at first glance. Although the section on ritual purity describes the subject matter as being applied to

---

35. Remember that only holiness and impurity were considered dynamic!
The transferring or the lack of transferring impurity may be the reason why the section on *zāraʿat* and its purifications are located in the center of the laws of ritual purity.

36. Compare *m. Neg.* 3:1 and 3:2, where the rabbis not only declared that the laws on *zāraʿat* do not apply to non-Jews but also that a (Jewish) groom during his wedding week and folks gathered for pilgrim festivals do not need to undergo the procedure of priestly examination: הכל מיטמאין בנגעים חוץ מן העובדי כוכבים וגר תושב . . . חתן שנראה בו נגע נותנין לו שבעת ימי המשתה לו ולביתו ולכסותו וכן ברגל נותנין לו כל ימות הרגל.

37. One could also interpret the instruction in Exod 12:7 in this way—that is, the application of the blood to the two doorposts and the lintels (על שתי המזוזת ועל המשקוף) is an indication of boundaries (inside: Israel; outside: Egypt); see my "Funktion der 'Verstockung' Pharaos in der Erzählung vom Auszug aus Ägypten (Ex 7–14)," *BN* 93 (1998) 56–76, esp. pp. 71–75.

38. Only in later literary layers of the Hebrew Bible as well as in other texts from the Second Temple Period (especially in the *Temple Scroll* and in *Miqṣat Maʿaśê ha-Torah*) have the texts been understood and/or even revised in this way.

and valid for the common space or, better yet, for a person's private space, ritual purity is tightly bound to the narrative about the erection of the tabernacle and the installation of the cult by means of its textual frames. A woman in childbed should not touch consecrated things (in later Jewish literature, particularly sacred food).[39] A person who has been contaminated by a carcass should not approach the sanctuary, and so on. Concerning the most private issues, such as seminal emissions and menstrual bleeding—contamination with which is not even under someone's control except for the impure person him- or herself—the *sanctuary intrudes into human lives*, because defilement causing impurity acquires its relevance only with reference to the sacred space. It is for this reason that later rabbis declared the prohibition of touching an animal to be relevant only when the person in question is going to the temple.[40]

Therefore, contrary to Christophe Nihan's argument that "the legislation on impurities stresses the fact that the boundaries defining this cosmic order are continuously threatened by the intrusion of organic . . . and therefore chaotic, anti-social forces,"[41] thereby emphasizing the horizontal level, our investigation turns out to demonstrate quite the opposite: these texts set up a system of the ongoing *imagination of the sanctuary*, especially (but not necessarily only) in times when it no longer existed. Not chaotic and antisocial forces but the sanctuary is the entity that intrudes into humans' lives and minds. Certainly, manuals on dietary habits or the prohibition of sexual intercourse with menstruating women may have been part of a common social-cultural taboo.[42] However, in this context they constitute a *fictional* text within a text. They do not participate in the text simply as a factual report on Israel's cultic practices.

---

39. Compare S. Cohen, "Purity and Piety: The Separation of Menstruants from the Sancta," in *Daughters of the King: Women and the Synagogue—A Survey of History, Halakhah, and Contemporary Realities* (ed. S. Grossmann and R. Haut; Philadelphia: Jewish Publication Society, 1992) 103–15; S. Pfann, "A Table Prepared in the Wilderness: Pantries and Tables, Pure Food and Sacred Space at Qumran," in *Qumran—The Site of the Dead Sea Scrolls: Archaeological Interpretations and Debates* (Proceedings of a Conference Held at Brown University, 2002; ed. K. Galor et al.; Leiden: Brill, 2006) 159–78.

40. See, e.g., *b. Roš Haš.* 16b (see also above, n. 35).

41. Nihan, *From Priestly Torah to Pentateuch*, 325.

42. See, e.g., S. S. Soroudi, "The Concept of Jewish Impurity and Its Reflection in Persian and Judeo-Persian Traditions," *Irano-Judaica* 3 (1994) 142–70; A. V. Williams, "Zoroastrian and Judaic Purity Laws: Reflections on the Viability of a Sociological Interpretation," *Irano-Judaica* 3 (1994) 72–89; see also Milgrom, *Leviticus*, 1000–1004.

On the other hand, these cultic "realities" portrayed in the text are not mere fiction. Their admission to the text arises from an 'act of fictionalizing' (Iser's *Akt des Fingierens*). The cultic system is not presented for its own sake. Rather, it functions as a reference or means to something that does not exist but is being made imaginable (sacred and common space). By means of fictionalizing, the authors present the world as an "as if." The fiction relinquishes any reference to the ritual practice in order to organize what seems impossible or is concealed in reality. Holiness is conserved within the only room that has been left to it: the realm of literature, that is, the "Holy" Scriptures. Leviticus 11–15 is thus far more than a written witness to regulations on ritual purity. These authors, probably in the 5th or 6th century, formed or even transformed their ritual practice into literature as one, if not the only space in which the categories of ritual purity mentioned were still valid.

Only by means of this literary fictionalization could the system of ritual purity, and thus *the idea of the sacred surrounded by the common*, be upheld. Whether this was the biblical authors' aim or not, this structure mirrors the state of affairs exactly as it is today. Every (educated) Jew today is well aware of the fact that (s)he stays in the state of impurity permanently (at least due to corpse impurity). If there were a sanctuary, Jews in this state of impurity would have to undergo certain purifications (ablutions, sacrificial rites). Because there is no sanctuary today, the only thing that remains is the awareness of the Jewish person's impure condition, which does not matter at all but is grounded in these texts.

Fiction and Imagination in Early Christian Literature

The Acts of the Apostles as a Test Case

UTE E. EISEN

Justus-Liebig-Universität Gießen

> No one can transcend the verbal character that the present and the past become, and no one can reach what *actually* is or *really* was. "Since Friedrich Nietzsche," says Hayden White in an interview, "it is all metaphor," figurative language.[1]

Until recently, the literary-critical categories *fiction* and *fictionality* have only seldom been used in New Testament research and, then, cautiously.[2] Definitions of these terms in literary-critical debates are legion and sometimes quite contradictory, thus making extensive discussion

---

1. H.-J. Goertz, *Unsichere Geschichte: Zur Theorie historischer Referentialität* (Universal-Bibliothek 17035; Stuttgart: Reclam, 2001) 13 (translation Margaret B. Lampe).

2. This changes increasingly; see most recently K. Backhaus and G. Häfner, *Historiographie und fiktionales Erzählen: Zur Konstruktivität in Geschichtstheorie und Exegese* (Biblisch-Theologische Studien 86; Neukirchen-Vluyn: Neukirchener Verlag, 2007); A. Leinhäupl-Wilke, "Lebendige Erinnerung: Evangelien als Erzähltexte," *Bibel und Kirche* 62 (2007) 142–44; B. Schmitz, "Die Bedeutung von Fiktionalität und Narratologie für die Schriftauslegung," in *'Der Leser begreife': Vom Umgang mit der Fiktionalität biblischer Texte* (ed. H.-G. Schöttler; Münster: LIT, 2006) 137–49; J. Schröter with A. Eddelbüttel, eds., *Konstruktion von Wirklichkeit: Beiträge aus geschichtstheoretischer, philosophischer und theologischer Perspektive* (Theologische Bibliothek Töpelmann 127; Berlin: de Gruyter, 2004); J. Schröter, "Neutestamentliche Wissenschaft jenseits des Historismus: Neuere Entwicklungen in der Geschichtstheorie und ihre Bedeutung für die Exegese der urchristlichen Schriften," *TLZ* 128 (2003) 855–66; idem, "Von der Historizität der Evangelien," in *Der historische Jesus: Tendenzen und Perspektiven der gegenwärtigen Forschung* (ed. J. Schröter and Ralph Brucker; BZNW 114; Berlin: de Gruyter, 2002) 163–212; L. Alexander, "Fact, Fiction and the Genre of Acts," *Acts in Its Ancient Literary Context* (Library of New Testament Studies 298; London: T. & T. Clark, 2005) 380–99; E. Plümacher, "TERATEIA: Fiktion und Wunder in der hellenistisch-römischen Geschichtsschreibung und in der Apostelgeschichte," in *Geschichte und Geschichten: Aufsätze zur Apostelgeschichte und zu den Johannesakten* (ed. J. Schröter and R. Brucker; WUNT 170; Tübingen: Mohr Siebeck, 2004) 33–83.

215

impossible within the framework of this essay.[3] One thing is clear: in recent literary criticism, the terms *fiction* and *fictionality* are no longer being limited to entirely imaginary narratives, such as detective stories or
novels. In the present study, I will expand on this concept, supported by
a consideration of the Latin meaning of *fictio* and its derivatives. Recourse to the Latin meaning provides considerably more leeway in dealing with the concept than has commonly been thought. In the Latin
dictionary of *Lewis and Short*, *fictio* is generally defined as "a making,
fashioning, forming, formation" as well as a rhetorical *terminus techni-
cus* that is translated 'an assumed or fictional case, a supposition, fiction'.
According to the *Oxford Advanced Learner's Dictionary*, *forming* and *formation* are defined as "the action of forming something" and *supposition*
can be paraphrased as "an idea that you think is true although you may
not be able to prove it"; the verb *suppose* can mean "to think or believe
that something is true or possible."

Already these definitions show the spectrum of *fictio*'s meaning.
Considering these translations and paraphrases, which could be expanded extensively, it is clear that understanding the word simply as
"fictitious" in the sense of "made up" is not sufficient to capture the
breadth of its meaning.[4] *Fictio* and *fingere* mean in the most general
sense a "creation, composition"—so, on the one hand, "to construct"

---

3. For the spectrum of definitions of the terms see, for example, F. Zipfel, *Fiktion,
Fiktivität, Fiktionalität: Analysen zur Fiktion in der Literatur und zum Fiktionsbegriff in der
Literaturwissenschaft* (Allgemeine Literaturwissenschaft: Wuppertaler Schriften 2; Berlin:
Schmidt, 2001) 13–29. Concerning the debate surrounding the term *fictionality* in literary
criticism, compare especially the two anthologies *Funktionen des Fiktiven* (ed. D. Henrich
and W. Iser; Munich: Fink, 1983); and *Fiktion, Wahrheit, Wirklichkeit: Philosophische Grund-
lagen der Literaturtheorie* (ed. M. E. Reicher; Paderborn: Mentis, 2006). Furthermore, from
all the abundance of literature, the following monographs and articles are suggested:
A. Assmann, "Die Legitimität der Fiktion: Ein Beitrag zur Geschichte der literarischen
Kommunikation," *Theorie und Geschichte der Literatur und der schönen Künste* (Texte und
Abhandlungen 55; Munich: Fink, 1980); eadem, "Fiktion als Differenz," *Poetica* 21 (1989)
239–60; K. L. Walton, *Mimesis as Make-Believe: On the Foundation of the Representational
Arts* (Cambridge: Harvard University Press, 1990); K. Kasics, *Literatur und Fiktion: Zur
Theorie und Geschichte der literarischen Kommunikation* (Reihe Siegen 94; Heidelberg: Carl
Winter Universitätsverlag, 1990); A. Kablitz, "Kunst des Möglichen: Prolegomena zu
einer Theorie der Fiktion," in *Poetica* 35 (2003) 251–73; E. Esposito, *Die Fiktion der wahr-
scheinlichen Realität* (Frankfurt am Main: Suhrkamp, 2007).

4. In connection with the question of fiction and fictionality, there are also the questions: What is truth? What is actuality? What is reality? This discussion is too lengthy to
be carried out within the framework of this essay. For an orientation to these questions,
see, for example, P. Lampe, *Die Wirklichkeit als Bild: Das Neue Testament als ein Grund-
dokument abendländischer Kultur im Lichte konstruktivistischer Epistemologie und Wissenssozi-
ologie* (Neukirchen-Vluyn: Neukirchener Verlag, 2006), especially pp. 30–43; or Goertz,
Unsichere Geschichte.

and, on the other hand, "to make up, to conceive."[5] The narrower understanding of the word has long entailed the categorical differentiation between fictional and factual literature; in other words: which literature is imagined (for example, novels) and which literature corresponds to happenings (for example, histories). This view focused on the dichotomy between *poetry* and *history* as understood since Plato, at the latest.

However, in recent literary and historical-critical research, the entire semantic field of *fiction* has increasingly been moving beyond purely imagined literature, extending especially to historiographical narratives. Several authors have adopted this well-established trend, for example, Hayden White in the Anglo-American context, Paul Ricoeur in the French, and Arnaldo Momigliano in the Italian.[6] Programmatically also the fictional character of historiography is clear in the German title of Hayden White's collection of essays, which is translated *Also Clio Writes Poetry, or the Fiction of the Factual* (*Auch Klio dichtet oder die Fiktion des Faktischen*).[7] According to White, it is the "constructive imagination" of the historian that narrates the past and thus selects from an unordered mass of data, emphases, subordinations, and constructs.[8] He compares the historian to a "competent detective" who unravels the case based on the available source materials and is "capable of putting the right questions to it."[9] According to White, every historical presentation thus has an element of fiction, but conversely, every fiction also contains an element of the "real."[10] Literary and historical narratives

---

5. Based on one possible translation of the Latin term from Quintilian's *Institutionis Oratoriae* in E. Zundel, *Clavis Quintilianea: Quintialian's 'Institutio oratoria' aufgeschlüsselt nach rhetorischen Begriffen* (Darmstadt: Wissenschaftliche Buchgesellschaft, 1989) 39.

6. P. Ricoeur, *Temps et récit* (3 vols.; Paris: Seuil, 1983–85), especially vol. 1; Arnaldo Momigliano, *Les fondations du savoir historique* (Paris: Les Belles lettres, 1992).

7. The German subtitle is: *Studien zur Tropologie des historischen Diskurses* (Einführung von R. Koselleck; Stuttgart: Klett-Cotta, 1986). The original English version: *Tropics of Discourse: Essays in Cultural Criticism* (Baltimore: Johns Hopkins University Press, 1978).

8. Compare H. White, *Metahistory: The Historical Imagination in Nineteenth-Century Europe* (Baltimore: Johns Hopkins University Press, 1973); and the two essay collections: idem, *Tropics of Discourse* and *The Content of the Form: Narrative Discourse and Historical Representation* (ed. H. White; Baltimore: Johns Hopkins University Press, 1987). The New Testament scholar Peter Lampe arrives at the same result but on the basis of other premises: he uses a constructivist paradigm. See especially the closing chapter, "Ausblick auf eine konstruktivistische Theorie der Geschichtsschreibung," in Lampe, *Die Wirklichkeit als Bild*, 180–89.

9. White, "The Historical Text as Literary Artefact," *Tropics of Discourse*, 81–100 (esp. p. 84).

10. See ibid., 97–98.

breathe the imaginary as well as the factual; they construct and interpret narrative(s).

Individual occurrences of events are selected and described from an
unending current of past events; that is to say, interpretive selection
and constructive memory take place. In the flow of the narrative,
events are newly created, because no event can be as congruently presented or retold as it actually occurred, because it is gone. Even eyewitnesses describe the same event differently according to their own
perspectives, as Thucydides already noted (1.22.3). In addition, historical events are largely nonverbal and are transformed and shaped in
the process of being verbalized. But even verbal events such as conversations or speeches are normally changed in the process of recounting
if no recording is made.

With every narrative of past events, things are changed and to a
certain extent newly created.[11] This modern realization was already
perceived in Greco-Roman historiography. Eckhard Plümacher aptly
summarizes this way: "[T]he presence of fictional elements, whether
in exaggerated accounts or even in fabricated details and events, was,
in any case, normal within a great number of historical works, especially in Greco-Roman historiography with what used to be called the
'tragic-pathetic'—better termed 'mimetic' or 'sensational'—mode of
historiography."[12] Lucian also assumed it to be quite normal that historical narrative cannot take place without some things being made
up, but he qualifies this by saying that, in a historical work, complete
fiction is not well received (*How to Write History* §10).

Pursuing the meaning of fiction further, one soon confronts the verb
fingere. The *Latin Dictionary* of *Lewis and Short,* for example, translates it
'to form, shape, fashion, frame, make', further distinguishing it as being 'with the access[ory] notion of arranging, adorning, etc., to set to
right, arrange; dress, trim'. An additional, separate meaning in conjunction with falsehood is: 'with the access[ory] notion of untruth, to
alter, change, with the purpose of dissembling'. These definitions alone,
which present only a limited selection, show the scope of the lexical
field. And this gives rise to the question can narrative texts, whether
literary or historical, be formed, configured, and conceived without the

---

11. Raymond Queneau demonstrated this impressively in his book *Exercises de style*
(36th ed.; Paris, 1959), by telling a story in 99 variations.

12. Plümacher, "TERATEIA," 276. The entire article addresses this thesis extensively
and with numerous examples. The author also goes into detail with regard to the ancient
understanding of miracles.

element of "make believe"? Just as White counted on arousing "the ire of historians who believe that they are doing something fundamentally different from the novelist, by virtue of the fact that they deal with 'real,' while the novelist deals with 'imagined,' events,"[13] so some theologians and believers will be provoked when original compositions, (new) creations, or even made-up things are considered in connection with biblical texts. Thus, in the exegetical practice of the past, biblical narratives were labeled as being made up only in a somewhat cryptic way. They were described as "legendary" or in Bultmann's time preferably as "mythical" or as 'church products' (*Gemeindebildungen*). These circumlocutions mean nothing more than that the stories are made up.

In connection with above-described departures from literary and historical criticism, I will argue this thesis:

> **1.** No narrative text, not even one that in the process of its transmission is declared a holy text,[14] comes into existence without being molded and fictionalized to some extent; in other words, every narrative is also made up. This is constitutive of narrative literature.

This holds true for every form of narrative, be it literary, historical, or religious, and in this respect, narrative is not distinguishable from speech. Since antiquity, speech has used explicit strategies of rhetoric to captivate and, ultimately, to convince the public.[15] The same holds true for narrative. Every story is stamped with a narrative interest, strategy, and perspective. Otherwise narration is not possible. Every narrative is a specific appropriation of reality, the two never being identical.[16] Aleida Assmann described reality in her book with the apt title *The Legitimacy of Fiction* as too little and at the same time too much.

---

13. White, "The Historical Text as Literary Artefact," 98.

14. The fact that the biblical texts are the holy Scripture of Christianity does not place their literary character in question. I consider the canonization of biblical books and letters to be a contingent act of the first centuries of the church that does not change the fact that these texts are literature and as such can be analyzed. Concerning the canonization process, compare, for example, B. M. Metzger, *The Canon of the New Testament: Its Origin, Development, and Significance* (Oxford: Clarendon, 1992); and H. von Lips, *Der neutestamentliche Kanon: Seine Geschichte und Bedeutung* (Zurich: Theologischer Verlag, 2004).

15. "History was a branch of rhetoric; it was the author's task to present the narrative in as felicitous a way as possible," J. Marincola asserts aptly (*Authority and Tradition in Ancient Historiography* [Cambridge: Cambridge University Press, 1997] 79–80).

16. "The narrative . . . is a form of explanation, as Arthur C. Danto already stated. What we perceive from the past is transmitted in stories. One cannot talk about the past 'realistically,' only 'metaphorically.' The metaphor does not portray the past reality; it represents it, or even better, it presents it" (Goertz, *Unsichere Geschichte*, 33; translation Margaret B. Lampe).

Primarily through fiction, which Assmann describes as a constructive attempt at understanding, the "too little" in the form of disjointedness and randomness is compensated for by the "too much" in the form of abundance and complexity. She writes:

> We [want] . . . to understand fiction as a model of reality, as a constructive design for understanding, which is characterized by the fact that at the same time it exceeds the contingence of the factual and falls short of it. The consistency and coherence of fiction thus are based on a double incongruence in view of the disjointedness and randomness of the real. First: Compared to fiction reality proves to be a 'too little.' Through interpreting connections and the creation of coherency the deficit of the circumstances is repaired. . . . Second: Compared to fiction, reality proves to be a 'too much.' . . . The necessity to choose and through the principle of selection to transform an unclear and meaningless entropy into a meaningful unity characterizes no less the basic situation of every writer.[17]

Reality is primarily a chaotic, amorphous flow of events that is first ordered and then shaped though interpretation. Narrative forms the memory of events or creates conceptions of possible or wished-for events. In this, it works with summarization, conversion, molding, expansion, opening up perspectives, overlapping, and much more. Every narrative has more or less to invent to make the transition, to bridge time, to bring events into succession, to construct monologues or dialogues. Real events cannot be identically represented, just as it is impossible to make up a story in every detail, because it always draws on at least something that is known. Figure 1 demonstrates this.

The real/ reality/ so-called factual report	←————————→ ←————————→ ←————————→	The completely imagined that has no reference to experienced reality/ fantasy literature
Not presentable	Possibilities of the account	Not presentable[18]

For the Acts of the Apostles, the creative and fictitious are clarified by the many speeches that form about one-third of the entire narrative work. Of course, there was no stenographer for the speeches of Peter or

---

17. Assmann, *Legitimität der Fiktion*, 14 (translation mine).

18. T. W. Adorno writes: "If one tries to imagine a totally non-existing object in, as the epistemological theory calls it, fantasizing fiction, one will not find anything, whose elements and even aspects of coherence cannot be reduced to something existing" (*Ästhetische Theorie* [Frankfurt am Main: Suhrkamp, 1970] 259), translation M. B. Lampe.

Paul. In the direct report of the words, the author of Acts conveyed his conception of what Peter or Paul could have said. Through the narrative strategy of direct speech, the author creates the illusion of having been a witness who heard what was said. In this way, the narrative comes across as much more immediate, but it is fictitious, a simulated directness that is so convincing that it is effective even today. Congregations and researchers still debate the question whether these discourses actually took place as presented in Acts.

But within a narrative, where does fact stop and fiction begin? To determine this is neither easy nor unequivocally possible. The decision depends on the imagination of the recipient. This leads to my second thesis:

2. It is characteristic of narrative literature that the lens of the observer (the imagination of the recipient) determines what is considered fictitious or given.

At least since Wolfgang Iser's studies in the 1970s and their *Wirkungs-geschichte* (history of effect), the collaboration of the reader in creating the meaning of a text can hardly be doubted. Iser ties in to the ideas of Roman Ingarden, who developed a dialectic of textual "schemata" and their receptive "concretization." According to Ingarden, texts communicate objects and actions that are only "schematized"; in other words, they are incompletely presented. They contain so-called "gaps" that must first be filled in by the completing, concretizing activity of the recipient.[19] Wolfgang Iser took up this approach in his classic essay "Die Appellstruktur des Textes" ("The Appeal Structure of Texts") as well as in later works[20] and showed how indefinite or (as Iser calls them) blank spaces invite us to different kinds of reception at the various levels of the textual structure.[21] Contrary to Ingarden, who speaks of the need to fill in the blank spaces, Iser emphasizes the need for combination,

---

19. R. Ingarden, *Das literarische Kunstwerk* (4th ed.; Tübingen: Max Niemeyer, 1972) 266 and passim.

20. W. Iser, *Rezeptionsästhetik: Theorie und Praxis* (ed. R. Warning; 4th ed.; Munich: Fink, 1994) 228–52; idem, *The Act of Reading: A Theory of Aesthetics Response* (Baltimore: Johns Hopkins University Press, 1978); idem, *Der implizite Leser: Kommunikationsformen des Romans von Bunyan bis Beckett* (2nd ed.; Munich: Fink, 1979); idem, *Das Fiktive und das Imaginäre: Perspektiven literarischer Anthropologie* (Frankfurt am Main: Suhrkamp, 1991).

21. Long ago, Lucian advised history writers: "Again, if a myth comes along you must tell it, but not believe it entirely; no, make it known for your audience to make of it what they will—you run no risk and lean to neither side" (*How to Write History* §60; LCL; Cambridge: Harvard University Press, 1959).

the schemata of the text are related to one another that the imaginary object can begin to be formed, and it is the blanks that get this connecting operation under way. They indicate that the different segments of the text *are* to be connected, even though the text itself does not say so. They are the unseen joints of the text, and as they mark off schemata and textual perspectives from one another, they simultaneously trigger acts of ideation on the reader's part. Consequently, when the schemata and perspectives have been linked together, the blanks 'disappear'.[22]

Just as events in narratives are consolidated, selected, ordered, expanded, condensed, or arranged with direct speech and the replay of thoughts, so this creative act is repeated in the process of reception (as a new creation), because in the act of reading these combinations, the narrated text is coordinated with the reader's experiences and view of the world. The author's creative composition of a narrative corresponds to the creative imagination of the recipient.

In the following pages, I will clarify these two theses by looking at the New Testament Acts of the Apostles and its exegesis. Acts is from a two-part work (the Lukan corpus), comprising the Gospel of Luke and the book of Acts, which is made clear by the two prologues (Luke 1:1–4; Acts 1:1–2), for example. This two-volume work is unique in the New Testament. Acts describes how the gospel message was carried from Jerusalem to Rome and ends with Paul's two-year stay in the capital city. I intend to use it as an example because for over 100 years a heated controversy has raged regarding the literary and historical character of this text. The point of contention lies in the special form of this text, because it is presented as a historical narrative and has often been viewed as the first church history. Within the scholarly debate, two opposing positions confront each other. One is the Anglo-Saxon school of thought, which includes the German exegete Martin Hengel and his followers. They regard the author of this text, whom together with Irenaeus of Lyon (*Adv. Haer.* 3.1.1) they identify as Luke (the doctor and companion of Paul) and consider him to be the first Christian historian. Acts is understood as a historical work that re-creates events with great historical dependability.[23] Second, the mainstream

---

22. Iser, *The Act of Reading*, 182–83.
23. Representative of this perspective: M. Hengel and A. M. Schwemer write: "Contrary to the widespread anti-Luke 'scholastic' scholarship, we consider Acts to be a work that was written soon after the third Gospel by Luke, the physician, who was Paul's travel companion from the time he brought the collection to Jerusalem. This means that Acts, at least partially, is the first-hand source of an eyewitness to Paul's late period, of which the letters only tell a little" (*Paulus zwischen Damaskus und Antiochien: Die*

German scholars estimate the historical value of Acts to be minimal and emphasize the self-dependent literary and theological formation of early Christian tradition as well as taking into consideration the partially new creations by the anonymous author of the Lukan composite work.[24]

A new controversial issue of the *Zeitschrift für Neues Testament* has the title "How Historical Is the Acts of the Apostles?"[25] The arguments exchanged there by Rainer Riesner and Daniel Marguerat are a representative example of the present situation in the field. Rainer Riesner, who belongs to the tradition of Martin Hengel, takes the position that Acts is a dependable historical work that was composed before the destruction of the temple, thus before 70 C.E., by an eye and ear witness and companion of Paul. Riesner draws on the prologues of the Lukan composite, the so-called "we passages," and the "particular density of chronological, geographical, and other details."[26] He concedes, however, that Luke must have done some inventing in speeches for which no one "took minutes." He also credits Luke with an "ironic tendency" to try to downplay the inner-Christian conflicts among different parties that are evident in other sources. Riesner maintains, however,

---

unbekannten Jahre des Apostels [with a contribution by Ernst Axel Knauf; WUNT 108; Tübingen: Mohr Siebeck, 1998] 10 [translation M. B. Lampe]); similarly M. Hengel, *Acts and the History of Earliest Christianity* (Philadelphia: Wipf & Stock, 1980). See also, for example, C.-J. Thornton, *Der Zeuge des Zeugen: Lukas als Historiker der Paulusreisen* (WUNT 56; Tübingen: Mohr Siebeck, 1991). Other representatives of this position can be found in J. A. Fitzmyer (he himself belongs to this group), *The Acts of the Apostles: A New Translation with Introduction and Commentary* (AB 31; New York: Doubleday, 1998) 51. Most recently: R. Riesner, "Die historische Zuverlässigkeit der Apostelgeschichte," *Zeitschrift für Neues Testament* 18 (2006) 38–43.

24. The commentaries of H. Conzelmann are the most representative, e.g., *Die Apostelgeschichte* (2nd rev. ed.; HNT 7; Tübingen: Mohr, 1972); and E. Haenchen, *Die Apostelgeschichte* (7th rev. ed. of this new interpretation; KEK 3; Göttingen: Vandenhoeck & Ruprecht, 1977; he sees Acts as an edifying book, p. 93). The majority of German exegetes belong to this same group. Among French scholars, D. Marguerat represents this school of thought: *The First Christian Historian: Writing the 'Acts of the Apostles'* (trans. K. McKinney, G. J. Laughery, and R. Bauckham; SNTSMS 121; Cambridge: Cambridge University Press, 2002); idem, "Wie historisch ist die Apostelgeschichte?" *Zeitschrift für Neues Testament* 18 (2006) 44–51. E. Plümacher takes a stimulating, original position in the German discussion by seeing the author of Acts as a historian but at the same time not denying the multifaceted fictional character of Acts; instead, he considers it constitutive, not only for this work, but also for the entirety of ancient mimetic historiography (see idem, TERATEIA).

25. *Zeitschrift für Neues Testament* 18 (2006) 37–51.

26. Riesner, "Die historische Zuverlässigkeit der Apostelgeschichte," 42 (translation M. B. Lampe).

that despite the definitely "panegyric mood of Luke," a "positive evaluation of Lukan historiography is possible."[27]

The French New Testament narratologist Daniel Marguerat, on the other hand, raises the discussion to the level of the philosophical theory of history and thereby goes beyond the above-mentioned German discussion. With regard to Raymond Aron, Henri-Irénée Marrou, and Paul Veyne, he comments, "There is no history outside historical tradition, which is performed by the interpretation in the historian's mind. History is narrative and as such is constructed from a point of view."[28] With Ricoeur, he differentiates three basic forms of historical writing: first, the documentary; second, the descriptive; and third, the poetic. He places Acts in the third category and identifies it more precisely as a so-called fundamental narrative (French: _récit fondateur_), the primary function of which is the endowment of identity on a people or group, although he concedes that Acts also carries traits of other types of history. However, the primary importance of the identity-bestowing aspects of the narrative, according to Marguerat, appears not only in the prologue but also in the use of the first-person plural in the so-called "we" passages. Marguerat writes, "The 'we' is not the handwriting of a chronicler but the identity-creating reassurance of a group that is reclaiming its legitimacy with the inheritance of the Pauline tradition."[29]

In the following, I will develop my two above-formulated theses with selected passages in Acts: the prologues of Luke–Acts, the "we" passages, and a single narrative from Acts—the story of Ananias and Sapphira.

As scholars have already shown, the prologues of the Lukan corpus play a central role in the debate, because the narrator (not to be mistaken for the author) explicitly, and unlike the other Gospels, provides information about his reason for writing his narrative. The prologue of the Gospel of Luke says (Luke 1:1–4):

> [1]In as much as many have undertaken to compile a narrative of the things that have been accomplished among us, [2]just as those who from the beginning were eyewitnesses and ministers of the word have delivered them to us, [3]it seemed good to me also, having followed all things closely for some time past, to write an orderly account for you, most excellent Theophilus, [4]that you may have certainty concerning the things you have been taught.[30]

---

27. Ibid., 41.
28. Marguerat, "Wie historisch ist die Apostelgeschichte?" 45 (trans. M. B. Lampe).
29. Ibid., 50.
30. English Standard Version (2001).

In his prologue, the first-person narrator alludes to already-existing attempts to write a narrative of the events that happened "among us." He also reports that he decided to write down everything. His characterization of his actions shows that he wants to be convincing about giving a better recounting of the events. He wants to accomplish this by carefully researching (*akribōs*) and narrating the events in the right sequence (*kathexēs*), whereby he implies that his forerunners neglected these aspects. With the mention of exactitude (*akribeia*), he moves his work onto the horizon of ancient historiography. Earlier, Thucydides emphasized this virtue in his methodological chapter on the reproduction of actions (1.22).

The narrator of Acts speaks about himself in the first person in the prologue of Acts but remains anonymous throughout the entire Lukan corpus. However, he names the person to whom he dedicates his writings. It is the high-born Theophilus (*kratiste Theophilos*). The narrator formulates the purpose of his report as enabling Theophilus to see that the tradition he was taught is credible.

Hence, in the Lukan prologue the writer formulates a narrative contract to which he again refers at the beginning of Acts. The prologue states (Acts 1:1–2):

> [1]In the first book, O Theophilus, I have dealt with all that Jesus began to do and teach, [2]until the day when he was taken up, after he had given commands through the Holy Spirit to the apostles whom he had chosen.[31]

Here the narrator speaks again in the first person, still as an anonymous "I," to his narrative addressee, Theophilus, who was already referred to in Luke 1:3. He summarizes the contents of his first book in a few words.

Based on narrative analysis, it can be said of the writer of the Lukan corpus, according to the prologues, that he (in Gérard Genette's terms) is an extradiegetic-heterodiegetic narrator.[32] He stands outside the story and is initially not a figure in the narrative. He presents himself as a narrator who, after all previous attempts, now wants to communicate the events with all exactitude and in the correct order. With this, he slips into the role of a thorough researcher, who with his methodical procedure proves himself superior to the "many" who have tried before him. By reminding the reader at the beginning of Acts who he is

---

31. Ibid.
32. See G. Genette, *Narrative Discourse* (Oxford: Blackwell, 1980); idem, *Narrative Discourse Revisited* (Ithaca, NY: Cornell University Press, 1990).

and what his thorough methods are, he creates a kind of *primacy effect* regarding his special narrative authority.[33]

Furthermore, he creates a communication-situation with the specifically named narratee, Theophilus, and thus the narrative acquires the function of an appeal. In addition, Theophilus is characterized as *most excellent* and thus as a person of power and influence. Together with the reader, the narratee is put in a receptive position to recognize the dependability of the teachings. By again mentioning Theophilus directly, (1) the communication channel between the narrator and the narratee is stabilized, and (2) the formula used in the first prologue is recalled. What held true for the first book now also holds true for the second. This connection gives the work cohesion and is intended to make the books' contents dependable.

We have before us a self-confident narrator who wants to prove the credibility of the teachings with his narrative. But he remains anonymous in the prologue. This holds true also for the narrative passages in which he—quite suddenly—places himself in the scene as an eyewitness of the events. This happens in the "we" passages (Acts 16:10–17; 20:5–15; 21:1–18; 27:1–28:16). Here the extradiegetic-heterodiegetic narrator of Acts becomes a homodiegetic narrator. Quite abruptly, he jumps "Mary Poppins–like" into the scene and as Paul's companion becomes an eyewitness to the events: he becomes a figure in the story. This is surprising, because in the prologue he did not appear as an eyewitness. The volume of these "we" narratives, compared with the whole of Acts or even the two books, is limited; there are only four of these passages, sometimes comprising only a few verses. They are scattered throughout 13 chapters. But since the days of the early church, they have been very precisely observed and have inspired not only Irenaeus of Lyon to speculate about the possible author.

In scholarly work, there are also very different interpretations to be considered.[34] (a) The traditional perspective reads these passages with Irenaeus as authentic eyewitness accounts of the author. The passages are taken literally. (b) Within the framework of source-critical

---

33. For *primacy effect*, see the excellent article by M. Perry, "Literary Dynamics: How the Order of a Text Creates Its Meaning," in *Poetics Today* 1 (1979) 35–61, 311–61. On the concept of *authority* in ancient historiography, see the detailed study by Marincola, *Authority and Tradition*.

34. See the excellent overviews of scholarly work by S. M. Praeder, "The Problem of First Person Narration in Acts," *Novum Testamentum* 29 (1987) 193–218; S. M. Sheeley, "Getting into Act(s): Narrative Presence in the 'We' Sections," *Perspectives in Religious Studies* 26 (1999) 203–20, esp. pp. 204–7.

and redaction-critical studies, the "we" passages are often construed as adaptations of "we sources." (c) Vernon K. Robbins represents the hypothesis that the author is using an ancient convention found in tales of sea voyages, because "we" passages are also used to describe these journeys. (d) Recently the "we" passages have increasingly been considered within the context of narratological methodology as a textual strategy. This poses the questions: Which narrative effect does this "we" create? Which narrative strategy does it follow?[35]

Note that the narrator is here alleging to have been a participant in the events and thus an eyewitness, so it is not surprising that these passages were often received in this way.[36] However, no matter whether they are authentic or not (which we can never know with certainty), the narrator gains additional authority as a (fictitious or actual) eyewitness. In Hellenistic historiography, it was considered an honor for the historian to have "experienced 'the spray and swell of the waves' like Odysseus" (*Od.* 12.219);[37] it even "should be an indispensable obligation of every historian to really deserve this title."[38] It is no coincidence that the "we" passages have to do with sea voyages; the dramatic narrative of Paul's shipwreck, which the writer is supposed to have witnessed, is especially impressive (Acts 27).

In summary, in the prologue the author claims the authority of a historian. Now, although subordinate, the authority of the eyewitness emerges at the end of the narrative. According to Robert Scholes and Robert Kellogg, this conforms to the hierarchy of ancient conventions, which valued the report of the historian over that of the eyewitness.[39]

---

35. For more detail, see my *Poetik der Apostelgeschichte: Eine narratologische Studie* (NTOA 58; Fribourg: Academic Press / Göttingen: Vandenhoeck & Ruprecht, 2006); W. S. Campbell, *The "We" Passages in the Acts of the Apostles: The Narrator as Narrative Character* (Studies in Biblical Literature 14; Leiden: Brill, 2007); H. Hupe, *Lukas' Schweigen: Dekonstruktive Relektüren der "Wir-Stücke" in Acta* (Vienna: Passagen, 2008).

36. See, for example, Thornton, *Zeuge des Zeugen*.

37. This concept was popular among ancient historiographers, as is shown, for example, by Lucian's allusion to this Homerian quotation; Lucian, however, distanced himself from it (*How to Write History* §4).

38. See E. Plümacher, "Wirklichkeitserfahrung und Geschichtsschreibung bei Lukas: Erwägungen zu den Wir-Stücken der Apostelgeschichte," in *Geschichte und Geschichten* (WUNT 170; Tübingen: Mohr Siebeck, 2004) 85–108, esp. p. 103, translation M. B. Lampe (see references to Polybius et al., pp. 100–104).

39. R. Scholes and R. Kellogg, *The Nature of Narrative* (London: Oxford University Press, 1966) 242–72; and in reference to the "historian's inquiry," see in detail Marincola, who on the contrary emphasizes that *autopsy was* highly regarded (*Authority and Tradition*, 63–86).

Our narrator claims both authorities for himself, although the emphasis rests on that of the historian, as the prologue in Luke 1:1–4 shows.

The function of the omniscient and eyewitnessing "we" is to put the narrator in the story as a character. However, even in the "we" passages, the narrator is no more identifiable than in the prologues or elsewhere in the narrative. In these passages he plays the minor role of an anonymous supporting actor whose primary characteristic is being Paul's companion. Thus it is not surprising that the narrative of Acts is still read as an authentic report of an eyewitness.

In literary-critical interpretation, the "we" in the passages is understood as a fictitious "we" serving the function of giving particular authority and force to the author and his account. The narrative strategy is *narration* as *reliable narration*. The *reliable narrator* correlates with the just-as-reliable *narratee*, who is characterized as a highly elevated person; in this way, the book is allocated to a corresponding social milieu. Possibly the character Theophilus is also purely fictitious and owes his existence to his textual function alone.

Is the literary-critical perception of the narrative of Acts less valuable or convincing than the conservative perception represented, for example, by many Anglo-Saxon scholars? Quite the contrary, because it portrays an intelligent author who attempts to convince readers and strengthen their faith through his version of the history and at the same time tries to prevail against competing interpretations.

On the level of reception, we found very different possibilities for an interpretation of Acts that depends specifically on the imagination of the recipient. And with this, I return to my second thesis. The conservative reader takes the narrative contract literally; for others, a narrator appears who presents his theological interpretation to men and women with great skill.

Similarly, the narrative of Ananias and Sapphira is perceived in different ways. Acts 5:1–11 says:

> [1]But a man named Ananias, with his wife Sapphira, sold a piece of property, [2]and with his wife's knowledge he kept back for himself some of the proceeds and brought only a part of it and laid it at the apostles' feet. [3]But Peter said, "Ananias, why has Satan filled your heart to lie to the Holy Spirit and to keep back for yourself part of the proceeds of the land? [4]While it remained unsold, did it not remain your own? And after it was sold, was it not at your disposal? Why is it that you have contrived this deed in your heart? You have not lied to men but to God." [5]When Ananias heard these words, he fell down and breathed his last. And great fear came upon all who heard of it. [6]The young men rose and wrapped him up and carried him out and buried him. [7]After an interval of about three

hours his wife came in, not knowing what had happened. [8]And Peter said to her, "Tell me whether you sold the land for so much." And she said, "Yes, for so much." [9]But Peter said to her, "How is it that you have agreed together to test the Spirit of the Lord? Behold, the feet of those who have buried your husband are at the door, and they will carry you out." [10]Immediately she fell down at his feet and breathed her last. When the young men came in they found her dead, and they carried her out and buried her beside her husband. [11]And great fear came upon the whole church and upon all who heard of these things.[40]

Daniel Marguerat describes this narrative as the "most tragic episode in the book of Acts."[41] It is a tragic, not to mention shocking narrative indeed, for the concealment of part of the money that was held back from the sale of the property is not in proportion with the consequences. Both marriage partners suffer death one after the other because of the concealment of the money. Both vv. 5 and 11 state that all who heard of the deaths were greatly frightened (*phobos megas*). Robert O'Toole speaks aptly here of "shock therapy."[42] On the pragmatic level, shock is probably what was supposed to be accomplished by means of this narrative.

This episode must first be defined within its context. A few chapters earlier, the ideal of community property as practiced in the congregation in Jerusalem is described in two summaries (Acts 2:42–47, especially v. 44; 4:32–35[43]). The tenor of these summaries is that the people of the congregation "were of one heart and soul, and no one said that any of the things that belonged to him was his own, but they had everything in common" (Acts 4:32). In both summaries, the ideal of community property is emphasized, and the majority of interpreters are in agreement that these verses present the fiction of a healthy, unified congregation.

---

40. English Standard Version (2001).

41. D. Marguerat, "Ananias and Sapphira (Acts 5,1–11): The Original Sin," *The First Christian Historian* (SNTSMS 121; Cambridge: Cambridge University Press, 2002) 155.

42. R. O'Toole, "'You Did Not Lie to Us (Human Beings) but to God' (Acts 5,4c)," *Bib* 76 (1995) 190.

43. [32]Now the full number of those who believed was of one heart and soul, and no one said that any of the things that belonged to him was his own, but they had everything in common. [33]And with great power the apostles were giving their testimony to the resurrection of the Lord Jesus, and great grace was upon them all. [34]There was not a needy person among them, for as many as were owners of lands or houses sold them and brought the proceeds of what was sold [35]and laid it at the apostles' feet, and it was distributed to each as any had need. (English Standard Version [2001])

Directly following the second idealized summary, two stories from the early Christian congregation are presented and are to be understood as contrasting narratives. First the story of Joseph, named Barnabas, is told. He is a Levite from Cyprus who sells his field and lays his money "at the apostle's feet" (Acts 4:36–37). This narrative of a positive example serves as a foil to the story of Ananias and Sapphira. This married couple violates the ideal of complete community ownership by holding back money from the field they sold. Peter directly confronts Ananias, who falls to the ground and dies. How the death comes about remains a question and is unspecified. It is simply stated that the man fell to the ground, died, was carried out, and was buried. In his speech, it is true that Peter judges Ananias's actions as being lies to God, but he delivers no death sentence on Ananias. Three hours later, Sapphira comes and stands before Peter. She also falls to the ground dead after Peter condemns her actions, and she is carried out by men and buried.

Before I present various interpretations of this narrative, I want to make an observation about the literary form of the text. This story belongs to the genre of miracle stories and especially to the group of "rule miracles of punishment."[44] According to Gerd Theißen, they are more frequent than the "rule miracles of reward," because in antiquity the enforcement of norms relied "more on fear of punishment than on encouragement through praise."[45] In the New Testament, this kind of text appears only twice.[46] In the milieu of early Christianity, miracles involving punishment for going against norms appear primarily in the inscriptions at Epidaurus and also in the writings of Lucian.[47] In Epidaurus, these stories serve to establish the appropriate norms in the temple area. Miracles involving punishment are told in relation to behaviors of people who spied on the *Abaton*, expressed doubt, or misappropriated offerings of thanksgiving. These narratives appear in inscriptions and served as warning signs. Furthermore, numerous narratives about punishment miracles appear in the Talmud: for example, a judge who violates procedural law dies quite suddenly (*Mekilta Mishp.* §20), just as a student who dares, in the presence of the teacher,

---

44. For the following, see G. Theißen, *The Miracle Stories of the Early Christian Tradition* (Philadelphia: Fortress, 1983) 108–11.

45. Ibid., 109.

46. The only other punishing miracle is found in the story about the cursing of the fig tree (Mark 11:12–14).

47. See Theißen, *Miracle Stories*, 109–10.

to decide *halaka* (*b. 'Erub.* 63b) or a Roman who pushes a rabbi aside in the bathroom (*b. Ber.* 62b). Gerd Theißen summarizes: "in the Jewish rule miracles the issue is almost always one of life or death."[48]

These quotations present our narrative of Ananias and Sapphira in a less exotic light than before, proving it to be related especially to narratives in the Talmud. In the Talmud, there is a lack of proportion between actions and consequences, in that comparatively small offenses lead to death. Talmudic scholars and classical historians presumably would be skeptical that these stories from the Talmud and inscriptions from Epidaurus reflect historical reality. These texts clearly have an agenda. Their aim is good conduct, and they achieve this by pointing out the gravity of the situation in drastic terms.

In the following paragraphs, I will present an overview of the reception of the Ananias and Saphira narrative in modern biblical commentaries. The discussion revolves around the question of whether the story is based on a historical event. Thus, Jacob Jervell writes in his 1998 commentary: "It is impossible to dismiss the story as non-historical";[49] he does not elaborate.[50] As an argument for the historicity of the narrative, Walter B. Cannon's ethnological research can be used; he documents the historicity of curses resulting in death.[51] However, the fact that in our story there is no curse speaks against this argument. Nonetheless, I concede that, within a magical understanding of the world, this story is perhaps historically conceivable.

In contrast, some scholars do not consider the entire narrative historical but only its core: a married couple in the congregation withheld money; they were convicted and excluded from the group. In retelling the story, the exclusion from the congregation became death. One argument against the historicity of the entire narrative is that it is hard to imagine that Ananias could have been buried in such a short time and furthermore without informing his wife.

---

48. Ibid., 110.

49. J. Jervell, *Die Apostelgeschichte* (17th ed.; KEK 3; Göttingen: Vandenhoeck & Ruprecht, 1998) 199.

50. It is only clear that he opposes H. Conzelmann and M. Dibelius. Conzelmann writes: "We cannot reconstruct a historical nucleus" (*Die Apostelgeschichte*, 45) and Dibelius labels the story a "legend" (see "Stilkritisches zur Apostelgeschichte," in *Aufsätze zur Apostelgeschichte* [ed. H. Greeven; FRLANT 60; Göttingen: Vandenhoeck & Ruprecht, 1951] 21).

51. See G. Lüdemann, *Das frühe Christentum nach den Traditionen der Apostelgeschichte: Ein Kommentar* (Göttingen: Vandenhoeck & Ruprecht, 1987) 71.

It is also conceivable to understand the entire narrative as fiction. The writing becomes the narrative depiction of Deuteronomy's requirement to purge evil from the midst of the congregation (Deut 13:6, 12; 17:7, 12; 19:19; 21:21; 22:21, 24; 24:7; compare Acts 3:23). The fact that the carrying out of the bodies by young men occurs twice and is strongly emphasized lends this interpretation plausibility, because, as stated, it is actually quite improbable that the removal of the body of Ananias and the burial could have occurred so quickly and without first informing his wife, Sapphira. The narrator's point is simply to demonstrate what happens to those who are not of "one heart and mind," who do not uphold the rules and norms of the group: they will be removed from the congregation.

All of the presented interpretations work with constructions, whether intertextual references, ethnological insights, or recourse to customs, and so on. These ways of interpreting have to do with the imagination involved in producing the text. They interact with the uncertainties, such as the question of how to imagine the death happening in relation to Peter's speech or how to explain the rapid transition from the burial of the husband to the appearance of the wife. Such indefiniteness is filled in by the imagination. So during the process of reception, a new creation takes place. What is read is correlated with one's own experience and knowledge of the world. A person with a magical world view can more easily imagine that the narrative happened as presented. For others, the narrative is the author's creation or is based on an existing tradition that follows the pattern of the given genre of punishment miracles, just as the other miracle stories of Acts are shaped by the context of early Christian miracle stories. The different kinds of reception—whether as a factual event or as a fiction that dramatically illustrates the "gravity" of immoral behavior—allow the narrative to have different effects. Whether a text relates history or makes things believable that did not occur is decided by the manner of reception, which fills in blank spaces through imagination and construction, according to one's own world view.[52]

It can thus be maintained that narratives are constituted more or less through invention, because the past is ultimately lost and can only be found again through creative composition and creative reader-reception. Every narrative entails constructive composition; it selects

---

52. For this constructive process, see, e.g., P. Lampe, *Die Wirklichkeit als Bild* (see also the review by P. Busch, "Der erinnerte Jesus," *Zeitschrift für Neues Testament* 20 [2008] 75–76).

specific events from the ocean of past proceedings and relates these events more or less convincingly by means of narrative strategy—for example, by being true to the details with the goal of a realistic effect or by creating closeness to the events by presenting speeches as direct discourses. The exegesis of the prologues, the "we" passages, and the Ananias and Sapphira narratives in Acts have demonstrated how different composition strategies and receptions can be.

In the act of reception, narrative and imagination begin a game of probabilities and possibilities, and biblical narratives are not excluded from this process. They, too, use constructive remembrance. From the flow of past events, specific incidents are singled out or created by analogy, and narrative strategies are used in different ways to form and interpret. Narratives are constructive annexations, allowing themselves to be heard in the choir of other annexation processes. This interplay calls for dialogue about plural interpretations and should animate the present theological discourse. Recall the polyphony of interpretations regarding Jesus' crucifixion in the New Testament. No longer must each of these narrative interpretations be understood as an exhaustive representation of the actual event; instead, it can be understood as a creative attempt to take hold of a date in history that in the process of acquisition promises salvation.

Fictions and Formulations:
The Talmud and the Construction of Jewish Identity

DAVID KRAEMER

Jewish Theological Seminary, New York

Recognition of the Talmud's literary qualities emerged decades ago, beginning in earnest with the works of Avraham Weiss, followed then by Shamma Friedman and others.[1] *Literary*, in this context, was a very rough term, a term the meaning of which was assumed to have a kind of common sense taken-for-grantedness. It was entirely untheorized, as these scholars showed little or no awareness of the theoretical debates that swirled around them. Used by them, the term *literary* meant that the text in question was sometimes formulated for stylistic as opposed to legal or logical reasons—as though legal writing was not also literary and literature was not driven by logic.

For some involved in this work, recognition of the Talmud's literary qualities also included recognition of fictions in the talmudic text, though this latter point has been far more controversial. To be sure, few have disputed that there are at least occasional fictions in the Talmud's recounting of rabbinic deliberations, as even medieval rabbinic commentators admit. But there has been little agreement with regard to the extent of these fictions, and most mainstream scholars of the Talmud, wondering why the sages of the Talmud would "lie," grant the veracity of talmudic reports and representations unless there is reason to believe otherwise. But whatever an individual scholar's opinion regarding the question of fictions, that the Talmud is, in its way, "literary" is today barely challenged.

---

1. For Weiss's contribution, see, in particular, *Al ha-yetzirah ha-sifrutit shel ha-amoraim* (*Studies in the Literature of the Amoraim*) (New York: Horeb Yeshiva University, 1962). Friedman's method and assumptions are outlined in his introduction to *Pereq ha-isha rabba bebavli* (Jerusalem and New York: Jewish Theological Seminary of America, 1977). Among other contributions, of particular note is the work of David Halivni. See especially his introduction to *Meqorot umesorot: Eruvin-pesahim* (Jerusalem: Jewish Theological Seminary, 1982).

Nevertheless, it may fairly be questioned why the Talmud's "literariness" matters, and, more importantly in this context, what the literary nature of the Talmud's formulation has to do with the construction of rabbinic-Jewish identity. A number of years ago, I began to offer an answer to these questions, though the fact that the question of identity was central to my project was not fully appreciated. In my book *Reading the Rabbis: The Talmud as Literature*, I sought to offer far more than a collection of literary readings of selected talmudic texts. The texts I chose, read through a self-consciously literary lens, were intended to tell the story of an identity unique to the talmudic rabbis.

Before elaborating the argument I made, I must say a word about my theoretical orientation.[2] I am inclined to agree with theorists such as Terry Eagleton, who ultimately deny the possibility of defining a distinct category of writings that we might call *literature*.[3] Instead, literature is defined by the lens we bring to a text—the way one reads, the questions one asks, the qualities one notices, and so forth. I also find particular value in the sort of reader-response criticism that seeks to imagine the intended, competent reader of a text—a reader who may be identified, at least in large part, by what we know of the historical context in which a text was produced, by whom it was produced, and from the signals embedded in the text itself, particularly what the text expects of the reader before, in the partnership of text and reader, its sense can be discerned. Because a text will mean different things to different readers, if we want to state something about what an author wished to say, we must first do all we can to recover his intended audience. With respect to the Talmud, it seems to me that we can go quite far in accomplishing just this. And by putting ourselves in the position of that audience, we can take significant steps toward recovering not only the reader's responses but also the talmudic author's intended communications.

With respect to my earlier work, permit me to elaborate the trajectory of my program for recovering the rabbinic "identity-narrative." The shank of my book comprises these chapters: (2) "Torah, Written and Oral"; (3) "The Rabbis and Scripture"; (4) "Rhetorics of Tradition and Innovation"; (5) "On Truth, Human and Divine"; and (6) "Pluralism and Pragmatism." Perhaps it will not be obvious from the titles of these

---

2. A far more complete exposition of the positions taken in this paragraph may be found in *Reading the Rabbis* (Oxford: Oxford University Press, 1996) 3–17.

3. See Terry Eagleton, *Literary Theory: An Introduction* (Minneapolis: University of Minnesota Press, 1983) 7–8.

chapters, but together they are meant to tell a story, one that follows the following trajectory: the central identifier of rabbinic as opposed to other Judaisms in antiquity was the claim that God revealed two Torahs, one written and one oral. But the oral, which, in the rabbinic view, is ultimately the privileged Torah, is not revealed in the same sense as the written Torah. According to the Babylonian Talmud (the Bavli), much of what is called the oral Torah is the product of interpretation—that is, of applied human reasoning. In fact, when reasoning faces Scripture, reasoning often prevails. Read with a keen and discerning eye, the rabbis, in the Talmud, illustrate the fact that central rabbinic principles and laws do not originate in Scripture or even in revelation. In fact, the Talmud admits, rabbinic method yields genuine innovation—innovation that, despite the other Talmud's (the Yerushalmi's) claim to the contrary, was not revealed to Moses at Sinai. Admitting the outcomes of this ever-so-human process, the rabbis behind the Bavli allow that their method yields multiple possible truths. Indeed, a human method, as opposed to a divine one, could only yield such multiplicity. And this is a reality the rabbis affirm, at least in theory. But the question then arises: what is to be done in practice? Here the answer is genuinely surprising. Though one could imagine a rabbinic insistence on practical uniformity—despite theoretical multiplicity—this does not turn out to be so. The same rabbis who affirm multiple theoretical opinions allow for multiplicity in practice as well, on the condition that different communities observing different regulations respect the legitimacy of the alternative. The rest of my book is spent exploring several specific examples in which this multiplicity finds expression.

I hope it will not be difficult to see that this narrative describes a unique rabbinic identity. By identifying themselves with an oral Torah, these rabbis distinguished themselves from the majority of ancient Jews who, in the 5th or 6th century, still knew only one Torah, a written Torah. By insisting that this oral Torah comprises significant human elements, that it is often the product of human reasoning, and that it yields genuine innovations, they even distinguished themselves from their rabbinic colleagues in Palestine, who accepted only a far more traditional, more divine oral Torah. And by affirming the legitimacy of multiple truths or outcomes, theoretical and practical, they distinguished themselves from the variety of religious leaders, Jewish and non-Jewish, who continued to insist on a single truth and a single legitimate practice.

I admit that this narrative is merely one interpretation of the literature left us by the rabbis in the Talmud. But it is a plausible and even powerful interpretation that is supported by the approaches and insights that buttress any literary reading (I invite you to read the book to evaluate my claim here). So why has the identity of the talmudic rabbis never been characterized in quite this same way before? Because readers have never read their record in quite this way before. I claim, in fact, that only by reading these texts and others like them through this, the literary lens, does one fully appreciate the identity of the rabbis, whose identity came to define virtually all of medieval Judaism in the centuries to follow.

Here I offer another example of a text that, read with a literary lens—a lens that is attentive to the text's fictions and manipulations—yields important information about the rabbinic-Jewish identity, in this case, an identity that only ambivalently distinguishes itself from the Gentile identity. The text, found in tractate *'Abodah Zarah*, folio 30a, discusses details of a larger prohibition, that is, wine that was prohibited to Jews because of Gentile contact.

According to rabbinic law, as recorded already by the end of the 2nd century in *Mishnah 'Abodah Zarah*, any wine that has been handled by a Gentile is prohibited to Jews for two reasons: (1) because it may have been handled with the intention of offering it as a libation to an idol, and (2) because drinking wine with a Gentile might lead to overly familiar relations with the Gentile or, more particularly, with his daughter. To these, the Mishnah elsewhere (*Terumot* 8:4) adds a third reason: (3) the Gentile may have left his wine uncovered and a snake might, therefore, have drunk from it and left its venom behind. This, presumably, would represent a danger to life (8:6).

The present talmudic text discusses various limits on or compromises of the wine prohibition as here described. The limits pertain, in different ways, to "boiled" and to what the rabbis call mixed (that is to say, diluted) wines. "Boiled" (or "cooked"), in this context, means not literally boiled but heated to the level that the hand would be scalded by coming into contact with the liquid. "Mixed" or diluted refers to the common Roman practice of mixing wine and water, at least in formal settings.[4] For reasons we may not recover, the rabbis were of the opinion that heating or diluting the wine would affect the Gentile's willingness to use said wine in rituals of worship and the snake's willingness to drink from it.

---

4. For a brief discussion of Roman practice, see Tom Standage, *A History of the World in 6 Glasses* (New York: Walker, 2005) 78.

The central part of the Talmud's discussion is this (italicized sections are in Aramaic in the original; sections printed in roman typeface are originally in Hebrew):[5]

II.4 A. *Both Rabbah and R. Joseph say,* "Mixed wine is not prohibited out of fear that it was left uncovered, and boiled wine is not prohibited out of fear that it was poured as libation wine."

B. *The question was raised:* Is boiled wine prohibited out of fear that it was left uncovered, or is it not prohibited out of fear that it was left uncovered?

C. *Come and take note:* R. Jacob bar Idi testified concerning boiled wine that it is not prohibited out of fear that it was left uncovered.

II.5 A. *R. Yannai bar Ishmael was sick. R. Ishmael b. Zerud and rabbis came to call on him. They sat and raised this question:* Is boiled wine prohibited out of fear that it was left uncovered, or is it not prohibited out of fear that it was left uncovered?

B. *Said to them R. Ishmael b. Zerud, "This is what R. Simeon b. Laqish said in the name of a major authority, and who is that?* It is R. Hiyya: 'Boiled wine is not prohibited out of fear that it was left uncovered.'"

C. *They said to him, "May we rely upon this?"*

D. *Gestured R. Yannai b. R. Ishmael,* "Rely on me and on my shoulders."

II.6 A. *Samuel and Ablat were sitting together. Boiled wine was brought for them, and Ablat drew back his hand.*

B. Samuel said to him, "Lo, they have said: boiled wine is not prohibited out of fear that it was poured as libation wine."

II.7 A. *The servant girl of R. Hiyya found boiled wine that had been left uncovered. She came before R. Hiyya, who said to her,* "Lo, they have said: boiled wine is not prohibited out of fear that it was left uncovered."

II.8 A. *The servant of R. Adda bar Ahba found diluted wine that had been left uncovered. He said to him,* "Lo, they have said: diluted wine is not prohibited out of fear that it was left uncovered."

B. *Said R. Pappa, "They have made that statement only of wine that has been well diluted, but if it is only slightly diluted, [a snake] might drink of it."*

---

5. This translation is based on Jacob Neusner's and modified for the purposes of this essay.

C. *And if the wine is only slightly diluted, is it a fact that a snake will drink of it? And lo, Rabbah bar R. Huna was going along in a boat and he had some wine with him. He saw a snake swimming through the water and approaching, so he said to his servant, "Drive it away." The servant took some water and poured it into the wine, and the snake turned away.*

D. *[What this proves is only that] for pure wine the snake will take risks, but for diluted wine it won't take risks.*

E. *And won't it take risks for diluted wine? And lo, R. Yannai was at Akbori. They were sitting and were drinking diluted wine. Some was left in the jug, so they tied a rag upon it. He saw a snake carrying water, which it poured into the cask, until the cask was so filled that the wine rose above the rag, and then it drank.*

F. *[What this proves is only that] if the snake itself dilutes the wine, it will drink the wine, but if others dilute it, it won't drink the wine.*

G. *Said R. Ashi and some say, R. Mesharshiyya, "Does one insist on such solutions in a matter in which danger to life is involved?"*

H. *Said Raba, "The decided law is this:* mixed wine is prohibited out of fear that it was left uncovered and is prohibited as libation wine. Boiled wine is not prohibited out of fear that it was left uncovered, and is not subject to the prohibition that pertains to libation wine."

The gemara here explores the status of wine in various combinations: diluted and uncovered, boiled and possibly libated, and boiled and uncovered. The sequence begins with two assumptions (4.A—one need not worry lest diluted wine has been left uncovered or boiled wine libated), yielding a question (4.B—what about boiled wine left uncovered?), and ends with a definitive, categorical answer (8.H—one need always worry about diluted wine but not about boiled wine). More importantly, it begins with theoretical dialogues between rabbis and continues with what are represented as "real life" exchanges between a rabbi and a Gentile. It is the latter that are of particular interest in this discussion.

We must recall that, in the broader talmudic discussion, the wine prohibition is not merely about idolatry. It is most significantly about separation from Gentiles. In the Talmud's own words, as it explains a variety of related food prohibitions: "Their bread and oil [were forbidden] on account of their wine, and their wine [was forbidden] *on account of their daughters*, and their daughters [were forbidden] on account of 'another thing'" (*b. 'Abodah Zarah* 36b). That is to say, if a

Jew shares bread and oil with a Gentile, he is likely also to share wine. And if he shares wine, he will become an intimate of the Gentile and thus come to know his daughter. Under these circumstances, he might be attracted to her and even seek her hand in marriage; at the very least, he may sleep with her. And if he is smitten with her, he may be tempted to cooperate in her idolatrous rites. The length of this chain makes it clear that idolatry is not the *only* thing the rabbis were worried about. In fact, elsewhere in this same talmudic deliberation, they admit as much, saying that both Gentile bread and strong drink were prohibited out of fear of marriage (*b. ʿAbod. Zar.* 31b and 35b). Jews must be vigilant about maintaining their separation from Gentile neighbors. The consequences of not doing so, in the judgment of the sages behind these regulations, are disastrous.

This gemara, as I read it, hints that what is at issue here is not just two human cultures—one approved and one condemned—but a human culture and an animal-like poison. Permit me to elaborate. The gemara's discussion of uncovered wine follows immediately upon and is intimately tied to its discussion of 'libated wine' (*yayn nesekh*). The two go hand-in-hand; when one discusses the former, it is natural to discuss the latter. On the surface, the avoidance of Gentile wine seems to be justified on "rational" grounds. But, as this gemara makes clear, rationality is hardly the point.

From our perspective, the two stories about the aggressive snakes (8.C and E) are patent fiction. Of course, what is obvious to us (that these are ridiculous stories) may not have been obvious to them, but it is difficult to believe that even they would have believed a story about a snake who added water to a cask in order to gain access to the wine contained therein. Moreover, even if they believed these stories, they approached the problem with an irrational fear. After all, we could easily inquire into a Gentile's practice with respect to covering liquids. Yet they do not direct us to examine his practice in this matter any more than we are directed to inquire whether particular wine has or has not been used in worship. Regardless of the reality, their wine, when not first boiled, is prohibited as though it had been poisoned by a snake. That is to say, the wine of the Gentile is deemed venomous. And if the wine is venomous, then the Gentile must in some way be the source of the venom. The Gentile is, by association, the snake.

This symbolic association, as outrageous as it may sound, is supported by an explicit talmudic teaching, found earlier in the very same chapter of *ʿAbodah Zarah*. In the course of a discussion regarding the Mishnah's law prohibiting entrusting one's animal to an idolater, the gemara quotes a teaching that declares, "the animals of Jews are more desired by them [for sex] than their wives." Why is this so? Because,

> when the snake came upon Eve [and had sex with her] he left his filth [= venom] in her [and this filth infected all of her offspring for generations to come]. Israel, who stood at Mount Sinai, their filth was removed. But idolaters, who did not stand at Mount Sinai, their filth was not removed. (22b)

Gentiles are "snake-like" in that they are permanently infected with the filth of the original snake. Their wine, and, as our text makes clear, even their water must thus be avoided as though a snake had drunk from it.

So, on the one hand, the present talmudic text, through both its law and the symbolic association that its formulation implies, counsels extreme separation from the Gentile and his dangers. But that is only one side of the work it does. There is another side, again, both legal and literary, that erodes the foundation of the wall it has built.

First, the law. As I suggested at the beginning, the present law, even according to Rava's relatively strict conclusion, represents a significant compromise. Even if we assume that Gentiles would not have used boiled wine in their worship, and even if we accept the notion that snakes would have distinguished boiled wine and refused to drink from it, we cannot forget that there is a third, equally important reason behind the wine prohibition: the avoidance of relations with Gentiles. And, as anyone who has ever drunk so-called boiled wine knows— and I speak here from personal experience—its powers are in no way diminished. Whatever the diminution in the quality of its taste may be, its alcohol remains potent, and it therefore continues to function as a social lubricant. If a Jew were to pour such wine, I have no doubt that his Gentile neighbor would agree to join him. And if a Gentile were to pour it, I have no doubt that a Jew would find himself every bit as much at ease.

But it is not just the practical, legal loophole that opens up the prospect of Jewish-Gentile relations here. In fact, the present stories as herein formulated make certain we know that such relations were relatively common. Simply consider the exchanges as they progress. The first two (4 and 5) involve exclusively rabbinic interlocutors. But the latter three involve a rabbi and a Gentile each. It is the first (6) that is perhaps most remarkable. In this story, Samuel sits with a Gentile named Ablat who is sufficiently learned in Jewish practice to know that he should withdraw his hands lest he touch wine that is served to

Jews. He does not, however, know that the prohibition does not pertain to boiled wine, so Samuel teaches him this refinement in the law, and they presumably go on to enjoy the wine together. Whether Ablat has a daughter we do not know. But he, as Gentile, should be problematic enough. It is significant, therefore, that Samuel, one of the greatest of talmudic sages, is willing to share wine with him.

Now we might think that Ablat (or perhaps Samuel) is exceptional. It is for this reason, I think, that we are then introduced to two stories in which the Gentile in question is the servant of the sage. Evidently, we are to assume that relationships of this sort between Jewish house-holders and Gentile servants were common. What this reveals, which the Samuel-Ablat story does not, is that the social structure of the so-cieties the rabbis inhabited made for regular Jew-Gentile contact. And the exceptions to the broad prohibition on Gentile-tainted wine that they each support assure that contact would remain possible because the most onerous restrictions would be limited. In other words, *restriction* has been at least partially replaced by *relationship*.

Now, though it is impossible to be sure, I do not assume that the stories told here simply convey the "facts" as they were. It seems to me far more likely that the stories are formulated in the present composi-tion to make the points just illuminated. But even if we assume that the stories are "true," we still must be mindful of the fact that they are ordered and combined to make this same point. Even the most non-critical reading of this text allows its purpose, as conveyed by its for-mulation, to shine forth.

In the end, this text makes two points in tension with each other: one that beckons the reader to view the Gentile as poisonous and the other that invites him or her to understand the Gentile as person, and even as neighbor. I say that the *text* does this because both seemingly contradictory messages are the product of my engagement with this text as reader. In my experience as an informed reader of good will, one who does not consciously seek to impose my own meaning on the text, these are the points that emerge.

I do not believe that I am reading against the grain of this text. I am not aggressively deconstructing it. But even if, at some level, the mean-ings I have described are my own, this does not change the "reality" of what "the text says." If we subscribe to the theoretical position that it is the reader who ultimately constructs the meaning of a text, we have to subscribe to this position in all readings. And here, as elsewhere, I can defend the reading I may or may not have constructed by reference to the evidence of the text as I discover it. This text-as-read is no different from any other text-as-read, at least with respect to the way meaning is communicated and/or construed.

In this example, as in so many others, we may readily see that the Talmud is law that is literature. It is theory that is, by virtue of its theoretical quality, fiction. But it is also, on account of its normative connotations—that is to say, *on account of the way it has been read*—fact. Because of its power to spark the Jewish imagination and regulate the Jewish body, it is the Talmud more than any other rabbinic composition that has "written" Jewish identity, for its own time and for time to come.

Are Vocation Texts Fictional?
On Hesiod's Helicon Experience

GERRIT KLOSS
University of Heidelberg

The first deities that Hesiod mentions in his *Theogony* are—right in the first line—the Muses with whom a genealogy of the gods is to begin (Μουσάων Ἑλικωνιάδων ἀρχώμεθ᾽ ἀείδειν). The reason for this, as the poet tells us a little later (lines 22–35), is purely personal: the Muses themselves once turned Hesiod into a poet and, at the same time, prescribed for him the topic of his song, that is: the immortal gods. His poem was, however, both to begin *and* to end with the Muses—and this is precisely what the *Theogony*, as it is transmitted, does. Hesiod's "Heliconian Narrative" constitutes the earliest example of the poet's initiation (*Dichterweihe*) by the Muses and has become the model for all subsequent accounts of poetic initiations in Greek and Roman poetry (for instance, in Archilochus, Epimenides, Parmenides, Callimachus, Ennius, Propertius, and others).[1] While in later poetry the initiation narratives, on account of their obvious reference to Hesiod, are a priori suspected to function as a mere literary topos, in Hesiod's own case scholars have repeatedly investigated the nature of the event described by him: is it pure invention by Hesiod, meant to couch in mythical images a subjective process of awakening, or are we looking at the description of an actual experience? And if Hesiod felt the presence of the Muses to be real, did he encounter them in a dream or in a vision?[2] These are no doubt interesting questions, but they lead us into the realm of psychology, where it is hardly possible to give positive answers.

Author's note: I am grateful to Farouk Grewing and Alexander Kirichenko for their translation of my text.

1. See A. Kambylis, *Die Dichterweihe und ihre Symbolik: Untersuchungen zu Hesiodos, Kallimachos, Properz und Ennius* (Heidelberg: Carl Winter, 1965).

2. See K. Latte, "Hesiods Dichterweihe," *Antike und Abendland* 2 (1946) 152–63; F. Dornseiff, *Antike und Alter Orient: Kleine Schriften I* (Leipzig: Koehler & Amelang, 1956) 37–38 and 76; K. von Fritz, "Das Prooemium der hesiodeischen Theogonie," in *Festschrift Bruno Snell* (Munich: Beck, 1956) 32; Kambylis, *Die Dichterweihe und ihre Symbolik*, 52–61; M. L. West, *Hesiod: Theogony* (Oxford: Clarendon, 1966) 158–61; C. Calame, "Énonciation:

All that we have is the text, and any interpretation can only aim at answering the question of how the author wanted the text to be perceived by his audience. That is to say, our primary concern is not so much how and in what sense the described event took place or whether Hesiod invented it but (much more) whether its account *claims* to be authentic. Hence, we do not investigate the event's nature but the mode in which it is related. To use narratological jargon: we are not interested in whether what the text describes is *authentic* or *fictitious* but whether the text's communicative intention itself is *factual* or *fictional*. Since the term *fiction*, in the English-speaking world is used in a broader sense than in the German world, I first want to clarify the terminology, before actually embarking on an analysis of Hesiod's passage.

In keeping with common usage in German scholarship, by *fictional* I mean a text's particular mode of speech suggesting to the recipient that he will gain an adequate understanding of the text only if he refrains from verifying the statements made in the light of empirical facts (as s/he would do in everyday life). Thus, the empirical author of a fictional text requires of his audience to comprehend that these statements are not to be considered his own personal affirmations. At the same time, however, the intellectual game between author and recipient can succeed only if the latter, on a second level, allows himself to think of the statements of the text *as if* they were authentic expressions. Those who try to read a novel in the same way as a documentary claiming to be true, and measure, point by point, its created world by real life misjudge the fictional nature of the statements and must inevitably conclude that the author either lies or is wrong. On the other hand, those who are not willing to suspend, for the time of reception, their awareness of the fact that the details and events related in the text are merely made up fundamentally refuse to engage in the game that the author invites them to play.

Véracité ou convention littéraire? L'inspiration des Muses dans la Théogonie," *Actes sémiotiques (documents)* 4/34 (1982) 5–24; S. R. Slings, "Poet's Call and Poet's Status in Archaic Greece and Other Oral Cultures," *Listy filologické* 112 (1989) 72–80; J. Rudhardt, "Le préambule de la Théogonie: La vocation du poète. Le langage des Muses," in *Le métier du mythe: Lectures d'Hésiode* (Cahiers de philologie 16; Lille: Presses Universitaires du Septentrion, 1996) 25–27; J. B. Hainsworth, "Hesiod's Vision: *Theogony* 1–35," in *Desde los poemas homéricos hasta la prosa griega del siglo IV d.C.* (ed. J. A. López Férez; Madrid: Ediciones clásicas, 1999) 14–15. Compare with the typological parallels from other cultures given by Z. Ritoók, "Dichterweihen," *Acta Classica Universitatis Scientiarum Debreceniensis* 6 (1970) 17–25.

Thus, while the author of a factual text indicates that the statements made in that text are his own and that he himself is responsible for their truth-value, the fictional text signals that it is to be considered a sequence of authentic statements *only* in the sense of an intellectual experiment. The fictional text is, as it were, an act of openly pretended factual communication: "openly" means that the recipient, by way of implicit or explicit signals of the text's fictionality, can—or even *must*—comprehend the "as-if-ness" of its statements; because, for the sake of the intended understanding of such a text, it is virtually required that the recipient grasp the rules of the proposed game.[3]

The definition I have just put forward makes clear that, by using the terminological pair "factuality" and "fictionality," we are operating in a realm that borders on the notions of "truth" and "lie." However, only factual statements claim that their empirical truthfulness can be verified. Fictional statements, as a matter of principle, evade this claim: they claim authenticity solely at the level of the fictional speaker introduced by the author; at the author level, they are confessedly nonauthentic. Consequently, poets—insofar as they write poetry—cannot lie because they do not affirm anything but only pretend to do so: they can only invent. After all, it took until the 16th century for poetic theory to become conscious of this fundamental rule: "The Poet, he nothing affirms, and therefore never lieth," as Philip Sidney put it in his 1595 *Defence of Poesie*.

Hence, even in cases where, by modern standards, questions of factuality and fictionality are concerned, to ancient poetics only the terms *truth* and *lie* were available. 'Poets tell many lies' (πολλὰ ψεύδονται ἀοιδοί), says Solon (fr. 29 W.) around 600 B.C.E.. And also, when in the 5th century Gorgias of Leontinoi (according to my knowledge, for the first time in literary criticism) formulates the chief principle of fictional communication, he employs the notion of deception: regarding tragedy, he says (fr. 23 D.-K.), 'the deceiver [that is, the poet] is more just than the nondeceiver, and the deceived [that is, the audience] is wiser than the undeceived' (ὅ τ᾽ ἀπατήσας δικαιότερος τοῦ μὴ ἀπατήσαντος καὶ ὁ ἀπατηθεὶς σοφώτερος τοῦ μὴ ἀπατηθέντος). This is important with

---

3. For this definition, see especially M. Martinez and M. Scheffel, *Einführung in die Erzähltheorie* (Munich: Beck, 1999) 9–19; L. Rühling, "Fiktionalität und Poetizität," in *Grundzüge der Literaturwissenschaft* (ed. H. L. Arnold and H. Detering; 3rd ed.; Munich: Deutscher Taschenbuch, 1999) 27–36; W. Iser, *Das Fiktive und das Imaginäre: Perspektiven literarischer Anthropologie* (Frankfurt a.M.: Suhrkamp, 1993) 37–45 ("Als-Ob").

regard to the fact that Hesiod, too, as we shall see shortly, speaks of
truth and lie in poetry.

I turn now to the passage from Hesiod that I want to examine
(*Theog.* 22–35):

αἵ νύ ποθ᾽ Ἡσίοδον καλὴν ἐδίδαξαν ἀοιδήν,
ἄρνας ποιμαίνονθ᾽ Ἑλικῶνος ὑπο ζαθέοιο.
τόνδε δέ με πρώτιστα θεαὶ πρὸς μῦθον ἔειπον,
25   Μοῦσαι Ὀλυμπιάδες, κοῦραι Διὸς αἰγιόχοιο·
„ποιμένες ἄγραυλοι, κάκ᾽ ἐλέγχεα, γαστέρες οἶον,
ἴδμεν ψεύδεα πολλὰ λέγειν ἐτύμοισιν ὁμοῖα,
ἴδμεν δ᾽ εὖτ᾽ ἐθέλωμεν ἀληθέα γηρύσασθαι.”
ὣς ἔφασαν κοῦραι μεγάλου Διὸς ἀρτιέπειαι,
30   καί μοι σκῆπτρον ἔδον δάφνης ἐριθηλέος ὄζον
δρέψασαι, θηητόν· ἐνέπνευσαν δέ μοι αὐδὴν
θέσπιν, ἵνα κλείοιμι τά τ᾽ ἐσσόμενα πρό τ᾽ ἐόντα,
καί μ᾽ ἐκέλονθ᾽ ὑμνεῖν μακάρων γένος αἰὲν ἐόντων,
σφᾶς δ᾽ αὐτὰς πρῶτόν τε καὶ ὕστατον αἰὲν ἀείδειν.
35   ἀλλὰ τίη μοι ταῦτα περὶ δρῦν ἢ περὶ πέτρην;

And one day they taught Hesiod glorious song while he was shepherd-
ing his lambs under holy Helicon, and this word first the goddesses said
to me—the Muses of Olympus, daughters of Zeus who holds the aegis:
"Shepherds of the wilderness, wretched things of shame, mere bellies,
we know how to speak many false things as though they were true; but
we know, when we will, to utter true things." So said the ready-voiced
daughters of great Zeus, and they plucked and gave me a rod, a shoot of
sturdy laurel, a marvellous thing, and breathed into me a divine voice
to celebrate things that shall be and things there were aforetime; and
they bade me sing of the race of the blessed gods that are eternally, but
ever to sing of themselves both first and last. But why all this about oak
or stone?[4]

After the (somewhat puzzling) 'break-off formula' (*Abbruchformel*) in
line 35, Hesiod at first continues singing of the Muses, of their relation
to their father, Zeus, and of their song among the Olympic gods, before
in line 116 the actual account of the cosmogony and theogony begins.

Which are, then, the essential features of the poet's initiation?[5]

1. Hesiod is a shepherd grazing his sheep at Mt. Helicon when the Muses
   address him.
2. The Muses impart to him the gift of beautiful song.

---

4. All translations from Hesiod in this paper are taken from H. G. Evelyn-White,
Hesiod, The Homeric Hymns and Homerica (Cambridge: Harvard University Press, 1964).

5. See West, *Hesiod: Theogony*, 159–60; J. T. Kirby, "Rhetoric and Poetics in Hesiod,"
Ramus 21 (1992) 37–41.

3. The Muses talk to Hesiod but do not come into his sight.
4. The Muses give Hesiod a rod, a σκῆπτρον, as a symbol of his new dignity as a poet—and they do so "by plucking a branch of laurel." The identification of a σκῆπτρον with a branch of laurel is surprising, because a σκῆπτρον is a stick of a certain thickness one can lean on, whereas a laurel branch (δάφνης ὄζος) is thin and pliable. However, Andreas Patzer showed convincingly that epic rhapsodes carried a σκῆπτρον as a sign of their authority as poets. But Hesiod is not an epic rhapsode but a proponent of a new kind of poetry that—as we shall see shortly—competes with epic. Thus, the Muses hand over to him a symbol of his authority (σκῆπτρον) but one of a different kind: the symbol of Apollo himself. It is in this deviation that Hesiod's special affinity to the god of poetry manifests itself.[6]
5. The Muses "breathed into him a divine voice" so that he can "celebrate things that shall be and things that were aforetime" (lines 31–32). The latter formulation has unleashed hot debates in scholarship, because Hesiod's *Theogony* does not contain any prophecies. The best explanation of this is, I think, Heinz Neitzel's:[7] the phrases "things that shall be" and "things that were aforetime" do not refer to separate events in the future and in the past. Rather, the expression as a whole, "things that shall be and were aforetime," is equivalent to "things that are through all time," that is: the eternally divine (compare in the next line: 'the race of the blessed gods that are eternally' μακάρων γένος αἰὲν ἐόντων), and this is exactly what Hesiod describes.

The three notorious lines that the Muses speak to Hesiod before giving him the σκῆπτρον belong to the most-often-discussed passages in Greek literature: "Shepherds of the wilderness, wretched things of shame, mere bellies, we know how to speak many false things as though they were true; but we know, when we will, to utter true things" (26–28). This brings us to the core of our investigation. In the first line, Hesiod is reproached for being a useless shepherd, totally subject to his lowly bodily desires. The plural comes somewhat as a surprise but can be explained by the fact that Hesiod is, in a generalizing way, addressed as a typical exemplar of his kind; almost in the sense of a deep sigh: "Oh no, those shepherds. . . ."[8]

---

6. A. Patzer, "Hesiod als Rhapsode," in *Ut poesis pictura II* (ed. N. Holzberg et al.; Bamberg: Buchner, 1993) 83–98.

7. H. Neitzel, "Hesiod und die lügenden Musen: Zur Interpretation von Theogonie 27f.," *Hermes* 108 (1980) 396–98. Compare with J. S. Clay, "What the Muses Sang," *Greek, Roman, and Byzantine Studies* 29 (1988) 330.

8. For line 26, and the phrase γαστέρες οἶον in particular, see M. B. Arthur, "The Dream of a World without Women: Poetics and the Circles of Order in the *Theogony* Prooemium," *Arethusa* 16 (1983) 101–4; J. T. Katz and K. Volk, "'Mere bellies': A New Look at *Theogony* 26–28," *JHS* 120 (2000) 123–29. Both discussions seem overly subtle to me.

In the subsequent two lines, an opposition is set up between two kinds of poetry that are both inspired by the Muses: in the first, the Muses breathe into the poet "many false things as though they were true"; in the second, they "utter true things," but with an apparent limitation added: "when we will." It is clear that the truth-telling type of poetry must be the one, to which Hesiod's *Theogony* belongs.[9] The tenor of the entire passage, especially the handing-over of the σκῆπτρον that immediately follows, makes this evident. But what kind of poetry operates with lies that look like the truth? The great majority of scholars believe—and rightly so, I think—that this refers to heroic epics of the Homeric type.[10] Is Hesiod here, then, sharply polemicizing against Homer by calling him a liar? Most scholars believe so, but this would be a strange reproof, for it would, by extension, reflect badly on the Muses, who say of themselves that they inspire this kind of poetry as well. The Muses, then, would habitually breathe falsehoods into the epic poet and only, by means of an exception ("when [they] will"), the truth.

Not only does this idea contradict the traditional image of the Muses, but as a consequence, Hesiod himself could not be sure whether

---

9. See R. Kannicht, "Der alte Streit zwischen Philosophie und Dichtung," *Der altsprachliche Unterricht* 23/6 (1980) 14 (against W. Stroh, see n. 10).

10. See, e.g., Kannicht, "Der alte Streit," 15–20; A. M. Buongiovanni, "La verità e il suo doppio (Hes., Theog., 27–28)," in *Ricerche di filologia classica III: Interpretazioni antiche e moderne di testi greci* (Pisa: Giardini, 1987) 11; M. Puelma, "Der Dichter und die Wahrheit in der griechischen Poetik von Homer bis Aristoteles," *Museum Helveticum* 46 (1989) 75; E. L. Bowie, "Lies, Fiction and Slander in Early Greek Poetry," in *Lies and Fiction in the Ancient World* (ed. C. Gill and T. P. Wiseman; Exeter: University of Exeter Press, 1993) 21–22; M. Finkelberg, *The Birth of Literary Fiction in Ancient Greece* (Oxford: Clarendon, 1998) 157; Hainsworth, "Hesiod's Vision," 13. "Dass Hesiod hier seine eigene neue Poesie als Poesie der Wahrheit pointiert der homerischen Poesie gegenüberstellt, die die Wirklichkeit nur täuschend ähnlich abzubilden vermag, hätte man nie bezweifeln sollen" (A. Patzer, "Hesiod als Dichter: Das Proömium der *Theogonie* als Musenhymnus," in *Weltbild und Weltdeutung* [ed. P. Neukam and B. O'Connor; Munich: Bayerischer Schulbuch, 2002] 126). The idea of W. Stroh that Hesiod attributes both ψεύδεα and ἀληθέα to his own *Theogony* has been nearly unanimously rejected (W. Stroh, "Hesiods lügende Musen," in *Studien zum antiken Epos* [ed. H. Görgemanns and E. A. Schmidt; Meisenheim am Glan: Hain, 1976] 85–112). Equally unconvincing is Neitzel, "Hesiod und die lügenden Musen," 387–91: beginning with the unnecessary presupposition that Hesiod in line 28 makes the Muses only arbitrarily (εὖτ' ἐθέλωμεν) inspire poets with truth, he concludes that both line 27 and line 28 must refer to non-Hesiodic poetry. I will deal with the problem of the supposed arbitrariness that seems to undermine Hesiod's own claim to truthfulness below in this essay.

the Muses were deceiving him as well.[11] It seems that we cannot gain control over this interpretive difficulty as long as we assume that the Muses could be ready to deceive the poets. I believe that line 27 is not talking about lying in the true sense of the word at all. As we have seen, in contexts reflecting on poetry, the terms ψεῦδος and ἀπάτη stand for what we would in modern times call "literary fiction." And this is, I think, what Hesiod has in mind here: he puts the fictional poetry of Homer opposite his own, factual poetry. To consolidate this thesis, we need first of all to answer two questions: (1) What function did the Muses have for the early Greek poet? (2) Was there, in Hesiod's time, any significant consciousness at all of literary fictionality?

1. *The Muses.* In Book 8 of the *Odyssey*, the singer Demodocus is introduced with the following words (62–64):

> Then the herald drew near, leading the good minstrel, whom the Muse loved above all other men, and gave him both good and evil; of his sight she deprived him, but gave him the gift of sweet song.

> κῆρυξ δ᾽ ἐγγύθεν ἦλθεν ἄγων ἐρίηρον ἀοιδόν, / τὸν περὶ Μοῦσ᾽ ἐφίλησε, δί-δου δ᾽ ἀγαθόν τε κακόν τε· / ὀφθαλμῶν μὲν ἄμερσε, δίδου δ᾽ ἡδεῖαν ἀοιδήν.[12]

Hence, the Muse is apparently responsible for the singer's talent. The phrase ἡδεῖαν ἀοιδήν (64) indicates that what is meant here is most of all the esthetic quality, the beauty of the song.[13]

Moreover, the Muse's goodwill also guarantees the correctness of the details that the singer processes.[14] This follows from the words with which Odysseus praises Demodocus's song of Troy (487–91):

> Demodocus, verily above all mortal men do I praise thee, whether it was the Muse, the daughter of Zeus, that taught thee, or Apollo; for well and truly dost thou sing of the fate of the Achaeans, all that they wrought and suffered, and all the toils they endured, as though haply thou hadst thyself been present, or hadst heard the tale from another.

---

11. The problem is well set out by G. Arrighetti, "Esiodo e le Muse: Il dono della verità e la conquista della parola," *Athenaeum* 80 (1992) 46–48; compare with Neitzel ("Hesiod und die lügenden Musen"); see n. 10.

12. Translations of the *Iliad* and the *Odyssey* are taken from Samuel Butler (London: Longman Green, 1898 and 1900).

13. See L. H. Pratt, *Lying and Poetry from Homer to Pindar: Falsehood and Deception in Archaic Greek Poetics* (Ann Arbor: University of Michigan Press, 1993) 30–32.

14. See H. Maehler, *Die Auffassung des Dichterberufs im frühen Griechentum bis zur Zeit Pindars* (Göttingen: Vandenhoeck & Ruprecht, 1963) 17–19; Stroh, "Hesiods lügende Musen," 98–99; Puelma, "Der Dichter und die Wahrheit," 67–73; Pratt, *Lying and Poetry,* 47–53; Finkelberg, *The Birth of Literary Fiction,* 71.

Δημόδοκ᾽, ἔξοχα δή σε βροτῶν αἰνίζομ᾽ ἁπάντων· / ἢ σέ γε Μοῦσ᾽ ἐδίδαξε, Διὸς πάϊς, ἢ σέ γ᾽ Ἀπόλλων· / λίην γὰρ κατὰ κόσμον Ἀχαιῶν οἶτον ἀείδεις, / ὅσσ᾽ ἔρξαν τ᾽ ἔπαθόν τε καὶ ὅσσ᾽ ἐμόγησαν Ἀχαιοί, / ὥς τέ που ἢ αὐτὸς παρεὼν ἢ ἄλλου ἀκούσας.

The divine authority of inspiration is, thus, responsible for the factual accuracy of the account. Odysseus, because he himself was at the gates of Troy, can of course judge if Demodocus's account accords with the truth. But because the singer was not present at Troy and because he did not have an opportunity to ask an eyewitness either, there can be only one reasonable explanation for the authenticity of his account: namely, that it is of divine origin. The Muse replaces, as it were, the eyewitnessing of the events about which Demodocus wants to sing. Thus, in the invocation of the Muses in Book 2 of the *Iliad*, right before the catalog of ships, it says (485–86):

> For you are goddesses and are present and know all things, but we hear only a rumor and know nothing.

> ὑμεῖς γὰρ θεαί ἐστε πάρεστέ τε ἴστέ τε πάντα, / ἡμεῖς δέ κλέος οἶον ἀκούομεν οὐδέ τι ἴδμεν.

2. *The consciousness of literary fictionality.* Martin West remarks in his commentary on *Theogony* 26–28:

> This distinction which the Muses make between truth and plausible fiction is somewhat problematic. It is sometimes understood as a distinction between epic and didactic poetry. . . . This is certainly wrong; no Greek ever regarded the Homeric epics as substantially fiction.[15]

Here, two things are being confused: the mythical material was indeed considered by the Greeks as authentic, not *fiction*. But it is certainly possible to compose, in fictional mode, texts the contents of which must be regarded as essentially authentic (compare historical epic).[16]

Another possible objection is of a more fundamental nature. In two often-quoted articles, Wolfgang Rösler tried to demonstrate that in the times of early Greek oral poetry a consciousness of literary fictionality

---

15. West, *Hesiod: Theogony*, 162. Compare Stroh, "Hesiods lügende Musen," 90: "Denn für schlichtweg fiktiv hat wohl kein antiker Mensch die homerischen Epen gehalten."

16. This distinction has been clearly drawn by Kannicht, who states "daß auch für ihn [= Hesiod] der heroische *Stoff* des Epos selbstverständlich Historie war und insofern selbstverständlich 'substantially true'" (Kannicht, "Der alte Streit," 16); at the same time, the Muses with ψεύδεα, "umschreiben . . . die spezifische poetische Qualität der epischen ἀοιδή: die *Gedichtetheit* nämlich *ihrer Wahrheit*, terminologisch also: ihre *Fiktionalität*" (ibid., 20; italics mine).

simply did not exist; rather, the poet—in the face-to-face situation of his performance—guaranteed the authenticity of his account. The option of writing fictional poetry, Rösler argues, developed only with the beginning of written, or book culture.[17] However, contrary to Rösler's contention, there are a variety of passages in Homer plainly showing that such a consciousness of fictionality did indeed exist.[18] I will here confine myself to looking at the proems to both Homeric epics.

The *Iliad* begins with the words: 'The wrath sing, goddess, of Peleus' son Achilles' (μῆνιν ἄειδε θεὰ Πηληϊάδεω Ἀχιλῆος); the *Odyssey* with: 'Tell me, O Muse, of the man of many devices' (ἄνδρα μοι ἔννεπε, Μοῦσα, πολύτροπον). First of all, right from these initial wordings, with the themes being stated, and from the summaries of the subject matter that follows in each of the two proems, one can infer that the poet knows at least in outline the contents of what is to follow. That is, he himself chooses the object of his song.

In both proems, he additionally states at which point of the story the song is supposed to begin. In the *Iliad*, he says (6–7): 'Of this sing from the time when first there parted in strife Atreus' Son, lord of men, and noble Achilles' (ἐξ οὗ δὴ τὰ πρῶτα διαστήτην ἐρίσαντε / Ἀτρεΐδης τε ἄναξ ἀνδρῶν καὶ δῖος Ἀχιλλεύς); this statement is rather precise—not so that of the *Odyssey* (10): 'Of these things, goddess, daughter of Zeus, beginning where thou wilt, tell thou even unto us' (τῶν ἁμόθεν γε, θεά, θύγατερ Διός, εἰπὲ καὶ ἡμῖν). The exhortation to the Muse in the *Iliad* shows that the extent of the poet's control over his material goes at least so far as to include his ability to prescribe to the Muse the starting

---

17. W. Rösler, "Die Entdeckung der Fiktionalität in der Antike," *Poetica* 12 (1980) 283–319; idem, "Schriftkultur und Fiktionalität: Zum Funktionswandel der griechischen Literatur von Homer bis Aristoteles," in *Schrift und Gedächtnis: Beiträge zur Archäologie der literarischen Kommunikation* (ed. A. Assmann, J. Assmann, and C. Hardmeier; Munich: Fink, 1983) 109–22.

18. For an attempt different from mine to prove the consciousness of fictionality in the Homeric poems, see E. Pöhlmann, "Dichterweihe und Gattungswahl," in *Candide iudex: Beiträge zur augusteischen Dichtung—Festschrift für Walter Wimmel* (ed. A. E. Radke; Stuttgart: Steiner, 1998) 247–51. Rösler's hypothesis has met with some criticism but (as far as I know) has never been seriously put to the test. Bowie's arguments are not entirely convincing, because he thinks of the poet's and the Muses' claim to truth as not being explicit and universal ("Lies, Fiction and Slander," 11–20). In my opinion, however, it *is* explicit and universal, there being no contradiction between a claim of this sort and the fictionality of the poems. S. R. Slings, in his excellent article "The I in Personal Archaic Lyric: An Introduction" (in *The Poet's I in Archaic Greek Lyric: Proceedings of a Symposium Held at the Vrije Universiteit Amsterdam* [ed. S. R. Slings; Amsterdam: Vrije University Press, 1990] 1–30), restricts himself to some brief critical remarks (pp. 8–9, 13–14).

point of his poem. The poet of the *Odyssey* could have certainly done the same thing. What he does instead, however, is to let the source of his inspiration choose the beginning for him.

The parallels both in the proem to the *Iliad* and elsewhere in the *Odyssey* itself demonstrate that this refusal to name the exact starting point of the narrative was most likely not in accordance with common practice. How can one explain this exceptional and seemingly unnecessary decision by the poet of the *Odyssey* to entrust the Muse with the task of choosing the poem's beginning? My answer is that already at the very outset the poet knows exactly how his poem will be organized. The main reason that he departs from the tradition of providing the exact temporal starting point must be that Odysseus's travels that chronologically precede all other episodes of his story are postponed until Books 9–12, where they are introduced as a lengthy flashback. Because the objective of the *Odyssey* was to include the entire story of Odysseus's return to Ithaca beginning with his departure from Troy, it was impossible for Homer to ask the Muse to begin the narrative at a later point. What may look at first like the poet's indifference to the way his narrative will begin is in fact conditioned by the work's overall plan, of which he is of course perfectly aware while composing its proem.

Thus Homer's alleged refusal to take responsibility for the planning of his own work emerges, on closer scrutiny, as a direct consequence of that very plan, which he pretends not to have. Thus, everybody familiar with the plot of the *Odyssey* will perceive the address to the Muse, not as a serious request for inspiration based on deeply felt piety but as a traditional element of the epic genre, which in this particular case, due to the compositional peculiarities of the poem, cannot be formulated in the conventional way. The logical precedence of the poetic concept over the source of inspiration that we have uncovered in the proem to the *Odyssey* presupposes the corresponding precedence of the poet over the Muse. He knows beforehand what she will dictate to him. In other words, she is nothing but a fictional entity created by him. From this viewpoint, the address to the Muse clearly emerges as nonauthentic, that is, a fictional statement that every recipient is in a position to recognize as such.[19]

What does this imply for Hesiod's understanding of epic poetry? If, on the one hand, the Muses are supposed (in accordance with the

---

19. Pratt rightly speaks of "the possibility that truth claims in archaic poetry are themselves fictional, part of the narrative game" (*Lying and Poetry*, 53).

Homeric commonplace) to guarantee the veracity of the narrative, but, on the other hand, the fictionality of the Homeric epics is presented as self-evident, then it follows that Hesiod was capable of making the Muses responsible for the contents of fictional poetry. (At the same time, he consciously leaves out of consideration the fact that the Muses themselves are the object of fictional speech; I will discuss this issue in more detail below.) Of course, what Hesiod means by fictional poetry is (first and foremost) the Homeric epics. This becomes especially apparent if one recalls that line 27 presents an almost literal quotation from Homer.

In Book 19 of the *Odyssey*, Odysseus introduces himself to Penelope under the false identity of a Cretan named Aithon, who claims to have met Odysseus. The basic information that Odysseus imparts to his wife—that he is still alive and is currently on his way home—is unquestionably true, while all the details that the speaker uses to communicate this message are manifestly false. The story, however, is told in such a convincing way that Penelope cannot help but believe it. For this reason, the epic narrator concludes this scene with the following words (203): 'Thus he made the many falsehoods of his tale seem like the truth' (ἴσκε ψεύδεα πολλὰ λέγων ἐτύμοισιν ὁμοῖα). Thus, Odysseus's story is plausible but untrue.

I find it highly significant that it is in connection with his narrative at Alcinous's banquet that Odysseus is compared with an epic singer. Odysseus's report of his wanderings that spans over more than two books is thus commented on at the end by the narrator (11.333–34): "So he spoke, and they were all hushed in silence, and were held spellbound throughout the shadowy halls." Enchantment of the listeners is repeatedly mentioned among the typical characteristics of the divinely beautiful song. Alcinous's judgment of Odysseus as a singer is particularly revealing (11.363–69):

> Odysseus, in no wise as we look on thee do we deem this of thee, that thou art a cheat and a dissembler, such as are many whom the dark earth breeds scattered far and wide, men that fashion lies out of what no man can even see. But upon thee is grace of words, and within thee is a heart of wisdom, and thy tale thou hast told with skill, as doth a minstrel, even the grievous woes of all the Argives and of thine own self.

> ὦ Ὀδυσεῦ, τὸ μὲν οὔ τί σ' ἐΐσκομεν εἰσορόωντες / ἠπεροπῆά τ' ἔμεν καὶ ἐπί-κλοπον, οἷά τε πολλοὺς / βόσκει γαῖα μέλαινα πολυσπερέας ἀνθρώπους / ψεύδεά τ' ἀρτύνοντας, ὅθεν κέ τις οὐδὲ ἴδοιτο· / σοὶ δ' ἔπι μὲν μορφὴ ἐπέων, / ἔνι δὲ φρένες ἐσθλαί, / μῦθον δ' ὡς ὅτ' ἀοιδὸς ἐπισταμένως κατέλεξας, / πάντων Ἀργείων σέο τ' αὐτοῦ κήδεα λυγρά.

Of course, Alcinous cannot deduce from the content of Odysseus's narrative whether or not he has told the truth. For him, the chief criterion of the account's authenticity is its beauty, which leads to the enchantment of the listeners. Because, according to Alcinous's logic, beauty and truth can be united only in a song composed by a singer held in high esteem by the Muse, beauty must be a sign of truth. The main reason that Odysseus's story must be true is that he told it in such a convincing way.[20]

What Alcinous fails to notice, however, is that the *apologoi* are not inspired by the Muse at all because Odysseus was an eyewitness of all the events that he narrates and, therefore, there is in no need of a Muse. Thus, when speaking on one's own behalf, one can tell stories that are untrue but plausible. The stories that Odysseus tells the Phaeacians are not quite of this kind, but those he later on tells Penelope certainly are. If Odysseus as the narrator of his wanderer tales can be compared with the rhapsode Demodocus, and epic singers portrayed in the *Odyssey* (as has been often pointed out) can be perceived as self-reflexive images of Homer himself, then it becomes possible to compare Homer himself with Odysseus. Every now and then, Odysseus tells stories that, however plausible, are true only in a limited sense, their individual details being a product of pure invention. I find it very likely that Homer's indirect self-identification with Odysseus as a storyteller is not coincidental but reflects what may be self-ironic intention. Above all, however, I argue that, by almost literally quoting *Odyssey* 19.203, Hesiod directly alludes to this (to borrow a phrase from Wolfgang Iser)[21] *Selbstanzeige* 'self-exposure' of Homer.

So, what Hesiod indeed is doing is to contrast his own factual poetry with the fictional Homeric epics. Unlike the majority of scholars, however, I claim that this contrast does not necessarily imply that Hesiod had a polemic intent.[22] This would be the case if Hesiod directly accused

---

20. See Kannicht, "Der alte Streit," 17; G. B. Walsh, *The Varieties of Enchantment: Early Greek Views of the Nature and Function of Poetry* (Chapel Hill: University of North Carolina Press, 1984) 6–14. Pratt (*Lying and Poetry*, 67–69 and 92–93) argues that the equation "formal skill = truth" cannot be "a general principle of archaic or even of Odyssean poetics" (ibid., 69), since Odysseus in his later tales is presented as a skillful liar. Alcinous only "implies that he can judge not the truth-value of Odysseus' narrative but the character of the speaker" (p. 93). The equation may not be valid for all formally convincing tales, but it is certainly valid for songs inspired by the Muses, and Alcinous, by comparing Odysseus with a singer, shows that he credits him with this kind of trustworthiness.

21. Iser, *Das Fiktive und das Imaginäre*, 35–36.

22. Rudhardt ("Le préambule de la Théogonie," 30), while unnecessarily skeptical that Hesiod is aiming at poems of the Homeric type, is right in stating that he doesn't

Homer of lying. But as we have seen, all he does is to describe the fictional character of epic poetry in general—and he does so in the same terms as used, in his indirect self-referential remarks, by the poet of the *Odyssey*, to whom the Muses are nothing but his own poetic creations. Thus one cannot ascribe to Hesiod the assumption that the Muses deceive some poets and inspire them with truth only "when they will." For, as Hesiod knew, neither poetry nor the Muses are guilty of lying.

The word ψεύδεα that Hesiod uses does not characterize the communication between the Muses who grant and the poet who receives the divine inspiration; it refers to the fictional communication between the poet and his audience: the poet is a creator of fictions who is assisted by the Muses. If anything is polemical, it is Hesiod's description of epic poetry as *merely plausible*, that is, as indifferent to truth; it is of no importance whether it contains true or untrue things; what matters is whether or not it is plausible. At the same time, the Muses are able, "when they will," to inspire poetry based on true facts—that is, factual poetry.[23] Thus, the addition of 'when we will' (εὖτ' ἐθέλωμεν) does not denote the sheer arbitrariness of the Muses, who rely on some inscrutable set of rules in choosing whether to present poets now with truth, now with falsehood. Much rather, the Muses promise the poet that *if* they choose to inspire factual poetry they will not confuse ψεύδεα with ἔτυμα but will always respect the criteria of truth.[24]

Let us now finally turn to the question of whether Hesiod's description of his *Dichterweihe* is a fictional text. My analysis has produced results that at first glance may appear confusing: by writing a genealogy

---

polemicize against poetry full of ψεύδεα: "il ne me paraît certain que l'auteur de la *Théogonie* condamne la poésie mensongère; comme la véridique, elle est inspirée par les Muses auxquelles il n'adresse pas aucun reproche. Il distingue deux types de poésie entre lesquels il établie simplement une hiérarchie."

23. The much disputed semantic difference between ἔτυμος and ἀληθής in this context fits in with the contrast that is established between fictional and factual poetry. See Buongiovanni, "La verità e il suo doppio," 15:

> Ἀληθής è usato essenzialmente per indicare che un *racconto* è veritiero nel senso che contiene *tutti gli elementi nel giusto ordine*, dall'inizio alla fine, senza omettere nulla e senza riportare nulla in maniera infedele. Ἔτυμος invece non implica un racconto ordinato ed esauriente, ma si riferisce essenzialmente *all'accuratezza di un'informazione*; esso punta piuttosto verso la sfera della precisione che verso quella della completezza.

Thus ψεύδεα may be blended with ἔτυμα, but not with ἀληθέα ('the whole truth').

24. "We know, when we will, to utter true things" is therefore equivalent to "when we are willing to utter true things (i.e., to inspire factual poetry), we know how to do that." The infinitive γηρύσασθαι is to be understood both with ἴδμεν and ἐθέλωμεν.

of the gods, Hesiod is obviously claiming to produce a factual text. There is not the lightest hint in the *Theogony* that Hesiod could be self-ironically undermining his claim to truth. The narrative of his poetic initiation on Mount Helicon, however, by which he purports to authenticate his claim to truth, is quite different in this respect. Hesiod clearly reveals his awareness of the fictionality of the Homeric epics. This, as we have seen, must have entailed the view that the Muses are not the subject but the objects of the fictional discourse. Consequently, the Muses that turn Hesiod into a poet are also, from his own viewpoint, just fictional entities. If one analyzes the narrative of Hesiod's poetic initiation in this way, one cannot help but conclude that this account is a fictional text. Thus, we are confronted with a paradox: a fictional text (the *Dichterweihe*) serves to authenticate a factual text (the genealogy of the gods). How is this possible?

If we want to answer this question, we must take into account the fact that Hesiod is only implicitly pointing to the fictionality of the Helicon episode, disclosing it only to those who, in their approach to the text, equip themselves, as it were, with the tools of philological analysis. His original audience, on the other hand, consisted for the most part of listeners whose understanding of poetry was fostered by the Homeric epics. Furthermore, among his immediate addressees one must count his fellow-poets, the Homeric rhapsodes. It is to this audience, both knowledgeable and constrained by deep-rooted conventions, that he had to communicate his new way of composing poetry. The crucial point is that there was one thing that neither poets nor admirers of traditional epic poetry were able to do, irrespective of whether or not they really believed in the existence of the Muses, which was to renounce the traditional rhetoric of inspiration associated with them. We could even say that this "rhetoric of the Muses" lay at the very foundation of epic poetry and, for this reason, could not be disregarded. Even though, as we have seen, it was possible for an epic poet to make an indirect reference to the fictional nature of his inspiration by the Muse, it would have been utterly unthinkable for him to admit in a poetological discourse that the Muses were objects of his fictional speech. Hesiod uses this taboo in a highly elegant way when he describes his poetic initiation.

His main goal here is to draw a clear line between himself as the creator of a factual text and the poets of fictional epic poetry. In order to make this distinction understandable to his audience, however, he must formulate it in terms of the traditional "rhetoric of the Muses." Simply to express doubt that epic poets are inspired by the Muses would not help him to support the claims of his own poetry. His task is thus to reveal that the traditional epic rhetoric of inspiration is based on tenuous premises without, however, completely destroying it. Every epic poet, as well as every attentive listener knows that the Muses are *objects* of *fictional* texts. Nevertheless, everyone pretends that they are the *subjects* of *factual* texts.

Hesiod's strategy in dealing with this dilemma is to reveal the fictionality of the epic text but to preserve the status of the Muses as subjects of poetic communication. Thus, Hesiod declares the Muses to be capable of poetic invention. Furthermore, by making them responsible for texts whose content is, strictly speaking, nonfactual, he has found a very clever way of telling his fellow-poets that, even though they are inspired by the Muses, the result of this inspiration has nothing to do with truth. This division between epic poetry and factual truth opens up a gap that Hesiod now purports to fill: the Muses obviously have to be capable of more than just poetic invention—they also must be able to "proclaim the truth." It is this uncompromising claim to truth on which he bases his *Theogony*. In order to prevent epic poets from questioning the veracity of his own poetry on the same grounds, he presents his contact with the Muses as a personal experience. In so doing, he attempts to make his position as unassailable as possible. From the position of the "rhetoric of the Muses," in response to anyone accusing him of having invented the Helicon episode, he can now point out that, although the Muses may inspire every poet, it is only some of them (the composers of factual poetry) that they inspire with nothing but truth.

At the same time, the "rhetoric of the Muses" implies that Hesiod could not have composed the *Theogony* without the Muses' assistance. Otherwise, his work would contain conspicuously untrue elements and thus betray itself as a human artifact designed to deceive. One can see now how Hesiod's attribution of poetic deceptions to the Muses combined with his assertion that his poetic initiation is a biographical fact produces the effect of a reliable authentication of his claim to truth. The only way to undermine it would be to call into question its very foundation, which is the idea of poetic inspiration by the Muses. However, one can hardly imagine a participant in the traditional "discourse of the Muses," particularly a poet, who would be interested in doing this.

Thus, Hesiod relies on an ambivalent mode of communication in his Helicon narrative: on the one hand, the fact that the text communicates indirect signals of fictionality (particularly by quoting the *Odyssey*) allows one to analyze it as fictional. On the other hand, from within the "rhetoric of the Muses" (that is, the traditional locus of epic discourse), it can only be understood as a factual text. Hesiod successfully demarcates his own poetry from the Homeric ideology of inspiration, without openly condemning it, and simultaneously manages in his own way to heighten the status of the Muses. While resorting to the rhetoric characteristic of the kind of poetry that he wants to leave behind, he achieves three things at the same time: he devalues traditional fictional epic poetry, forestalls criticism, and provides authentication for his factual *Theogony*.

It would be interesting to investigate to what extent the conclusions that I have reached are applicable to other "vocation texts." I must limit myself here to a few brief observations. It has been repeatedly pointed out that Hesiod's poetic initiation finds parallels in the Old Testament narratives of prophetic vocation.[25] The best comparative material can be found in Isaiah 6, Jeremiah 1, and Ezekiel 1–2, where the vocation accounts are narrated in first person, and in Exodus 3–4, which is reported in third person. Isaiah and Ezekiel have a vision of the Lord; Jeremiah and Moses can only hear him. What all these accounts have in common is the act of endowing the prophet with persuasive speech, parallel to what we have seen in Hesiod (in the case of Isaiah and Jeremiah, the Lord touches the mouth of the future prophet; Ezekiel eats a scroll, "and it was in my mouth sweet as honey"; Moses receives assistance from his eloquent brother Aaron).[26] It is also interesting that all four future prophets, just as Hesiod, start out as social outsiders. None of them has previously belonged to any of the guilds traditionally responsible for prophetic activities, which may explain why the vocation could only come from God himself.[27]

The Exodus account presents an additional similarity to Hesiod in that it names a mountain as the place where the vocation occurs (Exod 3:1), that the one called upon is a shepherd (3:1), and that he receives a rod as a token of his vocation (4:1–5). It is not my aim here to determine whether these parallels indicate a common origin in the ancient

---

25. See Dornseiff, *Antike und Alter Orient*, 76; I. Trencsényi-Waldapfel, "Die orientalische Verwandtschaft des Prooimions der hesiodeischen Theogonia," *Acta Orientalia Academiae Scientiarum Hungaricae* 5 (1955) 45–74 (still the best treatment of this topic).

26. Isa 6:6; Jer 1:9; Ezek 3:3; Exod 4:14.

27. See Trencsényi-Waldapfel, "Die orientalische Verwandtschaft," 51–52; G. von Rad, *Theologie des Alten Testaments*, vol. 2: *Die Theologie der prophetischen Überlieferungen Israels* (9th ed.; Munich: Chr. Kaiser, 1987) 61–63.

Near East or whether they are merely typological. The only question that I would like to raise is whether or not the biblical texts can be regarded as either fictional or factual in the same sense as Hesiod's account. My answer is: perhaps. It is quite significant that all five texts are based on a similar mode of communication:

1. The purpose of the vocation narrative is to authenticate a factual text with religious content.
2. The speaker is likely to meet with social resistance from influential opponents willing to preserve old conventions. Hence, it is essential to adopt the language and rhetoric of the powerful in order to make his own cause as safe from attack as possible.

However, can one find in the biblical texts the Hesiodic symbiosis between the fictional speech-mode, which undermines the foundation of the traditional system from without, and the factual speech-mode, which supports this foundation from within? In other words: would it accord with the authors' intentions if the critical recipients of their writings, who do not believe in God's epiphanies, were to perceive them as fictional texts, whereas those who read them from the position of the Old Testament "rhetoric of prophecy" saw them as factual narratives? The main reason why this question cannot be answered is probably that the biblical authors, unlike Hesiod, do not even consider the possibility of the reception of their texts from outside the system. The characteristic topoi of the biblical accounts, if they were recognized as such by their contemporary recipients, could at least point to a possible intention of fictional communication.[28] It is the reflective distance from his own vocation communicated through signals of fictionality that distinguishes Hesiod's text from the Old Testament accounts. This complex blend of factual and fictional speech may be at least partly responsible for the fact that the *Dichterweihe* has elicited such a great variety of critical responses. In this respect, Hesiod's text can be considered truly unique.

---

28. "Structural intertextuality" may be an indicator of the fictionality of a text: see F. Zipfel, *Fiktion, Fiktivität, Fiktionalität: Analysen zur Fiktion in der Literatur und zum Fiktionsbegriff in der Literaturwissenschaft* (Berlin: Erich Schmidt, 2001) 237–38.

PART 4

Rereading Biblical Poetry

From Aristotle to Bakhtin

The Comedic and the Carnivalesque in a Biblical Tale

NEHAMA ASCHKENASY
University of Connecticut

Reading the book of Ruth in light of theories of dramatic comedy involves interpreting the scriptural text against its grain and in contradiction to traditional views. Unlike classical or Shakespearean drama, the biblical tales, Ruth included, were meant to be read not performed, and therefore they have not been imprinted with the conventions of drama and the theatre. Further, Ruth deals with the important issues of the redemption of the land and of the childless widow, and Boaz has always been cast in the role of a respectable pillar of the community. Therefore, identifying Ruth's plot as generic dramatic intrigue enacted by prototypical comic characters with the spirit of carnival underlying it reverses long-established conceptions of the story.

Nevertheless, the book of Ruth lends itself to the dramatic genre by virtue of the centrality of its dialogue and its narrator's limited omniscience. The tale is structured as a series of short, eventful scenes animated by spirited, dynamic dialogue that can be easily adapted for the stage. The conversation in Ruth is either between two protagonists or between a protagonist and "chorus" (in the form of the women of Bethlehem or the workers in the field or the elders at the gate); but there are usually no more than two principal interlocutors in any given scene. The story's narrator offers brief historical information and intervenes periodically to provide pieces of information—more like a dramatist or theatrical director setting the stage (season, time of day, backdrop) than like an all-knowing author privy to his protagonists' internal thoughts or feelings.

Drama has been defined as the representation of the protagonist in conflict either with an antagonist, with circumstances, or with the self. The book of Ruth reveals all three forms of conflict but concentrates mainly on the second: that is, people in conflict with circumstances. One

265

might argue that Naomi and Ruth are also in conflict with an antagonist, the Bethlehem community at large, which no doubt condemns Naomi for abandoning it in a time of famine and distress and is suspicious of Ruth for being an intruder, a member of a despised nation.

It is therefore appropriate to study Ruth in light of the long history of dramatic tradition. The book can be illuminated through attention to Aristotle's *Poetics*, the classical practitioners of drama from Shakespeare to Molière, and modern theorists including Henri Bergson, Northrop Frye, and Dorothea Krook. Ruth meets the major criteria of the dramatic form: it fulfills Aristotle's requirements of "unity" of the plot, of pyramid structure, and of reversal of fortune and epiphany.[1] Ruth displays Aristotle's primary tragic elements except for its plot line, which, as in every comedy, moves from distress to happiness. Ruth's author manifests kinship with Shakespeare and other dramatists in his understanding of comedy as verging on the tragic, and with Northrop Frye in his conception of comedy as "the Mythos of spring."[2]

Furthermore, when Ruth is read in the light of Dorothea Krook's mapping of tragedy—which begins with an "act of shame or horror" and concludes with "affirmation"[3]—Ruth emerges as comedy in the deepest sense—that is, as tragedy in reverse. Whereas tragedy is the mimesis of the ritual of death, charting the hero's journey from success to disaster, comedy follows the reverse trajectory, beginning with disaster and ending with triumph.[4] Ruth further offers scenes in which human frailty, trickery, the unexpected, and the incongruous all coalesce to evoke laughter and a sense of merriment. As to the nature of the dramatic resolution, as Frye suggests, in comedy "the erotic and social affinities of the hero are combined and unified in the final scene," since comedy is "much concerned with integrating the family

---

1. All references to Aristotle's *Poetics* are to G. M. A. Gruss, trans., *Aristotle on Poetry and Style* (New York: Bobbs Merrill, 1958) 5–100. A reconstruction of Aristotle's views on comedy, based on the *Poetics* and the *Tractatus Coislinianus,* is offered by Richard Janko, *Aristotle on Comedy: Towards a Reconstruction of Poetics II* (Berkeley: University of California Press, 1984); see also Dana F. Sutton, *The Catharsis of Comedy* (Boston: Rowman & Littlefield, 1984).

2. Northrop Frye, *Anatomy of Criticism* (Princeton, NJ: Princeton University Press, 1957) 163, 178. See especially Frye's theory of comedy in the chapter "The Mythos of Spring: Comedy," 163–86.

3. Dorothea Krook, *Elements of Tragedy* (New Haven, CT: Yale University Press, 1969) 8–18.

4. Northrop Frye, *A Natural Perspective: The Development of Shakespearean Comedy and Romance* (New York: Columbia University Press, 1965) 73.

and adjusting the family to society as a whole."[5] Ruth's marrying Boaz and bearing a son to carry her dead husband's name suggests that Elimelech's family, which was estranged from his people and seemingly severed from them forever (since all the males have died), has miraculously become reintegrated into Israelite history and society.

The comedy in Ruth elevates the female figures to the role of the *eiron*, the conscious creators of the comic spirit, rather than its victims, buttressing a woman-centered or even feminist understanding of the story.[6] The comic mode further allows for an irreverent perspective on the elderly patriarch and thus on patriarchy in general. Ruth is only one example of comedy resulting from the fooling of the patriarch, a recurrent biblical situation and a universal laughter-inducing motif representing the Bergsonian "inversion."[7] The cycle of women's lives is an underlying pattern in the tale that enhances the central role of women, who become not only the passive beneficiaries of charity but the epistemological and textual heart of the tale. The story of Ruth itself is placed within the context of the spring season. The initial narrative is morbid as it chronicles the rapid series of disasters that befall Naomi's family and the three widows' agonizing dialogues spoken somewhere in the desolate landscape between Moab and Judah. Yet immediately after these bleak narratives, we enter Bethlehem with its bustling town life and curious crowds. Here we are also informed cryptically that this is the season of plenty, the beginning of harvest time. Thus the cycle of nature, leading from winter to spring, is paralleled by the cycle of the women's lives, which moves from death and emptiness to rebirth and fullness of life.

In this context it is relevant to remember that Greek drama grew out of the worship of Dionysus, the god of fertility, and that the theme of fertility, both of the soil and of the woman, is pivotal to our biblical story. Ruth begins with the land of Israel barren and fruitless, causing famine and forcing Elimelech's family to leave it, and culminates in the celebration of the plentiful harvest. It opens with childless women

---

5. Idem, *Anatomy*, 218.

6. Several scholars have suggested that Ruth may have originated in the female community; see E. F. Campbell's introduction to *Ruth* in the Anchor Bible series (AB 7; Garden City, NY: Doubleday, 1975). André LaCocque has argued in a number of his publications that Ruth was written by a woman, most recently in "Subverting the Biblical World," in *Scrolls of Love: Ruth and the Song of Songs* (ed. Peter Hawkins and Lesleigh Cushing; New York: Fordham University Press, 2006) 332.

7. Henri Bergson, "Laughter," in *Comedy* (ed. Wylie Sypher; Garden City, NY: Doubleday, 1956) 121.

who have no prospect of becoming mothers—Naomi because she is past her prime and Ruth because there is no redeemer in sight—and closes with Ruth giving birth to a son, thus making Naomi a grandmother and providing the necessary link in the family's once-broken genealogical line.

Another element of comedy pointed out by Northrop Frye and others is the Saturnalia (named after Saturn, the Roman god of agriculture), which usually happens at a crucial juncture in the comic action.[8] The Saturnalia is a moment of chaos that is characterized by the breaking of all boundaries, making merry, and eating and drinking excessively. One of the participants leads the festivities and assumes the role of the Lord of Misrule. Traditional commentary on Ruth sees Boaz as dignified and straight-laced, but I suggest that in a comic reinterpretation of Ruth it is Boaz who plays the role of the Lord of Misrule.

The tale's Saturnalian moment may also be examined in light of Mikhail Bakhtin's theory of carnival, a cultural phenomenon in medieval and Renaissance Europe that dates back to pagan times. Bakhtin argued that folk celebrations that allowed for rowdy humor and a parody of authority offered the oppressed lower classes relief from the rigidity of the feudal system and the church and an opportunity for expressing nonconformist, even rebellious views. The carnivalesque spirit, therefore, is a form of popular, "low" humor that celebrates the anarchic and grotesque elements of authority and of humanity in general and encourages the temporary "crossing of boundaries." In carnival, the town fool is crowned, the higher classes are mocked, the differences between people are flattened, and their shared humanity, the body, becomes the subject of crude humor. Bakhtin moved beyond the Freudian view of jokes as a form of emotional release from existential and social anxieties and saw in carnivalesque humor a social force that allowed a text to enter a sociopolitical discourse while enjoying impunity and thus to bring about cultural transformation.[9] While there is

---

8. Frye, *Anatomy*, 171; see also Cesar L. Barber, *Shakespeare's Festive Comedy: A Study of Dramatic Form and Its Relation to Social Custom* (Princeton: Princeton University Press, 1959) 15, 36.

9. Mikhail Bakhtin developed his theories of the carnivalesque and the dialogic imagination in *Problems of Dostoevsky's Poetics* (ed. and trans. Carl Emerson; Minneapolis: University of Minnesota Press, 1984), *Rabelais and His World* (trans. Helene Iswolsky; Bloomington: Indiana University Press, 1984), and *The Dialogic Imagination* (ed. Michael Holquist; trans. Caryl Emerson and Michael Holquist; Austin: University of Texas Press, 1981). For illuminating analyses of Bakhtin, see Gary Saul Morson and Caryl Emerson, *Mikhail Bakhtin: Creation of Prosaics* (Stanford, CA: Stanford University Press, 1990); and Michael Holquist, *Dialogism: Bakhtin and His World* (London: Routledge, 1990).

no indication in Ruth that its narrator(s) aimed at radical cultural transformation, the tale represents several cultural adjustments undergone by the Bethlehem community, such as the acceptance of the foreign wife, the condoning of women's sexual trickery, and the expansion of the meaning of the familial redeemer to include a kin other than a brother-in-law.

The end-of-harvest celebration may be seen as a mini-carnival in which existing structures are mocked and parodied, bringing about a social, psychological, and theological transformation. Without the spirit of unrestrained revelry that exists during the spring celebrations, when men become so intoxicated that they are unable to return home to their own beds and therefore must remain overnight in the open field, the scheme of Naomi and Ruth would never have worked. Indeed, Naomi must be acquainted with this harvest custom of reversal of normal behavior, knowing that the most respectable and disciplined citizen of the community becomes the leader of the celebration and loses control of his senses. The success of her daring plan depends entirely on this fact. In the earlier two biblical stories that also revolve around the deception of the patriarch by women in order to keep the family alive—the Genesis tales of Lot and his daughters and of Judah and Tamar—the women depend on the patriarch's losing his clearheadedness and becoming aroused erotically, whether by wine, in the case of Lot, or by the excessive eating and drinking during the sheep-shearing festivities, in the case of Judah.[10]

For proper dramatic structure, Aristotle requires a tightly knit story in which all events are causally connected, reflecting a great conflict and an entanglement leading to a climax, after which there is a movement toward a denouement, or resolution. Underlying this dynamic movement are elements of mystery and suspense, an epiphany, and the reversal of fortune. This structure is evident in Ruth; the protagonists' nocturnal encounter is the culmination of all events preceding it and marks the beginning of the resolution. As the true dramatic center of the tale, this encounter is very suspenseful because Naomi and Ruth have put their reputation at risk; if their maneuver does not succeed, both may be destroyed forever in this community. Even if Boaz is not upset or vengeful and decides to send Ruth on her way, the women's

---

10. On the affinities between these stories in terms of their genealogical links, literary motifs, and cultural practices, see Harold Fisch, "Ruth and the Structure of Covenantal History," *VT* 32 (1982) 425–37; see also my *Eve's Journey: Feminine Images in Hebraic Literary Tradition* (Philadelphia: University of Pennsylvania Press, 1986) 85–88.

plot has failed, and they are back where they started: destitute and hopeless. As in Shakespearean comedy, the situation in which the heroine finds herself could as easily have ended tragically. Yet because this is a comedy, the tragic potential is held at bay and eventually stunted; Boaz does not denounce Ruth and her mother-in-law, and instead, the story shifts gears at midpoint to reach a happy ending for its women protagonists.

The Aristotelian "unity of action" is also evident here: there are no secondary protagonists, nor is there a subplot mirroring the main plot. Reminiscent of Shakespeare's practice, in the biblical story Aristotle's "unity of time" is somewhat relaxed, but we may say that all events take place during the spring season, from the beginning to the end of harvest. The principle of "unity of place" is also somewhat relaxed, but in a general way it is the town of Bethlehem that offers a unity of location. The women of Bethlehem serve as the counterpart of the Greek chorus, commenting on Naomi's appearance when they first see her and naming the newborn child and rejoicing with Naomi at the end of the story.

Another modern theory of drama, offered by Dorothea Krook, also reinforces the placement of Ruth within the dramatic genre as well as my argument that Ruth as comedy is tragedy in reverse. Tragedy, says Krook, is triggered by an "act of shame or horror" that is followed by great suffering.[11] Although the biblical narrator does not comment on Elimelech's departure from Bethlehem, it is clear that this desertion, made years before the present time of the story of Ruth, is still considered horrendous, perhaps even unforgivable in its lack of faith in Israel as the divinely promised land. The family's departure before the tale properly begins casts a pall on the entire narrative. And while the sons' marriages to non-Israelite women are similarly narrated matter of factly, these unions contribute to the sense that the family offended God and therefore was punished by him. Thus the first two dramatic elements mapped out by Krook are met in Ruth: the initial shameful act(s) and the suffering that ensues.

Naomi herself understands her predicament to be God's deliberate action against her, not merely random catastrophe: "The hand of the Lord is gone out against me," she cries (Ruth 1:13). As in Greek drama, the question of divine retribution arises in the dialogue between the protagonist and the chorus. Naomi says to the women of Bethlehem: "For God has testified against me / and Shaddai has pronounced an

---

11. See Krook, "The Scheme of Tragedy," in *Elements of Tragedy*, 8–34.

evil sentence on me" (1:21). Even as she expresses her wretchedness, Naomi frames her present misery as part of an ongoing dialogue between herself and God. This is not simply colloquial speech in a God-fearing culture. Rather, it is a well-thought-out argument on the part of Naomi, whose rhythmic lament reverberates with echoes of the book of Job, thus endowing her plight with larger, even colossal significance. Naomi's language, at once polemical and philosophical, evokes a vision of the divine court in which God is both witness for the prosecution and judge determining the verdict. In this scene, Naomi imagines herself to play a major role: the accused. Elsewhere, I have argued that Naomi's sense of self-worth is revealed precisely in these words.[12] Although she proclaims her wretchedness through them, she also claims that God has singled her out for persecution, couching her grievances in the language of Job, thus placing her predicament in the venerable biblical tradition of a man challenging a wrathful God regarding his undeserved suffering. Yet in terms of her personal complaint and dialogue with God, Naomi also recognizes that she is paying for the grave violation that occurred in her family. According to Krook, drama further involves the protagonist's coming to a heightened understanding or an epiphany followed by the affirmation of life and the dignity of humankind (even in defeat, in the case of tragedy). The happy resolution of Ruth cannot be attained apart from the manifold epiphanies that are enjoyed by each of the three main characters.

Naomi's epiphany relates to a realization that her predicament is a consequence of a sin—not sin committed by her directly but a sin in which she participated as part of her family. To make amends, she seeks not only material salvation for Ruth but redemption in the covenantal sense, *yibbum* through a male redeemer. Therefore, in her attempt to lift herself and Ruth from the jaws of poverty and destitution, Naomi is looking for more than a material solution to their problems. She does not sell her property, for instance, or try to reactivate her land so that it can once again become productive and a source of profit. Rather, she looks for a redeemer, a *gô'ēl*, for Ruth, who will provide more than just the comforts of a husband and a home. Her quest for redemption thus gives a spiritual turn to her search for material security and survival. Ruth's epiphany is akin to Naomi's, for she realizes that, truly to become

---

12. See my "Language as Female Empowerment in Ruth," in *Reading Ruth: Contemporary Women Reclaim a Sacred Text* (ed. Judith A. Kates and Gail Twersky-Reimer; New York: Ballantine, 1994) 111–24; see also my *Woman at the Window: Feminine Images in Hebraic Literary Tradition* (Detroit: Wayne State University Press, 1998) 146–56.

one of the Hebrew people whom she so passionately wants to espouse, she needs to enter the community through the time-honored custom of levirate marriage and that she must rebuild the family that has been devastated.

Boaz's epiphany, so important to the happy ending of the story, comes to him from Ruth herself. Here we find a reversal of traditional roles, for now the woman teaches the man and not vice versa. This reversal is one of the comic sources of the story, akin to the student lecturing his teacher or the accused chiding the judge, to use Bergson's examples. It becomes clear that, while Boaz shows compassion and charity toward Ruth when he first spots her among the poor in his field, he had already known about Naomi's arrival. However, he was not moved to help her before, nor does he show further interest in the two women once the harvest season ends. When Ruth asks Boaz why he has singled her out for special treatment, she is not just being modest or grateful. She elicits from Boaz an admission that he has heard that Naomi and her daughter-in-law have returned and that he knows much more about Naomi and Ruth than his actions so far have shown. But if Ruth's question is meant to stir in Boaz a sense of responsibility, perhaps even guilt, that would drive him to do more for her and Naomi than he has done so far, she is not completely successful. Therefore, when the season of harvesting is over and the women are again alone and desolate, they need to resort to action.

It is only during the nocturnal encounter between Ruth and Boaz that Boaz's education is completed and his long-awaited epiphany is finally achieved. Ruth designates Boaz as her "redeemer," although technically he is not. Ruth's choice of words and the nature of her argument are significant; she could simply ask Boaz to rescue her from misery or save her honor, because she has now been compromised. Rather, she evokes the levirate custom, making Boaz understand the spirit of the law, rather than simply its narrow meaning. Ruth presents herself not as a charity case but as a woman looking to find a place for herself within the community's religious framework: to enter the Israelite family through the institution of the levirate marriage. She makes Boaz realize that the law itself does not always cover all the cases confronted in real life. With Ruth's subtle help, Boaz broadens his conception of the levirate obligation to include not only the widow's brother-in-law but also her more distant relatives. Ruth teaches Boaz a lesson in the humanitarian interpretation of the law, which he readily accepts. She also creates a new reality with the aid of language; by naming Boaz a "redeemer," Ruth makes him one. Once Boaz finally perceives this lesson, he proceeds to do the right thing for his two widowed relatives.

The women's subtle, clever use of language is a means of self-empowerment, of creating a happy reality for themselves out of a situation of hopelessness and emptiness. Their lexicon, especially Naomi's nuanced and creative use of Hebrew, sustains the suspense; the various dramatic elements come to light only in the full course of the play. Thus the dramatic suspense in the story's plot line is not only how these two women, shunned by God and community alike, will lift themselves out of their misery; it is how they will find a redeemer, a *gôʾēl*, not just a protector. The concern is to revive Naomi's family through a male child who, legally and socially, will be regarded as her own natural grandson and thus preserve and renew the line of Elimelech. It is Naomi who initially introduces the way that the plot will unfold, although she does not do so directly but through a very innovative use of rhetoric. By calling Orpah Ruth's *yĕbāmāh* and talking about the impossibility of providing redeemers for her daughters-in-law, Naomi in fact introduces the concept of *yibbum*, the redemption of the childless widow. She uses the potential of words to send subliminal messages and create new realities, and the reader is left with the suspenseful question how Naomi's comically impossible scenario will nevertheless become a reality.

This suspense is further sustained by Naomi's creative and humorous use of Hebrew. When Naomi describes the improbable event of her marrying a man that very night and eventually bearing sons, her language is so outrageously exaggerated that it points to a subtext quite different from the statement that is ostensibly being made. Naomi describes at length what cannot happen, but her elaborating on the impossible—namely, that she will remarry and give birth to sons and that her daughters-in-law will wait for these sons to redeem them—points to hidden desires and hope. While on the face of it Naomi rules out any possibility of her daughters-in-law remarrying within her family, her protestations create an imaginary world in which the unlikely might indeed come true; behind the language of seeming desperation lurks the vision of a potential miracle. Naomi's comically absurd scenario plants for the actors and audience alike an idea and a hope that it be realized. And when she wrongly uses the term *yĕbāmāh* to denote the familial link between the two widowed sisters-in-law, Naomi does not misspeak; she speaks with tongue in cheek. She calls Orpah Ruth's *yĕbāmāh* the way we would call an idiot a "genius." While stating the improbable, she resorts to the comical, because it is only in the world of comedy that the impossible may still come true.

While dismissing the possibility of a levirate marriage for Ruth and Orpah, Naomi in fact introduces the concept into both the tale and the consciousness of the reader. Moreover, to build up her vision of the possible further, to enhance her subliminal message, and to create a world out of the word Naomi names the relationship between the two women using a term that technically does not denote the link between women whose husbands are brothers. Naomi tells Ruth to follow her sister-in-law, Orpah, who has finally taken Naomi's advice and headed back to Moab. But in the Hebrew, Naomi does not use the term 'sister' or 'sister-in-law'; rather, she calls Orpah *yĕbimtēk*, using the term *yĕbāmāh* to describe the familial relationship between the two women. In Biblical Hebrew, the noun *yĕbāmāh* designates the childless widow in relation to her dead husband's brother. He is the *yābam* or 'redeemer', as it is usually translated, and she is the *yĕbāmāh*, the feminine form of the same noun. But nowhere in the Bible is it suggested that sisters-in-law are each other's *yĕbāmāh*. This should not be taken as a slip of the tongue, a careless mistake on the part of a distraught woman. Naomi has taken liberty with the language, but in the process she has created a new frame of reference within the tale by filling the dialogue with intimations of *yibbum* 'levirate marriage', thus mitigating the language of the unattainable. Naomi creates a world with the force of her tongue, and the reader is left to wonder how the misnomer she uses will enter reality. Will a time come in which either of these two young women will indeed be rightfully called *yĕbāmāh*?

Naomi further creates suspense with regard to her own destiny in the short speech that she gives to the women of Bethlehem: "Call me not Naomi; call me Mara: for the Lord has dealt bitterly with me. I went out full, and the Lord brought me back empty; why then do you call me Naomi?" (1:20–21). These words may sound bitter, but they also disclose a humorous look on the part of Naomi at the discrepancy between her predicament and her name. Naomi claims that her name, which means 'pleasure', contrasts with her sorry reality, and that it therefore should be changed to mirror reality truthfully. Naomi is here in line with biblical tradition, which attributes great importance to names; but what she means, of course, is not that her name should be changed to reflect her sorry predicament but that her reality should be mended and altered to conform to her original name. Both when she introduces the theme of *yibbum* as an impossibility and when she laments about her name, Naomi sounds both sad and humorous.

Running through these august themes is an undeniable comic tone, casting the Ruth story as comedic drama, if read in light of Aristotle's

Poetics, or as a "carnivalesque" narrative, if read through Bakhtinian lenses.[13] Henri Bergson has suggested that the comic writer uses tricks such as discrepancies, deceptions, misunderstandings, mistaken identities, the unexpected, and stock comic types. In Ruth, it is possible to see in the three protagonists a variation of the conventional comic types featured in classical comedy as well as in later works, such as the plays of Molière. In this setup, Boaz plays the *senex*, the comic old man; Ruth is the *virgo*, the young girl often inaccessible for a variety of reasons; and Naomi is the *servus callidus*, the clever slave, or the *servus delusus*, the crafty servant whose inspired planning and improvisation bring about the happy comic resolution.[14]

The discrepancy in age and status between Boaz and Ruth, reflected also in the marked differences in their linguistic styles, is rife with comic promise. The attraction that a young woman holds for an old man has often been used by dramatists and stage directors for its hilarious, farcical possibilities. When the older Boaz notices Ruth among the people in his field, it is because he finds the young woman interesting, unusual, or perhaps even attractive. Furthermore, Boaz's lofty rhetoric, imbued with the concepts of morality, goodness, and charity contrasts with his inaction through most of the story. Boaz emerges as a pompous old man for whom talk is easy, but he is awkward and hesitant when it comes to interaction with a young woman that he obviously likes. In public, he praises Ruth for her good deeds, but he is too reluctant or protective of his good name to visit the women's home in private. Boaz's "comic flaw," the counterpart of the Aristotelian "tragic flaw," is excessive concern with his public image; his inclination is to make grand public gestures on which he does not follow through. His flaw may also lie in his timidity with women, in his sexual shyness, which creates a comic discrepancy between his status as a wealthy, powerful figure and his diffidence with women in private. Ruth and Naomi use these weaknesses to their own advantage.

Additionally, Boaz's style seems stale and rigid: he uses a set format of greetings (addressing his workers with the conventional formula "God be with you," to which they respond "God bless you," 2:4) and

---

13. For an exclusively Bakhtinian reading of the tale that argues that the entire Ruth narrative is permeated with the spirit of carnival, as theorized by Bakhtin, and that its speech displays the Bakhtinian "heteroglossia," see my article, "Reading Ruth through a Bakhtinian Lens: The Carnivalesque in a Biblical Tale," *JBL* 126 (2007): 437–53.

14. See Robert S. Miola, "Roman Comedy," in *Shakespearean Comedy* (ed. Alexander Leggatt; Cambridge: Cambridge University Press, 2002) 18; John Creaser, "Forms of Confusion," in ibid., 82.

customary blessings ("May God grant you due recompense; may your payment be full from the God of Israel, under whose wings you have come to seek refuge," 2:12). The old man sounds like a puppet repeating familiar formulas rather than expressing his own original sentiments. This renders him mechanical, robotic, and therefore comical in the Bergsonian sense.[15]

Frye distinguishes between two comic types, the *eiron*, the creator of comedy, and the *alazon*, the butt of it.[16] It goes without saying that, in the comic scheme of things, Ruth and Naomi play the role of the *eiron*, and Boaz, the *alazon*. In the very first encounter between Boaz and Ruth, the latter uses a playful, even teasing tone when she asks Boaz why he has singled her out. The old man embarks on a lengthy speech about how he has already heard of Ruth; his stilted, effusive language contrasts amusingly with Ruth's easy and straightforward tone. We can only imagine Boaz's young workers sneering at their old master behind his back. Ruth's strategy of gently embarrassing the old man who is so conscious of his status in the community culminates in the scene at the threshing floor. This is a classic example of the comic situation known as the "bed trick" or the fooling of the powerful male. The *alazon*, says Frye, is often the "heavy father" or a surrogate of this character (Boaz addresses Ruth as "my daughter"), who often displays "gullibility." Frye further describes the *alazon* as a "man of words rather than of deeds."[17] As noted, Boaz often uses a highly rhetorical language, lauding charity and good work, and yet, as we have seen, he stays within the realm of speech not deeds; it is the women who drive him to action. The *eiron*, according to Frye, is often the heroine, who brings about the dramatic resolution through disguise or some other trickery. According to this description, Ruth is the perfect *eiron*. Frye also speaks of the *eiron* as "the type entrusted with hatching the schemes which bring about the hero's victory." Often a female confidant, in the biblical story this type of *eiron* is Naomi.[18]

Indeed, the tale as a whole, framed by the spring festivities, is narrated from a carnivalesque perspective in several ways. First, the narrative gives voice to multiple and contradictory points of view expressed across a broad spectrum of dialect, from high to low, from elegant and euphemistic to direct and physical. Second, the spirit of

---

15. Bergson, "Laughter," 79–86.
16. Frye, *Anatomy*, 172–75.
17. Ibid., 172.
18. Ibid., 173.

revelry, mockery, and defiance underlies the entire Ruth narrative and is not limited to the night of drinking and merry-making. The mocking narrative voice is heard first in the rhyming names of Naomi's sons, מחלון 'little illness' and כליון 'destruction', which sound more like names created by the comic/macabre mind after the fact, in the process of narrating the events, rather than names given by hopeful parents. Orpah's synecdochic name is also comic, for we will forever see her as the back of a neck, ʿorep, rather than a full human being. Pĕlōnî ʾAlmōnî, Mr. So-and-So, is a comic moniker, a punishment meted out by the narrator to the person who has refused to fulfill his familial obligations.

The barley celebration marks the heart of the carnival and is characterized by chaos and loss of control. It is clear that the intoxicated Boaz becomes unsteady and forgetful when he sinks into deep sleep. Here the situation can easily develop into physical farce as the old man, usually buttoned-up and proper, wakes from his drunken stupor disoriented and alarmed to find a strange woman at his feet in the open field. Ruth, on the other hand, is sober, controlled, and purposeful; she asks—in fact, orders—the old man to "redeem" her. The comic possibilities envisioned by Bergson are numerous here: we find disguise, pun, comic repetition of verbal formulas, inelasticity of the body, and the manipulation of one person by another so as to appear "as a mere toy in the hands of another." Ruth expands on her mother-in-law's initial plan, and in response to Boaz's startled "Who are you?" she not only identifies herself but proceeds to make an audacious suggestion: "I am Ruth, your handmaid: spread therefore your skirt [or wing] over your handmaid; for you are a near kinsman [or, a redeemer]" (3:9). A woman asking a man to marry reverses the norms of patriarchal society and is inherently comic.

Bakhtin emphasized the importance of the physical to the carnival's challenge of authority, pointing out that Rabelais wanted to "return a reality, a materiality to language and to meaning."[19] The body brings the world back to a physical level, moving it away from dogma and authoritarianism.[20] Indeed we see that Ruth (perhaps more subtly than her two predecessors but as daringly) introduces carnival physicality to her encounter with the reluctant patriarch when she uncovers his legs, or feet, which is the biblical euphemistic code for the nakedness of the body. The reader inevitably laughs here, because, as Bergson suggests,

---

19. Bakhtin, *The Dialogic*, 171.
20. Idem, *Rabelais*, 3.

"our attention is diverted to the physical in a person when it is the moral that is in question" and when a person is "embarrassed by his own body."[21]

An alternative translation of Ruth 3:7 makes this scene even more flagrant. The standard translation of the Hebrew verb ותגל is 'she uncovered his legs', but an equally valid reading would be 'she uncovered herself', with the following word, מרגלותיו, indicating where this action takes place, at his feet, rather than functioning as the syntactic object, his feet.[22] According to this reading, Ruth makes a bold physical move: she uncovers her own body and exposes herself to the man. Ruth also introduces the physical to the language of her discourse when she tells Boaz to "spread" his "wing" over her. She uses the word "wing" not only as a metaphor for protection, the way Boaz used it metaphorically in an earlier scene, but in the physical sense of "the corner" of his blanket, or robe. Plainly put, Ruth brazenly suggests to Boaz that he take her under his blanket. Ruth sounds somewhat mischievous when she repeats the ceremonious phrase that Boaz himself had uttered earlier—"under [God's] wings" (2:12)—and jokingly alters the overstated "God's wings" simply to "wings," the corners of Boaz's garment.

In this verbal pun, Ruth makes fun of the old man's grand but shallow vocabulary, criticizing it as too lofty and insubstantial and implying that the only wings that matter to her in the present are not the esoteric "God's wings" but Boaz's "wings," meaning the protection that he can give her through marriage. She diminshes the metaphoric "wing" and brings it down to earth even more to the literal, physical meaning of Boaz's blanket or robe, suggesting physical contact. Thus, in the spirit of the carnival, Ruth reduces the "high" concept implied in Boaz's "God's wings" to the crudely physical. When Boaz regains his composure, he is still emotional and effusive; in a flowery speech, he blesses Ruth and commends her profusely, perhaps to cover up his embarrassment and discomfort at her presence. However, physical comedy resurfaces when, in a theatrical gesture, Boaz measures out a significant portion of barley and tells Ruth to hold up her apron so that he can fill it (3:15). One can only imagine the farcical, even bawdy visual possibilities of Ruth returning home with her apron bulging provocatively.

---

21. The three citations are from Bergson, "Laughter," 111, 135, and 93, respectively.

22. See also Ellen van Wolde, "Intertextuality: Ruth in Dialogue with Tamar," in *Feminist Companion to Reading the Bible: Approaches, Methods and Strategies* (ed. Athalya Brenner and Carole Fontaine; Sheffield: Sheffield Academic Press, 1997) 444–45.

Two conventional types are still missing in the present appraisal of Ruth as comedy: the romantic young man who wins the female protagonist at the end and the comic "scapegoat." In our biblical story, Boaz combines in himself two diametrically opposite comic figures: (1) the old man absurdly interested in a younger woman and (2) the object of the young woman's desire. His interest in Ruth is on the one hand ridiculous, but it is also reciprocated. He may try to cover up his embarrassment over her uninvited attraction, but the fact is that Boaz is the woman's romantic interest. Furthermore, in traditional comedy, the heroine is inaccessible to the male hero either because there is another figure to overcome—a rival for her affections or some other "blocking figure," such as his own father (as in Molière's *Miser*)—or because the woman is stigmatized socially (she is not freeborn, for instance).[23] Both factors are found in Ruth: Boaz is aware of a possible "rival," both in the form of a closer male kin who would have precedence if the question of *yibbum* ever came up, and in the form of the local young men who, as he notices, have shown an interest in Ruth (3:10). Boaz is also held back by Ruth's disdained foreignness as a Moabite. Once we realize that Boaz unites two clashing figures of comedy, the preposterous old man and the romantic hero, we understand that the book of Ruth is highly unusual in its fusion of two distinct forms: the universal genre of comic romance and the biblical narratives' covenantal history.

Finally, Northrop Frye argues that comedy often includes a communal scapegoat and a ritual of expulsion, whereby society purges itself of the spirit of chaos that has temporarily seized it. With moderation and harmony reestablished, a far better, well-integrated society emerges from the one we experienced at the beginning of the play.[24] The reader finds evidence of this in the scene that takes place at the city gate (4:1–12), which concludes the dramatic part of the book. Here we witness a public ceremony in which Naomi's male kin draws off his shoe, signaling that he wishes to excuse himself from performing the rite of *yibbum*, thereby "expelling" himself, if not from the community at large, then from his role as redeeming kinsman. This nameless man, humorously referred to as *pĕlōnî 'almōnî* ('so-and-so') quickly disappears, and his departure ushers in the festivity in which the elders and the crowd gather at the gate to bless and embrace Ruth.[25]

---

23. Creaser, "Forms of Confusion," 82–83.
24. Frye, *Anatomy*, 165.
25. On the festive ending of comedy, see idem, *A Natural Perspective*, 128–30.

I do not suggest that the Ruth narrator was in any way acquainted with the genre of comedy as practiced by the Greeks, nor do I propose that the narrator had in mind a stage production when composing the tale.[26] I argue that comedy provides an undergirding to the story of Ruth, the scroll traditionally read in synagogue during the holiday of Shavuot in recognition of its links to the agricultural gifts offered at the temple at this time. However, just as we recognize the ancient harvest festivals within the biblical holidays of Sukkot, Pesaḥ, and Shavuot, so we catch glimpses of comedy behind the sober surface of the biblical tale.

Ruth may be read as a romantic comedy with carnivalesque undertones, rooted in the seasonal celebration of nature and its cycles, and thereby connected to festivities outside the boundaries of respected society. It offers a humorous, even rebellious critique of law and authority that has been coated with a story of historical and covenantal significance to the people of Israel, yet its comedic mode and carnivalesque spirit have not been entirely suppressed. One may read the comedy in Ruth in light of Freud's concept of humor, which sees in jokes and laughter-causing situations an emotionally liberating device, a mechanism for the release of pressures and the temporary lifting of the fear of authority. The humor in Ruth, especially in its deception of a patriarch, offers a topsy-turvy moment in which the woman is licensed to manipulate the powerful man and teach him how to behave.[27]

One might also read the humor in Ruth through Mikhail Bakhtin's Marxist lens and become more aware of the tale's subversive and antinomian aspects, of the intent of its comic voice to destabilize society with its rigid laws and offer validity to the multiplicity of voices and groups existing in society, especially to two minority groups. We have on the one hand the antiestablishment groups who, in the time of the tale's composition, fought against the likes of Ezra and Nehemiah for the acceptance of foreign wives.[28] On the other hand is the disenfranchised half of Israel, the women, who are allowed in this story to assert

---

26. Shimon Levy studies the theatrical aspects of Ruth and its potential for stage performance but does not go into genre analysis. Though his chapter on Ruth paraphrases a famous Shakespearean title, he does not recognize the comedic elements of the tale. See "Ruth: The Shrewing of the Tame," in *The Bible as Theatre* (Brighton: Sussex Academic Press, 2000) 82–103.

27. See Sigmund Freud, *Jokes and Their Relation to the Unconscious* (trans. James Strachey; New York: Norton, 1963).

28. On this aspect of Ruth, see Campbell, *Ruth*, 26.

themselves, take center stage, and freely fashion their own destiny—a privilege mostly afforded to men in the biblical narratives.

The critical exercise I have engaged in here, applying classical and modern theories of drama and a Bakhtinian concept to Ruth, opens up for the reader novel and even countercultural avenues of discoursing with the ancient text. A humorous view of authority, comic self-disparagement in the midst of sorrow, and misrule serve as a catalyst of epiphany and self-knowledge in this ancient tale. A comedic or carnivalesque reading of Ruth should not be mistaken for an irreverent look at a sacred book. Shakespeare, Molière, and Bakhtin, among many others, have shown that humor and comedy, while producing laughter, are very serious business. The comic view illustrates the absurdities of the human condition and the pretentiousness of humanity; it is produced by very important and essential human needs to cleanse inner demons, control existential fears, make life under oppression possible, and protest against injustice.

Ruth may represent the benign and healing impact of the carnival, where the boundaries of transgression are clearly delineated, and a certain amount of misrule does not lead to chaos and anarchy but offers a mechanism to integrate protest and rebellion into a redemptive vision. In Ruth, the Bible offers a familiar, universal "folk" tale, patterned on the comedic mode, originating in and retold (and probably also enacted) during public festivities. While following the trajectory of comedy or even the carnivalesque genre, this form has been reshaped by the biblical narrator into a covenantal story. The elements of crude physical humor, the transformation of the figure of authority into an intoxicated, bumbling fool, and the women's double-talk bringing down the lofty semantics of divine reward are secondary to the tale's overarching theme of redemption. Yet these iconoclastic, rebellious, ironic perspectives are only thinly disguised and are still powerfully present, giving the tale its vigor and elasticity and its ability to speak to different generations with changing cultural views.

Where Is Isaiah in Isaiah?

FRANCIS LANDY
University of Alberta

In Isaiah, as in prophetic literature generally, questions of author-ship are inseparable from those of authority, reading, and readership: Are we dealing with thinkers, visionaries, poets, and revolutionaries, as in the old Protestant romantic tradition?[1] Or are we dealing with schools, communities, and the fictive invention of the prophet as a ret-rospective foreshadowing of ourselves?[2] These questions are not very

---

1. The tradition is not so old. For example, Marcus J. Borg (*Reading the Bible Again for the First Time* [San Francisco: HarperSanFrancisco, 2001] 111) begins his discussion of prophecy as follows:

> The classical prophets of ancient Israel are among the most remarkable people who have ever lived. Such is the indelible impression made by their words. Their lan-guage is memorable, poetic, and powerful. Their passion and courage are excep-tional. Their message combines radical criticism of the way things are with urgent advocacy of another way of being. They disturb our sense of normalcy in several ways—socially, personally, and spiritually. And, in their own words, they speak for God.

Similarly, Israel Knohl (*The Divine Symphony: The Bible's Many Voices* [Philadelphia: Jewish Publication Society, 2003] 55) cautions against a reductive approach to prophecy, citing the doyen of Israeli biblical scholarship, Yehezkel Kaufmann: "The primary sources of human creativity are beyond our ken and power to explain. An Amos or an Isaiah are not entirely accounted for by historical or social circumstances" (Yehezel Kaufmann, *The Re-ligion of Israel* [trans. Moshe Greenberg; Chicago: University of Chicago Press, 1960] 358). Likewise, Knohl, in his earlier book, regards the Holiness Codes as a reaction to the pro-phetic critique of social inequality and the cult (*The Sanctuary of Silence: The Priestly Torah and the Holiness School* [Minneapolis: Fortress, 1995] 214–15). A comparably traditional view of prophets as radical critics without ties to institutions is found in Rainer Albertz, *A History of Ancient Israel in the Old Testament Period*, vol. 1: *From the Beginnings to the End of the Monarchy* (trans. John Bowden; Louisville: Westminster/John Knox, 1994) 163: "The men who saw themselves as driven by God in the period from around 760 to 700 to react with an unprecedented degree of radicalism to the critical developments of the period all belong to the type of individual prophet with no ties to an institution."

2. Ehud Ben Zvi, for example, insists on the difference between the prophetic book, which alone is accessible to the critic, and the putative prophet. The book is the creation of literate elites, presumably in Achaemenid Jerusalem, who construct their own iden-tity by projecting it onto a fictive critical figure from the past: "Researchers never dealt

different from contemporary semiotic and deconstructive questions about the relationship of the real and implied author, real and implied reader, and the construction of the self in writing.[3] Paradoxically, an extreme focus on the act of writing is coupled with dissolution of the writing self into traces of other selves, texts, literary codes and conventions, and with the impact of impersonal drives and determinants, which may be psychic, economic, or political.[4] In the case of ancient

directly with historical speakers, nor with flesh-and-blood prophets, nor with those who had the good or bad fortune to listen to them. Scholars were never privy to any direct oral communication that could have happened in ancient Israel. Rather, they had and have access to written texts" (Ben Zvi, "The Prophetic Book: A Key Form of Prophetic Literature," in *The Changing Face of Form Criticism for the Twenty-First Century* [ed. Marvin A. Sweeney and Ehud Ben Zvi; Grand Rapids, MI: Eerdmans, 2003] 277). Elsewhere he argues that prophetic books were not "mimetic" (p. 289). Other scholars who have argued that historical prophets are reconstructions of later scribal communities are Philip R. Davies (*In Search of Ancient Israel* [JSOTSup 148; Sheffield: Sheffield Academic Press, 1992] 124): "I see no reason to attribute it [prophetic literature] to 'prophets' nor to anyone before the fifth century BCE"; and Robert Carroll, in numerous contributions, including his massive commentary on Jeremiah. In Isaiah scholarship, this point of view is represented by Edgar Conrad, who notes the inaccessibility of the real author and readers of the book of Isaiah (*Reading Isaiah* [Minneapolis: Fortress, 1991] 154) and suggests that it was primarily written for a community of survivors. Similarly, Peter D. Miscall (*Isaiah* [Readings; Sheffield: JSOT Press, 1993] 19) writes that "I use the term 'Isaiah' to designate the eighth-century prophet as a character in the book," though, as becomes clear in his later *Reading Isaiah: Poetry and Vision* ([Louisville: Westminster/John Knox, 2001] 19), he does not deny the historical existence of that prophet. A very thorough discussion of the issues of composition, poetics, and historicity may be found in James R. Linville, "On the Nature of Rethinking Prophetic Literature: Stirring a Neglected Stew," *JHS* 2 (1999).

3. For these issues, see the many works of Wolfgang Iser (e.g., *The Implied Reader* [Baltimore: Johns Hopkins University Press, 1974]; idem, *Prospecting: From Reader Response to Literary Anthropology* [Baltimore: Johns Hopkins University Press, 1989]) and Umberto Eco (e.g., *Six Walks in the Fictional Woods* [Cambridge: Harvard University Press, 1994]).

4. Deconstruction, like structuralism, is characterized by close reading combined with skepticism about the self-sufficiency of the author. All texts are palimpsests, bearing the traces of their history and the many persons and events that have contributed to them. For instance, Roland Barthes dissolves literary works into the codes that constitute them (*S/Z* [trans. Richard Miller; London: Cape, 1974]). However, few writers have been as poignantly aware of the intersection of life and writing as Derrida, from his early essay on Rousseau to his latest works (see, for example, Jacques Derrida, *Of Grammatology* [trans. Gayatri Chakravorti Spivak; Baltimore: Johns Hopkins University Press, 1974] 97–316). As Yvonne Sherwood and John D. Caputo write: "What Amos and Derrida share is the desire to mobilize the forces of writing in a way that cannot be annexed to the rhetoric of human mastery and the power of the subject" ("Otobiographies or How a Torn and Disembodied Ear Hears a Promise of Death," in *Derrida and Religion* [ed.

writers, we are aided as well as frustrated by our lack of knowledge, which allows scope for our imagination. I once published a mystical autobiography of Isaiah: I know whereof I speak.[5] So I am concerned here with the implied author and reader of Isaiah, their relation to the real author and readers—especially of interest when it comes to us academics—but also the points where the author intrudes, fictively and imaginatively, as in the vision of chap. 6, or the call scene in chap. 40, or is foregrounded in the third person, in the royal confrontations and reassurances in chaps. 7 and 37–39, and the sign of chap. 20.

The question is complicated by the presumption of multiple authorship over many centuries and the gap, in particular, between Proto- and Deutero-Isaiah—a gap that is in part self-conscious.[6] How can we, or should we, cross the fissures in the text? So when I speak of the implied author, I am speaking about a tone, a persona linking different

Yvonne Sherwood and Kevin Hart; New York: Routledge, 2005] 211). Julia Kristeva introduced the concept of *intertextuality* into Western literary discourse: "Any text is constructed as a mosaic of quotations; any text is the absorption and transformation of another" ("Word, Dialogue and Novel," in *The Kristeva Reader* [ed. Toril Moi; New York: Columbia University Press, 1986] 37), but she has also written numerous psycholiterary studies of individual authors and artists, as well as the relationship of writing, desire, and depression. Good starting points for the Marxist reading of literature are Frederic Jameson, *The Political Unconscious: Narrative as a Socially Symbolic Act* (Ithaca, NY: Cornell University Press, 1981), and Terry Eagleton, *Literary Theory: An Introduction* (2nd ed.; Minneapolis: Minnesota University Press, 1996). An excellent introduction to Marxist literary theory and the Bible is Roland Boer, *Marxist Criticism of the Bible: A Critical Introduction to Marxist Literary Theory and the Bible* (London: T. & T. Clark, 2005).

5. See my "Ghostwriting," in *Beauty and the Enigma and Other Essays on the Hebrew Bible* (JSOTSup 312; Sheffield: Sheffield Academic Press, 2001) 392–413. Also published as "Ghostwriting Isaiah," in *First Person: Essays in Biblical Autobiography* (ed. Philip R. Davies; Biblical Seminar 81; Sheffield: Sheffield Academic Press, 2002) 93–114.

6. I am thinking of references in Deutero-Isaiah to the "former things," for example, in 42:9; and also of the very marked caesura between chaps. 39 and 40. Much recent scholarship has focused on compositional links between Deutero- and Proto-Isaiah, for example: Odil H. Steck, *Bereitete Heimkehr: Jesaja 35 als Redaktionelle Brücke zwischen dem Ersten und dem Zweiten Jesaja* (Stuttgart: Katholisches Bibelwerk, 1985); Hugh G. M. Williamson, *The Book Called Isaiah: Deutero-Isaiah's Role in Composition and Redaction* (Oxford: Clarendon, 1994); and Antti Laato, *"About Zion I Will Not Be Silent": The Book of Isaiah as an Ideological Unity* (Stockholm: Almqvist and Wiksell, 1998). A useful corrective note is put forward by Benjamin Sommer (*A Prophet Reads Scripture: Allusion in Isaiah 40–66* [Contraversions; Stanford: Stanford University Press, 1998]), who argues that Deutero-Isaiah has as many allusions to Jeremiah as to Proto-Isaiah. See also Patricia Tull Willey, *Remember the Former Things: The Recollection of Previous Texts in Second Isaiah* (SBLDS 161; Atlanta: Scholars Press, 1997).

personalities, a prophetic performance, just as we may speak of many different Hamlets—a collective impersonation, wherewith we recognize a certain habit of mind,[7] a rhythm, metaphorical field, a mood conveyed by the nonsignifying aspects of language.

This is not to deny the prophetic experience. Every text, especially poetic text, is infused by experiences of many kinds, including the experience of writing. In the case of the prophets, we must assume some institutional context conducive to mystical or shamanic initiation and mediation, and also the experience of the context disappearing—of being called profoundly into question. I worry when scholars try to explain away Isaiah 6, for example, through the "retrojection" hypothesis, as if explaining away the inexplicable were not beside the point.[8] Isaiah 6 may be an account of a real event that happened in 734 (or whenever) to Isaiah,[9] but even if not, it is an account of an event of some kind. It is indeed an event articulated in language, communicated to an outside, even if that outside is told it cannot be communicated; it is subject to processes of interpretation and contextualization, just as it arises from these processes. But if we do not grant that Isaiah (or whoever) wrote these words, heard them spoken by God, we are nonhearers, at least of this particular fiction; we are outside the circle supposed by the text to be its readership, even if this readership is, paradoxically, nonhearers.

The words are God's; the "vision" of Isaiah is one of divine language. In this sense, God is the author, and to the extent that the prophet transmits God's message, even when he opposes God, he speaks for God. On the other hand, according to the projection hypothesis, God may be a fiction, an unacknowledged or split-off part of the prophetic self. God constructs the prophet as a resistant figure; the

---

7. By "habit of mind," I mean something like Pierre Bourdieu's "habitus," as a set of structuring dispositions (see, for example, *The Field of Cultural Production* [New York: Columbia University Press, 1993]).

8. The "retrojection" hypothesis or *Rücksprojizierungsthese*, first systematically developed by Friedrich Hesse (*Das Verstockungsproblem im Alten Testament: Eine frömmigkeits-geschichtliche Untersuchung* [BZAW 74; Berlin: de Gruyter, 1974]), holds that the strange command to speak so as not to be understood in 6:9–10 was retroactively imputed to God in Isaiah's commissioning scene so as to account for his subsequent failure. Most versions of this hypothesis are explicitly founded on the impossibility of ascribing perverse and paradoxical commands to God. See, most recently, Jan Joosten, "La prosopopée, les pseudo-citations et la vocation d'Isaïe (Is 6,9–10)," *Bib* 82 (2001) 232–43.

9. The dates of the kings of Israel and Judah are notoriously confused. However, 736–734 is a common consensus for the death of Uzziah (see Joseph Blenkinsopp, *Isaiah 1–39* [AB 19; New York: Doubleday, 2000] 224).

prophet experiences the word coming from some psychic abyss.[10] Or there may be a third party, the one who writes "the vision of Isaiah" and all the words of the book—for whom both God and prophet are fictional constructs—and is constituted by them. And at a fourth level, we as readers imagine, project ourselves, and take on the subject position of all three, insofar as readers and writers are constantly changing places. This makes our task as academics difficult, for we assume a distance, a certain whimsical detachment, even though this distance is already foreclosed, because we have the responsibility to be ideal readers.

In Isaiah, as in prophetic literature generally, there are stories about the prophet as well as places where the prophet intrudes into the text in the first person. As has been argued by Peter Ackroyd and Robert Carroll, among others, these stories have a rhetorical function.[11] They contribute to an image of the prophet as a suffering, thinking being; the prophet teaches as much through his life—for example, in heroic confrontations with kings and prophets—as through his words. He models for us what it is to be a reader, a prophet, a human being. A reader takes on the subject position of the prophet, as I have already noted, as a way of learning how to be a human being in a particular context. We might experience ourselves being called in chap. 6, for example, at a remove. This involves us in some contradictions.

As we read, we construct a personality that is familiar and unfamiliar at the same time. All prophets are alike, governed by conventions, in a tradition that insists on likeness. We know what to expect from prophets, and the text fulfills these generic expectations. At the same time, the prophet is demarcated as individual, for instance, through the title חֲזוֹן יְשַׁעְיָהוּ 'the vision of Isaiah'. The signature, as Derrida reminds us, is a sign of difference, of supplementarity; this body of text differs from others, such as Jeremiah and Ezekiel, and we can labor on the differences of style, imagery, and ideology. The book

---

10. The resistance may be experienced by both parties: "The text interacts with but resists the reader just as the reader interacts with but resists the text" (Elliot R. Wolfson, *Language, Eros, Being: Kabbalistic Hermeneutics and Poetic Imagination* [New York: Fordham University Press, 2005] 115).

11. Peter R. Ackroyd, "Isaiah I–XII: Presentation of a Prophet," in *IOSOT Congress Volume: Göttingen, 1977* (ed. J. Emerton; VTSup 29; Leiden, Brill, 1978) 16–48; idem, "Isaiah 36–39: Structure and Function," in *Von Kanaan bis Kerala: Festschrift für J. P. M. van der Ploeg* (ed. W. C. Delman; Neukirchen-Vluyn: Neukirchener Verlag, 1982) 3–21. Robert Carroll's views are represented throughout his oeuvre; see, however, especially his commentary on *Jeremiah* (London: SCM, 1986).

is pervaded by the attribution to the prophet, as a guarantee of truth: "this is true because it comes from the famous prophet Isaiah." None-theless, it also suggests the mystery of the person outside the confines of the book: the conflict between the paternal affiliation, as Isaiah, son of Amoz, and the divine calling, the obscure and fraught relation be-tween the work and the self, the distinction and interaction between the persona of the writer and his or her multiple imaginal and in-timate lives. It is also complicated by the title 'Vision'. The word חזון refers to prophetic vision, or even to a book, a vision translated as a book.[12] The vision (חזון) is distinct from normal vision (ראה); it is the vision of that which is invisible.[13] It introduces the world of poetry and of the imagination—not least as a marked, poetic term. One who sees a vision already has access to a different world, already differs from his or her everyday self—as does the reader of these words.

The construction of identity is complicated further as we progress through the book. "The vision of Isaiah" is followed by הדבר אשר חזה ישעיהו בן אמוץ 'the word/thing that Isaiah, son of Amoz, saw' in 2:1, and משא בבל אשר חזה ישעיהו בן אמוץ 'the burden of Babylon, which Isa-iah, son of Amoz, saw' in 13:1. What do all these different beginnings do?[14] Do they suggest different identities, selves, or a different starting

---

12. For the relationship of the vision and the book, see my article "Vision and Voice in Isaiah," *JSOT* 88 (2000) 19–36, reprinted in *Beauty and the Enigma*, 371–91, with an ex-tensive bibliography. Some scholars, such as Ehud Ben-Zvi (*A Historical-Critical Study of Obadiah* [BZAW 244; Berlin: de Gruyter, 1996] 12), consider חזון to be a dead metaphor, simply a title for a book. However, this is to minimize the importance of *vision* as a the-matic problem in the book. Apart from my article above, see Robert Carroll ("Blindsight and the Vision Thing: Blindness and Insight in the Book of Isaiah" in *Writing and Reading the Scroll of Isaiah*, vol. 1 [ed. Craig C. Broyles and Craig A. Evans; Leiden: Brill, 1997] 79–93), who comments, "The fact remains that the writers of the scroll (or final redactor as author) marked the traditum of Isaiah as 'vision'" (p. 84). Peter Quinn-Miscall, *Reading Isaiah: Poetry and Vision* (Louisville: Westminster/John Knox, 2001), studies the relation of image and text in detail.

13. Wolfson (*Language, Eros, Being*, xxiii–xxiv) pellucidly discusses the relation of the visible and the invisible in Merleau-Ponty's phenomenology, that all vision is a "tele-vision," a "seeing afar," a mode of transcendence through which the invisible becomes visible.

14. Ackroyd ("Isaiah I–XII," 32) regards the title in 2:1 as intrusive, while John Gol-dingay ("Isaiah i.1 and ii.1," *VT* 48 [1998] 326–32) argues that 2:1 is in fact the conclusion to chap. 1, not the beginning of a new discourse. Goldingay's main argument, that חזון can only refer to a single vision, begs the question both of the coherence of the chapter and the incoherence of the book as a whole. As Willem A. M. Beuken (*Jesaja 1–12* [HTKAT; Herder: Freiburg, 2003] 59) points out, the title asserts that the whole book is ultimately unified.

point? It is easy enough, for instance, to contrast Isaiah 1 and Isaiah 2, the first of which begins with an appeal to creation, the primary constituents of heaven and earth, as well as to the legacy of the archetypal prophet, Moses,[15] while the second begins at the end, with the אחרית הימים 'the lattermost days'.[16] Similarly, 13:1 turns to Jerusalem's antithesis, Babylon.

These different beginnings in turn represent different poetic voices in the book. Chapter 1, despite the clairvoyance suggested by חזון, is this-worldly, on the hither side of disaster; the prophet sees through this world and condemns it. Chapter 2 is utopian, an anticipation of a new age characterized by political union, disarmament, and a single language, the word of YHWH, emanating over the whole earth. The two voices are in dialogue with each other throughout the book and are projected syntagmatically in the relation between Proto- and Deutero-Isaiah. Between the new age and ours, there is no continuity. The problem of the book, the poetic problem, is how to pass from one to the other. The disjunction between what I have elsewhere called Prophet A and Prophet B[17] makes poetic unity and the unity of the implied personality behind it inaccessible, at least on this side of the disaster. Prophet A is the harbinger of Prophet B in our world; Prophet B signifies the end of time (אחרית הימים) in time. Poetic unity could only occur with the abolition of Prophet A; but because it is the union of Prophets A and B, this cannot be fulfilled without logical contradiction. The vision of the book, of a world at peace, is beyond the horizon of the

---

15. As already recognized by the rabbis, Isaiah begins where Moses left off in Deut 32:1 (*Midraš Tanḥuma*, ad loc.). The relationship between the two texts is frequently discussed in commentaries, e.g., Hans Wildberger, *Isaiah 1–12* (trans. Thomas Trapp; Minneapolis: Fortress, 1991) 13.

16. Some critics think that there is no implication of ultimacy in this phrase; e.g., Marvin Sweeney (*Isaiah 1–39* [FOTL 16; Grand Rapids, MI: Eerdmans, 1996] 99), who considers it simply to refer to the future. However, in the context of an end to conflict, and also given parallels in the Hebrew Bible such as Gen 49:1 and Num 24:14, it must have an eschatological dimension. An extensive discussion can be found in Wildberger, *Isaiah 1–12*, 92. Bernard Gosse ("Michée 4,1–5, Isaïe 2,1–5 et les rédacteurs finaux du livre d'Isaïe," *ZAW* 105 [1993] 100) notes that the phrase does not occur elsewhere in Isaiah or in Micah but is frequent in Jeremiah, in the context of the return of displaced peoples. He thinks that both the text in Isaiah and the parallel passsage in Micah (4:1–3) draw upon this correlation. As W. Werner (*Eschatologische Texte in Jesaja 1–39: Messias, Heiliger Rest, Völker* [Würzburg: Echter Verlag, 1982] 154–55) remarks, context determines whether a particular passage refers to an indeterminate future or an eschatological future.

17. See my "Torah and Anti-Torah: Isaiah 2:2–4 and 1:10–26," *Biblnt* 11 (2003) 319.

book. Or to put it differently, the vision of 1:1 is split, and the 'vision of everything' (חזות הכל) of 29:11 is only possible when the book is sealed, enigmatic, with its ultimate closure.

Correspondingly, 13:1 introduces a new section of the book, the oracles concerning the nations, in chaps. 13–23. Discourse about the nations—the paradigmatic other with regard to Israel—places Isaiah in their position, because he articulates their doom, their desires and passions, and their voices, in part through fictitious quotations (as shown to great effect by Hanna Liss in her recent book),[18] in part through alliterations, the sonorous nonsignifying aspects of language, and in part through the generic title משא. The word משא 'burden' suggests the weight of grief upon the poet/prophet,[19] that the prophecy is an imposition laid upon him, and confounds, perhaps ironically, our expectation—equally generic—of chauvinistic *Schadenfreude*. More important, as the oracles proceed, so the difference between Israel and the nations breaks down. Chapter 22 is a משא גיא חזיון 'valley of vision', an epithet for Jerusalem. In chap. 17, an oracle against Damascus slides seamlessly into an oracle against Israel—either the Northern Kingdom or the collective people. Chapter 19 concludes with a federation of Israel, Egypt, and Assyria. The switch to the other as a mirror of the self—a familiar prophetic rhetorical trick—results in an alienation of God and prophet. In 21:11, for instance, a mantic voice calls from Seir, reminiscent of archaic traditions,[20] from Israel's alter ego, Esau. In chap. 18, the people who are קו־קו,[21] beyond the rivers of Kush, are reminiscent of or articulate God's strange language, צו לצו קו לקו,[22] in

---

18. Hanna Liss, *Die Unerhörte Prophetie: Kommunikative Strukturen prophetische Rede im Buch Yeshaʿyahu* (Leipzig: Evangelische Verlag, 2003), and her English summary in "Undisclosed Speech: Patterns of Communication in the Book of Isaiah," *JHS* 4 (2002).

19. Most scholars still regard משא as a technical term for an oracle, with no metaphorical connotations. Exceptions are mostly from the literary-critical perspective. A recent stimulating example is Sherwood and Caputo, "Otobiographies," 214–15.

20. E.g., Deut 33:2, Judg 5:4, Hab 3:3.

21. The expression—and indeed the identity of the people—is very obscure. Suggestions include 'very tall', 'muscular', 'ship-going', or that it is an onomotopoeia for their language. See the extensive discussions in Hans Wildberger, *Isaiah 13–27* (trans. Thomas Trapp; Continental Commentary; Minneapolis: Fortress) 208; and Meir Lubetski and Claire Gottlieb, "Isaiah 18: The Egyptian Nexus," in *Boundaries of the Ancient World: A Tribute to Cyrus Gordon* (ed. Meir Lubetski, Claire Gottlieb, and Sharon Keller; JSOTSup 273; Sheffield: Sheffield Academic Press, 1996) 374.

22. There have been many attempts to interpret this strange idiom, including references to infantile babble, necromantic ventriloquism, the abecediary, and vomit. A recent detailed discussion appears in John Emerton, "Some Difficult Words in Isaiah 28.10

28:10 and 13, and ultimately pay homage to God—an alienation that is also identification.

What are the fundamental drives of the book? One is destructive: the author imagines a world pervaded by death and the death drive, impersonated, for instance, by the Assyrians as a surrogate for God—who, here at least, is the Shiva-like destroyer rather than the creator. In 1:4–7, the punishment of the sons exceeds all possible justification:

> Woe, sinful nation, people heavy with iniquity, seed of evildoers, corrupting sons. They have forsaken YHWH, they have spurned the Holy One of Israel, they have recoiled backwards. Why are you still struck, do you continue going astray? Every head is sick, every heart faint. From the sole of the foot to the head, there is no gap; wounds, stripes, fresh blows; they are not pressed out, they are not bound up, nor soothed with oil. Your land is desolate, your cities burnt with fire; your ground before you, strangers are consuming it, desolate like the overthrow of strangers.

Paternal violence against sons is a familiar trope of the wisdom tradition; patriarchy reproduces itself—sons in the image of the father—through chastisement. The suppurating body, beaten, burned, empty, and devoured, is open, exposed; the boundaries between inside and outside, self and other, are breached. Images of cannibalism, conflagration, and desolation render the land (coterminous with the maternal body) moribund—a site of death rather than life. The strangers who devastate the land are agents of God (who has turned himself into a stranger) against sons who do not acknowledge that they are sons. The מהפכה, the inversion of all normal values, including family values, results in what Julia Kristeva calls "abjection," whereby the maternal body becomes loathsome.[23] Disgust carries over to the description of the temple courts in the following scene, and of Jerusalem as prostitute in 1:21. Abjection suggests humiliation as the obverse of idealization; it is because it is desirable that the body is abjected—literally, cast out— as in images of exile. The libidinal economy, as in the wisdom tradition

---

and 13," in *Biblical Hebrew, Biblical Texts: Essays in Honour of Michael P. Weitzman* (ed. Ada Albert-Rapoport and Gillian Greenberg; JSOTSup 333; Sheffield: Sheffield Academic Press, 2001) 39–56.

23. Kristeva delineates her theory of abjection in *Powers of Horror: An Essay on Abjection* (trans. Leon S. Roudiez; New York: Columbia University Press, 1983). An interesting application of Kristeva's theory of abjection to the prophetic experience is Timothy Beal, "The System and the Speaking Subject in the Hebrew Bible: Reading for Divine Abjection," *BibInt* 2 (1994) 171–89. See also Fiona Black's monograph, *Artifice of Love: The Grotesque Bodies and the Song of Songs* (LHB/OTS 392; London: T. & T. Clark, 2009).

generally, links sexual constraint to sado-masochism. Why is the child beaten? We do not know, but we may suspect a certain gratification, on either side.

This is clearer in the following chapter, in the protracted dystopia, the account of the Day of the Lord in 2:6–22, juxtaposed to the utopian vision of 2:2–4. There God rises up "to terrify the earth" (2:19, 21). Again, we do not quite know why he does this, or what is the basis for his wrath against human achievement, but the repetition of the refrain, the recurrent stress on the "splendor of his pride" (2:10, 19, 21, and so forth), suggests an emotive and esthetic element that may be related to the theory of the sublime.

Derrida argues, in common with Kristeva and Blanchot, that an "archiviolithic" element accompanies all writing, because it displaces lived reality and preceding wholes.[24] Writing is a counterdepressant that preserves the past and is a record of the attempt of past writers to think through the complexities of their existence; it risks failure and despair, especially in the case of literature of catastrophe, such as prophetic literature.[25] Catastrophe presents the imminence of the death not only of a culture but of the entire web of significance on which that culture is based, especially when, as in the case of Israel, it is held to convey universal truth or Torah. In the literature of catastrophe, all words become meaningless, are reduced to the single signifier, death.[26] Isaiah, like prophetic literature generally, is haunted by the horizon of utter absurdity.

On the other side of the violence, there is the desire for a new relationship with Israel and the world, founded on "justice and righteousness." An ideal society, governed by proper affective ties and

---

24. The neologism *archiviolithic* comes from Jacques Derrida, *Archive Fever* (trans. Eric Prenowitz; Chicago: University of Chicago Press, 1995) 10. Julia Kristeva (*Revolution in Poetic Language* [trans. Margaret Waller; New York: Columbia University Press, 1984]) argues for the ambiguity of language, especially poetic language, that both is a defensive formation against violence and is infused with it. See also Maurice Blanchot (*The Writing of the Disaster* [trans. Ann Smock; Lincoln: University of Nebraska Press, 1982]), for whom writing must necessarily be fragmentary, because it speaks for that which cannot be comprehended within an overall unity.

25. Throughout her work, Julia Kristeva conceives of writing as a counterdepressant, as an attempt to seek a language for our profoundest maladies. See in particular the essays in *Black Sun: Depression and Melancholia* (trans. Leon S. Roudiez; New York: Columbia University Press, 1989).

26. Edith Wyschogrod, *Spirit in Ashes: Hegel, Heidegger, and Man-Made Mass Death* (New Haven: Yale University Press, 1985) 31: "At the same time, the signified is also and always death. The signifier collapses into the signified."

responsibilities is the basis for the divine-human relation. Ethics is first philosophy, for Isaiah as well as for Lévinas.[27] Ethics is, however, transposed immediately into the sexual and familial passions of the book, into the ecstatic correlate of abjection. For example, the nuptial celebration of the union of God and the daughters of Zion in 4:5 follows their purification with the רוח משפט 'the spirit of justice' in 4:4. Similarly, justice and righteousness are the erotic substance at stake in the love song of 5:1–7.

There are two interconnected problems here. The first is how the ethical demand can be reconciled with divine violence, manifest for instance in the misogyny of 3:16–26. The second is that there is a tension between ethics as the object of desire and pleasure for its own sake. Ethics, as expressed in justice, means renunciation, an acceptance of boundaries and limits. Pleasure, which may take the form of pleasure in poetry even at its most nihilistic, as well as in the beauty of the world and of human beings, potentially conflicts with ethical responsibility, just as violence, the discharge of hatred and horror, exceeds its occasion.

I want to go somewhere else, however: how the poet/prophet invents himself in the text. What happens when the "I" intervenes, fugitively, autobiographically? What happens, for instance, when the prophet says, "I have heard this," as in 22:10 and 28:22? For a moment, the prophet is focalized as the subject of hearing a message that may incorporate the end of the world, the decimation of the people, or the fall of empires. We listen to his hearing, as someone separate from a message that comes to him, as it were, from a great distance. In 28:22, "for destruction and doom I have heard from YHWH of hosts over all the earth," he may or may not be included in the forthcoming disaster. But he is a witness, whose self-approbation is directed at people who are urged "not to scoff" (28:22), as a way of averting or mitigating their fate. His voice may thus articulate a resistance to the inevitability of the decree, a countervoice within the voice or to the voice of God. This voice may indicate that a resistance within God, insofar as the prophetic voice is

---

27. According to Emmanuel Lévinas, God is only to be found in the ethical relation. Philosophy has primarily been concerned with ontology, which results in the discourse of totality. However, before we are, we are already responsible to an other. The ethical relation then precedes being. For this reason, ethics is first philosophy. The formulation is repeated with many variations throughout Levinas's work and is the basis for the title of his essay, "Ethics as First Philosophy," in *The Levinas Reader* (ed. Seán Hand; Oxford: Blackwell, 1989) 75–87.

constructed by him, is part of the vision. The prophet hears "destruction and doom." What is it to hear "destruction and doom"? Insofar as כלה means annihilation, it is to hear nothing. To hear the end is to hear silence, as in the burden of silence in 21:11, itself intricately connected to a self-authentication message in 21:10.

Similarly, in באזני ה' צבאות 'in my ears, YHWH of Hosts' in 5:9, the evocation of the ears is a metonymy for his entire aural experience. Again, what is heard is absence, "if many houses shall not be desolate, great and goodly, without inhabitant" (5:9), framing the list of woe-oracles in 5:8–24, and anticipating, verbatim, the prediction of depopulation in 6:11. Absence speaks, and what is spoken is absence.

Inevitably, the book of Isaiah turns round chap. 6, the so-called call vision. Biblical scholarship muddles itself interminably on whether it really is a call vision, but at the very least I would say—and Hanna Liss would agree with me—that it is an initiation scene, one in which Isaiah learns and teaches us what it is to be a prophet and is inducted into his role.[28] Both Hanna Liss and I have written extensively on this chapter, on the communication and noncommunication processes between prophet and God, on rhetorical techniques whereby both characters are constructed and deconstructed.[29] It is a *mise-en-abyme* of the book, as several critics have argued, a metapoetic key that teaches us how to read and listen.[30] But it is equally a metapoetic vortex that makes read-

---

28. The issue is whether the chapter conforms to the genre of the prophetic call scene (like Jeremiah 1 or Ezekiel 1) or is a commissioning scene. Related to this is the question whether it is Isaiah's initial prophetic encounter or whether chaps. 1–5 precede it chronologically or rhetorically as well as in the current sequence of the book. For a full discussion, see Liss, *Die Unerhörte Prophetie*, 55–60; and Jörg Barthel, *Prophetenwort und Geschichte: Die Jesajaüberlieferung in Jes 6–8 und 28–31* (FAT 19; Tübingen: Mohr Siebeck, 1997) 82–88.

29. Francis Landy, "Strategies of Concentration and Diffusion in Isaiah 6," *BibInt* 6 (1999) 58–86; reprinted in idem, *Beauty and the Enigma* (JSOTSup 312; Sheffield: Sheffield Academic Press, 2001) 298–327. All references are to the latter edition. Whereas Liss concentrates on structures of communication, I focus on the rhetoric of the chapter, but our conclusions are, in fact, very similar.

30. The phrase "mise-en-abîme" is taken from Miscall, *Isaiah*, 34. The concept *mise-en-abîme* (spelled also *mise-en-abyme*) was introduced into biblical studies by Mieke Bal, in an essay on Ruth, in her book *Lethal Love: Feminist Literary Readings of Biblical Love Stories* (Bloomington: Indiana University Press, 1987) 68–88. A *mise-en-abyme* is "a microstructure that contains a summary of the overall fabula in which it functions" (p. 75), like Chinese boxes. The perception that Isaiah 6 has a similar function in the book of Isaiah is pervasive. Hugh Williamson (*The Book Called Isaiah*, 30–56), for instance, regards Isaiah 6 as structurally central to the entire book. Jean-Pierre Sonnet ("Le motif de l'endurcissement [Is 6,9–10] et la lecture d' 'Isaïe,'" *Bib* 73 [1992] 208–39) has pointed to the transfor-

ing and listening impossible. It raises preeminently our questions of fictionality and identity. Did Isaiah really see this vision and hear these
words? Many scholars have worked to extricate themselves from the
immediacy of the vision, in order to avoid the implication of an evil or
perverse God. Von Rad and Brevard Childs, for instance, show how the
vision fits into preexisting theological paradigms and hence can be
comfortably nestled in "salvation history";[31] others, mostly in the tradition of German scholarship, see it as a retrospective justification of the
prophet's failure, as I have already noted.[32] Both may be true, but both
equally displace and avoid the question: why did God act so strangely?
Why set up the prophets, or anybody, to fail, as indeed happens to almost every figure in the Hebrew Bible, paradigmatically Moses? Why
the exile, and history as exile?

One can easily accept the facticity of visions—mystics always have
visions—but also that visions are imaginative experiences (were Isaiah's
lips really scorched?) and are translated into dense, poetic language. Indeed, what is experienced is in part the birth of poetry, as language that
strives (as in a koan or haiku) to make a human, local habitation for that
which is transcendent and ineffable.

So we see Isaiah seeing Yhwh, the hem of his robes filling the
temple, seeing and hearing the seraphim singing (their blind experience at one remove, as it were), the temple quaking, Isaiah's fear, his
purification and his volunteering his services: "Here I am, send me!"—
very untypical of prophets. Hanna Liss has pointed to the noncommunication between God and prophet in this part of the chapter—God is
at a great distance—as well as Isaiah's identification with the people, as
being of "unclean lips," which renders the sight of God traumatic.[33] But
I must add that it is also conventional. The sovereign God sits on his
throne, surrounded by attendants, whose praise, rich as it is, is theo-
logically unexceptional. The seraphim have a long history, for instance

---

mation of the motif as a key to reading an esoteric and occluded text in the last stages of
redaction (pp. 234–37). See also my "Strategies," 322; and Liss (*Die Unerhöhrte Prophetie*,
19), for whom the necessary failure of the people provides a reserve for future exegesis
and thought.

31. Gerhard von Rad, *Old Testament Theology* (trans. John Bowden; London: SCM,
1975) 152–55; Brevard S. Childs, *Isaiah: A Commentary* (OTL; Louisville: Westminster/John
Knox) 56–57.

32. There are also different versions of the *Rücksprojizierungsthese*. For example,
Barthel (*Prophetenwort und Geschichte*, 114) argues that revelation is always accompanied
by interpretation.

33. Liss, *Die Unerhöhrte Prophetie*, 42–52.

as uraei.[34] The prophet also is constructed, as passing through fear to acceptance of his mission. We know what to expect: more of what he has been saying for the last five chapters.

I should add that the chapter, as an initiation, has much in common, cross-culturally, with initiations of ritual, mystical, and shamanistic specialists: adoption by a spiritual or otherworldly master, who takes over the paternal role, the passage through death to a new reality, the acquisition of a new and often bizarre language.[35] As many have pointed out, Isaiah thus becomes a survivor, a representative of the new age; he cannot communicate, because he lives in a different world.[36]

What follows, however, is bewildering. Again, as readers, we must imagine Isaiah as hearing it for the first time:

> And he said: Go, say to this people: hear attentively, but do not understand; look intently, but do not perceive. Fatten the heart of this people, weigh down its ears, delude its eyes, lest it see with its eyes, and hear with its ears, and its heart understand, and it return, and be healed. (Isa 6:9–10)

The commission is paradoxical: Isaiah is to speak but only in double talk, because every word is designed not to communicate; the people are to hear and see but not to understand or perceive (literally, "know"). The more they understand, the less they understand; faithful obedience would consist of nonhearing. We are into the cloud of unknowing, indeed, and may never escape its foggy embrace. Moreover, v. 9 grants the people autonomy, because they have the responsibility to listen intensely; v. 10 takes this autonomy away, because the prophet is charged with ensuring that they cannot hear and works to obstruct their senses. Most disturbing of all, from any normative theological point of view, is the conclusion: "lest they return and be healed."[37]

---

34. The literature on the seraphim is quite substantial. Many scholars regard the seraphim as being modeled on the protective cobra, or uraeus, depicted on Egyptian regalia. Examples have been found on seals from 8th-century Judah. Representative discussions are M. Görg, "Die Funktion der Serafen bei Jesaja," *BN* 5 (1978) 28–39; and Philippe Provençal, "Regarding the Noun 'sarap' in the Hebrew Bible," *JSOT* 29 (2005) 371–79.

35. Cross-cultural comparison of prophetic initiation with that of other ritual experts has been somewhat neglected in the last decades. This is unfortunate in view of the veritable explosion in studies of shamanism. See, for example, the long review essay by Robert Adlam and Lorne Holyoak, "Shamanism in the Postmodern World: A Review Essay," *Studies in Religion* 34 (2005) 517–68. Little has been published since Thomas W. Overholt's fascinating *Channels of Prophecy: The Social Dynamics of Prophetic Activity* (Minneapolis: Fortress, 1989)

36. This is the thrust of Liss's argument. See also Conrad, *Reading Isaiah*, 111–13.

37. From early times, translators and interpreters have sought to avoid the implications of the conclusion by reading it as a positive prediction: they will return and be

Why not? If healing is against God's will, at the base of the entire prophetic experience is a malevolent deity.

Isaiah responds, "Until when, my Lord?"—a conventional but also, as it turns out, problematic reaction that invites the prospect of utter desolation. The response, "until the cities are laid waste, without inhabitant," is mitigated in the last verse, in which a tenth returns or survives, only to be subject to further devastation, but in which, however, "the holy seed" is planted.

I do not think there is any escape from the difficulty of this chapter, nor should there be. But I shall point out three things:

1. The seraphim sing that God's glory fills the whole earth; at the end of the chapter, this earth is a wasteland. Are the two visions the same? The plenitude of glory is manifested, then, in annihilation.
2. Any attempt by the prophet to communicate is contrary to the divine will. Equally, any attempt by God to communicate through the prophet is contrary to his own will. We then have a possibility that God is talking to God through the prophet, or a conflict between his יצר הטוב and יצר הרע, his 'good and evil inclinations'.
3. We learn to be readers and critics when we realize that we can never fully understand. Isaiah models for us what it is to be readers and critics.

However, I will go a step farther. Each of the key words in 6:10 is totally ambiguous, combining opposite meanings or connotations. The word השע 'delude' (or 'smear over') may mean 'to gaze'; the 'heaviness' (הכבד) of the ears reflects the divine 'glory' (כבוד) of v. 3; the 'fatness' (השמן) may refer to the 'oil' of blessing and anointing. It is easy to construct irony here. But it also suggests something akin to Paul de Man's 'Blindness and Insight," as proposed by Robert Carroll in his marvellous essay on "blindsight" in Isaiah.[38] The more one hears, the less one hears; conversely, only in silence can one begin listening.

But the conclusion is irrefragable, irrespective of its apparent and ambiguous reversal[39] three verses later: "lest it return, and be healed." There is here a sense, I think, that healing is not healing; that repentance, Israel living on its land, leading normal, happy, ethical lives, is too easy. Or too unreal.

---

healed. See Craig A. Evans, *To See and Not Perceive: Isaiah 6.9–10 in Early Jewish and Christian Interpretation* (JSOTSup 64; Sheffield: JSOT Press, 1989). A recent instance of this interpretation is Shizuka Uemura, "Isaiah 6.9–10: A Hardening Prophecy?" *Annals of the Japanese Biblical Institute* 27 (2001) 23–57. Even if Uemura's somewhat intricate argument is accepted, however, it contradicts the rest of the commission.

38. Carroll, "Blindsight and the Vision Thing," 92–93.

39. In 6:13 ושבה והיתה לבער could mean 'and it [the tenth] shall *return* and be for a burning/grazing' or 'it shall *repent*' or 'it shall *once again* be for a burning/grazing'. For the multiple ambiguities of this part of the verse, see my "Strategies," 318–19.

From wherever we are, death and exile gape before us.

A further observation: the chapter concludes זרע קדש מצבתה 'the holy seed is its stump'. The treble holiness that signifies divine transcendence in 6:3 is here immanent in the survivors, the returnees from exile, and in the prophet.[40] Isaiah projects himself into the future, for instance in the persona of the Davidic king, who judges "not according to the hearing of the ears" in 11:3; and in the first-person voice singing at the end of time in 12:1. Beyond the horizon of the *Verstockungsauftrag*, the opacity of poetic language, there is the clear unanimity of the end. We do not know what this clear language is (the שפה ברורה of Zeph 3:9). One is reminded of the Jewish mystic, Abraham Abulafia, who was obsessed by the idea of transparent language but for whom also pure language was no language at all but merely a play of phonemes.[41]

Some people say that Isa 40:1–11 is a self-conscious reversal of chap. 6.[42] I am not sure that this is entirely valid, though it has an element of truth (as with everything in Isaiah). To begin with, Deutero-Isaiah has its own share of mysteries, not least the mystery of the servant, and ends inconclusively, on this side of the disaster (at least if you include Trito). But more important, it begins with voices, summoning to speech: קרא אמר קול (40:6) 'A voice says "Cry"' and the response, "What shall I cry?" The response is full of the plangency of human mortality: "All flesh is grass. . . ." Again, this is fully embedded in the discourse, the transformation of the 'flesh' (בשר) into 'proclamation' (מבשרת) in 40:9, for instance.[43] There is an immediate counter,

---

40. Jonathan Magonet, "The Structure of Isaiah 6" (*Proceedings of the Ninth World Congress of Jewish Studies*, division A: *Period of the Bible* [Jerusalem: World Union of Jewish Studies, 1985] 91–97 [esp. pp. 93–94]), points out the relationship between the triple קדוש 'holy' of 6:3 and the 'holy [קדש] seed' of 6:13.

41. For Abulafia's views on language and hermeneutics, see Moshe Idel, *Language, Torah and Hermeneutics in Abraham Abulafia* (Albany: State University of New York Press, 1989).

42. The relationship between Isaiah 6 and 40 has become something of a commonplace in contemporary Isaianic scholarship. A comprehensive discussion and list of correspondences may be found in Burkhard M. Zapff, "Jes 40 und die Frage nach dem Beginn des deuterojesajanischen Corpus," in *Gottes Wege Suchen* (ed. Franz Sedlmeier; Würzburg: Echter Verlag, 2003) 355–73, and references therein. See also Williamson, *The Book Called Isaiah*, 37–38; and Barthel, *Prophetie und Geschichte*, 114. Further references may be found in my article, "The Ghostly Prelude to Deutero-Isaiah," *BibInt* 14 (2006) 332–63.

43. The wordplay is noted by Joseph Blenkinsopp, *Isaiah 40–55: A New Translation with Introduction and Commentary* (AB 19A; New York: Doubleday, 2000) 185; and Jan L. Koole, *Isaiah III*, vol. 1: *Isaiah 40–48* (Kampen: Kok Pharos, 1997) 70.

that there is an eternal language: "The word of our God lasts for ever" (40:8). But, one wonders, which word?[44]

Deutero-Isaiah, no matter how much it claims to be new, cannot escape from the past. In its memory, there is a dead mother, Jerusalem, with her dead children. The children imagine the mother experiencing their resuscitation, a proliferation; just as in 40:11, the ascent to Jerusalem coincides paronomastically with the nursing of the flock.[45] Lament, desire, and language, returning to the site of birth as if for the first time, but only as a ghost.

There are of course real children in the book: Isaiah's children, themselves signs of a new age. The children mean, especially through their names, but they bear with them the traces of lives. Shear-Yashuv strolls with his father on the road to the fullers' field, to meet King Ahaz (7:3).[46] Maher-shallal-hash-baz will say, "Daddy, Mummy," and perhaps learn how to pronounce his own name (8:4). The Immanuel child will enter the dangerous world of knowledge (7:16).

There is also the autobiographical narrative of the sexual conjunction of prophet and prophetess in 8:3. The prophetess embodies the divine word, as does the prophet. It suggests perhaps a confluence of two different kinds of prophecy or divine speech: God speaking through or as a woman. Sex parallels the writing of the child's name in 8:1 and is a possibly more intimate kind of prophecy. But this is to leave out the most intriguing aspects. Who are these people, what did they experience, what residue was there apart from the divine imperative? Or is the erotic imperative a sign of the prophetic imperative?[47]

Isa 5:1 introduces the poet, for the first time, as singer of a love song that is a parabolic microcosm of the relation of God and Israel as well as of the book. The prophet is ostensibly singing his beloved's song to his vineyard. As the parable progresses, the lovers are decoded as God and Israel, respectively. But what is the position of the prophet? As the one who sings the lover's song, he (or she) is speaking in a male voice

---

44. See John Goldingay's very stimulating article, "Isaiah 40–55 in the 1990s, among Other Things Deconstructing, Mystifying, Intertextual, Socio-Critical, Hearer-Involving" (*BibInt* 5 [1997] 225–46), for the problematics of "the word" here.

45. In 40:11 there is a wordplay between עֲלוֹת 'nursing' and עֹלוֹת 'ascending'. See my "Ghostly Prelude," 351 n. 58.

46. For the ambiguity of the name *Shear Yashuv*, see Liss, *Die Unerhörte Prophetie*, 72–82.

47. A more detailed discussion is to be found in my article "Prophetic Intercourse," in *Sense and Sensitivity: Essays on Reading the Bible in Memory of Robert Carroll* (ed. Alistair G. Hunter and Philip R. Davies; JSOTSup 348; Sheffield: Sheffield Academic Press, 2002) 262–70.

about the vineyard's failure to meet his expectations and his resulting retribution. But as a lover, for whom God is the דוד, the 'beloved', he is speaking of his own love. If God is the male lover, the prophet is coded as female. The vineyard is, however, a conventional symbol for the woman, for instance in the Song of Songs, of which 5:1 is a direct echo. The prophet may then be singing of God's love for himself/herself and his/her failure to meet his expectations. He identifies with Israel and shares in its fate. Or on the contrary, he is a third party, singing of his lover's affair with his vineyard, with the other woman. He/she sings for both and neither.[48] So Isaiah is everywhere and nowhere.

Two conclusions: Heidegger famously thinks of the thought of being. Isaiah is preeminently a process of thinking, thinking what it is to be human, which is passed through us.

Second, a suicidal Jewish poet, much influenced by Heidegger, Paul Celan, argues with God, for God, who did all this, who thought all this. God who is *das Nichts*, the *Niemandsrose*, in the wake of Kabbalah. The Nothing. The blank slate, the גליון גדול (8:1), on which everything writes.

---

48. See also my article, "The Parable in the Vineyard (Isaiah 5:1–7), or What Is a Love Song Doing among the Prophets?" *Studies in Religion* 34 (2005) 147–64.

Job 28 and the Climax in Chapters 29–31: Crisis and Identity

JAN FOKKELMAN
Leiden University

> [I]t is indeed our most authentic identity,
> the one that makes us who we are,
> that demands to be recognized.
> —Paul Ricoeur

In the globally used Stuttgart edition, the Hebrew Bible contains 1,574 pages. More than 35 percent of the texts is formal poetry, though it is not sufficiently visible in the typography of the current translations.[1] The book of Job takes up a unique position in the many collections of poetry. The poems in chaps. 3:1–42:6 are more than a collection; they are a consistent and well-sustained composition, and they throw light on a serious theme from several points of view.[2] Some passages

---

1. In the 4th ed. of *BHS* (1967–77), the five generally recognized poetic books of Psalms, Job, Proverbs, Song of Songs, and Lamentations (Job minus chaps. 1–2, 32:1–5, and 42:7–17, because these three passages are narrative prose) cover 253 pages of poetry. A rough estimate for the three Major Prophets comes to over 160 pages of poetry, for the 12 Minor Prophets 88 pages; in the narrative portion of Genesis up to and including Kings, there are about 18 pages of poetry.

2. The unity of the book can now be proved via a new dimension: hard figures. In my tetralogy *Major Poems of the Hebrew Bible* (Assen: Van Gorcum, 1998–2004), especially in vol. 4, many forms of numerical perfection become visible in the book of Job, as a result of the counting of the original (i.e., pre-Masoretic) syllables. A number of examples of this prosodic precision will follow; see below.

Poetry in the Hebrew Bible consists mainly of collections of separate poems: for example, Isaiah and the Psalter. Yet, one should also recognize the fact that some poetry is a unified work of art, such as Lamentations, the Song of Songs, and Second Isaiah (Isaiah 40–55). However, these texts are considerably less extensive than Job 3:1–42:6. Collections such as the Psalms of Asaph or the Songs of Ascent are not tight compositions, though recently more attention has been paid to the connection between the poems in these groups; these poems retain their individuality.

Regarding the articulation of Canticles in seven units and their concentric design, which is determined by the dominance of the voice (the boy in units 3 and 5, the girl in

are of a lyrical nature (for example, hymnic), but in general this poetry
is didactic. Chapters 4–27 are a debate: the tone is often excited, and
the text is mostly argumentative. Later, in the discourses of Elihu and
God, the genre is given a bit more space.

All the poems are speeches. They are set within a narrow but definitive framework of narrative prose. This envelope is governed by a
plot, which is to be expected in a narrative text; and this also means
that the prose follows a course that begins with the formulation of a
problem in chap. 1 and ends with a solution in chap. 42. In this way we
are also presented with a quest. The inclusio challenges us readers to
examine to what extent the body of the book—the long series of
speeches in poetry—contributes to the plot. And what this poetry
achieves is that it does indeed bring up the content of the quest for discussion in all sorts of ways. What then is the object of value to which
the quest must lead us?

Chapters 1–2 report on a heavenly council that is focusing on the
integrity of the mortal Job. God is in discussion with his public prosecutor. The quest arises from a question, and so does the plot. It arises
at precisely the moment when "the *śatan*" formulates the problem, in
the words: "Does Job fear God for nothing?" (1:9). The venom of this
question is in the quasi-innocent adverb *ḥinnām* ('for nought') which
in the Hebrew clause has conspicuously been fronted.

The reader is not unprepared for this. He has been informed by two
authorities—the narrator and the character God—so he knows what
the answer to the question of Job's faith must be: an affirmation. The
prosecutor's insinuating question, however, has opened a window on
another possibility, negation: perhaps his faith is not pure? A dimension of threat arises by means of this challenge. God himself has provoked the angel by praising Job excessively (1:8), and he does not
withdraw from his challenge. The contact between God and accuser
becomes a wager; Job becomes a target, and he is actually saddled with
the burden of proof. The celestials and the reader are in analogous positions: they have to wait and see how the test will end. Will Job remain
faithful to God, or will he abandon God under the pressure of unbear-
able and undeserved misery, because his faith secretly presupposed
reward for good behavior? Job becomes the guinea pig of an ugly *Spiel*;
he is robbed of his property, his children, and his health.

1–2, in the center = unit 4, and in 6–7), see my description in *De Bijbel Literair* (ed. Jan
Fokkelman and Wim Weren; Zoetermeer, 2003). The seven units are 1:2–2:7, 2:8–3:5, 3:6–
5:1, 5:2–6:3, 6:4–7:6, 7:7–8:4, 8:5–14.

The first paragraph of the book creates a paradoxical connection between the introductory prose (chaps. 1–2) and the body of the book (the 40 poems). The concepts plot and quest assume a crew; who is the hero who must cover the course in quest of the object of value? The answer seems to be so simple; the first sequence of the story (in the text it is the first paragraph, 1:1–5) pushes the man Job and his unimpeachable attitude to the fore. But this expectation is falsified by everything that follows in chaps. 1–2. Our attention shifts to the heavenly council. The problem with which the book opens is not Job's, but it is the problem of the parties there, and it is their discussion from which the plot arises. Their plot, moreover, largely resembles a conspiracy now that we are so well informed about Job's excellence. We observe that the problem and the test are formulated by the angel and that this prosecutor and his master are responsible for the instigating of the action, the quest, and the plot. Job is not the hero of the plot and the quest but their butt, their victim, and their guinea pig: a radical change of position.

Job himself is, in the first place (1:8–12), "only" someone under discussion; next (vv. 14–19) he is someone spoken to, the addressee of four[3] pieces of bad news; and finally, he as the victim is only allowed to react by speech. Comparable experiences occurred in chap. 2, where even his body and his health were affected. In both parts of the story, the climax of being addressed consists in his wife's urging him to curse God. That is the first and verbal form of his being put to the test; the remainder of the book—a treat in verbal skills because of the quality of the discourse (intense poetry) and the gravity of the matter discussed—is the second and definitive form of the test. Here 3 + 1 friends[4] function as executors of the test—after the prosecutor and Job's wife.

In the two prose chapters, Job does not get around to acting in the strict sense, for he is the target of the blows that are dealt him by the prosecutor. But it is striking that the narrator does not report the disasters to us; instead, he informs Job by means of other people—eyewitnesses, now a servant of his, now an anonymous person. From the beginning, the disasters have the status of a message in the text; they are verbal entities. And this linguistic mode of being is now given a counterpart by the author: he lets Job speak, and moreover, he introduces Job's wife as a speaker twice. The only room for action that is

---

3. The pattern of (the report of) the disasters is climactic, and it complies with the literary pattern of 3 + 1: first three sorts of cattle are stolen, and then Job is deprived of his children by death.

4. The three friends of the debate proper in chaps. 4–27, and then in chaps. 32–37 the (unsuccessful) mediator, Elihu.

given Job is (as said above) that of speech, and it seems to be small. But his verbal activity is soon given a great opportunity. The book immediately switches to quite a different mode of language and text—that is, poetry. The first long poetic discourse is given to Job. It comprises the bitter complaint and the heavy curses that put chap. 3 in a class by itself. His debate with three friends follows in chaps. 4–27. This section is concluded by a long poem, spoken by Job, which again assumes a position of its own (chap. 28) and forms a transition to the finale of the debate proper, chaps. 29–31. These are three poems and are again spoken by Job, and they are a powerful climax.[5]

In other words, the only thing Job can do in chaps. 1–2 is speak, and the opportunities to speak are increased a great deal in the body of the book. What the true meaning of this choice for poetry is and how formidable the importance of Job's verbal contribution is become very clear when we begin measuring. It is no accident that the poetry in this book consists of 40 poems.[6] The longest poem contains 40 verses, and it falls to Job himself: it is chap. 31. All the poems together consist of 412 strophes, and half of them are given to the man who has yet to become the hero of the book: 206 of these units. Job speaks 103 S-strophes and 103 L-strophes.[7] Thus Job's one voice has been given as many strophic units by the author as the other five characters who speak in Job 3:1–42:6. This is a salute by the writer to his hero's verbal power.

The first person that describes Job in the text is the narrator himself. He uses no less than four terms, which work together in pairs. The first pair is entirely positive; it consists of two synonymous adjectives: Job is 'blameless and upright' (*tām wĕyāšār*, 1+1 words). The second pair is 'fearing God and turning away from evil', so it is longer, 2+2 words. These terms allow some negativity to come to the surface,[8] and they further elaborate on Job's qualities by referring to behavior and introducing dimensions of religion and morality. All these characteristics of

---

5. After this, there are another six literary units that are spoken by a fourth friend, Elihu, but that do not provoke any reaction (chaps. 32–37), and finally four long poems with God as a speaker: his "answer from the storm," plus two short reactions by Job.

6. See vol. 4 of my *Major Poems* (2004) chap. 12, particularly p. 335.

7. All this is documented in ibid. The S for *short* and the L for *long* indicate units of two and three full poetic lines, respectively; see the concise but complete theory of biblical poetry presented in my *Reading Biblical Poetry: An Introductory Guide* (Louisville, KY, 2001). Chapter 5 discusses the strophe and its characteristics.

8. This negativity becomes apparent when we place fear/awe (a term that denotes some ambiguity in emotional respects) of God in opposition to the idea of the love of God, which we know from Deuteronomy 6, the *Shemaʿ*. The last pair of words plainly points to evil; Job rejects it, but the author recognizes it as a relevant factor by indicating it.

Job are repeated by the character God in their entirety and literally, and so we are told of 4 + 4 = 8 praiseworthy attributes in the first paragraph. This is no accident; I will say more below about the important convention of using the number 8. The pair "fearing God and turning away from evil" will return much later in the text in a special way, as words by God that are quoted by the hero himself. It is the crucial concluding line of the uncommonly important poem in chap. 28. One authority takes the other's side again, now in reverse order. What is the importance or consequence of this duplication, at such a crucial moment of transition?

When Job (end of chap. 2) sits down in the dust and dirt, three friends come to comfort him. "When they saw him from afar, they did not recognize him." Their first contribution, silence for seven days, is excellent; however, when the debate gets under way, they turn out to be fundamentally incapable of recognition. The friends look at Job through blurred glasses. Their reasoning betrays a vision of God and of man that can be characterized in four progressive statements: (1) this disaster was caused by God; (2) it means punishment; (3) there must be a reason for it: guilt or sin on your part; (4) only confess, then God may forgive you. This approach enrages Job. He keeps protesting, and he demands a fair trial from and with God. His total dedication and the assertiveness with which he stands up for himself are amazing.

The main issue of the book now seems to be clear. Is it not the classic, simplistic message of wisdom? It is the doctrine of commensurate retribution: doing good has its reward; the evildoer will certainly be punished—in other words, the doctrine that is part of theodicy. This is an easy symmetry, and the reader knows, just as Job does, that this view is often refuted by reality. The authors of the books of Job and Ecclesiastes observe the prosperity of the evildoer and the suffering of good people, and their heroes openly complain about it.

That the three friends exert pressure on Job and judge him with their pedantic attitude means lack of openness and empathy. Job defends himself passionately, and only on the first point does he agree with his friends: this misfortune was sent to him by God. But their interpretation (punishment > guilt > your sin) has become impossible for him, and he feels obliged to formulate new answers to questions such as: What drives God? Is God responsible for disasters on earth?

Behind the doctrine of retribution, there lurks the so-called economic model, which is: we adore you, O God, who gives us the good life. If, however, we add some venom and cynicism, it is: we adore you *as long as* you guarantee us fortune. Now the underlying truth has come to the surface. This way of relating to God is a vulgar tit-for-tat scheme. The contact between God and the alleged faithful appears to be open to manipulation: God has to deliver the goods, and then we are willing to recognize him. Such a mentality is abhorrent to Job, who instinctively turns away from it.

In the meantime, Job is completely ignorant of the heavenly wager. *We* are in the know, however, and therefore we are able to read the unfolding drama from a double perspective. We sympathize with the victim, we understand his ordeal, but at the same time we have superior knowledge and see the larger picture.[9] After chaps. 26–27, the debate gets stuck. The author will grant Job a grand finale. But first the hero makes a reflective speech, in which he measures wisdom. It is the exceptional text of chap. 28.

This poem about wisdom is remarkably independent, and its verses do not mention any addressee. Biblical scholars have speculated that this text should be an interpolation and often called it a hymn *to* wisdom. This is a hopelessly wrong label, because there is not a word of praise and not a verse or strophe of a laudatory nature to be found in the entire chapter. Moreover, most scholars have underestimated the poem's function in the completion of the debate proper and its relation to the climactic chaps. 29–31. They have neglected its contribution to the plot and overlooked the tyrannic force of the negation.

The correct division of the text is of the utmost importance. We are helped by a form of repetition that turns a double interrogative sentence (one bicolon) into a stanza-initial refrain. I am referring to v. 12, which returns in v. 20 and is practically identical there; it asks where wisdom can be found. In this way, the poem is divided into three sections; they contain 5 + 3 + 3 strophes with 11 + 8 + 9 verses,[10] respectively.

---

9. Compare the positions of Abraham and the reader in the beginning of Genesis 22. The patriarch is given an impossible and immoral order, and he does not know what the reader knows, thanks to the first sentence: that it is "only" a test. The difference in level of knowledge here, too, creates a double perspective.

10. The analysis justifying this is found in my *Major Poems*, 4:146–62. Stanza I has the exceptional length of five strophes. The arrangement of these strophes, however, guarantees that they remain one stanza: they follow the pattern AB X B'A'. The same model governs the only stanza of five strophes to be found in the whole Psalter; it is the theophany in the beginning of Psalm 18; see *Major Poems*, vol. 3, chap. 2, and also the analysis of the parallel text, 2 Samuel 22 in my *Narrative Art and Poetry in the Books of Samuel: A Full Interpretation Based on Stylistic and Structural Analyses* (4 vols.; Assen: Van Gorcum, 1981–93), vol. 3, chap. 8, §1.

A recent volume in Supplements to Vetus Testamentum offers a good rendering of Job 28. The author does justice to the connection of this chapter with its context, the position it takes in relation to the plot, and the unity of the book. Alison Lo, *Job 28 as Rhetoric: An Analysis of Job 28 in the Context of Job 22–31* (VTSup 97; Leiden, 2003) 197–204.

The tripart division of Job 28 is accompanied by three essentially different levels of observation and knowledge, three characters, and three situations. The ternary principle governs.[11] Stanza I is about mining. The ambitious and tireless *homo faber* leaves animals famous for their sharp sight far behind in exploratory power, knowledge, and technology. Stanza II takes us to the marketplace, where disillusionment lies in wait: even with a bag full of gold, humans are unable to buy a gram of wisdom. The conclusion follows in stanza III. Wisdom is not to be found in the sublunary world, and even one-time gods such as Yam, Mot, and the primeval Deep do not know the way leading to it; only God has access to it, as can be concluded from the miracles of creation. Parts I and III are connected by a striking analogy. Just as humankind differs essentially from the animals because of knowledge, God differs from humans because of wisdom. This is indicated by repetitions of the elements "see," "eye," "bring to *light*," and *"find* access"; thus, stanzas I and III are parallel units on each side of stanza II. A diagram makes the three levels visible:

	sharp sight	knowledge	wisdom	stanza
animals	yes	no	no	I
human beings	yes	yes	no	II
God	yes	yes	yes	III

The poet really has something of the systematic philosopher about him. He has not only thought out this system of almost entirely separate orbits, but he has also given it a successful poetic form with its three stanzas covering both the horizontal and the vertical entries of the diagram.

Thanks to the poet's subject, the contemplative nature of this speech, and the closely-knit design, the poem rises above the communication level of chaps. 4–27. In this regard, it is a counterpart to chap. 3, the bitter complaint with its fierce curses. That poem does not have an addressee either, so it is not restricted by it as a form of communication, and it also exceeds its specific context.

---

11. A fine example of the ternary principle in narrative prose is Genesis 38. See my contribution "Genesis 37 and 38 at the Interface of Structural Analysis and Hermeneutics," in *Literary Structure and Rhetorical Strategies in the Hebrew Bible* (ed. L. J. de Regt, J. de Waard, and J. P. Fokkelman; Assen: Van Gorcum / Winona Lake, IN: Eisenbrauns, 1996) 152–87.

Job 28 has another remarkable quality. This text has something in common with narrative prose: there is a clear quest at work—or rather, there are two. During the first stage, the miner is goal-oriented in searching for precious stones and gold, and the second stage takes him to the marketplace, where he is looking for wisdom. On a higher level, the speaker's quest is fulfilled: all through the poem, Job himself has also been searching for wisdom, and it is fitting that he is doing so by means of the genre and style of Wisdom. Will his search end in disillusion as well? Yes and no. The last verse of chap. 28 offers a solution of sorts.

The third stanza has this unambiguous conclusion: "Wisdom is hidden from the eyes of all living." In stanza I, concrete matter that was *hidden* could still come to light; in III, a subtle and nonmaterial entity such as wisdom remains *hidden* from the eyes of all—except from God's eye.[12] The quests of *homo faber* and of Job coincide and end in a deadlock. But then comes v. 28 of chap. 28—what a miraculous escape! Unexpectedly and at the last moment, there is a solution after all. A word of God, quoted by the man who in chap. 1 was emphatically recognized by two authorities as "fearing God and turning away from evil." Now, if this man says "Behold, the fear of the Lord, that is wisdom; to shun evil is understanding," there can be no argument. The concluding verse is already very striking by virtue of the fact that it is embedded speech. But what makes this verse even more extraordinary is that it offers a confluence of authorities; and not a confluence of two but of three authorities. The pronouncement is signed by the characters Job and God as well as their maker, the author. This has great consequences within and outside the text.

Now the power of negativity is at stake. The central stanza is imbued with negation, which is used no less than 12 times.[13] This lexical form of negativity is widened by the semantics of the surrounding parts. The not-knowing of animals, the not-finding of wisdom by the humans, the motif of hiding that supports the analogy of I and III, the impotence of the one-time gods—all these elements work together with the tyrannical negation of stanza II to give Job 28 the nature of a reckoning. Wisdom as an ideal and a genre may have a prestige that

---

12. See the connections between I and III that are brought about by the repetition of "eye" (vv. 7, 10, 21a), "see" (vv. 7, 24ab, 27a), the root of "conceal" (vv. 11 and 21a), and "light" (v. 11 and compare 26b); and observe the inclusio of vv. 3b and 27b: man as *ḥoqer* tries to become equal to God.

13. Ten times *lōʾ* (plus once virtually in v. 16b), twice the nominal negation *ʾên*, and then *lōʾ* four times in strophe *four* (the four cola of vv. 7–8).

has obtained in the ancient Near East for over more than two millennia; Job terminates it completely. He turns against the pretensions
and contents of metaphysics and speculative theology. The poem of
chap. 28 deconstructs wisdom using the means of Wisdom. The force
of negativity was indicated explicitly and explored systematically for
the first time in the history of thought by the philosopher Georg
Wilhelm Friedrich Hegel; we will meet him again twice. The force of
the negation has been underrated so dramatically by biblical scholars,
however, that they gave this poem the title "A Hymn *to* Wisdom,"
which sent us 180 degrees in the wrong direction.

The massive *no* to metaphysics does not have the last word. The last
word is a modest *yes*, which is really of use to humankind. The beginning or the principle of wisdom is fear of God and turning away from
evil, says Job, and it is not his finding.[14] Opposite the unfortunate situation that speculative theology and metaphysics defy verification
and thus can lead to failing debates such as in chaps. 4–27, Job with his
quotation places practical, effective ethics for daily life within the
community. In this way, the concluding verse of chap. 28 makes a good
transition to the long speech of chaps. 29–31. These three poems mean
a drastic change of direction for Job. He turns away from useless
squabbles with biased friends and their arrogant or snorting ideas, and
he turns to hard facts—to the highly personal speech that reveals his
own experience with reality. Instead of speculative reasoning, he en-
riches his audience with a crystal clear, verifiable discourse that remains experiential from A to Z.

Job 28 has no heading and no quotation formula for an introduction.
The absence of this sort of marker means that the passage is not separate from the preceding one. This means in my opinion that this radical
exploration is still just part of the communicative unit of chaps. 4–27
and that it is meant to be the conclusion of the debate proper with its
deconstruction of wisdom.[15] Job ends contact with the three friends
with the conclusion: I do not appeal any longer to the doctrines of wisdom, for we cannot convince each other in that way. I wish to fall back
on facts that cannot be denied: my life, my experience, my pain. Job's

---

14. The syntax of 28:28, for that matter, has the order PCS: predicate – copula[tively
used personal pronoun] – subject in 28a, and also P + S in the B colon. Many exegetes do
not see this.

15. Compare Lo, *Job 28 as Rhetoric*, 197, "The author wants chapters 27–28 and chapters 29–31 to be understood as two distinct speeches of Job." On p. 223, she calls chap. 28
a bridge between the beginning and the end of the plot.

drastic change of direction is an important intermediate station in the long course from chap. 1 to chap. 42.

In the meantime, the author has made good progress in sketching the hero's portrait. He has *his* agenda, and I consider it completely incredible that he would disagree with the analysis of wisdom by the hero. In his own pose of omniscient narrator, the author himself has certified Job as an authority by posing and recognizing his integrity, and he has had the certification confirmed by another authority: the person that is both his and Job's God. So this long poem, the book of Job itself, is a milestone in that it makes a settlement with the speculations and pretensions of wisdom and a plea for practical ethics and modest behavior. The turning away from metaphysics finds confirmation surprisingly and paradoxically in unexpected quarters. In chaps. 38–41, the author allows the character God to speak four long poems. It is a spectacular demonstration of transcendence. With a barrage of rhetorical questions, God makes Job feel that God is beyond human understanding and that, therefore, the categories of justice, complaint, plea, and justification can have no effect. Job listens carefully, and in his concluding speech he shows that he gives up his persistent efforts to have a fair trial: '*al-kēn 'em'as*, 42:6a—an ellipse (of the object) that must be respected.

After the powerful *no* and the modest *yes*, the hero tries to put the real problem into words. In chaps. 29–31, Job turns to his own experience and places his present situation in perspective. These poems are the conclusion and the climax of the debate, even though there is not a trace of a "you" (meaning the friends) to be found in the language any longer.[16] The content of the three chapters is easy to summarize. In 29, we find the happiness of and respect from the past; in 30, we follow the misfortune and suffering of the present; and in 31, Job defends his record of service and maintains his innocence.

The passage is a Hegelian triad.[17] In relationship to one another, the poems are a series of thesis, antithesis, and synthesis. Chapter 29 reports

---

16. So strictly speaking there is a double conclusion to the debate: chap. 28 leaves the foundation of wisdom and the arena of the friends; chaps. 29–31 crown the exchange with an alternative: Job's experiential testimony.

17. Compare my introduction to the analysis of Job 29–31 in *Major Poems*, vol. 4; there are also some appropriate quotations from Charles Taylor's extensive study, *Hegel* (Cambridge: Cambridge University Press, 1975) and from the famous *Introduction to the Reading of Hegel* by Alexandre Kojève (trans. J. H. Nichols; New York: Basic Books, 1969), who was the great Hegel scholar in Paris before World War II. That the writer "knows his

the naïve existence of former days, when everything went smoothly and when Job considered happiness and respect to be a matter of course. This existence was static, "immediate," as Hegel would put it. It is the phase of Being, of an unreflected identity. In chap. 30, negativity hits with frightful force. Happiness is wiped out. Change is inevitable. Job is the target of misjudgment on all sides, and this leads to a severe crisis in his self-image. This hour of opposition is in Hegel's term an instance of "mediation," for the way to a new mode of life is open and must be ventured. Chapter 31 describes the search for a new identity, a non-naïve life that must be organized under the pressure of negation. It is the phase of *Aufhebung* (dialectical overcoming) and totality, Hegel would say, and of *Werden* (becoming). The three poems deserve characterization on their own terms. Their structure and prosody demand further study.

Chapter 29 is the poem of the *conjunctions*. It begins in a tone of painful longing, "O that I were as in months gone by, in the days when God watched over me." Job is looking back from a present full of pain. In the first half, we see all those who were backing him: God (vv. 1–5), his offspring (v. 5b), and the whole community (vv. 7–13). It was the time

> when Shaddai was still with me, when my lads surrounded me,
> when my feet were bathed in cream, and rocks poured out streams of oil for me.

With the metaphors in this last line (v. 6), Job shows what his naïve existence actually brought him: paradise. The town worshiped him (strophes 3–5 = vv. 7–13) and looked up to him, full of admiration, awaiting his decisions (strophes 9–10 = vv. 21–25). Gradually the Job of chap. 29 was growing toward the position of king de facto (*mlk* in v. 25). In the beginning, he was the beneficiary of exquisite liquids (v. 6); at the end, liquids go out from him, when he speaks in the meeting: "My words were as drops upon them, they waited for me as for rain, for the late rain, their mouths open wide." Thus he has become benefactor.

This poem contains 49 cola: it is the square of the sacred number 7, an interesting figure—as many as in Job 10. In an odd number of cola, there is one colon in the middle, number 25, and both in Job 10 and here

---

Hegel" does not surprise me. In *Narrative Art and Poetry*, vol. 2, I have shown that the three oaths in the Nabal-David-Abigail triangle are also a dialectical triad. The remarkable thing about the third oath is, moreover, that it is in counterfactual mode and yet is decisive.

it is of unusual importance.[18] The immediate context of v. 14a is formed by strophes 5–6–7 (= vv. 11–13/14–15/16–17), and its theme is the heart of the composition: it is justice and how Job upholds it. Justice is primary in Job's relation with the community, and the community is the horizon of his administration of justice. Colon 25 does something with the language that is striking and remarkable; in this way, it becomes the axis of the center and the peak of the whole poem. The verb *lābaš* is used in two opposite directions within a half-verse of only three words. "I dressed in righteousness and it dressed me," says colon A; after these two verbal forms, the synonymous colon B chooses two nouns for the purpose of a perfect balance: "Justice was my cloak and turban." These decisions of style turn v. 14 into the peak of conjunctivity. The language of the verse demonstrates that Job and justice are completely one. And the immediate context shows what is the main application of justice: defending the weak. This administration of justice has the warmth of solidarity.

Chapter 30 is the poem of *disjunctions*. God's support turns into enmity, the community's respect becomes derision and malicious pleasure at Job's misfortune, and what happened to his offspring Job does not even dare to bring up for discussion. The refreshing liquids change into the exact opposite, according to v. 30: "My skin, blackened, is peeling off me; my bones are charred by the heat." The poem as a whole is characterized by a painful inclusio. It is the opposition of youthful scum that "laughs at me" (v. 1) versus: "my lyre is given over to mourning / my pipe, to accompany weepers" (v. 31). At the same time, the words that I plucked from the edges of chaps. 29 and 30 show how well they are tuned to one another. The laughter in 30:1 immediately follows the "mourners" of the last colon of chap. 29. For Job, this is a change of maximal sharpness; all at once, the king is the one despised most. Moreover, a parallelism on the high level of literary units has been produced now, because chap. 30 also ends in mourning. And this figure (*'bl* in 29:25 and 30:31) also contributes to the total reversal of Job's fate: the comforter cannot be comforted anymore.

Now I also go searching for the center; this time, however, for the center of the entire speech in chaps. 29–31, because the text of the ca-

---

18. The 25th colon of Job 10 is v. 12a, with the sweet-sounding but ever so sarcastic word-pair *ḥayyîm wāḥesed*. In *Major Poems*, vol. 2, ad loc., I explain how central its meaning is and that colon B appropriates the negative meaning of *šamar*; a bit further down, it is also negative: in v. 14. The traditional view ("your care has guarded my spirit"—thus, e.g., Good) is respectable but desperately wrong. In the Psalter, there is one poem of 49 cola, and again the 25th colon is of crucial importance: Psalm 74 uses a nominal sentence in v. 12a for the testimony *wēʾlōhîm malkî miqqedem*.

tastrophe is the middle one of the three.[19] The middle verse of the speech, which contains 97 verses, is v. 49 (!!), which is 30:23, and this verse says: "I know You will bring me to death, / the house assigned for all the living." The last words—that is, the words of colon B—are also the middle colon of all 201 cola in the triad.[20] Three aspects of 30:23 are now worth mentioning. The verse is part of the only passage in Job 29–31 in which Job speaks directly to God in a bitter complaint, and only here do we find the second-person singular for God. The verse deploys the antithetical word-pair life/death, and this maximal opposition conveys everything about the dynamics in the life of the tormented speaker. All this is syntactically subjected to growing consciousness or awareness: the verb *ydʿ* governs the sentence, and the fact that this verb occurs exactly 70 times in a book about wisdom, knowledge, and recognition may not be accidental.

Chapter 31 is the climax of the climax and the negation of the negative. In the longest poem of the book, 40 (!) verses, Job runs counter to all false surmises and implicit allegations. The chapter is a gigantic litotes, because time and again Job uses the formula "minus times minus equals plus." This is how it works: Job sums up all sorts of crimes and next denies committing them or even considering them. The structure, then, is a sustained enumeration. The tiny word *ʾim* is maximally exploited, with splendid flexibility. It has three uses that all take a turn: as a conjunction of conditional clauses, here especially present in the form of negative oaths (self-imprecations); as an interrogative particle; and as a negation.[21] Out of the 16 strophes of which the poem consists, exactly 12 begin with this word; so it has become a factor of structural importance.

Crossing out one misdeed or crime after another means that justice is restored to its normative position every time. Job reaffirms his loyalty to justice and solidarity. Chapter 31 executes *Aufhebung* (dialectical overcoming). *Aufhebung* means many things at the same time. The

---

19. The three poems of Job 29–31 have 24 + 33 + 40 = 97 verses; they have 49 + 68 + 84 = 201 cola, and 164 + 227 + 307 = 698 words.

20. The middle pair of words of the altogether 698 words are the numbers 349 + 350, and they are words 185–86 of chap. 30: the last word of v. 25 and the first word of v. 26, about the middle of strophe 11. Verse 25 speaks of solidarity with the weakest people, and thus it connects with the axis of chap. 29; 30:26 is about thwarted expectations.

21. See for more data not only the analysis in *Major Poems*, vol. 4 but also my contribution to the Muraoka Festschrift entitled "The Structural and Numerical Perfection of Job 31," in *Hamlet on a Hill: Semitic and Greek Studies Presented to Professor T. Muraoka on the Occasion of His Sixty-Fifth Birthday* (ed. M. F. J. Baasten and W. T. van Peursen; Leuven, 2003) 215–32.

typically Hegelian concept indicates "the dialectical transition in which a lower stage is both annulled and preserved in a higher one."[22] This lifting to a higher stage can be a form of sublimation. What does it mean for Job 29–31? Job takes leave of and annuls the naïve identity, the naturalness of bliss. This happens under the pressure of the negativity of chap. 30. In chap. 31, he preserves his loyalty to God and to his principles of justice and solidarity by saving them from chap. 29. He reaffirms them. They become part of his new, reflected and tried identity. It provides him with a ripened self-confidence.

It is useful for us to realize what position Job assumes both grammatically and with respect to the action in the three chapters. It is true that in chap. 29 he is regularly beneficiary, insofar as people look up to him full of admiration and attention, yet he comes across mainly as a subject—as a man in power, whose word is law. He does actually show solidarity, and he does do justice. In chap. 30, his position has changed to the opposite. He is object, for he is a target, beaten, attacked, and mocked by God and the people around him. But then there is chap. 31, where he scores his most impressive mark as a speaker and where he resumes his strength by expressing powerful denial or negation so often that the *yes* paradoxically becomes stronger and stronger. I will illustrate Job's way with justice and his increased self-confidence with an example. In the sixth strophe (vv. 13–15), he meditates on the treatment of slaves. This time the word *'im*, which marks the unit by *opening* it, is functioning as the interrogative particle, and the order of the words following it (abc–c' b'a' in the original) points the way to beautiful enjambment:[23]

> Did I ever reject justice for my slave /
>   and my maid when they complained against me?
> What should I do when El rises up /
>   when He calls to account, what should I answer Him?
> Did not He who made me in the belly make him? /
>   Did not One form us both in the womb?

This is a revolutionary strophe, for the reference to the equal birth of every man lays a bomb under the institution of slavery. And the crite-

---

22. Taylor, *Hegel*, 119.
23. This enjambment is overlooked in the rendering of the verse in the Job commentaries by Delitzsch (1864); Terrien (1963); L. Alonso Schökel and J. L. Sicre Diaz (1983); Edwin M. Good (1990), who quotes three short lines; Hans Strauss, BKAT (1998); and also in the RSV.

rion for the recognition of the rights of slaves lies in the vertical dimension: in the relationship with the Creator.[24]

Chapter 31 has a body of five stanzas (vv. 7–34) in which virtually all oaths of clearance are to be found. This mass is surrounded by stanzas I and VII, each consisting of six verses. They form a ring and a wide inclusio, because of the fact that in the head and tail of the poem Job directs defiant words at God. The 8th colon from the beginning and the 8th colon from the end are connected by a chiasm in which Job criticizes God's nasty attitude. Here is the original word order in a literal translation:

| v. 4b | and all my steps | He counts |
| v. 37a | the account | of my steps I will give Him |

From the beginning, God has lain in wait to catch me in mistakes and sins, says Job defiantly, but it has not provided him with anything. He need not even have bothered, for I myself am willing to provide him with a complete survey of my actions. This complete survey, the author now implies, corresponds with this chap. 31, this enumeration of uncommitted injustices. And in order to show how much he backs his hero, the author has made chap. 31 the height of numerical perfection. First hints of this are the number 8 for the verses about "my steps" and the use of the root "counting." Their places in v. 4b and in v. 37a are an iconic sign of the importance of counting and measuring.

The number 8 is the central normative figure of biblical prosody; it indicates the average number of syllables per colon. Thus is a guideline that is not obligatory but that is often followed. In the original (that is, pre-Masoretic) Hebrew, Job 31, with its quintuplet of 8 verses, has 672 syllables in 84 cola.[25] This can be read as $7 \times 8 \times 12$ syllables in 7×12 cola. There are 7 stanzas and 16 strophes. Eight of these strophic units are short, and they have precisely 8 syllables average per colon; the other 8 are long, and they score the same integer as an average. Furthermore, it is no accident that the verb *sāpar* ('to count') appears 8

---

24. Robert Gordis, *Book of Job* (Moreshet 2; New York: Jewish Theological Seminary, 1978) 339: "Verse 15 contains the most striking affirmation in the Bible—unsurpassed anywhere else—of the equality of all human beings."

25. See my *Major Poems*, vol. 4, chap. 12 for a detailed justification of the numerical aspects of the book of Job, and chap. 27, §3 for the figures of Job 31. In vol. 2 (2000), the reader will find the underlying theory (with a definition of *colon* and a fully developed formula for counting the pre-Masoretic syllables); see chap. 2.

times in the book of Job and that the noun *mispār* ('number') appears 12 times in poetry.[26]

Measures and proportions are very important for the poet, but the most important thing for him and for us are meaning and sense. What drives Job? What is he after? Again I look at the ring that stanzas I and VII form around the body of chap. 31 with Job's oaths of clearance. Here Job ventures to challenge his God. After he has portrayed God as a disgusting spy in v. 4, the punch line of stanza I (v. 6)[27] follows, in which he says almost teasingly, in a frontal attack: "let Him weigh me on the scale of righteousness;[28] then Eloah will know my integrity!" Aha, Job seeks the complete recognition of his *tummâ*. This word reminds us of the very first characteristic that Job was given by the author in the initial paragraph of chap. 1: Job was introduced to us as being *tām*.

In stanza VII, Job challenges God to come out with a lawsuit against him. He is not afraid of "a true bill drawn up by my accuser," and he says defiantly: "I would carry it on my shoulder, tie it around me for a wreath. I would give Him an account of my steps, offer it as a commander to Him." The Job that had become de facto king to his community in chap. 29, thanks to his honesty, here restores his appeal by calling himself *nāgîd*—a sacral title.[29] He straightens up from his enor-

---

26. It is striking to me that the proper name *Job* appears 56 times in the book; *'ôr* (light), the noun *drk*, and the proper name *yhwh* 32 times—again, multiples of 8.

Significant words or roots that occur 7 times are: *bth*, *qll*, *hdl*, *hyl*, *hps*, *škh*; and words such as *hōmer*, *hēqer*, *sur*, *saddîq*, *yātôm*, *šāhat*, *nĕšāmâ*, or the verbs *bāhar*, *hāzaq*, *hālap*, *yārâ*, *kihēd*, *pāqad*.

Appearing 14 times: *'ānōkî*, *'āwen*, *'hl*, *'ehād*, *yhd*, *ksh*, *npl*, *śātān*, and *phd*.

Eight times: both *'ēš* and *'iššâ*, the verb *š'l* and the name Sheol, the adjective *hākām*, the verbs *b't*, *gw'*, *glh*, *yhl*, *brk*, *ng'*, *nhm*, *nkr*, *str*, *'md*, *spn*, *rhq*, and *lbš*.

Sixteen times: *'mn*, *'bd*, *beten*. Life and death: *mwt* as a verb also appears 16 times; as a noun 8 times; together 24. The root for 'live, life, living' also appears 24 times (the word *hayyâ* which is characteristic of Elihu and a synonym of *nepeš* has not been included).

Twelve times the verbs *p'l*, *ryb*, *hpk*, and *ht'* occur, and the roots *ryb*, *sph*, *zkr*, *šrš*, *šmr*, *hzh*, *m's*, *'rh*, *shq*, *y's*. *Seventy* times: *pānîm* and the verb *yd'*.

27. Some translations (e.g., F. Delitzsch 1864; S. R. Driver and G. B. Gray, ICC, 1921; the RSV; Marvin Pope, AB 15, 1979; Georg Fohrer, KAT, 1961; A. de Wilde, OTS 21, 1981; and compare the artificial, counterfactual mode chosen by H. Strauss in BKAT) translate the crucial *'im* of v. 5 conditionally, so that vv. 5–6 become a compound sentence with this complete lack of logic: "If I have walked with worthless men . . . , let Him weigh me." Illogical: if someone were so guilty, he/she would not be so stupid as to ask to be weighed!

28. The "balance of *sedeq*" is a fine example of ambiguity. On the one hand, the scale is accurate (it has not been tampered with; it is *saddîq*); on the other hand, the speaker means that employing a scale is meant to establish (his own) *sedeq*: *his* purity.

29. The adjunct *kĕmô nāgîd* is not a simile that refers to God (as the rendering of the NJPSV has it, based on unnecessary theological timidity); it refers to the subject of the two cola of 31:37, Job himself.

mous crisis of identity and regains his pride. He recognizes himself and with rhetorical power, he corners his adversary to such an extent that it will be very difficult for God not to take his side by recognizing him.

Recognition—that is what Job is after. The catastrophe that threatened to bulldoze him under was that "people" were no longer interested in him and his integrity: his wife was not, the friends looking through their theodicy glasses were not, the entire community was not, and apparently God, as highest or primary authority, was not either. On all sides Job was awash in lack of recognition. The book of the Bible that was named after him reports that he defends himself to the last gasp and that he only succeeds in doing so, after a great deal of pain, by the firm practice of self-recognition; and note how he is vindicated in chap. 42! Recognition—in the history of thought this concept was for the first time introduced as a theme and distinguished as fundamental by Hegel (my third reference to the philosopher). *Der Mensch ist Anerkennen* 'Man is nothing but desire for recognition'; we humans are driven by *Begierde nach Anerkennung*.[30] Is it coincidental that the verb *nkr* 'recognize' appears 8 times in this book and in doing so follows the literary pattern 7 + 1 by reversing it?[31]

Against everything and everyone, Job has fought with and for his integrity, and he wins. The recognition that he is given follows the self-recognition that he has achieved despite all opposition.[32] His knees have not become weak under the enormous pressure; he has

---

30. Compare Taylor, *Hegel*, 153; and Kojève, *Introduction to the Reading of Hegel*, 192.

31. *Nkr* and 1 + 7: that is, 1× in the introductory prose, in 2:12, quoted before, about the friends who see Job's suffering but "do not recognize him"; 7× in the poetry. Moreover, 1 + 7 times *'ēš*: in prose 1× (in 1:16) and 7× in poetry; and strikingly enough, the same holds for *'iššâ* 'woman': in prose 1× (in 2:9 so 1× in prose) and 7× in verse. The pattern 7 + 1 may also be working with the root *š'l*, which occurs 1× as a noun, *šĕ'ēlâ* ('question') and 7× as a verb; with *ḥārâ*, also 1× as the noun *ḥārôn*, but 7× as a verb; with *naḥēm*, 7× verb, 1× fem. noun; with the verb *brk*, which has God for an object 7×, but in 42:12 God is subject; Job mentions *Sheol* 7×; Zophar does so 1×.

Note well: the composition of Samuel (which runs up to and including 1 Kings 1–2) begins and ends with *ša'al* 7× (in 1 Samuel 1 with Hannah; in the Adonijah-Bathsheba scene in the middle of 1 Kings 2), while this form of inclusio is continued in the first literary unit of the books of Kings: in 1 Kings 3, *ša'al* occurs 8× (moreover, as 7 + 1). After the first 7 in 1 Samuel (mainly in connection with Hannah's vow and name-giving), the word *Sheol* occurs just after the axis of her psalm (in chap. 2).

32. I am indebted to the last book that Paul Ricoeur (died May 2005) wrote, which is also the first book-length discussion of *recognition* in philosophy: *Parcours de la Reconnaissance* (Paris, 2004); see the translation by David Pellauer, *The Course of Recognition* (Cambridge: Harvard University Press, 2005). The epigraph at the beginning of this article is from p. 21 of the English edition.

Some quotations from Ricoeur: on pp. 76–77, he writes about *Oedipus at Colonus* and

kept a straight back, and at last God performs the weighing he has demanded. For God, there is nothing for it but to recognize that Job is
blameless; in 42:7, it is *dabber nĕkônâ kĕʿabdî ʾiyyôb* 'speaking the truth
as did my servant Job'. Stepping out of the text and the world of
words, we see the author, who is responsible for everything. He has
honored his hero's integrity by realizing numerical perfection in chap.
31, the composition that is the climax, as an iconic sign of Job's moral
perfection.

Weak knees: we do encounter them in the tradition of the more than
one and a half millennia in which 42:6 was translated incorrectly. It is
totally inconceivable and completely out of character that a man of
strong principles, an exquisite man such as Job should say in his last
words, which are also the last words of poetry in the book: "Therefore
I despise myself and repent in dust and ashes." This rendering (by the
RSV) contains three serious mistakes: the prepositional adjunct with
"dust and ashes" is not a locative, the verb *naḥēm* goes altogether in the
wrong direction, and the reflexive rendering of the verb *māʾas* is without any foundation.

Fortunately, a movement to evaluate the verse differently has got-
ten underway since the 1970s.[33] I have joined in, and in vol. 4 of my
Major Poems I have drawn attention to the following. The verb *māʾas*,
the opposite of *bāḥar* 'to choose' is known well; it does not mean 'despise' but 'reject', and the reflexive rendering is not only a last resource

---

about "the reversal . . . on the plane of the recognition of responsibility," which also
applies to Job:

> [T]he tragic character, however overwhelmed he may be by the feeling of the
> irresistible character of the supernatural forces that govern human destiny, re-
> mains the author of that innermost action consisting of his evaluating his acts,
> particularly retrospectively. . . . this misfortune becomes a dimension of the action
> itself, in the sense of being endured in a responsible manner. Across this trajec-
> tory of endurance, the play builds a progression from misfortune undergone to
> misfortune assumed.

Thinking of Job's speech in chaps. 29–31 and especially of his series of oaths, I read on
p. 91: "There is a close semantic kinship between attestation and self-recognition"; on
p. 92: "self-recognition belongs to the semantic field where it is related to recognition—
identification and recognition—*Anerkennung*." On p. 93: "Self-recognition, by virtue of
the dialectic [between identity and otherness] . . . puts us on the way toward the problematic of being recognized, implied by the request for mutual recognition." Beside Job
31, I place: "The proud assertion 'I will do it' expresses in language the risky posture of
ipseity, as self-constancy that goes beyond the safety of mere sameness" (p. 103).

33. D. Patrick, "The Translation of Job xlii 6," *VT* 26 (1976) 369–71; and P. A. H. de Boer,
"Haalt Job bakzeil?" *NTT* 31 (1977) 181–94. But the Peshiṭta already knew what *māʾas* was
aiming at and translated it as *ʾeštoq* 'I will keep silent'.

and a somewhat embarrassing decision ad hoc, but it is also simply wrong. The verb is used as an absolute verb here. In other words: there is an ellipsis of the object that can only be appreciated if one reads the form within the context. Then it appears that the stylistic figure of the ellipsis is a main feature of the concluding poem, 42:1–6. What we are asked to do is to tolerate the use of the verb as an absolute verb.[34]

For the correct view of v. 6, one also needs to listen well to the phrase in front. The word 'therefore' (*ʿal-kēn*) makes an explicit connection with the preceding verse. This means that 42:5 is the base on which Job is standing when he concludes with v. 6. Thus, the content of v. 5 is fundamental. It is about first-rate and second-rate knowledge of God. "With ear's hearing I heard you, but now I see you with my eyes." All the talking about God, all the way from chap. 3 to chap. 37, by three, four mortals was of a speculative nature. It presupposed and furthered knowledge of God that was only hearsay and thus of an indirect nature. But now God has just spoken four poems, chaps. 38–41, "the answer from the storm." It can be appreciated in different ways. I will present two. The author has had the kindness to give God a speech, or put differently: God was allowed by the author to say something as well. Another way of phrasing it will please believing readers better, with their need to show devotion: God has deigned to speak and to address Job personally.

I am counting again. In chaps. 38–41 we find no less than 36 + 21 + 41 + 0 = 98 morphemes in the second-person masculine singular with which the speaker, God, addresses Job directly. That is an exceptional intervention, an event that is of decisive importance to the completion of the plot of the book. It cannot be evaluated less than as a real meeting of God with the man Job. Beside this, the question whether Job, the speaker of 42:6b, has seen God with his *physical* eyes pales as irrelevant. Job has now met God, and he renders the meaning of this encounter in 42:6 in two word pairs: hearing versus seeing, ear versus eye—which

---

34. Reading the end of Exodus 2 helps us to practice tolerating it. Literally, the text says: "God saw the Israelites, and God knew," and the reader understands that leaving out the object of the last verb is an effective means of giving room to the comprehensiveness of God's understanding and commitment.

Ps 89:39, which has two verbs in the A colon (with a pseudo-redundant *ʾattâ* in front) is sometimes quoted to defend the view that the adjunct in Job 42:6b is the object of *both* verbs. But I, for one, think that it is precisely for the expressive value of Ps 89:39a that the verbs have been used absolutely; this, too, must be put up with, and there are translations of Psalms that do exactly that, such as Buber, RSV, M. E. Tate (also see the data in his note on p. 411 of WBC 20, 1990), and F. L. Hossfeld and E. Zenger (HTKAT, 2000).

this time function as an antithesis.[35] Thus, he also acknowledges that he has understood the unique meanings of the encounter. God has demonstrated in an elaborate way what the first thing is that a man must realize in a contact with God: that his being and his works are beyond comprehension. The elaborate demonstration of transcendence in chaps. 38–41 renders Job's endeavors to confront God in court for a fair trial (thus, in one way or another on equal terms) completely obsolete. Now we can fill in the elliptic object of his *'em'as*: 'Therefore, I reject [my argumentation so far, my efforts to drag God to court, my indignation, etc., etc.]'. . . .

The verb *naḥēm* has a surprising ambiguity in its semantic field, of pain and change for the good, with emotional satisfaction as a result.[36] Here it means, in the spirit of the context and in accordance with the positive signal that God's intervention gave to Job, that Job will be comforted for [his state of] dust and dirt, that is, for the tortured and humiliated state of survival to which he had been condemned for weeks.[37] God places unexpected, beneficial, and total comfort, *niḥam*, opposite the prosecutor's ominous and foul *ḥinnām*, which provoked the whole tragedy. Thus, the beginning and end of the book of Job are connected by a beautiful anagram in addition to other forms of word repetition. Is it a coincidence that the root of *naḥēm* (which as a verb connects 2:11 with 42:11, another inclusio) occurs a total of 8 times in Job?

---

35. What sort of parallelism is realized by the complementary pair hear/see should be assessed case by case. The words in the pair are often shown to be synonymous, as in Job 13:1 (with a beautiful third term, "knowledge," in v. 2); Exod 2:24–25; and Pss 22:25, 34:16, 84:9–10, and 102:20–21; but they can also signify an antithesis or a difference, as in this case. Thus Ps 48:9 can indicate difference and progression. See, for the difference, again Job 42:5a and b (and especially for the inferior quality of second-hand knowledge of God: Job 28:22 and 26:14).

36. A striking test case is 2 Sam 13:39, where one is used to thinking and translating the words as David 'was consoled' about Amnon's murder; after which it is illogical for Joab to have to go to so much trouble in chap. 14 to get David and Absalom together. As I argued in *Narrative Art and Poetry*, vol. 1, David was in reality still so *sad* about his loss that he wanted to set out after the fled murderer, Absalom.

37. Lo (*Job 28 as Rhetoric*, 32–33) offers a critical discussion of the problems with 42:6, but in her own conclusion, unfortunately, she sticks to the aspect of *repentance*. Moreover, she speaks of Job's "dejected worldview" and his "dejected outlook." What matters, however, is not his views but something much more objective, his being: suffering, humiliation, having one foot in the grave. This condition is now removed by God's vindication, the result of which is reported by the narrator in the prose of 42:7–8 but which had already been sensed and understood by Job in the preceding verses. On p. 33, Lo mentions the possibility of taking *niḥam* in 42:6 as a Piel with the meaning 'to find consolation'. This is not possible: the form is a Niphal.

The traditional rendering of *naḥēm* as 'to repent' is whimpering and insipid. At the last moment, it spoils the hero's portrait along with a great part of the point of the book. What Job really says is this: 'therefore, I reject / and I am[38] consoled about dust and dirt'. The verse (and all the poetry of this book) ends in a strongly alliterating word pair, which is an excellent metaphor for the state and the suffering in which Job has found himself until this moment. I consider it improbable that the pair (a type of hendiadys) is the object of *both* verbs in 42:6.[39] It would mean that we have a zeugma here. Because the first verb is transitive and usually governs its object directly, whereas the second verb governs a prepositional object, the zeugma would ignore an awkward inequality, and my surmise is that this is undesirable in Hebrew. The burden of proof, however, does not rest with me but with authors who hold the view that dust and dirt are governed by both verbs.

The important difference between direct and indirect contact, with the difference in quality between first-hand and second-hand knowledge of God as a possible outcome, is also under discussion in the last part of the book of Job, the concluding prose of 42:7–17. Commentators and translators seem to have grown so tired of their year-long labor on the poetry that they are not paying close attention for a moment. But even with the seemingly easy Hebrew of prose, one must be precise.

There is not a scholar that would dream of rendering *the beginning* of v. 7 other than: 'After the Lord had spoken these words to Job, . . .' and rightly so. The preposition *'el* in the construction *dabber 'el* simply means 'to', not 'about'. It is true that we know that this *'el* is frequently used "promiscuously," with the meaning of *'al* (for example, in the books of Kings and in Jeremiah), but for us that would be option 2. From the point of view of method and correct reasoning, option 1 is to take *'el* as *'el*, with the meaning 'to'. Therefore, it is mind-boggling to see how *the end* of v. 7 is rendered. A few words after the combination *dabber 'el*, we read this translation of God's words to Eliphaz: "My

---

38. The form *wĕniḥamtî* does not have a Masoretic accent on the last syllable, so it is not a *perfectum consecutivum*. It is an "ordinary" copulative perfect, and at the same time it can be taken as a performative form: as a speech act, just as *'āmartî* can mean 'herewith, I decide'.

39. Pace D. Patrick, "The Translation of Job xlii 6"; Edwin Good, *In Turns of Tempest: A Reading of Job* (Stanford, CA, 1990); Leo Perdue, *Wisdom in Revolt: Metaphorical Theology in the Book of Job* (JSOTSup 29; Sheffield, 1991) 232; Ellen van Wolde, "Job 42,1–6: The Reversal of Job," in *The Book of Job* (ed. W. A. M. Beuken; BETL 114; Leuven, 1994) 223–50; and K.-J. Illman, "Theodicy in Job," in *Theodicy in the World of the Bible* (ed. A. Laato and J. C. de Moor; Leiden, 2003) 330–31. Regarding Lo (*Job 28 as Rhetoric*, 32–33), it is not clear whether she follows the zeugma.

anger has flared up against you and your two friends, for they have not spoken the truth *about* Me as did My servant Job." The authors all parrot each other, and hardly anybody takes the trouble to account for this deviant 'speaking about'. At the end of v. 8, God repeats the causal clause in identical words.

The verb *dābber* occurs 39 times in Job, and approximately 10 times it is used as an absolute verb, which fits well within colometric practice. It occurs 7 times with the preposition *'el*, and in *all* these places it means 'speaking *to*'.[40] The result of this careful analysis is that God is not complaining about the friends' delivering incorrect assertions *about* him (though they have not done differently whenever it was their turn in chaps. 5–37). God is complaining about something quite different, which is that the friends have not spoken *to* him. Nowhere have they spoken directly to him, and this is presented in full relief by the contrast with Job himself. Several times Job has spoken entire strophes to God, and so he has used the second-person masculine singular. He did so in the middle of chap. 29 and, especially, in the first round of the debate, which was in chaps. 7, 9, 10, 13, and 14. This cannot be regarded separately from God's decision (in the poetry section) to speak elaborately himself to Job personally.

The interpreter of the book of Job can now draw conclusions: the friends' speaking *about* God is regretted explicitly by God because it was hearsay, the traditional arguments and slogans (including the triple[41] train of thought of the theodicy) that decorate themselves with the age-old prestige of Wisdom as a genre and practice but that are in reality of a speculative nature. And God has as little respect for this hearsay and second-hand speaking as did the speaker of chap. 28, the man Job.

---

40. The combination *dabber 'al* does not appear in Job. The combination *dābber 'el* is found in 2:13, 13:3, 40:27, 42:7 (2×), and in 42:8–9. Observe that the words 'as the Lord had told them' (*dibber 'ălêhem*) in v. 9 and the words *dibber . . . 'el 'iyyôb* in 7a form a frame round the double *dibbartem 'ēlay* of vv. 7b//8b!

41. Actually, there are three variations of the theodicy: (1) your misery is a punishment by God, so you must have sinned; (2) you were punished because the fact is that as a creature you are inferior (as Eliphaz said in chap. 5 and Bildad in chap. 25); and (3) this pain is meant by God to be a lesson in humility, so be grateful.

PART 5

Modeling the Future by Reconstructing the Past

Samuel's "Farewell Speech": Theme and Variation in 1 Samuel 12, Josephus, and Pseudo-Philo

JOACHIM VETTE

University of Heidelberg

Introductory Remarks

The title of the conference, "Literary Fiction and the Construction of Identity in the Ancient Near East," would have been a great context for the well-known Old Testament scholar Martin Noth to present his thoughts on 1 Samuel 12. For Martin Noth, this chapter was one of the pillars of the Deuteronomistic History, a Deuteronomistic piece of writing that provided its original readers with a theological reflection and evaluation on the course of Israel's history.[1] For Noth (to use my own phrasing), 1 Samuel 12 was a piece of Deuteronomistic literary fiction that took part in shaping Israel's identity at a certain point in time. In the following pages, I will deal with the story told in 1 Samuel 12 along with its retellings in *Jewish Antiquities* by Josephus and in the *Biblical Antiquities* by Pseudo-Philo. By comparing these three texts, I wish to address the connection between narrative shape and communicative intent and take issue with an all-too-simple connection between literary fiction and identity.

A comparison between the Masoretic Text of 1 Samuel 12 and its retellings in Pseudo-Philo and Josephus confronts us with a basic truth: the communication of narrative content (the story) is highly dependent on the narrative shape of the text (the discourse).[2] How Pseudo-Philo

---

1. M. Noth, *Überlieferungsgeschichtliche Studien: Die sammelnden und bearbeitenden Geschichtswerke des Alten Testaments* (3rd ed.; Tübingen, 1967) esp. pp. 59–60.

2. Although the distinction between *what* is told and *how* it is told is meanwhile a commonplace in literary studies, a wide range of terminology is used to describe this distinction: story – plot (E. M. Forster, *Aspects of the Novel* [London, 1927]), Stoff – Erzählung (W. Kayser, *Das sprachliche Kunstwerk* [Bern, 1951], fabula – sujet (T. Todorov, *Théorie de la littérature: Textes des formalistes russes* [Paris, 1965]), story – discourse (S. Chatman, *Story*

and Josephus shape their narrative has a decisive impact on what they are telling us. Both narratives leave very different impressions on us as readers. By comparing and contrasting 1 Samuel 12 (commonly referred to as Samuel's farewell speech) with these retellings, I intend to sharpen our observation with regard to the structure and intention of the biblical text.

Pseudo-Philo:
Liber Antiquitatem Biblicarum *(LAB 57)*

The retelling of Samuel's "farewell" in the *Biblical Antiquities* of Pseudo-Philo[3] is the shortest of these texts; it allows us to gain an overview of the basic story:[4]

> [1] Samuel sent and gathered all the people and said to them, "Behold you and your king. I am in your midst [*in medio vestri sum*] as God commanded me.
>
> [2] "And so I say to you before your king, as my master Moses the servant of God said to your fathers in the wilderness when the company of Korah rose up against him, 'You know that I have not taken anything from you, nor have I harmed any one of you.' Because they lied then and said, 'You did take,' the earth swallowed them up.
>
> [3] "And now you, who have not been punished by the Lord, testify before the Lord and before his anointed whether you have sought a king because I treated you badly; and the Lord will be the witness against

---

and Discourse: Narrative Structure in Fiction and Film [Ithaca, NY, 1978]), source – discourse (M. Sternberg, *The Poetics of Biblical Narrative: Ideological Literature and the Drama of Reading* [Bloomington, 1985]), histoire – récit (G. Genette, *Narrative Discourse: An Essay in Method* [Ithaca, NY, 1983]).

3. On Pseudo-Philo's *Liber Antiquitatem Biblicarum*, see: L. Cohn, "An Apocryphal Work Ascribed to Philo of Alexandria." *JQR* (1898) 277–332; G. Kisch, *Pseudo-Philo's Liber Antiquitatum Biblicarum* (Notre Dame, 1949); A. Spiro, "Pseudo-Philo's Saul and the Rabbis' Messiah ben Ephraim," *Proceedings of the American Academy for Jewish Research* 21 (1952) 119–37; M. James, *The Biblical Antiquities of Pseudo-Philo* (New York: Ktav, 1971); D. Harrington, "The Biblical Text of Pseudo-Philo's *Liber Antiquitatum Biblicarum*," *CBQ* 33 (1971) 1–17; C. Dietzfelbinger, *Pseudo-Philo: Antiquitates Biblicae. Jüdische Schriften aus hellenistisch-römischer Zeit* (2 vols.; Gütersloh, 1975); G. Nickelsburg, "Good and Bad Leaders in Pseudo-Philo's *Liber Antiquitatum Biblicarum*," in *Ideal Figures in Ancient Judaism: Profiles and Paradigms* (ed. J. Collins and G. Nickelsburg; Society of Biblical Literature Septuagint and Cognate Studies 12; Chico, CA, 1980) 49–65; D. Harrington, "Pseudo-Philo: A New Translation and Introduction," in *The Old Testament Pseudepigrapha* (2 vols.; ed. J. Charlesworth; Garden City, NY, 1983–85) 2:297–377; H. Jacobson, *A Commentary on Pseudo-Philo's Liber Antiquitatum Biblicarum* (2 vols.; Leiden, 1996).

4. The text is quoted from Jacobson, ibid., 1:185.

you [*Dominus erit testis vobis*].[5] But if now the word of the Lord has been fulfilled, I and the house of my father are free from blame [*ego excusatus sum*]."

4 The people answered, "We are your servants and our king along with us. Because we are not worthy to be governed by a prophet, we said then, 'Now appoint over us a king who will govern us.'" All the people and the king wept with great lamentation and said, "Long live Samuel the prophet!" and the king stood by. And they brought sacrifices to the Lord.

5 Afterwards Saul fought with the Philistines for one year and the battle went well.

Samuel opens his speech by clearly defining the constellation of characters: "Behold you and your king. I am in your midst as God commanded me." Samuel clearly sketches the opposing camps: *your* king, not mine. Israel and its king stand over against God and his prophet. The Latin *in medio vestri sum*, translated here 'I am in your midst' can also and perhaps even better be translated 'I stand between you', understanding *in medio* along the lines of Hebrew בין, as is often the case with Pseudo-Philo.[6] It remains to be seen whether Samuel positions himself between the people and their king to mediate or to separate.

The separation into two camps of those involved is carried into the following statement: "I say to you before your king, as my master Moses the servant of God said to your fathers. . . ." Without further discussing the fact that Pseudo-Philo revises Num 16:15,[7] where Moses speaks not to the fathers but to God, I notice that Samuel continues to delineate the opposing "teams": God is now joined by Moses, who also stands beside the prophet. We are faced with a situation where God, Samuel, and Moses stand on one side, the people and their king on the other. Once these opposing teams are clearly demarcated, Samuel launches into his main accusation: the people are compared with Korah and his company, who rebelled against their faultless leader. In chap. 16 of his *Biblical Antiquities*, Pseudo-Philo emphasizes that Korah and his company did not rebel against Moses but against God. This subtle distinction falls by the wayside in this context: here, God and the faultless leader are one and the same target of the rebellion. Just as Korah and his company received their due punishment without delay, Samuel

---

5. The dative *dominus erit testis vobis* should be read as *dativus incommodi*: "The LORD will be a witness *against* you" (see ibid., 2:1158).

6. See ibid., 2:1157.

7. "Moses was very angry and said to the LORD, 'Pay no attention to their offering. I have not taken one donkey from them, and I have not harmed any one of them'" [NRSV].

threatens the people with a similar fate: You are still unpunished, so be careful what answer you give! And only then, after clearly defining the context and the conditions of the following exchange does Samuel pose his question: Did you seek a king because I treated you badly? The subsequent biblical quotation is interesting in this context: "before the Lord and before his anointed" (1 Sam 12:3). In the context of 1 Samuel 12, this passage clearly refers to Saul. In the context of Pseudo-Philo's *LAB*, however, this reference is not without ambiguity, because Pseudo-Philo never actually narrates that Saul is anointed. He does, however, explain in great detail that Samuel is anointed (*LAB* 51.7). Thus, we at least have the option of reading "his anointed" as a change of referent and an allusion to Samuel himself.[8]

The people answer, and their answer is surprising because we find no equivalent in the biblical text: "We are your servants and our king along with us. Because we are not worthy to be governed by a prophet, we said then, 'Now appoint over us a king who will govern us.'" This confession is accompanied by loud expressions of lament and an explicit confirmation of Samuel's authority, even "in the presence of the king." In the end, Samuel's speech is a complete success. To speak of a farewell speech in this context would be absurd. Samuel does refer to the end of his office once God's word is fulfilled, but at the same time he emphasizes that this has not yet occurred. On the contrary, the people shout in acclamation: "Long live Samuel the prophet!" while the king stands by.[9] Samuel thus weakens the position of the king and, in consequence, the unity between the king and the people. The king was only appointed because the people were unworthy of being led by the prophet: Saul is clearly the second choice, a makeshift solution for a people who deserved no better. This also clarifies the intention of the *in medio* at the beginning of the speech. Samuel breaks the constellation apart that existed at the beginning. Now the people, God, Moses, and Samuel stand together on one side, and the king, Saul, only wields power under the auspices of prophetic authority.

We need to be careful not to accuse Pseudo-Philo of an attitude generally critical of the monarchy. Pseudo-Philo's criticism is not directed toward the monarchy as a whole but toward Saul personally. A brief overview of his statements on Saul makes this clear:

---

8. See Jacobson, *Commentary*, 2:1158.

9. This acclamation is especially striking when compared with 1 Sam 10:24, where we read יְהִי מֶלֶךְ ('Long live *the king*!').

- Pseudo-Philo's narration on Saul's election opens with the statement that the people demanded a king "before the appointed time" (*LAB* 56.1; compare 58.4).[10]
- According to Pseudo-Philo, Saul is elected precisely as a punishment for the people's untimely demand for a king. God says to Samuel: Saul should be "a king to consume them, and he himself will be consumed thereafter" (56.3). This attitude determines Pseudo-Philo's entire portrayal of Saul.
- As briefly mentioned above, Pseudo-Philo completely omits the fact that Saul was anointed.
- He also omits Saul's heroic victory over Nahash.
- In his retelling of 1 Samuel 15, Pseudo-Philo explains that Saul spared Agag, king of the Amalekites, because Agag had promised to show him hidden treasures (58.2). The son of Agag is later identified as the person who dishonors Saul by impaling him with his own sword (65.3).
- In the Endor episode, Pseudo-Philo reports that Saul cleansed the land of necromancers and magicians, not to honor God, but to create a reputation for himself (64.1).
- Before Saul dies, Pseudo-Philo narrates that Saul was a coward who had given up on himself and his people even before he was hopelessly surrounded by the enemy (65.5).

The combination of these and further elements creates a very negative portrait of Saul. It is quite appropriate to say with Abram Spiro: "Pseudo-Philo was one of the great geniuses of ancient Israel and supreme master of the black art of character assassination."[11] His retelling of 1 Samuel 12 fits perfectly into this picture.

Josephus: Jewish Antiquities (Ant. 6.5.5–6)

We are faced with a completely different portrait of Saul in *Jewish Antiquities* by Josephus.[12] For Josephus, Saul is a military genius of the

---

10. The enigmatic statement "if the word of the Lord has already been fulfilled, I am free" can also be read in this context. As Jacobson has shown, the Latin *ego excusatus sum* is best understood as "excused from public office and responsibility" (Jacobson, *Commentary*, 2:1159). The word of the Lord would thus be fulfilled once the appointed time for the king has arrived and Samuel has departed from public office.

11. Spiro, "Pseudo-Philo's Saul," 120.

12. On Josephus's *Jewish Antiquities*, see E. Schürer, *The History of the Jewish People in the Age of Jesus Christ* (rev. and ed. G. Vermes and F. Millar; 3 vols.; Edinburgh, 1973–87) 1:44–50; L. Feldman, "Josephus' Portrait of Saul," *HUCA* 53 (1982) 45–99; P. Alexander, "Retelling the Old Testament," in *It Is Written: Scripture Citing Scripture. Essays in Honour of Barnabas Lindars* (ed. D. Carson; Cambridge, 1988) 99–121; E. Ulrich, "Josephus' Biblical Text for the Books of Samuel" and L. Feldman, "Josephus' *Jewish Antiquities* and Pseudo-Philo's *Biblical Antiquities*," both in *Josephus, the Bible, and History* (ed. L. Feldman and

first order; a biblical hero who can easily hold his own when compared with Greek or Roman heroes. He is an example for all, especially for all kings. Again, a brief overview of relevant passages makes this agenda clear:[13]

- Already when introducing Saul, Josephus expands the biblical text by telling his readers that Saul was of slender build and "gifted with a spirit and mind, surpassing these outward advantages" (6.4.1).
- Josephus expands the ambiguous biblical proverb "Is Saul also among the prophets?" (1 Sam 10:11) by adding: "How has the son of Kis come to this degree of happiness?" (6.4.1).
- MT 1 Sam 10:16 leaves the question open why Saul did not tell anyone of his anointing. Josephus answers this question for us:

    But concerning the kingdom and all relating thereto, deeming that the recital thereof would excite jealousy and distrust, he held his peace; even to one who seemed most loyal of friends and whom he loved more affectionately than all those of his blood, he judged it neither safe nor prudent to disclose this secret— reflecting, on what human nature in truth is, and how no one, be he friend or kinsman, shows unwavering loyalty or preserves his affection when brilliant distinctions are bestowed by God, but all men straightaway regard these eminences with malice and envy. (6.4.3)

- Whereas Pseudo-Philo omits Saul's victory over Nahash, Josephus expands this narration as a case example for Saul's tactical prowess and personal courage.
- Even Saul's end appears in a positive light:

    King Saul and his sons fought courageously and with great endurance, seeking to find their honor in fighting valiantly and dying bravely. They broke through the lines of the enemies and created a bloodbath among the Philistines. In the end, they succumbed to the superior numbers of the enemy. (6.14.7)

- Josephus does recognize Saul's negative attributes, yet he tends to diminish their importance: Saul's depression is not punishment by God but a disease that is treated by "doctors" with David's music. Whereas 1 Samuel 19 reports that Saul sends his men to Michal's house to find and kill David, Josephus reports that these messengers only have orders to bring David to court. Many other alterations follow this pattern.[14]

Against this background, it is now interesting to see what Josephus does with Samuel's so-called farewell speech. In Josephus, as in Pseudo-Philo, Samuel opens this episode by referring back to Moses and Aaron.

G. Hata; Detroit, 1989) 59–80 and 81–96, respectively. L. Feldman, *Studies in Josephus' Rewritten Bible* (Leiden, 1988); S. Mason, ed., *Understanding Josephus: Seven Perspectives* (Journal for the Study of the Pseudepigrapha Supplement 32; Sheffield, 1998).

13. The English translation is taken from Josephus, *Jewish Antiquities*, Books I–IV (trans. H. St. J. Thackeray; Cambridge, MA: Harvard University Press / London: Heinemann, 1957).

14. For a detailed discussion of Josephus's treatment of Saul, see Feldman, "Josephus' Portrait of Saul."

Whereas Pseudo-Philo uses this reference to compare the people with the band of Korah, however, Josephus follows quite a different line of reasoning:

> I adjure you by the most High God, who brought those excellent brothers, I mean Moses and Aaron, into this world, and rescued our fathers from the Egyptians that without showing favor through respect, without suppressing anything through fear, without giving room to any other feeling, ye tell me, if I have done anything sinister. (6.5.5)

What follows is a list of crimes that Samuel may have committed, before the prophet concludes by saying: "If you know of such things, speak freely in the presence of your king" (6.5.5). Samuel demands that the people affirm his actions and emphasizes that this affirmation must happen *without* timidity and fear but in the presence of honored witnesses: God *and* the king. The two belong together in this context. Whereas with Pseudo-Philo, Samuel first threatens the people and then poses his question, Josephus has his Samuel choose an opposite course of action. This course of action pays off; the people freely grant him a positive affirmation of his leadership (6.5.6).

Samuel uses the authority thus granted to him to confront the people with their sin of turning from God by requesting a king. Following this confrontation, the people experience God's wrath directly in a thunderstorm. Fear gives birth to a confession, and the prophet is asked "as a kind and gentle father" (6.5.6) to plead on behalf of the people for God's mercy. At this point, we should note the fact that Samuel has not spoken one word of criticism against the king. His criticism only concerns the demand of the people; the king is merely witness to the events.

After the thunderstorm, Samuel promises to do what he can, but he also has words of warning: the people are called to "to be righteous and good" (6.5.6) from now on. But why? Samuel provides a reason. They are to heed this warning for the sake of their continued happiness under the rule of the king. Josephus then concludes this episode with a statement that has no parallel in either Pseudo-Philo or the biblical text: "Samuel dismissed them to their homes, having for the second time confirmed the kingdom to Saul" (6.5.6).

This text also gives one pause about calling Samuel's words a "farewell speech." The situation presented to us is a public gathering initiated by the prophet that has the purpose of leading the people to a certain behavior by means of evaluation and judgment. Samuel achieves two goals: the people confess their sins and learn what they must do to ensure happiness under royal rule. The king himself is not attacked or criticized at any point. On the contrary, even though the people's demand for a king is subject to harsh criticism, the king himself is confirmed in his office by Samuel—with the condition that the people continue to walk in the way of God. Samuel combines two things: the criticism of the demand for a king and a strengthening of the present king. We may indirectly conclude that Samuel is taking his leave after these words of strengthening, but the text never makes this assumption explicit.

With Pseudo-Philo and Josephus, we have two texts that are retelling the same biblical episode while drawing very different portraits of the events retold. What remains for us is a look at the narrative in 1 Samuel 12.

1 Samuel 12

1 Samuel 12 has traditionally been seen as a historical and literary caesura. The period of judges has come to a close, and the monarchy has begun. There have been scholars who have seen traces of an old covenant tradition in Gilgal in this text,[15] but recent discussion has generally understood 1 Samuel 12 to be a late Deuteronomistic meditation on the theology of history that provides us with a blanket condemnation of the monarchy as such.[16] In this view, the material in this chapter is created by the Deuteronomistic redaction in order to convey a certain theology of history to the reader. Following Martin Noth, the chapter is understood in analogy to such texts as Joshua 23 and 1 Kings 8 as one of the crucial pillars that support the large narrative structure of the Deuteronomistic History.[17] I do not want to enter into the debate on the existence, scope, or purpose of a Deuteronomistic History. In the context of Pseudo-Philo and Josephus, I would instead like to point out an important distinction, the distinction between the narrator's voice and the voice of the acting characters. I believe we must clearly differentiate

---

15. See J. Muilenburg, "The Form and Structure of the Covenant Formulations," *VT* 9 (1959) 361–64; K. Baltzer, *Das Bundesformular* (WMANT 4; Neukirchen-Vluyn, 1960) 74–76; recently Y. Amit, "The Saul Polemic in the Persian Period," in *Judah and the Judeans in the Persian Period* (ed. O. Lipschits and M. Oeming; Winona Lake, IN: Eisenbrauns, 2006) 647–62.

16. H. Hertzberg, *Die Samuelbücher* (ATD 10; Göttingen, 1968) 76; T. Veijola, *Das Königtum in der Beurteilung der deuteronomistischen Historiographie: Eine redaktionsgeschichtliche Untersuchung* (Helsinki, 1977) 84–85; A. Mayes, "The Rise of the Israelite Monarchy," *ZAW* 90 (1978) 10–11; D. Edelman, *King Saul in the Historiography of Judah* (JSOTSup 121; Sheffield, 1991) 66; P. Mommer, *Samuel: Geschichte und Überlieferung* (WMANT 65; Neukirchen-Vluyn, 1991) 123–25.

17. Noth, *Überlieferungsgeschichtliche Studien*, 5–10.

between a possible speech *given by the Deuteronomistic redactor to the reader* and a speech *given by Samuel to the people*. These two levels do not necessarily exclude each other, but they are not the same and should be separated in our dealing with the text—unless, of course, we assume that Samuel himself *is* the Deuteronomistic redactor. As with Pseudo-Philo and Josephus, I will approach the text on this second level as a speech given by Samuel to the people. How are we to understand and evaluate this process of communication in relation to its narrative shape, especially in comparison with the two texts discussed above?

The first issue that arises when we read this text is the medieval chapter division. There are few arguments that speak for starting a new pericope with 12:1. The ויאמר שמואל begins abruptly with no explanatory context. There are several arguments, however, for beginning the pericope two verses earlier. In 11:14, we encounter a change of characters as Samuel reappears for the first time since 10:24; we encounter a change of location as the events move to Gilgal; we encounter a slight change of addressee from העם to כל־העם; and we encounter a change of subject matter from the victory over Nahash to a public gathering initiated by Samuel. By beginning the pericope in 11:14, I follow the observations already made by Fokkelman, McCarthy, Tsevat, and Vannoy,[18] as well as the retelling by Josephus, who interestingly enough begins his version of this story precisely with the gathering at Gilgal. Once we read 11:14–15 as the narrative introduction to Samuel's speech, we discover an interesting context: Samuel gathers the people at Gilgal in order to renew the kingdom. The text explicitly lists three groups who participate in the action: Samuel, Saul, and the people. We hear how two of these participants react to what has occurred: 'And Saul and all the men of Israel rejoiced greatly'[19] (וישמח עד־מאד, 11:15)— Saul and all the men of Israel. But what about Samuel? ויאמר שמואל 'And Samuel said' (12:1).... Whereas the people and Saul rejoice, Samuel initiates a lengthy speech. By reading 11:15 and 12:1 together, we close a gap that is only created when these two verses are taken from their narrative sequence in the Masoretic Text. On the occasion of

---

18. M. Tsevat, "The Biblical Account of the Foundation of the Monarchy in Israel," in *The Meaning of the Book of Job and Other Biblical Studies* (ed. D. McCarthy; New York, 1980) 83–97; D. McCarthy, "The Inauguration of Monarchy in Israel: A Form-Critical Study of 1 Samuel 8–12," in *Institution and Narrative: Collected Essays* (ed. D. McCarthy; Rome, 1985) 401–12. J. P. Fokkelman, *Narrative Art and Poetry in the Books of Samuel: Vow and Desire (1 Sam 1–12)* (Studia Semitica Neerlandica 31; Assen, 1993) 481ff.

19. All translations of the Masoretic Text, unless otherwise noted, are my own.

the renewal of the kingdom, Saul and the men of Israel rejoice greatly, and Samuel speaks. This provides a general context for the prophet's speech in 1 Samuel 12.

In this speech, there is no question that Samuel is dealing with the evaluation of the very kingdom he has just renewed. But Samuel is faced with a dilemma in this evaluation. This dilemma is expressed most clearly in 12:12–13:

> Adonai, your God is your king.
> Now behold the king you have chosen, whom you have desired.
> Behold, Adonai has given you a king.

God himself is king, and yet God has given a king. How does this fit together? This dilemma is not new. It first appears in 1 Sam 8:7, when God says to Samuel:

> Listen to the voice of the people in all they say to you!
> For they have not rejected you,
> but they have rejected me from ruling over them.

Listen to the voice of the people, for they have rejected me. Or more to the point: the people do not want me as king, so give them what they want. Is God agreeing to his own rejection? In the face of this dilemma, we are not surprised that Pseudo-Philo comes to the conclusion that Saul is from the beginning a divine punishment for the people's rebellion. This is a very plausible solution to this dilemma.[20]

With this dilemma in the background, several elements of Samuel's speech combine into a unified whole. Because the dilemma was created by the demand of the people, the people must come to recognize their mistake. The theophany in the thunderstorm beautifully meets this need. It is very interesting that it is Samuel who initiates this theophany; the text does not explicitly say that he is acting on God's behalf: אקרא אל־יהוה ויתן קלות ומטר ('I will call to ADONAI and he will give thunder and rain', 1 Sam 12:17).[21] The theophany produces the desired response from the people (12:19):

---

20. See also Hos 8:4. Many modern scholars continue this line of interpretation. See, e.g., H. Donner, *Geschichte des Volkes Israel und seiner Nachbarn in Grundzügen* (ATD Ergänzungsreihe 4/1; Göttingen, 1984) 175–76: "Mögen die Israeliten sehen, welche Erfahrung sie damit machen werden! Jahwe weiß natürlich, dass es schlechte Erfahrungen sein werden." It is quite reductionistic, however, to understand Saul's kingship one-dimensionally as divine punishment (see the treatment of 1 Sam 10:17–11:13 in my *Samuel und Saul: Ein Beitrag zur narrativen Poetik des Samuelbuches* [Beiträge zum Verstehen der Bibel 13; Münster, 2005] 161–89).

21. See H. Stoebe, *Das erste Buch Samuelis* [KAT 8/1; Gütersloh, 1973] 239.

Pray for your servants to Adonai your God[22] that we may not die.
For we have added to all of our sins the evil
that we have desired a king.

Following this confession, Samuel is able to comfort the people ("Do not be afraid," 12:20) and assure them of God's forgiveness ("ADONAI will not abandon his people, for the sake of his great name," 12:22), while showing them the righteous path for the future ("Fear ADONAI and serve him in truth with your whole heart," 12:24). All this creates a wonderful narrative sequence: a dilemma, created by the people → punishment → confession → forgiveness → exhortation for the future.

These elements are indeed present in Samuel's speech, but they do not cover everything contained in this text. Besides the narrative sequence sketched above, there is a second thematic progression of equal importance. Once again, I will begin with the dilemma stated in 12:12–13:

Adonai, your God is your king.
Now behold the king you have chosen, whom you have desired.
Behold, Adonai has given you a king.

A second opposition, expressed in 12:2, runs parallel to the opposition between ADONAI and the king:

Now behold the king walks before you (מתהלך לפניכם).
. . .
And I walked before you (אני התהלכתי לפניכם).

The opposition here is between the king and Samuel. As with the first opposition, this one also refers back to 1 Samuel 8:

And they said to him: Behold, you have grown old and your sons do not walk in your ways. Now appoint a king over us that he may judge us as all the nations. And the word was evil in the eyes of Samuel when they said: Give us a king that he may judge us. And Samuel prayed to Adonai. . . . And Adonai said: not you, but me. . . . (1 Sam 8:5–7)

With other interpreters, I ask what exactly was "evil in the eyes of Samuel"—the rejection of God or the rejection of him and his sons?

---

22. It is interesting to note the suffix אל־יהוה אלהיך ('pray to ADONAI your God'), instead of אל־יהוה אלהינו ('ADONAI our God'; see 1 Sam 7:8). What is the reason for the mutation from *our* to *your*? Has Samuel's speech contributed to a distancing between the people and their God? This theory is stengthened by the fact that the people now refer to themselves as "servants of Samuel" and no longer as "servants of God" (compare 12:14 with 12:19).

The latter seems to have weighed heavily in Samuel's mind, otherwise ADONAI's rebuke in 1 Sam 8:7 would not have been necessary.[23] Samuel, however, did not either understand or accept this rebuke, for we read in 12:2:

> I am old and gray,
> but my sons, behold, they are with you.

An old, gray Samuel with his sons: the constellation at the beginning of chap. 8 repeats itself in chap. 12, a constellation that was the immediate reason for the people's demand for a king in the first place:[24]

> And his sons did not walk in his ways and turned aside after gain; they took bribes and perverted justice.
> . . .
> Then the elders said to him: Behold, you have become old and your sons do not walk in your ways. Now appoint a king over us! (1 Sam 8:3, 5)

The opposition between the king and Samuel also determines the following narrative sequence. 1 Sam 12:3 contains a vow of purification, which is strongly reminiscent of a reversal of the warnings that Samuel gave the people about the behavior of a king in chap. 8, even if the donkey is the only direct verbal link between the two texts.[25] Samuel's behavior is without blemish, but this comes as no surprise. After all, chap. 8 mentioned that Samuel's sons did *not* follow the ways of their father. Samuel's reference to past salvation history is noteworthy. This reference differs from the retellings in both Pseudo-Philo and Josephus, especially toward the end of Samuel's account:

> Then ADONAI sent Jerubbaal, Bedan, Jephthah and Samuel
> and saved you from the hands of your enemies. (1 Sam 12:11)

---

23. L. Eslinger, "Viewpoints and Points of View in 1 Sam 8–12," *JSOT* 26 (1983) 260; A. Schulz, "Narrative Art in the Books of Samuel," in *Narrative and Novella in Samuel* (ed. D. Gunn; JSOTSup 116; Sheffield, 1991) 123; J. Ackerman, "Who Can Stand before YHWH, This Holy God? A Reading of 1 Sam 1–15," *Prooftexts* 11 (1991) 9. For an opposing view, see U. Berges, *Die Verwerfung Sauls: Eine thematische Untersuchung* (FB 61; Würzburg, 1989) 62.

On the issue of repeated speech in this passage, see Sternberg, *Poetics of Biblical Narrative*, 421; G. W. Savran, *Telling and Retelling: Quotation in Biblical Narrative* (Bloomington, IN, 1988) 104.

24. For an interesting, different reading of this passage, see Fokkelman, *Narrative Art and Poetry*, 496–97.

25. 1 Sam 8:16 and 12:3. The donkey also appears in Moses' vow of purification in Num 16:15. For a rabbinic interpretation of this connection, see *Midr. Sam.* 14.9 (see also the above discussion on Pseudo-Philo, pp. 326–29).

This list of these judges is striking. Without entering into the discussion about the much-debated identity of Bedan,[26] we can see clearly that Samuel presents himself as the last link in the chain of the men who were sent by God to save his people. He thus presents himself not as prophet or priest but explicitly as judge (and we hear in the background the people's words in 8:6: "Give us a king to be judge over us"). The punch line follows in 12:12:

> But you saw that King Nahash the Ammonite came against you
> and you said to me:
> No! But a king shall be king over us.
> But Adonai is king over you.

Samuel is the judge, but the people come to him and say, "No, a king instead!" Samuel understands the demand of the people for a king as the rejection of his own authority. True, he also recognizes the rejection of God, but his personal issues have not disappeared, despite God's admonishment in 8:7. God's prophet has a very human problem with relinquishing power and authority. Even in the end, he clings to his position of power by stating (1 Sam 12:23):

> I will instruct you in the good and right way.

Josephus does not know of such a continuing role for Samuel, yet we are strongly reminded of Pseudo-Philo: "Long lives the prophet Samuel, even in the presence of the king." Again, we would do a great disservice to the text to subsume it under the heading "Samuel's farewell." We can hardly speak of a farewell; but if we do, then only with a very limited definition of *farewell*.

Concluding Remarks

We have seen that the narrative structures of all three texts are closely connected to the complex interaction between the characters Samuel, Saul, Adonai, and the people. For Martin Noth, 1 Samuel 12 was literary fiction, a piece of writing that does not report actual historical events but presents readers with a reflection on these events by means of a fictionalized speech placed in the mouth of Samuel. However, of the three different Samuels we are faced with in our three texts,

---

26. There are striking text-critical variants for this passage: the LXX reads Barak instead of Bedan, and one LXX manuscript adds Samson. The Peshitta reads Deborah, Barak, Gideon, Jephthah, and Samson. The targums read Gideon, Samson (Bedan), Jephthah, and Samuel. Because only the Peshitta omits Samuel in combination with several other changes, we should read Samuel as the last in the list of judges mentioned here.

it seems to me that the biblical Samuel with his personal issues least fits the role of the Deuteronomist's mouthpiece. By reducing Samuel to the mere medium by which a possible Deuteronomistic message is conveyed, we ignore the complexity of the literary character, of the *homo fictus*, as E. M. Forster called it,[27] which we refer to as Samuel. I do not want to deny that the text has purposes that transcend the narrative matrix and contribute to the shaping of identity. But in determining these purposes, I do not believe that we should transcend this narrative matrix and the complexity it contains.

How does Samuel's speech function within the context of 1 Samuel 8–12?[28] The prophet's monologue follows the events that undoubtedly constitute the high point of the biblical portrayal of Saul. In chap. 11, the spirit of God overwhelms Saul in response to the threat posed by Nahash to the inhabitants of Jabesh-gilead. He gathers the people of Israel and Judah behind him "as one man" (11:7) and leads them to a glorious victory. This chapter is witness to a subtle transfer of authority. Whereas certain individuals had previously questioned Saul's authority ("Who is he that he can save us?" 10:27), these questions have now been silenced. And whereas only Samuel had addressed the people prior to the campaign against Nahash, Saul himself now speaks while Samuel says nothing. At the end of the Nahash episode, the people pose a question *to Samuel* ("Who is it who said . . . ?" 11:12), but it is *Saul* who answers ("No one shall be killed on this day . . . ," 11:13). Samuel's authority was never challenged to such an extent as in this context. In this situation, he speaks out and says: "Come, let us renew the kingdom." In most cases, חדשׁ speaks of renewing something already in existence that has taken a turn for the worse and must be restored.[29] If Samuel speaks of renewing or restoring the kingship and then effects this renewal by means of his following speech, then it is a plausible reading of the text to conjecture that Samuel is attempting to restore previous power structures that had existed before Saul attained the status of a hero.

1 Samuel 12 ends with the people in a state of fear ("Then the people feared ADONAI *and Samuel* greatly," 12:18). This fear has a major part in driving a wedge between the king and his people, who now continue on in fear. Whereas we read in 11:7 that the people stood behind

---

27. Forster, *Aspects of the Novel*, 55.
28. For a full discussion of this issue, see my *Samuel und Saul*, 109–220.
29. See Isa 61:4; Lam 5:21; Job 10:17; Ps 51:12; 104:30; 2 Chr 15:8; 24:4. See also M. Buber, "Die Erzählung von Saul's Königswahl," *VT* 6 (1956) 113–73, esp. p. 155.

Saul *as one man,* we read in 13:7 that the people can only follow "trembling with fear after him." Samuel has succeeded in weakening the bond between Saul and Israel and Judah. The Saul cycle and especially the reasons for Saul's failure should also be understood in this context.

The Exile

Biblical Ideology and
Its Postmodern Ideological Interpretation

ADELE BERLIN

University of Maryland

Exile, in one way or another, left an enormous impact on the Hebrew Bible. The Babylonian Exile in 586 B.C.E. became a transforming moment, a linchpin in the Bible's construction of postexilic Jewish identity. All biblical literature written after it and the various exilic and post-exilic revisions of earlier literature were written under the influence of the exile.[1] The grand narrative that stretches from the books of Genesis through Kings records near its beginning the expulsion—the exile—of Adam and Eve from their home in Eden and ends with an account of the destruction of Jerusalem and the exile of the Kingdom of Judah.[2] Prophetic literature has destruction and exile and the restoration from it constantly on its mind. And exile dominates all but a few books in the Writings, most obviously Ezra, Nehemiah, Daniel, and Chronicles, but also a number of Psalms and, of course, Lamentations. Yet, despite the pervasiveness of the theme of exile throughout the Bible, there is no continuous account of this event (Albertz 2003a: 3). Nor does the Bible present a monolithic portrayal of what happened or what its significance is.

---

1. R. P. Carroll (2001: 103) goes as far as saying, "Thus we may read the Hebrew Bible from beginning to end as a series of narratives, tales, and depictions of deportation and displacement." A number of Carroll's points appear in multiple publications, but I will generally cite only one source.

2. The narrative is framed by the word אדמה 'ground' or 'land', the place from which one is exiled. Just as the אדמה is cursed because of Adam and then Cain, so the land is defiled because of Israel's sins. Just as Adam, Eve, and Cain were banished from the אדמה, the ground (Gen 3:17, 23; 4:12), so Judah was exiled from its אדמה, its ground/land (2 Kgs 25:21). This אדמה theme is used by the prophet Amos in 9:14–15 in his comforting vision of the future return from exile: "I will restore My people Israel. . . . And I will plant them upon their אדמה [their land], nevermore to be uprooted from their אדמה that I gave them."

The study of the exile has garnered increasing scholarly attention during the last few decades. In this essay, I will examine some post-modern studies of it. Postmodernism has brought a number of important benefits to biblical studies, but, like anything taken to an extreme, it also has its dangers. I will focus here on what I see as some post-modern excesses and errors. This will be, then, an ideological critique of some contemporary writings on the exile along with a brief look at some of the ways the Bible constructs its ideology of exile.

It is widely accepted among scholars today, except for the very con-servative among them, that the Bible in general and more specifically its portrait—or more correctly, portraits—of the exile are not to be taken as objective historical records but are ideologically informed re-tellings of the past, literary works that take liberties with "the truth" of the events described. The focus on texts as ideological constructs and the inquiry into their ideology is largely a postmodern phenomenon and an extremely useful one for interpreting the Bible.

A small group of scholars, however, go too far in their reading of the Bible as an ideological text, essentially claiming that it is all ideology and no history. In their discussions, the exile is taking its place in the un-history of ancient Israel—another in a growing list of biblical events that never occurred but that was made up for ideological pur-poses. This is the position of scholars often called "minimalists," "revi-sionists," or "nihilists" by those who oppose them and called New Historians by those in sympathy with them.[3] Lest you think I exag-gerate their position, I quote one of them, Niels Peter Lemche, who in praising recent progress in the study of the history of Israel says, "[T]here is no premonarchic history of Israel worth speaking about; the Davidic and Solomonic empire is in jeopardy; the history of the di-vided kingdom—particularly the Judean part—is being dramatically rewritten, the exile is suspected of being mostly an ideological con-struct" (Lemche 1997: 124). In the same article, Lemche, going to an even greater extreme, praises two of his colleagues who "showed that

---

3. The minimalists generally include Philip Davies, Niels Lemche, Thomas Thompson, and Keith Whitelam. John Van Seters is sometimes included in this group, and some of Hans Barstad's work should be. Robert Carroll is a postmodernist with sympathy toward some of the minimalists' work, although I am not sure I would call him a minimalist. I dis-cuss Carroll's writings on the exile below. Lester Grabbe (1998b: 12–13) objects to the use of the term *minimalist*, which he considers polemical. But those generally known as min-imalists seem to enjoy being polemical, or at least to be intentionally provocative, so I see no reason to spare them from a polemical term.

the ancient Israelites themselves were also fictitious creations of the imagination of the biblical historians" (1997: 138). The statement that "the exile is suspected of being mostly an ideological construct" implies that the entire notion of an exile—the event itself—is a literary fiction made up to give legitimacy to the so-called "restored" Judean province and the small group of people who dominated it. Philip R. Davies (1998: 136) explicitly says: "'Exile' is not an episode in the 'history of Israel'; it is an ideological claim on behalf of a certain population element in the province of Judah during the Persian period."[4] This statement, and others like it, reflects the notion that, if a piece is ideological, it cannot be based on any historical event but must be entirely fictional. James Barr (2000: 82) has already addressed the absurdity of this position, and I need not mention it further.

Most biblical scholars hold more moderate views. They accept that the exile was an actual event and that some, although limited, historical information about it can be recovered both from biblical and from extrabiblical sources. Actually, the moderates and the minimalists agree on a number of the "facts" but disagree on the weight they should be given. For instance, all acknowledge that the Babylonians conquered Judah, destroyed some part of it, and, in keeping with standard Assyrian and Babylonian practice, deported a portion of the population. There is also general agreement that only a portion of the Judean population was deported to Babylonia (estimates range from 10% to 25%). Opinions differ, however, on the effects of these events on Judah and its remaining population. Some scholars conclude that there was a breakdown of the major institutions that had a devastating effect, while others, largely the minimalists, insist that life in Judah went on as before, basically uninterrupted.[5]

Despite their admission that destruction and a deportation occurred, the minimalists want to avoid the term *exile* as being too heavily freighted with ideology. They prefer the term *deportations*, which they take as a more neutral term.[6] Moreover, they seek to minimize the impact of the deportations. They point out that there were a great many deportations and population exchanges in the ancient world and that this one was nothing special. Robert Carroll (2001: 112) puts it this way:

---

4. Carroll (1998a: 77) calls "exile" an "ideologically contaminated term." The title of his article reinforces the notion that the exile never happened.

5. On this point, see Barstad 1996: 19, 42–43, 79.

6. See Grabbe's "Reflections on the Discussion" (1998b: 147–48).

"There are just too many stories in the Bible about the deportations of peoples—too many exiles as it were—but only one exilic event seems to be singled out for the focus of the biblical writers . . . and this . . . tends to conceal from us the extraordinary ordinariness of such events and to privilege just one group in history."[7] Carroll is an example of a postmodernist who adamantly refuses to espouse the Bible's view. But it seems to me that it's one thing to read against the biblical presentation in order to get at "what really happened" (that is, how important this exile was compared with other similar events) and quite another to do what Carroll is doing—deny the Bible its right to formulate an ideological position on the exile. After all, the Bible was not attempting to write a history of deportations.

On the face of it, it is rather amazing that postmodernists, so interested in ideology, are so reluctant to examine in any depth the Bible's ideology of exile. They are satisfied simply to call it ideology, as opposed to history, and to condemn it on these grounds. But an understanding of the Bible's ideology is crucial to the understanding of the Bible. Indeed, *exile* carries a lot of ancient ideological baggage. The ideology of exile did not originate in the 6th century B.C.E., nor is it an Israelite or Judean invention. While we have most of our historical documentation from Neo-Assyrian and Neo-Babylonian sources, the threat of destruction and exile for disobedience to one's sovereign goes back at least as far as Hammurapi. In the epilogue to Hammurapi's laws, among the curses against anyone who would disobey his laws, we read: "May he [Enlil] order . . . the destruction of his city, the dispersion of his people, the transfer of his kingdom, the disappearance of his name and memory from the land" (*ANET* 179, lines 71–73). So the biblical idea of exile, the clearest expression of which is in Leviticus and Deuteronomy, is grounded in ancient Near Eastern thought, adjusted to Israelite religious views, where God is the king, and his laws are those that he is said to have commanded Israel to follow. When the actual deportations occurred, this "ideology" was already there, waiting to be called upon. In that sense, part of an "ideology of exile" already existed and was not particularly Judean, let alone the creation of an elitist segment of the Judean returnees.

Why do the minimalists work so hard to deny the exile and undermine its ideology? For one thing, they want to be *enfants terribles,* overturning the approaches of their predecessors, undermining the

---

7. See also Thompson 1998: 110; Davies 1998: 129, 132–33.

simplistic acceptance of the accuracy of the Bible's historiography. But there is more to it than this. Lurking behind their scholarship is a political agenda. It is, as has already been recognized, an anti-Israel and anti-Zionist agenda. Their writings reveal (although they never admit it) that, for their own anti-Zionist political reasons, they are not in sympathy with the Bible's constructed exile and the ideology it embodies. The biblical ideology of exile and return, a staple in Jewish tradition especially after the destruction of the Second Temple, was used by modern Zionists to justify their own return to the land (Eisen 1986); and so, the minimalists appear to think, if they can undermine the Bible's ideology of the exile, they will undermine the modern Zionist cause.

Other scholars have pointed out the minimalists' political subtext, albeit they value it differently. Whitelam's defender, Lemche (1997: 149), is pleased that Whitelam has written "a very politically correct book, timely according with the establishment in Palestine of the first institutions of a Palestinian state." Another supporter of Whitelam's efforts, Robert Carroll (1998b: 55), says, "Current events in the Middle East where the Palestinians are suppressed and without a state of their own obviously play a strong part in shaping Whitelam's approach to reading the scholarship of biblical historiography." Among those critical of the minimalist enterprise, John Collins (2005: 66; see also 2004: 206) criticizes Whitelam's book for, among other things, offering "too facile a continuum between the ancient story and the modern situation."[8] Bustenay Oded (2003a: 56) similarly observes that, in many of the minimalists' writings, "the present [Middle East] political conflict is quite openly projected onto the ancient past and onto biblical studies . . . under the aegis of pretentious academic research."[9] Stefan Reif states trenchantly that, in trying to free themselves of older Christian bias in biblical scholarship, the nihilists, or minimalists, have substituted political ideology for religious ideology. "Alas," says Reif (2002: 243), "most Jews will find little evidence of disinterest in their writings, especially with regard to the State of Israel and the nature of

---

8. Ironically, Whitelam and others criticize the Bible's representation of continuity between the deportees and the returnees, and they seek to minimize the historical or biological connections between them. Whitelam's drawing of continuity for the modern scene is exactly what he rejects in the Bible.

9. Oded cites Pastor 1998. The anti-Zionist stance of these authors, as Oded points out, is most obvious in their anachronistic use of the terms *Palestine* and *Palestinian* when referring to ancient Israel.

Israeli scholarship. For such 'nihilists', a whole history of ancient Israel has apparently been invented to justify modern Christian and Zionist thinking."[10] Reif goes on to cite passages from minimalist sources to support his statement.

The scholars whose comments were just quoted here are themselves working in a postmodernist mode, uncovering the unstated ideological underpinnings of the contemporary writings they discuss, just as the minimalists did for the biblical text and for their own scholarly predecessors. Yet, surprisingly, the minimalists themselves seem either unaware of these underpinnings in their own work or are unwilling to acknowledge them. For instance, Whitelam (2002) vehemently attacked scholars who found his work to be politically or ideologically driven, specifically anti-Zionistic or anti-Semitic.[11]

This position of denying one's own agenda is inconsistent with postmodernism, in which "explicit advocacy of political ends" is a hallmark (Adam 1995: 45). New historians, in the words of A. K. M. Adam (1995: 46–47), "show that the context that *modern* (*not* New) historians posit for a given work will actually reflect not only the prevalent ideas of the past historical moment, but also, in concealed form, the prevalent assumptions of the historicist's own day." It appears that the minimalists are guilty of the same offense of which they accuse modern historians—inscribing in a concealed (or perhaps not so well-concealed) manner their own ideological views into their reconstruction of the past. The only difference is that their ideology is not the old variety of patriarchal, ruling-class advocacy but, in the case of the minimalists, a more fashionable ideology, especially in Western Europe (home of most of the minimalists), that is antithetical to the State of Israel and to Zionism.

Were it only a matter of an anti-Zionist political agenda, which might be dismissed as the personal view of a small group of scholars (although I worry that the intentional insertion of any political view into scholarship may undermine that scholarship).[12] But there is something more insidious about the postmodernist approach to the exile espoused by this same group of scholars—something that is at the heart of postmodernism and that leads to a misunderstanding, I think, about

---

10. It is ironic that Reif's essay appeared in a memorial volume for Robert Carroll.

11. Whitelam begs for proof in the form of specific references to back up the claims against him of anti-Zionism and anti-Semitism. Ironically, a number of them are provided by Stefan Reif in his contribution to the same volume.

12. I am not so naïve or perverse as to suggest that we can be totally objective, but to go to the opposite extreme is, to my mind, a flaw of postmodernism.

the Bible's concept of exile. Postmodern scholars are bothered by what they take to be the imposition of exile ideology or, more precisely, the ideology of return by a small exclusivist minority, the temple establishment, on the majority. As Carroll put it in one of his more provocative passages (1992: 89), "It makes the rebuilt temple community look like a Leninist seizure of power without adequate representation of other interests."[13] This is typical of postmodernism or New Historicism. As Carroll himself explained elsewhere (1998b: 55): "New Historicist approaches to the Bible seek to redress history in favor of the silenced and repressed of (somebody else's) history, usually the wretched of the earth." So Carroll is trying to restore the voice of those silenced by the powerful elite of Jerusalem. But were these voices ever really silenced? Did the Jerusalem temple community stamp out all opposing views? Was there a "resistance movement" to the mainstream view?

Carroll supports his contention by dividing writings about the exile into two camps: the literature of exile and return, according to which the return has already taken place; and the literature of exile with no return (yet)—that is, literature in which the return is yet to take place in the future. He posits two opposing schools of thought: the dominant ideology of exile and return, promoted by the rebuilt temple community, who see the exile as completed; and a second ideology, of those alienated from the center, that speaks of exile without return. The examples of the latter that Carroll (1992: 89–90) cites are the Qumran writings, especially the *Damascus Document*, and pseudepigraphal literature such as *Enoch, Baruch, 4 Ezra,* the *Syriac Apocalypse of Baruch,* and the *Testaments of the Twelve Patriarchs.* Note that none of these works is in the Hebrew Bible and that Carroll is building on the work of Michael A. Knibb, who focused on how the idea of exile played out in the Greco-Roman period, not in the Persian period, whence most of the biblical texts about exile originated. It is not immediately clear where Carroll would place the diaspora stories of Esther and Daniel, which also speak of exile but not of return, but elsewhere he indicates that

---

13. See also Carroll 1998a: 79: "[T]he tendency of the 'canonical' text is for the Jerusalem writers to have contaminated all other writings with their own ideological holdings and values." Against the argument that a small group of Jerusalem elite imposed its will upon the majority, Ben Zvi (2003: 33) notes that "the actions and ideologies of the elite are of importance to, and have an impact on, non-elite members of society too. Ideological (or theological) worlds have to be shared—at least to some extent—by elite and non-elite members of the community or polity to be socially and historically successful."

they belong in the "exile without return" category. Carroll (1992: 90) says of the two bodies of literature that he identifies:

> If one category has tended to dominate biblical literature, that should not mislead scholars into imagining that only one viewpoint has any legitimacy. . . . What is even more important is the fact that the literature of "deportation without restoration" allows us to recognize in the alternative literature an ideological hegemony which has systematically distorted our accounts of the intellectual, social, political and religious history of the period of the second temple.

Elsewhere (2001: 108) he states:

> It has to be recognized that the kind of literature incorporated into the Bible tends to favor the "end of exile" approach to ancient history and probably represents the propaganda literature of the temple community in Jerusalem as opposed to other ancient literature which represents Diaspora communities for whom there had been no end to exile (see in particular the Dead Sea Scrolls).

Carroll got it wrong here, apparently because he was operating with the notion of the hegemonic power of the Jerusalem temple community as preserved in the Hebrew Bible and, like other postmodernists, was too much concerned with defending the powerless, recouping their suppressed voices, and resisting the ideology of "hegemonic" texts. Actually, the biblical evidence shows that the idea of an ongoing exile, with the return in the future, is very much present within the Hebrew Bible, even in books that are centered on the restoration and written after it occurred. It was a common postexilic view, not at all repressed or dominated by the idea of exile with return in the present. In place of Carroll's dichotomy between two contemporaneous views, I see a chronological development, with the historical return of 539 as its watershed. Before 539 and in the years immediately following it, the idea of exile and return (or imminent return) is typical and natural (for example, Lamentations; Psalms 74, 79, and others; Second Isaiah). More interesting is the idea of a never-ending exile that is evident in the later Persian period and beyond, after the historical restoration.[14] The restoration was never considered complete, even by those who participated in it.

I offer here a brief selection from the Hebrew Bible of passages in which the notion of an ongoing exile is found. Ongoing exile may be expressed both in eschatological and noneschatological frameworks.

---

14. Bedford (2001: 28 and 62) warns of the danger of reading ideas from later texts into the early exilic and postexilic period, which is exactly what Carroll has done.

Perhaps the clearest example is Psalm 126, as it is most often inter-preted currently, according to which the opening verses speak of the restoration as having occurred, "When the Lord restored the fortunes of Zion" (NRSV), while the second part of the psalm prays for restora-tion in the future ("Restore our fortunes").

The book of Chronicles, clearly a postexilic work whose ideology of exile has been aptly described by Sara Japhet (1999), is an interesting case. Unlike the rest of the Bible, Chronicles does not play up the depor-tations to Babylonia. On the contrary, Chronicles minimizes them, lim-iting the deportation to only King Jehoiachin himself and some of the temple vessels (2 Chr 36:10; compare with the extensive list of deportees in 2 Kgs 24:12–16). As for the destruction, it was confined to Jerusalem and did not include the other towns of Judah (2 Chr 36:17–19). In similar fashion, Chronicles sees the Assyrian Exile of the Northern Kingdom as applying only to the Transjordanian areas (1 Chr 5:26). These smaller exiles serve Chronicles' ideology, according to which Israel remained continuously in the land after the settlement. To be sure, elsewhere Chronicles mentions the exile of Judah, but, explains Japhet, the crucial term for Chronicles is "all Israel," not "Judah," when referring to the people. Moreover, the exile of Judah is temporary, lasting 70 years, to give the land its sabbatical rest (2 Chr 36:20–21).

As for the restoration, Japhet points out that, by ending with the no-tice of the edict of Cyrus, Chronicles puts itself and its implied au-dience at the time of Cyrus, *before the restoration has taken place. Thus, the restoration is in the future.* "For the Chronicler, the restoration of Israel's destiny is not a matter of the past but a program for the future—it has not yet occurred, but is to be expected and awaited" (Japhet 1999: 43). The restoration in Chronicles will not look like the restoration pre-sented by Ezra–Nehemiah. It will be a return to the idealized monarchy of David and Solomon with a broad definition of "all Israel," not limited to Ezra's returned Israel. It will be a time of peace and of Israel's obser-vance of the Torah.

We turn now to Ezra and Nehemiah, taken by most scholars as the primary exemplars of the idea of exile and return. Ezra opens with the notice that Jeremiah's prophecy of return had been fulfilled (Ezra 1:1; cf. Jer 25:11 and 29:10) and goes on to describe the rebuilding of the Jerusalem community. Yet even in this book, which certainly sees the historical exile as having ended and which most obviously represents the view of the rebuilt temple community, the idea of an ongoing exile is found. *Exile* here does not mean living outside Judah (the term גלה is not used); it means living in Judah under conditions that fall short of restoration. According to Ezra 9:6–7 and Neh 9:32–37, the restoration is marred by the fact that Judah is not an independent nation but is subservient to Persia: *"Today* we are slaves, and the land that you gave our fathers to enjoy its fruit and bounty—here we are slaves on it." These passages speak of the restoration as only a temporary respite in a story of continuous exile ("But now, for a short while, there has been a reprieve from the Lord our God, who has granted us a surviving remnant and given us a stake in His holy place" [Ezra 9:8])—an idea diametrically opposed to the Chronicles view that the norm is living in the land of Israel, and exile is a temporary aberration. But because of Israel's current sins, says Ezra, this respite threatens once again to give way to another exile. The history of Israel is here defined by exile in the past and the present: "all the suffering that has overtaken us . . . from the time of the Assyrian kings *to this day."* The message is that, although the audience is the returned Israel, the restoration is not yet fully complete and is not certain to be completed.

So we see that in some writings from the postexilic period, exile no longer signifies a historical event completed in the past but, instead, a concept describing the ongoing present condition. If the exile did not end with the edict of Cyrus or with the return of the Judeans to Judah or with the rebuilding of the Second Temple, when will it end? If the end of the exile can no longer be located in the past, it must be still to come in the future.

This future need not be eschatological, as we see from Chronicles and Ezra–Nehemiah, the future restoration of which does not come after a catastrophic change in the world order leading to the end time.[15] But as eschatology developed in the late Second Temple period, it became a ready-made home for thoughts of the future restoration. If the restoration could no longer be located in historical time, it must be located in eschatological time. Eschatological thought provided yet another context for the revision of the ideology of exile.

We find an example of this shift from a real-time return to an eschatological return in the book of Daniel, purporting to come from the Babylonian or Persian periods but actually written later, during the time of the Maccabean revolt. According to Daniel 9, the prophet Jeremiah's prediction that the exile would end after 70 years (which had already happened, according to Ezra 1:1, and was on the cusp of happening, according to 2 Chr 36:22) had been misunderstood and needed to be recalculated through the divine insight that Daniel was given.

---

15. Japhet (1999: 44) raises but rejects the possibility that Chronicles is eschatological.

The new calculation puts the end of exile in the future, which turns out to be the near future from the point of view of Daniel's actual audience, living in the time of Antiochus IV Epiphanes. Eschatological calculations often bring the eschaton to within striking distance of their audience. This passage is a good example of how a seemingly unfulfilled prophecy can be reinterpreted so as to maintain its validity. I want to call attention, however, to the fact that a *fulfilled* prophecy was perceived here as *unfulfilled*. The historical exile had indeed ended, but for the author of Daniel it had not yet ended, because he operated with the *concept* of an ongoing exile in the historical present and an idealized return in the future.

Daniel turns the notion of the *end of exile* into the notion of *ongoing exile* through interpretation of an authoritative text. Another example of how interpretation can alter the time frame of the return is the Qumran text 4QMMT, which contains a paraphrase of Deut 30:1–3. 4QMMT C 14–21 reads:

> And it shall come to pass, when all these things befall you, at the end of days (באחרית הימים), the blessings and the curses, [then you will take] it to heart and you will return unto Him with all your heart and with all your soul, at the end [of time (באחרית הימים) . . .]. (Qimron and Strugnell 1994: 58–61)

Deut 30:1–3 does not contain the phrase אחרית הימים, but the author of MMT reads it into the paraphrase, thereby interpreting the passage to mean that the blessings and curses of Deuteronomy, some of which have already come to pass (at least the curses), will be completely realized in the eschatological age. MMT was perhaps influenced by Deut 4:30, which says,

> When you are in distress, and when all these things have befallen you, in the future (באחרית הימים), you will return to the Lord your God and heed his voice.

The plain sense of the idiom אחרית הימים in Deut 4:30 and in most of the Bible is "in the future, the not-too-distant future," but in late biblical and postbiblical usage it becomes a technical term for the eschaton (*TDOT* 1:211–12). It is in this eschatological sense that the author of MMT understands אחרית הימים in Deut 4:30 and reads it into Deut 30:1–3. Thus, as in Daniel, the new concept of ongoing exile and eschatological return is read into an older traditional text about the exile.

Thus, in the course of time, exile came to be understood not merely as a historical event in the past but as an existential mode of being. This is certainly the case in the intertestamental literature and in the

Qumran texts, as demonstrated by Michael Knibb. But it did not begin there; it has earlier roots within the Hebrew Bible.

The explanations given to explain the growth of the concept of on-going exile are both historical and conceptual: the economic and political difficulties faced by the Jews in the Persian and Greek periods as well as the failure of the restoration to live up to its idealized expectations, especially as they had been described in the literature that had become or was in the process of becoming authoritative (Ben Zvi 2003: 39; see also Albertz 2003b). Jerusalem was not the "Emerald City" described in Isa 54:11–14, nor had the other prophetic visions of restoration come to pass: Jerusalem was not the spiritual center of the world; God's glory had not been declared by all the nations; peace and plenty were not yet realized; and the Davidic monarchy was nowhere in sight.[16]

I would give prominence to the latter factor, for as is well-known, the Second Temple period saw increasing involvement with traditional authoritative texts (soon to become canonical), invoking and updating their ideology for current application. Jeremiah's prophecy about the length of the exile seems to have been especially important, because it is cited in Ezra, Chronicles, and Daniel.[17] Postexilic restoration ideology was influenced by earlier ideology of the restoration as embodied in traditional texts. Again, as in the case of exile ideology, prior ideology played a role in the formation of new, revised, or extended ideology. Historical events in and of themselves do not generate ideology unless there already exists (or is created) an ideological context in which to place them. When the restoration did not live up to its billing, the notion of being in exile, already a strong concept central to Jewish identity, naturally extended its life into the future. The idea of an ongoing exile continued to grow as time passed, becoming an ongoing, never-ending condition of postexilic Jews—*all* postexilic Jews, not just an alleged opposition group whose existence is a postmodern fabrication.

To conclude, I have touched upon only a few parts of the Bible's ideology of exile. This ideology, with its many permutations, is worthy of the deeper study that some scholars give it for what it can tell us about

---

16. Whether Isaiah 54 or other similar passages are eschatological or simply idealized visions of the return is not material for my argument.

17. J. Hill (2004) finds that Jeremiah is the origin of the idea of unended exile, especially in the letter in Jeremiah 29 and the mythical construct of Nebuchadnezzar in Jeremiah 25 and 27. Hill suggests that the structure of the entire book reflects the idea of unended exile.

biblical thought. It should not be discarded as "just" an ideological construct, as a number of postmodernists do. More disturbing is the way certain postmodern assumptions may lead to erroneous conclusions about the nature both of the history and of the ideology of the exile. The minimalists claim that the Bible's ideological discourse has distorted earlier views of the history of the exile. I do not argue with this point. My claim is that the minimalists and other postmodernists, by means of their own ideological fixations, have distorted our view of the Bible's ideology of exile.

Bibliography

Ackroyd, Peter
1968   *Exile and Restoration: A Study of Hebrew Thought of the Sixth Century B.C.* Philadelphia: Westminster.
Adam, A. K. M.
1995   *What Is Postmodern Biblical Criticism?* Minneapolis: Fortress.
Albertz, Rainer
2003a *Israel in Exile: The History and Literature of the Sixth Century B.C.E.,* trans. David Green. Atlanta: Society of Biblical Literature / Leiden: Brill.
2003b The Thwarted Restoration. Pp. 1–17 in *Yahwism after the Exile: Perspectives on Israelite Religion in the Persian Era,* ed. R. Albertz and B. Becking. Assen: Van Gorcum.
Albertz, Rainer, and Becking, Bob, eds.
2003   *Yahwism after the Exile: Perspectives on Israelite Religion in the Persian Era.* Assen: Van Gorcum.
Barr, James
2000   *History and Ideology in the Old Testament.* Oxford: Oxford University Press.
Barstad, Hans
1996   *The Myth of the Empty Land: A Study in* the *History and Archaeology* of *Judah during* the *"Exilic" Period.* Symbolae Osloenses Fasciculi suppletorii 28. Oslo: Scandinavian University Press.
Bedford, Peter Ross
2001   *Temple Restoration in Early Achaemenid Judah.* Leiden: Brill.
Ben Zvi, Ehud
1995   Inclusion in and Exclusion from Israel as Conveyed by the Use of the Term "Israel" in Postmonarchic Biblical Texts. Pp. 95–149 in *The Pitcher Is Broken: Memorial Essays for Gösta Ahlström,* ed. S. Holloway and L. Handy. JSOTSup 190. Sheffield: Sheffield Academic Press.
2003   What Is New in Yehud? Some Considerations. Pp. 32–48 in *Yahwism after the Exile: Perspectives on Israelite Religion in the Persian Era,* ed. R. Albertz and B. Becking. Assen: Van Gorcum.
Blenkinsopp, Joseph
2002   The Age of the Exile. Pp. 416–39 in *The Biblical World,* vol. 1, ed. J. Barton. London: Routledge.

Carroll, Robert P.
  1992   The Myth of the Empty Land. *Semeia* 59–60: 79–93.
  1997a   Deportation and Diasporic Discourses in the Prophetic Literature. Pp. 63–88 in *Exile: Old Testament, Jewish, and Christian Conceptions*, ed. J. Scott. Leiden: Brill.
  1997b   Madonna of Silences: Clio and the Bible. Pp. 84–103 in *Can a "History of Israel" Be Written?* ed. L. L. Grabbe. JSOTSup 245. Sheffield: Sheffield Academic Press.
  1998a   Exile! What Exile? Deportation and the Discourses of Diaspora. Pp. 62–79 in *Leading Captivity Captive: "The Exile" as History and Ideology*, ed. L. L. Grabbe. JSOTSup 278. Sheffield: Sheffield Academic Press.
  1998b   Poststructuralist Approaches: New Historicism and Postmodernism. Pp. 50–66 in *The Cambridge Companion to Biblical Interpretation*, ed. John Barton. Cambridge: Cambridge University Press.
  2001   Exile, Restoration, and Colony: Judah in the Persian Empire." Pp. 102–16 in *The Blackwell Companion to the Hebrew Bible*, ed. L. G. Perdue. Oxford: Blackwell.

Collins, John J.
  2004   The Politics of Biblical Interpretation. Pp. 195–211 in *Biblical and Near Eastern Essays: Studies in Honour of Kevin J. Cathcart*, ed. Carmel McCarthy and John F. Healey. London: T. & T. Clark.
  2005   *The Bible after Babel: Historical Criticism in a Postmodern Age.* Grand Rapids, MI: Eerdmans.

Davies, Philip R.
  1997   Whose History? Whose Israel? Whose Bible? Biblical Histories, Ancient and Modern. Pp. 104–22 in *Can a "History of Israel" Be Written?* ed. L. L. Grabbe. JSOTSup 245. Sheffield: Sheffield Academic Press.
  1998   Exile? What Exile? Whose Exile? Pp. 128–38 in *Leading Captivity Captive: "The Exile" as History and Ideology*, ed. L. L. Grabbe. JSOTSup 278. Sheffield: Sheffield Academic Press.

Eisen, Arnold
  1986   *Galut: Modern Jewish Reflection on Homelessness and Homecoming.* Bloomington: Indiana University Press.

Fried, Lisbeth S.
  2003   The Land Lay Desolate: Conquest and Restoration in the Ancient Near East. Pp. 21–54 in *Judah and the Judeans in the Neo-Babylonian Period*, ed. Oded Lipschits and Joseph Blenkinsopp. Winona Lake, IN: Eisenbrauns.

Grabbe, Lester L.
  1998a   "The Exile" under the Theodolite: Historiography as Triangulation. Pp. 80–100 in *Leading Captivity Captive: The "Exile" as History and Ideology.* JSOTSup 278. Sheffield: Sheffield Academic Press.
  2002   "The Comfortable Theory," "Maximal Conservatism" and Neo-Fundamentalism Revisited. Pp. 174–93 in *Sense and Sensitivity: Essays on Reading the Bible in Memory of Robert Carroll*, ed. A. G. Hunter and P. R. Davies. JSOTSup 348. Sheffield: Sheffield Academic Press.

Grabbe, Lester L., ed.
1997   *Can a "History of Israel" Be Written?* JSOTSup 245. Sheffield: Sheffield Academic Press.
1998b   *Leading Captivity Captive: The "Exile" as History and Ideology.* JSOTSup 278. Sheffield: Sheffield Academic Press.

Hill, John
2004   "Your Exile Will Be Long": The Book of Jeremiah and the Unended Exile. Pp. 149–61 in *Reading the Book of Jeremiah: A Search for Coherence,* ed. M. Kessler. Winona Lake, IN: Eisenbrauns.

Hunter, Alastair G., and Davies, Philip R., eds.
2002   *Sense and Sensitivity: Essays on Reading the Bible in Memory of Robert Carroll.* JSOTSup 348. Sheffield: Sheffield Academic Press.

Japhet, Sara
1983   People and Land in the Restoration Period. Pp. 103–25 in *Das Land Israel in biblischer Zeit,* ed. G. Strecker. Göttingen: Vandenhoeck & Ruprecht.
1999   Exile and Restoration in the Book of Chronicles." Pp. 33–44 in *The Crisis of Israelite Religion,* ed. B. Becking and M. C. A. Korpel. Leiden: Brill.

Klein, Ralph
1979   *Israel in Exile.* Philadelphia: Fortress.

Knibb, Michael A.
1976   The Exile in the Literature of the Intertestamental Period. *Heythrop Journal* 17: 253–72.
1983   Exile in the Damascus Document. *JSOT* 25: 99–117.

Lemche, Niels Peter
1997   Clio Is Also among the Muses!—Keith W. Whitelam and the History of Palestine: A Review and a Commentary. Pp. 123–55 in *Can a "History of Israel" Be Written?* ed. L. L. Grabbe. JSOTSup 245. Sheffield: Sheffield Academic Press.

Lipschits, O., and Blenkinsopp, J., eds.
2003   *Judah and the Judeans in the Neo-Babylonian Period.* Winona Lake, IN: Eisenbrauns.

McConville, J. Gordon
1996   Faces of Exile in Old Testament Historiography. Pp. 27–44 in *After the Exile: Essays in Honour of Rex Mason,* ed. J. Barton and D. J. Reimer. Macon, GA: Mercer University Press.

Oded, B.
2003a   Where Is the "Myth of the Empty Land" to Be Found? History versus Myth. Pp. 55–74 in *Judah and the Judeans in the Neo-Babylonian Period,* ed. O. Lipschits and J. Blenkinsopp. Winona Lake, IN: Eisenbrauns.
2003b   הגלות—מציאות היסטורית או מיתוס? פרק בחקר ראשונה של גולת אשור ובבל. *Bêt Miqraʾ* 49: 103–23.

Pastor, J.
1998   When Is the End the Beginning? Or When the Biblical Past Is the Political Present. *SJOT* 12: 155–202.

Qimron, Elisha, and Strugnell, John
1994   *Qumran Cave 4, V: Miqṣat Maʿaśê Ha-Torah.* DJD 10. Oxford: Clarendon.

Reif, Stefan
2002   Jews, Hebraists and "Old Testament" Studies. Pp. 224–45 in *Sense and Sensitivity: Essays on Reading the Bible in Memory of Robert Carroll*, ed. A. G. Hunter and P. R. Davies. JSOTSup 348. Sheffield: Sheffield Academic Press.

Scott, James M.
1997a   Exile and the Self-Understanding of Diaspora Jews in the Greco-Roman Period. Pp. 173–218 in *Exile: Old Testament, Jewish, and Christian Conceptions*, ed. James M. Scott. Leiden: Brill.

Scott, James M., ed.
1997b   *Exile: Old Testament, Jewish, and Christian Conceptions*. Leiden: Brill.
2001   *Restoration: Old Testament, Jewish, and Christian Perspectives*. Leiden: Brill.

Smith-Christopher, Daniel L.
2002   *A Biblical Theology of Exile*. Minneapolis: Fortress.

Talmon, Shemaryahu
2001   "Exile" and "Restoration" in the Conceptual World of Ancient Judaism. Pp. 107–46 in *Restoration: Old Testament, Jewish, and Christian Perspectives*, ed. J. M. Scott. Leiden: Brill.

Thompson, Thomas L.
1998   The Exile in History and Myth: A Response to Hans Barstad. Pp. 101–18 in *Leading Captivity Captive: "The Exile" as History and Ideology*, ed. L. L. Grabbe. JSOTSup 278. Sheffield: Sheffield Academic Press.

Weinfeld, Moshe
2005   The Crystallization of the "Congregation of the Exile" (*kehal ha-golah*) and the Sectarian Nature of Post-exilic Judaism. Pp. 232–38 in *Normative and Sectarian Judaism in the Second Temple Period*, ed. M. Weinfeld. London: T. & T. Clark.

Whitelam, Keith W.
2002   Representing Minimalism: The Rhetoric and Reality of Revisionism. Pp. 194–223 in *Sense and Sensitivity: Essays on Reading the Bible in Memory of Robert Carroll*, ed. A. G. Hunter and P. R. Davies. JSOTSup 348. Sheffield: Sheffield Academic Press.

Index of Authors

357

Index of Scripture